Off to Work™ with

Excel 97

LABYRINTH
PUBLICATIONS

(800) 522-9746

Trademarks, Copyright

The Off to Work™ Series

Labyrinth Publication's Off to Work™ series includes self-paced tutorials for Microsoft© **Word 97**, **Excel 97**, **PowerPoint 97** and **Access 97**. This series is designed for vocational training yet provides the ease-of-use that sets Labyrinth books apart. Features of the series include...

- Business oriented projects
- Numerous exercises including Skills Builders, Assessments and Critical Thinking
- No file dependencies between lessons (allows you to "skip around")
- Inexpensively priced and exceptionally easy-to-use

Ask About Our Revolutionary New AutoGrade Technology!

Labyrinth Publications has developed a revolutionary new technology called AutoGrade to accompany the Off to Work series of textbooks. AutoGrade automatically grades the Assessment projects at the end of each lesson and records the results in an electronic database. AutoGrade completely automates the assessment and tracking process. So stop assessing students the old fashioned way and put AutoGrade technology to work now!

Other Labyrinth Textbooks and Software Include...

- Crowd Control (desktop control software for Windows 95)
- Laying a Foundation with Windows 95 (textbook)
- Discover the Internet with Netscape Navigator 3.0 (textbook)
- Welcome to the World of Computers (textbook)
- Mastering the Essentials of WordPerfect 6.1, Word 6.0, Word 7.0 and Excel 7.0 (textbooks)
- and more...

See Our Complete Product Listing on the Next Page

Or

Visit Our Web Site at www.labyrinth-pub.com

Or

Call (800) 522-9746

Labyrinth Publications Product Listing

	Title & Description	ISBN
	Discover the Internet with Netscape Navigator 3.0	1-887281-30-4
Windows	Laying a Foundation with Windows 95	1-887281-10-X
	Laying a Foundation with Windows 98	1-887281-65-7
Office 97	Off to Work with Office 97	1-887281-39-8
	Off to Work with Word 97	1-887281-33-9
	Word 97 Quick Course	1-887281-38-X
	Off to Work with Excel 97	1-887281-32-0
	Excel 97 Quick Course	1-887281-37-1
	Off to Work with PowerPoint 97	1-887281-41-X
	Off to Work with Access 97	1-887281-43-6
Software	AutoGrade 99	
	AutoCheck 99	
	TestWriter	
Office 95	Mastering the Essentials of Microsoft Word 7.0	1-887281-13-4
	Word 7.0 Quick Course	1-887281-18-5
	Mastering the Essentials of Excel 7.0	1-887281-19-3
	Excel 7.0 Quick Course	1-887281-06-1

Table of Contents

1 Creating and Editing a Simple Worksheet

Objectives:

- Create a simple worksheet

- Understand workbook and worksheet concepts

- Display, hide and move toolbars

- Enter text and numbers

- Edit cell entries

- Select cells

- Align cell entries

- Use AutoSum

- Open and close workbooks

What is Microsoft Excel?

Microsoft Excel is an electronic spreadsheet program that makes working with numbers a pleasure instead of a chore. Excel has powerful features to let you enter and edit text and numbers, perform an endless variety of calculations, produce charts and other reports and make informed financial decisions. Excel is the most widely used spreadsheet program in both homes and businesses.

Why Use Excel?

Excel provides a number of important features and benefits that make it a smart choice to use.

1. IntelliSense Technology - Excel's IntelliSense technology includes many automated tools to assist you in entering, editing and analyzing data. This speeds up the process of creating worksheets, so that you can focus on analysis and other tasks.

2. GUI - Excel's Graphical User Interface is so easy to use that even beginning computer users find it simple. The interface reduces the need to memorize commands and it will make you more productive.

3. Charting - Have you heard of the expression **"a picture speaks a thousand words"**? This is especially true with financial or numeric data. Excel's powerful charting and formatting features let you display your data in a powerful and convincing graphic format.

4. Widely used - Excel is the most widely used spreadsheet software. Excel is the right choice if you are trying to develop marketable skills and find employment.

5. Integration with other Office programs - Excel is part of the Microsoft Office suite of programs which also include Word, Access and PowerPoint. The ability to exchange data with these programs is one of the most powerful and attractive features of Excel.

It's Time to Learn Excel!

It's time to put your fears behind and learn this wonderful program. You will be amazed at the power and simplicity of Excel and how easy it is to learn. The knowledge you are about to gain will give you a marketable skill and make you the master of Excel.

The Project - Diane's Cafe

In this lesson, you will develop a worksheet for Diane's Café. Diane needs to track the weekly sales of her various menu items, so that she can better plan her inventory purchases. You will enter data including both text and numbers. You will compute Totals using the AutoSum button on the toolbar and you will widen the worksheet columns. You will also learn some preliminary techniques and concepts such as starting Excel, using toolbars and scrolling. You will create the following worksheet as you progress through this introductory lesson.

	A	B	C	D	E	F	G	H
1	Diane's Café - Weekly Sales Data							
2								
3			Wednesday	Thursday	Friday	Saturday	Sunday	
4	Soups							Totals
5		Vegetable	3	10	12	15	16	56
6		Chicken	4	8	10	13	14	49
7		Split Pea	6	13	15	18	19	71
8		Total	13	31	37	46	49	176
9								
10	Salads							
11		Mixed Greens	2	5	4	10	8	29
12		Cobb	3	7	5	12	10	37
13		Spinach	4	8	11	14	14	51
14		Fruit & Nut	2	3	5	5	3	18
15		Total	11	23	25	41	35	135
16								
17	Entrees							
18		Chicken Kiev	3	5	5	6	8	27
19		Pot Roast	6	1	2	3	7	19
20		Fish	8	2	3	4	5	22
21		Total	17	8	10	13	20	68
22								
23	Dessert							
24		Apple Pie	3	6	8	7	2	26
25		Key Lime Pie	5	3	2	2	1	13
26		Pecan Pie	2	2	6	8	3	21
27		Total	10	11	16	17	6	60

Starting Excel

There are several ways to start Excel. The three most common methods are listed below.

- Click the Start button and choose Microsoft Excel from the Programs menu.

- Click a desktop shortcut for the Excel program (if a shortcut is on the desktop).

- ♦ Click the Microsoft Excel button on the Microsoft Office toolbar (if it is displayed).

Hands-On 1.1 - Start Excel

In this exercise, you will start the Excel program.

1. Start your computer and the Windows desktop will be displayed.

2. **Click** the Start **Start** button and choose **Programs**.

3. Choose **Microsoft Excel** from the Programs menu.

   The Excel program will load and the Excel window will appear. Don't be concerned if your window appears different from the example shown below.

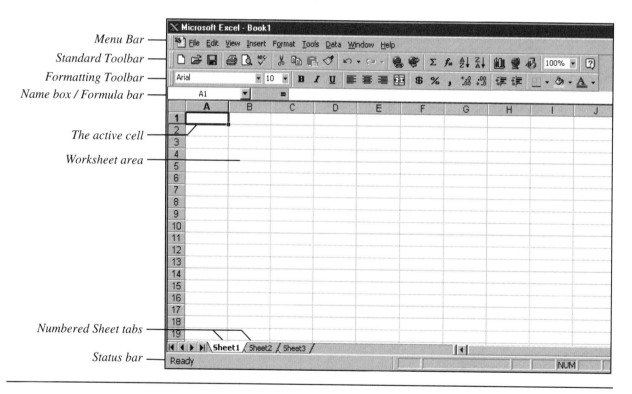

4

Workbooks and Worksheets

Excel displays a blank **workbook** the moment you start the program. A workbook is composed of **worksheets**. This is similar to a paper notebook that has many sheets of paper. You enter text and numbers and insert formulas, charts and other objects in the worksheets. Excel provides 3 worksheets in a new workbook. However, you can increase this number and have up to 255 worksheets in one workbook.

A worksheet is composed of rows and columns

A worksheet has a grid structure with horizontal rows and vertical columns. The intersection of each row and column is a **cell**. The worksheet actually has 256 columns and 65,536 rows although only a small number of the rows and columns are visible in the worksheet window. Each cell has a **reference** that is the column letter followed by the row number. For example, A1 is the reference of the cell in the top left corner of the worksheet. So we refer to this cell as cell A1.

Moving the Highlight and Scrolling

A thick line known as the highlight surrounds the active cell. You can make a cell active by clicking it with the mouse or by using the keyboard. Changing the active cell is important because data is entered into the active cell. You can also use the vertical and horizontal scroll bars to scroll through the worksheet. However, you must position the highlight in the desired cell after scrolling. The following table lists several important keystroke commands that are used to move the highlight and thus make a cell active.

Use these keys	To move the highlight like this
→　←　↑　↓	One cell to the right, left, up or down
Home	Column A of the active row
Ctrl + Home	Cell A1
PageDown	Down one screen
PageUp	Up one screen

Hands-On 1.2 - Move the highlight and check out the Excel window

In this exercise, you will use the mouse and keyboard to move the highlight around the worksheet.

Click in the desired cell

1. Slide the mouse and the pointer will have a thick cross ⊹ shape when it is in the worksheet area.

2. **Click** the pointer on **any cell** and the highlight will move to that cell.

3. Move the highlight **five times** by clicking in various cells.

Use the keyboard to move the highlight

*In the next few steps, you will move the highlight with the keyboard. You can use the keys on the main part of your keyboard or on the Numeric keypad at the bottom right corner. Keep in mind, however, that you must have the Num Lock key turned **off** if you want to move the highlight with the Numeric keypad. The word NUM will disappear from the Status bar when Num Lock is turned off.*

Continued...

4. Use the arrow ⟶ ⟵ ⬆ ⬇ keys to position the highlight in **cell F10**.

5. **Tap** the ⌂Home⌂ key and the highlight will move to cell A10.

   The Home key always moves the highlight to column A in the active row.

6. **Press** ⌂Ctrl⌂ ⌂+⌂ ⌂Home⌂ to move the highlight to Cell A1.

7. **Tap** the ⌂PageDown⌂ key two or three times.

   Notice that Excel displays the next twenty or so rows each time you tap PageDown.

8. **Press & Hold** the ⬆ key until the highlight is in cell A1.

Use the scroll bars

9. **Click** the Scroll Right ▶ button on the horizontal scroll bar until columns AA and AB are visible.

   Excel labels the first 26 columns A - Z and the next 26 columns AA - AZ. A similar labeling scheme is used for the remaining columns.

10. Take a few minutes to practice scrolling and moving the highlight.

Explore the Excel window

11. Use the following steps to explore the Excel window.

❶ *Notice the Name box on the Formula bar (don't worry if your Formula bar is not displayed. You will learn to display and hide the Formula bar soon.) The Name box displays the name or reference of the active cell. You will learn how to name cells in a later lesson.*

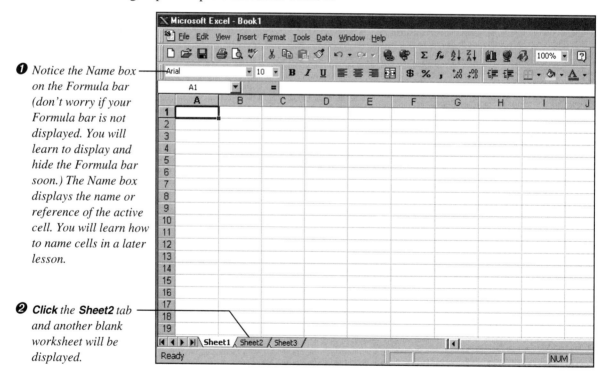

❷ *Click the **Sheet2** tab and another blank worksheet will be displayed.*

❸ *Click the **Sheet1** tab.*

12. **Press** ⌂Ctrl⌂ ⌂+⌂ ⌂Home⌂ to move the highlight to cell A1.

Using Toolbars

Excel has several **toolbars** that let you rapidly issue commands. The **Standard toolbar** and the **Formatting toolbar** are usually displayed at the top of the document window as shown in the following illustration. The illustration also shows the **Formula bar** that is located below the Formatting toolbar. Excel lets you display as many toolbars as desired.

The Standard toolbar ——

The Formatting toolbar ——

Name box / Formula bar ——

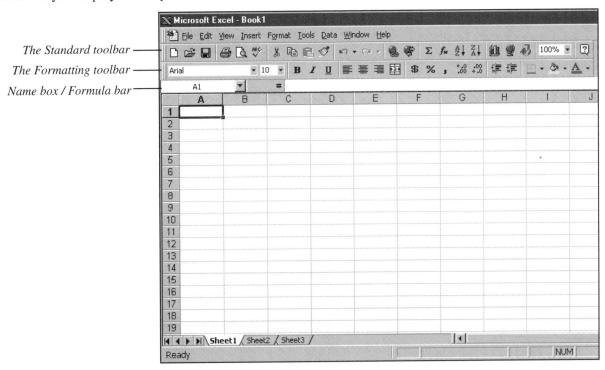

The toolbars can be customized

Excel lets you modify the toolbars by adding and removing buttons. You can also create your own customized toolbars with the buttons you use most often. You can even create your own buttons.

Displaying and Hiding Toolbars

Excel lets you display as many toolbars as you desire. It is usually better to limit the number of toolbars to prevent the document window from appearing cluttered. Most Excel users display the Standard and Formatting toolbars and the Formula bar. Most computers have this arrangement set as the default.

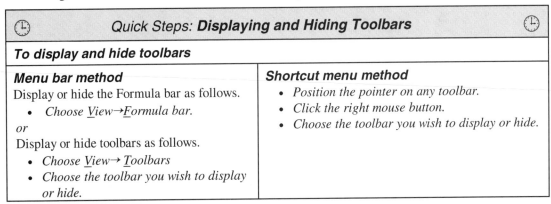

🕐	Quick Steps: **Displaying and Hiding Toolbars**	🕐
To display and hide toolbars		
Menu bar method Display or hide the Formula bar as follows. • *Choose View→Formula bar.* *or* Display or hide toolbars as follows. • *Choose View→ Toolbars* • *Choose the toolbar you wish to display or hide.*	**Shortcut menu method** • *Position the pointer on any toolbar.* • *Click the right mouse button.* • *Choose the toolbar you wish to display or hide.*	

Hands-On 1.3 – Displaying and hiding toolbars

1. Look at the illustration on the preceding page. Are the Standard and Formatting toolbars and the Formula bar displayed on your screen?

Use the <u>V</u>iew→<u>T</u>oolbars command to display and hide toolbars

2. Choose **<u>V</u>iew→<u>T</u>oolbars** from the menu bar and the Toolbar list will appear.

   Both Standard and Formatting should have a check next to them (don't be concerned if they are not checked). A check means the toolbar is displayed.

3. **Click** any toolbar name on the list.

   The toolbar you chose will be displayed or hidden.

Display or hide the Formula bar

4. Choose **<u>V</u>iew→<u>F</u>ormula bar** from the menu bar.

   The Formula bar will be either displayed or hidden.

5. Display the Formula bar if it is currently hidden.

Use the right-click method

   *In the next few steps, you will use the **right** mouse button to display the Toolbar list. Clicking the right mouse button is known as **right-clicking**.*

6. Position the mouse pointer anywhere on the Standard or Formatting toolbar and **click** the **right** mouse button (right-click).

   The Toolbar list will pop up.

7. Use the **left** mouse button to choose any toolbar from the list.

   The toolbar you chose will be displayed or hidden.

Now practice

8. Take a few minutes to practice displaying and hiding toolbars and the Formula bar.

   Use both the <u>V</u>iew menu and the right-click technique.

9. When you have finished experimenting, set up the Excel window so that only the Standard and Formatting toolbars and the Formula bar are displayed.

Moving Toolbars

Toolbars can be moved to various locations in the Excel window. Toolbars can be **docked** at the top, bottom, left or right side of the window. Docked toolbars are attached to an edge of the Excel window. Toolbars can also **float** anywhere in the Excel window.

Quick Steps: *Moving Toolbars*

To move a docked toolbar

- *Position the mouse pointer on the Move* *handle at the left edge of the toolbar.*
- *Drag the toolbar to a new location.*

To move a floating toolbar

- *Position the mouse pointer on the Title bar at the top of the floating toolbar.*
- *Drag the toolbar to a new location.*

Hands-On 1.4 – Moving toolbars

This exercise uses a series of illustrations to move the Formatting toolbar in the Excel window.

Move the Formatting toolbar to the center of the window

1. Position the mouse pointer on the Move 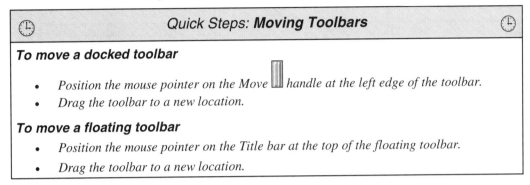 handle at the left edge of the Formatting toolbar.

2. **Press & Hold** the left mouse button, then **drag** the mouse into the center of the screen. A shaded rectangle will appear as shown in the following illustration.

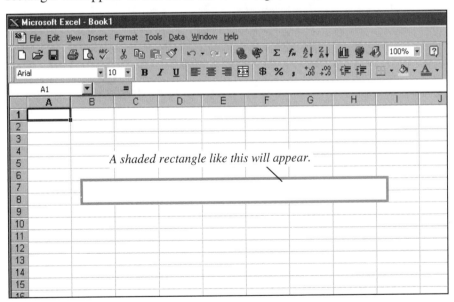

3. **Release** the mouse button and the toolbar will float in the worksheet area.

Continued...

Move the Formatting toolbar under the Standard toolbar

4. Position the mouse pointer on the Title bar of the toolbar as shown in the following illustration.

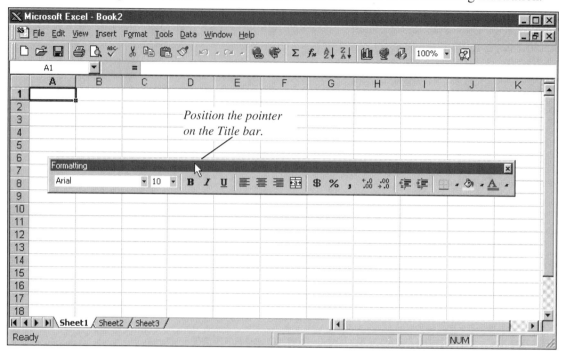

5. **Drag** the mouse up until the shaded rectangle is positioned just below the Standard toolbar. The rectangle will suddenly become thin when it is in the correct position.

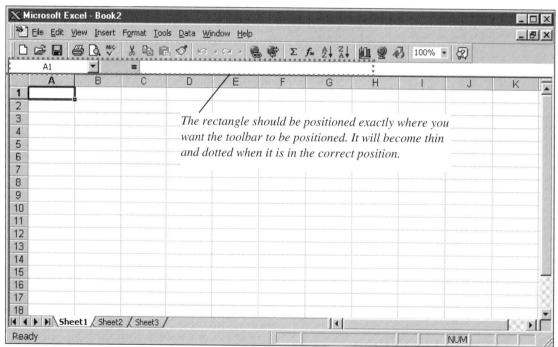

6. **Release** the mouse button and the toolbar should be docked below the Standard toolbar.

7. Now practice moving the toolbars to various locations in the Excel window.

   Don't try to move the Formula bar because its position cannot be changed.

8. When you have finished, position the Standard and Formatting toolbars at the top of the window (in their usual locations).

Entering Data

You can begin entering data the moment Excel is started. Data is entered into the active cell (the cell with the highlight). You can enter text, numbers or formulas into cells. Text and numbers are used for different purposes in a worksheet. Text is used for descriptive headings and entries that require alphabetic characters or a combination of alphabetic and numeric characters. Numbers can be calculated using formulas. Excel recognizes the data you enter and it decides whether the entry is text, a number or a formula. Text and number entries are discussed in detail below and on the following pages.

Entering Text

An entry is considered to be text whenever it contains alphabetic characters or spaces. Excel left aligns text entries in cells although you can change the alignment to center or right. The following table shows several examples of text entries. Notice that each example contains at least one alphabetic character or a space.

Examples of text entries	
1996 Budget	555 9090
Q1	Bicycle Sales

Long text entries

Text entries are often too long to fit in a cell. These entries are known as **long entries**. Excel uses the following rules when deciding how to display long entries.

1. If the cell to the right of the long entry is empty, then the long entry is displayed over the adjacent cell.
2. If the cell to the right of the long entry is **not** empty, then Excel shortens or **truncates** the display of the long entry.

Keep in mind that Excel does not actually change the long entry, it simply truncates the display of the entry. You can resolve this situation by widening the column that contains the long entry.

Deleting and Replacing a Cell's Content

You can delete the content of a cell by making the cell active (clicking the cell) and then tapping the Delete key. Likewise, you can replace the content of a cell by clicking the cell and entering the new data.

Undo and Redo

Excel's **Undo** button lets you reverse your last 16 commands or actions. You can reverse simple actions such as accidentally deleting a cell's content or you can reverse more complex actions such as deleting an entire row. You can Undo most commands or actions. However, there are a few commands that cannot be undone such as deleting entire worksheets, printing and saving workbooks.

Excel also has a **Redo** button that reverses Undo. Use Redo when you Undo actions but then decide that you want to go through with them after all. You will probably love Redo if you have a difficult time making up your mind.

The arrow buttons to the right of Undo and Redo let you Undo or Redo multiple actions. In fact, you can Undo or Redo up to 16 actions! You will use Undo, Redo and the arrow buttons soon.

Hands-On 1.5 - Entering text

In this exercise, you will begin creating a worksheet for Diane's Café. Diane needs to track the weekly sales of her various menu items, so that she can better plan her inventory purchases. You will create a worksheet for this purpose.

Type a long text entry and check out the Formula bar

1. Make cell **A1** active by clicking the mouse pointer ⇩ in it.

2. Type, **Diane's Cafe - Weekly Sales** (don't try to format the text) and **tap** ⌷Enter⌷.

   The text should be entered in the cell and the highlight should move down to cell A2. Excel moves the highlight down when you tap Enter because most people enter data column-by-column. Notice that the entry displays over cells B1 and C1. The long entry would not display over these cells if they contained data.

3. **Click** the mouse pointer ⇩ in cell A1 and the Formula bar will have the appearance shown below.

   *Notice that the Formula bar displays the name of the active cell (A1) and the cell's content. In this example, the cell's content is the title **Diane's Café - Weekly Sales**. The title is a long entry because it is wider than cell A1. Cells B1 and C1 are empty, so the long entry is displayed over them. Keep in mind; however, that the entire entry belongs to Cell A1. This concept will be demonstrated in the next few steps.*

Delete the entry and use Undo and Redo

4. **Tap** the ⌷Delete⌷ key and the entire entry will be deleted.

   Notice the entire entry was deleted because it belonged to cell A1.

5. **Click** the Undo 🔙 button to restore the entry.

6. **Click** the Redo 🔜 button and the entry will be deleted again.

   Redo always reverses Undo.

7. **Click** Undo 🔙 again to restore the entry.

Verify that the entry belongs to cell A1

8. **Tap** the ⇨ key to make cell B1 active.

9. Look at the Formula bar and you will see that cell B1 is empty.

   Once again, the long entry belongs to cell A1 even though it is displayed over cells B1 and C1.

Type additional text entries

10. Use the arrow ⇨ ⇦ ⇧ ⇩ keys to position the highlight in cell **C3**.

11. Type **Wednesday** and **tap** ⇨ once.

   Notice the entry is completed and the highlight moves to cell D3. You can always use the arrow keys to complete an entry and move the highlight in the desired direction.

Continued...

12. Type **Thursday** in cell D3 and **tap** ⤷.

Notice that the display of Wednesday is shortened or truncated. A long entry is always truncated when the cell to the right contains text or a number.

13. Enter the remaining text entries as shown below.

Use Undo if you make a mistake. Also, you can change any entry by clicking in the desired cell and retyping the entry.

	A	B	C	D	E	F	G
1	Diane's Café - Weekly Sales						
2							
3			Wednesda	Thursday	Friday	Saturday	Sunday
4	Soups						
5		Vegetable					
6		Chicken					
7		Split Pea					
8		Total					
9							
10	Salads						
11		Mixed Greens					
12		Cobb					
13		Spinach					
14		Fruit					
15		Total					
16							
17	Entrees						
18		Chicken					
19		Pot Roast					
20		Fish					
21		Total					
22							
23	Dessert						
24		Apple Pie					
25		Key Lime Pie					
26		Pecan Pie					
27		Total					

You will continue to enhance your worksheet in the next exercise.

Entering Numbers

Numbers can only contain the digits 0 - 9 and a few other characters. Excel right aligns numbers in cells although you can change the alignment to center or left. The following table discusses the characters you can use when entering numbers.

Characters which can be used in numbers
Digits 0 - 9
The following characters: + - ( ) , / $ % .

Don't type commas, dollar signs or other number formats

It isn't necessary to type commas, dollar signs or other number formats when entering numbers. It is easier to just enter the numbers and then use Excel's formatting commands to add the desired number format. You will learn how to format numbers soon.

Do type decimal points and minus signs

You should always type a decimal point if the number you are entering requires one and a minus sign (or parenthesis) if the number is negative.

The Confirm and Cancel Buttons

In the previous exercise, you used Enter and the arrow keys to complete an entry and move the highlight. The Confirm ☑ button on the Formula bar can also be used to complete an entry. Also, you can cancel an entry before completing it by clicking the Cancel ☒ button on the Formula bar or by tapping the Esc key.

Hands-On 1.6 – Entering numbers

In this exercise, you will add numbers to the worksheet.

Use the Confirm button
1. Position the highlight in cell **C5**.

2. Type **3** but **don't** tap Enter or the arrow keys.

3. Look at the Formula bar and notice the Cancel ☒ and Confirm ☑ buttons.
   These buttons appear when you begin entering data in a cell or when you edit data.

4. **Click** the Confirm ☑ button to complete the entry.
   Notice the highlight remains in cell C5. It is preferable to complete entries with the keyboard when building a worksheet. This is because the highlight automatically moves to the next cell. The Confirm button is actually most useful when editing entries.

Use the Cancel button and the Esc key
5. Position the highlight in cell **C6** and type **4** (but don't confirm the entry).

6. **Click** the Cancel ☒ button on the Formula bar to cancel the entry.

Continued...

7. Type **4** again but this time **tap** the (Esc) key on the keyboard.

The Escape key has the same effect as the Cancel button.

8. Type **4** once again and **tap** the (↓) key.

Notice the number is right aligned in the cell.

9. Enter the remaining numbers as shown below.

Keep in mind that some of the numbers you enter will cause entries in column B to be truncated. You will solve this problem by widening column B later in this exercise.

	A	B	C	D	E	F	G
1	Diane's Café - Weekly Sales						
2							
3			Wednesda	Thursday	Friday	Saturday	Sunday
4	Soups						
5		Vegetable	3	10	12	15	16
6		Chicken	4	8	10	13	14
7		Split Pea	6	13	15	18	19
8		Total					
9							
10	Salads						
11		Mixed Gre	2	5	4	10	8
12		Cobb	3	7	5	12	10
13		Spinach	4	8	11	14	14
14		Fruit	2	3	5	5	3
15		Total					
16							
17	Entrees						
18		Chicken	3	5	5	6	8
19		Pot Roast	6	1	2	3	7
20		Fish	8	2	3	4	5
21		Total					
22							
23	Dessert						
24		Apple Pie	3	6	8	7	2
25		Key Lime I	5	3	2	2	1
26		Pecan Pie	2	2	6	8	3
27		Total					

10. Take a few minutes to check the accuracy of your text and numbers.

It is very important to be accurate when entering data in worksheets. Excel's formulas, charts and other features are of no use unless your data is accurate.

You will learn how to save the workbook on the next page.

Saving a Workbook

One important lesson to learn is to **save your workbooks frequently!** Power outages and careless accidents can result in lost data. The best protection is to save your workbooks every 10 or 15 minutes and after making significant changes. It is recommended that you understand the concepts of files, folders and pathnames before attempting this exercise. These and many other essential Windows 95 concepts are discussed in Labyrinth Publications, *Laying a Foundation with Windows 95* textbook.

The Save and Save As Commands

Excel provides several commands that let you save documents. The **Save** command saves the current workbook onto a disk. If the workbook had previously been saved, then Excel replaces the old version of the workbook with the new edited version. If the workbook is new, then Excel displays the **Save As** dialog box. The Save As dialog box lets you name the workbook and it lets you specify the disk drive and folder that you wish to save it to. You can also use Save As to make a copy of an existing workbook by saving the workbook under a new name.

Excel 97 supports long filenames

Excel 97 supports long filenames. You can use up to 255 characters when naming a workbook in Excel 97. This is a huge improvement over the 8 character limitation in some earlier versions of Excel.

Hands-On 1.7 – Save the workbook

In this exercise, you will save the workbook. Your instructor will probably want you to use the diskette that is provided with this course. You will probably be saving workbooks onto the A: disk drive.

1. Choose **File→Save...** from the menu bar and the **Save As** dialog box will appear.

2. Use the following steps to save the workbook.

❶ *Click here and choose the disk drive with your exercise diskette. It is most likely 3 ½ Floppy [A:].*

❷ *Notice that Excel proposes the Filename, Book1.*

❸ *Type the name **Hands-On Lesson 1** and it will replace Book1. (If you switched disk drives, then you may need to click in the File name box, delete the name Book1 with the Delete and/or Backspace keys, then type the new name.)*

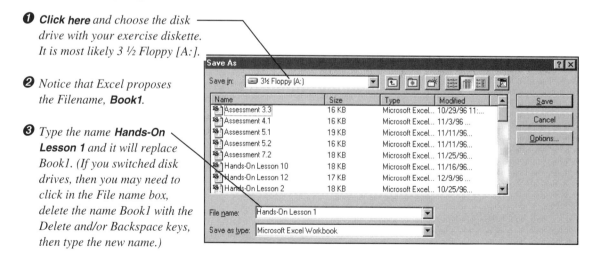

❹ *Click the **Save** button.*

Notice the workbook was saved and it also remains on the screen. You will continue to use the workbook throughout this lesson.

Editing Cell Contents

You can edit the active cell by clicking in the Formula bar and making the desired changes. You can also double-click a cell and then edit the contents directly in the cell. This technique is known as in-cell editing.

It may be easier to retype the entry

Editing a cell is beneficial if the entry is long and retyping it would be time consuming. Editing can also be beneficial with complex formulas and other functions that are difficult to recreate. However, it is usually easier to just replace an entry if the entry is small and requires little typing.

Using the Delete and Backspace Keys

You can use the Delete and Backspace keys to delete characters from an entry. The following table discusses the Delete and Backspace keys.

This key	Deletes like this
Delete	Character to the right of the insertion point.
BackSpace	Character to the left of the insertion point.

Hands-On 1.8 – Edit entries

The Hands-On Lesson 1 workbook should be open from the previous exercise.

Use the Formula bar to Edit the title

1. **Click** cell **A1**.

2. Use the following steps to edit cell A1 using the Formula bar.

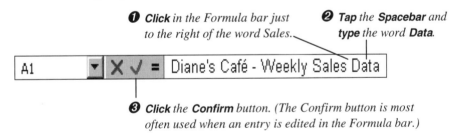

❶ *Click in the Formula bar just to the right of the word Sales.*

❷ *Tap the Spacebar and type the word Data.*

❸ *Click the Confirm button. (The Confirm button is most often used when an entry is edited in the Formula bar.)*

Use in-cell editing

3. **Double-click** cell **B14** (the cell with the word Fruit).

4. Use the mouse or the ⭢ key to position the flashing insertion point to the right of the word Fruit.

5. **Tap** the SpaceBar once and type **& Nut**.

6. **Tap** Enter or **click** the Confirm ☑ button to complete the change.

   The entry should now read **Fruit & Nut** *(although the entry may be slightly truncated).*

7. Change the entry in cell **B18** to **Chicken Kiev** and cell **A23** to **Desserts** (plural).

8. **Click** the Save 🖫 button to update the changes.

   The Save button automatically saves changes to a workbook that has previously been saved.

Selecting Cells

There are many ways to **select** cells in Excel. When you select cells, you are telling Excel which cells you wish to perform a command on. You can move, copy, delete, format and perform numerous other operations on selected cells. You can select with both the mouse and the keyboard.

Ranges

A range is a rectangular group of cells. Earlier in this lesson, you learned that each cell has a reference. For example, A1 refers to the first cell in a worksheet. Likewise, a range reference specifies which cells are included in the range. The range reference includes the first and last cells in the range separated by a colon (:). For example, the range C3:G3 includes all cells between C3 and G3. The following illustration shows several ranges and their corresponding range references. Notice that the ranges appear in black with white text (or reverse video as it is often called).

	A	B	C	D	E	F	G
1	Diane's Café - Weekly Sales Data						
2							
3			Wednesda	Thursday	Friday	Saturday	Sunday
4	Soups						
5		Vegetable	3	10	12	15	16
6		Chicken	4	8	10	13	14
7		Split Pea	6	13	15	18	19
8		Total					
9							
10	Salads						
11		Mixed Gre	2	5	4	10	8
12		Cobb	3	7	5	12	10
13		Spinach	4	8	11	14	14
14		Fruit & Nut	2	3	5	5	3

This is the range C3:G3 — (row 3)

This is the range B5:B8 — (column B, rows 5–8)

This is the range B11:C14 — (columns B–C, rows 11–14)

The following table describes the various methods of selecting cells in Excel.

Method	How to do it
Select a range	Drag the mouse pointer over the desired cells.
Select several ranges	Select a range, then press 【 Ctrl 】 while selecting additional ranges.
Select an entire column	Click a column heading (e.g. ▢ A ▢).
Select an entire row	Click a row heading (e.g. ▢ 1 ▢).
Select multiple columns or rows	Drag the mouse pointer over the desired column or row headings.
Select an entire worksheet	Click the Select All ▢ button at the top left corner of the worksheet.
Select using the Shift key	Position the highlight in the first cell you wish to select, then press & hold 【 Shift 】 and click the last cell in the range. You can also press & hold Shift while tapping the arrow keys on the keyboard.

Hands-On 1.9 – Practice selecting

Drag-select and deselect

1. Position the mouse pointer ⇧ on cell **C3**.

2. **Press & Hold** the left mouse button and **drag** to the right until the range C3:G3 is selected.

Continued...

3. **Deselect** the cells by **clicking** anywhere in the worksheet.

Select multiple ranges

4. **Select** the range **C3:G3** as you did in steps 1 and 2.

5. **Press & Hold** the ⌨Ctrl key while you select the range **B5:B8** as shown on the previous page.

   Both the C3:G3 and B5:B8 ranges should be selected. The Ctrl key lets you select more than one range at the same time.

6. **Press & Hold** while you select the range **B11:C14** as shown on the previous page.

   There should now be three ranges selected as shown on the previous page.

7. **Deselect** the ranges by **releasing** the ⌨Ctrl key and **clicking** anywhere in the worksheet.

Select entire columns and rows

8. Use the following series of steps to select various rows and columns.

   ❶ **Click here** on the Column A heading and the entire column will become selected.

   ❷ Position the mouse pointer on the Column C heading, then **drag** to the right until columns C, D and E are selected. Column A will be deselected.

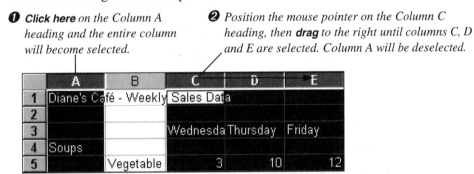

   ❸ **Click** the **Select All** button to select the entire worksheet.

   ❹ **Click** the **Row 4 heading** to select row 4.

   ❺ **Drag** the mouse pointer **down** over the row 10 - 15 headings to select those rows.

Use the Shift key methods

9. **Click** cell **B5**.

10. **Press & Hold** the ⌨Shift key, then **click** cell **G8** to select the range B5:G8.

11. **Click** cell **B11**.

12. **Press & Hold** the ⌨Shift key, then **tap** ⟶ five times and ⬇ four times.

   The range B11:G15 should be selected. Notice that the Shift key methods give you precise control when selecting. You should use the Shift key methods if you find it difficult to select with the mouse.

13. Take five minutes to practice selecting ranges, rows and columns.

Aligning Cell Entries

Excel makes it easy to align text and numbers within cells. Entries can be left, right or center aligned. You already learned that text entries are automatically left aligned and numbers are automatically right aligned. The alignment buttons on the Formatting toolbar let you change the default alignments as shown below.

Friday   Friday   Friday

Left aligned   Center aligned   Right aligned

Hands-On 1.10 – Align text entries and widen a column

In this exercise, you will align the entries in row 3. You will also widen columns B and C.

Select a range and change the alignment

1. **Select** the range **C3:G3** as shown below.

2. **Click** the Align Right button on the Formatting toolbar.

> *Each entry in the range (except Wednesday) should be right aligned. Wednesday does not appear right aligned because it is too wide for the cell. You will change the width of column C in a moment.*

3. Take a few moments to practice aligning entries in other cells or ranges. Use the Undo button after making each change.

Adjust the width of columns B and C

> *In the next few steps, you will adjust the width of columns B and C. This section provides a brief introduction to adjusting column widths. A complete discussion of adjusting column widths is given in a later lesson.*

4. Use the following steps to adjust the width of column B.

❶ *Position the mouse pointer on the border between column headings B and C and the Adjust pointer will appear.*

❷ *Drag the border to the right until the column is wide enough to display all the entries in column B.*

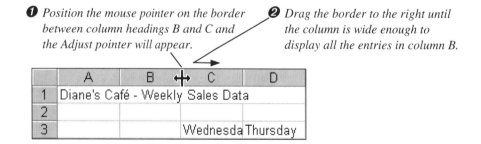

5. Widen column C until the word Wednesday is completely visible in cell C3.

> *You will need to drag the border between column headings C and D.*

6. **Click** the Save button to save the changes.

> *Continue with the topic on the next page where you will learn to use the AutoSum button.*

The AutoSum Button

The power of Excel becomes apparent when you begin using formulas and functions. The most common type of calculation is when a column or row of numbers is added or **summed**. In fact, this type of calculation is so common that Excel provides the AutoSum Σ button specifically for this purpose.

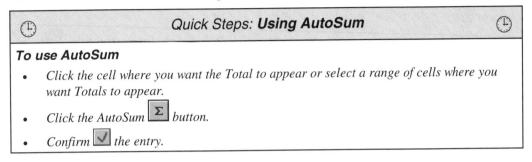

Quick Steps: *Using AutoSum*

To use AutoSum

- *Click the cell where you want the Total to appear or select a range of cells where you want Totals to appear.*
- *Click the AutoSum Σ button.*
- *Confirm ✓ the entry.*

Hands-On 1.11 – Use AutoSum to compute the column totals

In this exercise, you will use AutoSum to compute the Totals. Keep in mind that this section provides an introduction to formulas. You will learn more about formulas as you progress through this course.

Compute one column Total at a time

1. **Click** cell **C8**.

2. **Click** AutoSum Σ.

3. Use the following steps to check out the formula and confirm the entry.

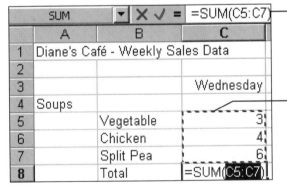

❶ **Notice** *that Excel proposes the formula =SUM(C5:C7) in cell C8 and in the Formula bar. All formulas begin with an equal = sign. SUM is a built-in function that adds up the numbers in a range (in this example the range is C5:C7).*

❷ **Notice** *the flashing marquee that surrounds the range C5:C7. AutoSum assumes you want to sum up all cells above C8 until the first empty cell is reached. The marquee identifies this range of cells.*

❸ **Click** *the Confirm ✓ button on the Formula bar to complete the entry.*

The Total should be 13.

4. **Click** cell **D8**.

5. **Click** AutoSum Σ, then **click** Confirm ✓.

6. Use the preceding technique to compute the column Totals in cells **E8**, **F8** and **G8**.

Continued...

Compute an entire row of column Totals with one command

7. **Select** the range **C15:G15** as shown below.

    This range will contain the column Totals for row 15.

8. **Click** AutoSum Σ.

    The column Totals should automatically be computed. AutoSum only displays the marquee and requires confirmation when you are computing a single Total.

9. Use the preceding steps to compute the column Totals in rows **21** and **27**.

Make column H a Totals column

10. **Click** cell **H4**, type the word **Totals** and Confirm ✓ the entry.

11. Use the Align Right ⬛ button to right align Totals.

12. **Click** cell **H5**.

13. **Click** AutoSum Σ and Excel assumes you want to add the cells to the left of H4 as shown below.

	A	B	C	D	E	F	G	H	
1	Diane's Café - Weekly Sales Data								
2									
3			Wednesday	Thursday	Friday	Saturday	Sunday		
4	Soups							Totals	
5		Vegetable	3	10	12	15	16	=SUM(C5:G5)	

14. Confirm ✓ the entry and the row Total should be **56**.

15. Use the preceding steps to compute the row Total in cell **H6**.

Override the range that AutoSum proposes

16. **Click** cell **H7**, then **click** AutoSum Σ.

    Notice that Excel assumes you want to sum the cells H5 and H6 that are above H7. This assumption is incorrect. The reason Excel made this assumption is there were two cells above H7, which is enough to make a range. Excel will always propose a column summation if it has a choice between a column and row summation.

17. Use the following steps to override the range that AutoSum is proposing.

    ❶ *Position the mouse pointer in cell **C7**, then drag to the right until the range C7:G7 is selected.*   ❷ *Notice the new range C7:G7 appears in the formula.*

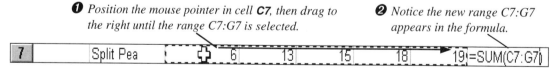

18. **Confirm** the entry and the row Total should be 71.

19. Use the preceding technique to compute the row Total in cell **H8** (the Total should equal 176).

    Actually, you could have accepted the formula that AutoSum proposed for cell H8. In this case, the column and row summations would have been the same.

Continued...

Sum the row Totals one range at a time

You can eliminate the problem of AutoSum proposing the wrong formula by summing a range of row Totals with one command. This is the same technique you used to sum the column Totals.

20. Select the range **H11:H15** as shown below.

	A	B	C	D	E	F	G	H
9								
10	Salads							
11		Mixed Greens	2	5	4	10	8	
12		Cobb	3	7	5	12	10	
13		Spinach	4	8	11	14	14	
14		Fruit & Nut	2	3	5	5	3	
15		Total	11	23	25	41	35	

21. Click AutoSum Σ.

The five row Totals should automatically be computed.

22. Use the preceding steps to compute the row Totals for the ranges **H18:H21** and **H24:H27**.
Your completed worksheet should match the worksheet shown below.

	A	B	C	D	E	F	G	H
1	Diane's Café - Weekly Sales Data							
2								
3			Wednesday	Thursday	Friday	Saturday	Sunday	
4	Soups							Totals
5		Vegetable	3	10	12	15	16	56
6		Chicken	4	8	10	13	14	49
7		Split Pea	6	13	15	18	19	71
8		Total	13	31	37	46	49	176
9								
10	Salads							
11		Mixed Greens	2	5	4	10	8	29
12		Cobb	3	7	5	12	10	37
13		Spinach	4	8	11	14	14	51
14		Fruit & Nut	2	3	5	5	3	18
15		Total	11	23	25	41	35	135
16								
17	Entrees							
18		Chicken Kiev	3	5	5	6	8	27
19		Pot Roast	6	1	2	3	7	19
20		Fish	8	2	3	4	5	22
21		Total	17	8	10	13	20	68
22								
23	Desserts							
24		Apple Pie	3	6	8	7	2	26
25		Key Lime Pie	5	3	2	2	1	13
26		Pecan Pie	2	2	6	8	3	21
27		Total	10	11	16	17	6	60

Continue with the next page where you will learn how to close and save the workbook.

Closing a Workbook

You can close a Workbook by choosing **File**→**Close** from the menu bar. Excel will prompt you to save the workbook if it is new or if you have changed it since the last time you saved it.

Hands-On 1.12 – Close the workbook

1. Choose **File**→**Close** from the menu bar.

2. **Click** the **Yes** button when Excel asks if you want to save the changes.

    Hands-On Lesson 1 should have been the only open workbook. The Excel window changes when you close the last open workbook as discussed in the following illustration.

    Most commands on the pull-menus are unavailable when all workbooks have been closed.

    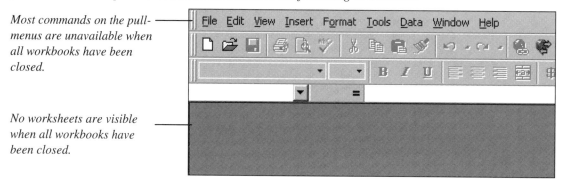

    No worksheets are visible when all workbooks have been closed.

    Your Excel window will most likely have the appearance shown in the preceding illustration. Don't be concerned if you still have an open workbook. You will learn to open new and existing workbooks and exit from Excel in the following sections.

Creating a New Workbook

You can create a new empty workbook at anytime by clicking the New ▢ button on the Standard toolbar.

Hands-On 1.13 – Create a New Workbook

1. **Click** the New ▢ button.

    A new empty workbook should appear. You could use this workbook to create a new worksheet, however, you will close this workbook in the next step.

2. Choose **File**→**Close** from the menu bar.

    The workbook is empty, so Excel will close it without asking you to save it.

Opening Existing Workbooks

The **Open** dialog box lets you open a workbook from a disk into the computer's memory. You can edit the workbook once it has been opened.

Hands-On 1.14 – Open the Hands-On Lesson 1 workbook

1. Choose **File→Open...** from the menu bar or **click** the Open 📂 button on the Standard toolbar. Take a few moments to study the following illustration but don't perform the steps yet.

You can click this list and choose a disk drive.   *This button moves you up one level in the file hierarchy.*   *This button launches your Web browser.*   *Use these buttons to create and access your favorite folders.*   *These buttons change the way the files are displayed in the dialog box.*

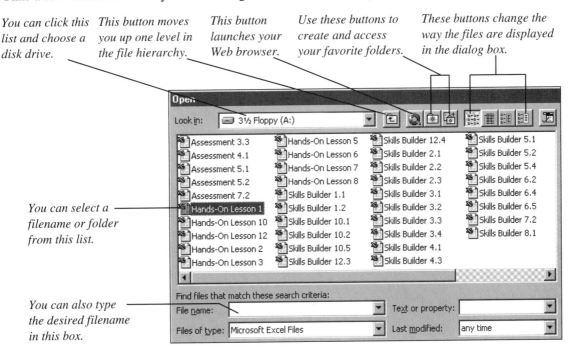

You can select a filename or folder from this list.

You can also type the desired filename in this box.

2. Use the following steps to open the Hands-On Lesson 1 workbook.

❶ **Click here** *and choose the disk drive that your diskette is in. It is most likely in 3 ½ Floppy [A:].*

❷ *Choose the* **Hands-On Lesson 1** *workbook.*

❸ **Click** *the* **Open** *button.*

Note: *You can also open a workbook by double-clicking it on the list. This saves you the effort of having to click the Open button.*

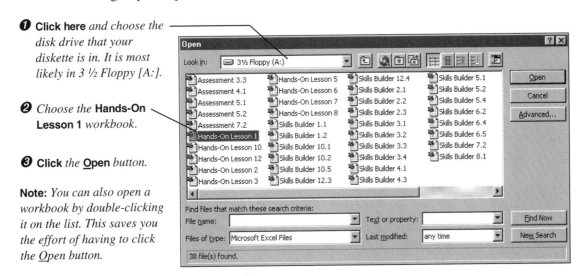

3. Take a few moments to scroll through the worksheet and you should notice that the most recent changes have been saved. You will exit from Excel on the next page.

Exiting From Excel

You should always exit from Excel when you have finished using the program. If you have one or more open workbooks and they have not been saved recently, then Excel will ask if you wish to save them.

Hands-On 1.15 – Exit from Excel

1. Choose **File**→**Exit** from the menu bar.

   The Excel program should close automatically and the Windows desktop should be displayed. Excel did not ask you to save the Hands-On Lesson 1 workbook because you did not change it after opening it in the previous exercise.

   Now continue with the questions and exercises on the following pages.

Concepts Review

True / False

1. Each workbook can have a maximum of one worksheet.

2. A worksheet is composed of horizontal rows and vertical columns.

3. Toolbars can be moved in the Excel window.

4. Text entries can contain spaces.

5. Numbers can only contain the digits 0 - 9 and not other characters.

6. The Undo button lets you reverse up to the last 16 changes.

7. A colon **:** is used to separate the beginning and ending cells in a range reference.

8. You can select an entire row by clicking the row header.

9. When given a choice, AutoSum will always sum the numbers to the left of the active cell instead of summing the numbers above the active cell.

10. The New button lets you open an existing workbook.

1. **T   F**
2. **T   F**
3. **T   F**
4. **T   F**
5. **T   F**
6. **T   F**
7. **T   F**
8. **T   F**
9. **T   F**
10. **T   F**

Multiple Choice

1. Which of the following keystrokes will always move the highlight to cell A1?
   a) Home.
   b) Ctrl + PageUp.
   c) Ctrl + Home.
   d) Ctrl + Insert.

   (   )

2. What happens when you enter a number in a cell that already has a text entry?
   a) The number replaces the text entry.
   b) Excel rejects the number and keeps the text entry intact.
   c) The cell contains both the number and text entry.
   d) The computer overheats and begins smoking.

   (   )

3. What happens when you insert an entry in the cell to the **right** of a long text entry?
   a) The display of the long entry is truncated.
   b) The long entry is permanently changed.
   c) It has no effect on the long entry.
   d) None of the above.

   (   )

4. What happens when you insert an entry in the cell to the **left** of a long text entry?
   a) The display of the long entry is truncated.
   b) The long entry is permanently truncated.
   c) It has no effect on the long entry.
   d) None of the above.

   (   )

5. Which button is used to confirm an entry?
   a)
   b)
   c)
   d) None of the above.

   (   )

Skills Builder 1.1

In this exercise, you will open and edit a workbook. The purpose of this exercise is to demonstrate that sometimes it is easier to replace entries while other times it is easier to edit them.

Open a workbook and replace several entries

1. **Start Excel** and **click** the Open ▣ button on the Standard toolbar.

2. Navigate to your exercise diskette and **double-click** the workbook named **Skills Builder 1.1**.

3. **Click** cell **A4**.

4. Type **Ralph** and **tap** ⌑Enter⌑.

    Notice it was easy to replace the entry because the name Ralph is easy to retype.

5. Replace the name **Calvin** in cell **A6** with the name **Steven**.

Use the Formula bar to edit several entries
6. **Click** cell **C4**.

7. **Click** in the Formula bar just in front of the telephone prefix 222.

8. **Tap** ⌑Delete⌑ **three times** to remove the prefix.

9. Type **333** and Confirm ✓ the entry.

10. Change the area code in cell **C8** from 714 to **814**.

Use in-cell editing to edit several entries
11. **Double-click** cell **D4**.

    The flashing insertion point should appear in the cell.

12. Use the ⌑→⌑ or ⌑←⌑ keys to position the insertion point in front of the word **Lane**.

13. Use the ⌑Delete⌑ key to remove the word **Lane**.

14. Type **Dam** (as in holds back water) and Confirm ✓ the entry.

15. Edit the next five addresses using either the Formula bar or in-cell editing. The required changes are shown in bold in the following table.

Cell	Make these changes
D5	2900 **Carlton** Drive, San Mateo, CA 94401
D6	**2300** Palm Drive, Miami, FL 33147
D7	888 Wilson Street, **Concord**, CA **94518**
D8	320 Main Street, **Pittsburgh**, PA 17951
D9	132nd Street, Los Angeles, CA **90045**

16. When you have finished, choose **File**→**Close** from the menu bar and **click** the **Yes** button when Excel asks if you wish to save the changes.

Skills Builder 1.2

In this exercise, you will open and edit a workbook. You will use AutoSum to compute totals and you will use the alignment buttons to align entries.

Open a workbook and compute the Totals

1. **Click** the Open ![open button] button on the Standard toolbar.

2. Navigate to your exercise diskette and **double-click** the workbook named **Skills Builder 1.2**.

3. **Click** cell **C10**.

4. **Click** AutoSum ![AutoSum button].

   Notice that Excel proposes the formula =SUM(C8:C9). Excel proposes this incorrect formula because there are empty cells in the range you need to sum. You will correct this by selecting the correct range in the next step.

5. **Drag** the mouse pointer over the range **C5:C9** as shown below.

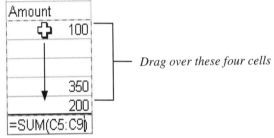

   Drag over these four cells

6. Confirm ![confirm button] the entry and the total should equal **650**.

7. Use the preceding steps to compute the totals in cells **E10**, **G10** and **I10**.

   You may need to scroll to the right ![scroll right button] *to see column I.*

Align the entries

8. Use the following steps to align the cell entries for Q1.

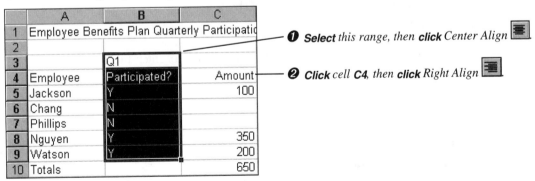

   ❶ **Select** *this range, then* ***click*** *Center Align* ![center align button]

   ❷ **Click** *cell* **C4**, *then* ***click*** *Right Align* ![right align button]

9. **Align** the entries for **Q2**, **Q3** and **Q4** as you just did for Q1. **Hint:** Use the ![Ctrl key] key to select multiple ranges that require the same alignment and align them with one command. You will also need to **right align** the word **Amount** in cells **E4**, **G4** and **I4**.

10. **Close** the workbook when you have finished and **save** the changes.

Skills Builder 1.3

In this exercise, you will create the worksheet shown at the bottom of this page. You will enter numbers that contain two decimal places. You will also use the alignment buttons to align the text and numbers.

Enter text and widen the columns

1. **Click** the New ⬜ button, then enter the text in rows 1-3 as shown below.

    *Make sure you enter the entire phrase **Order Tracking Sheet** into cell D1. Also, the entries in cells A3, B3 and E3 will be truncated. You will correct this by widening the columns in the next steps.*

	A	B	C	D	E	F	G
1				Order Tracking Sheet			
2							
3	Customer ID	Order Status	Item #	In Stock?	Order Total	Shipping Address	

2. Position the mouse pointer on the border between column headings A and B and the Adjust pointer A ↔ B will appear.

3. **Drag** the border to the right until the column is wide enough to display the entry **Customer ID**.

4. Widen columns **B** and **E** until the entries in those columns are completely visible.

Enter the numbers with decimal points

5. **Click** cell **E4**.

6. Type **100.91** and **tap** ⊡.

    You should always type the decimal point if your number requires it.

7. Type **45.87** and **tap** ⊡.

8. Enter the numbers shown below in cells **E6**, **E7** and **E8** (don't type the total 292.38 in cell E9).

Use AutoSum to compute the Total Orders

9. **Click** cell **E9**.

10. **Click** AutoSum Σ, then **click** the Confirm ✓ button.

    The total should be 292.38 as shown below.

11. Complete the worksheet as shown below. You will need to enter the numbers and text shown. Make sure you enter each shipping address into a single cell. For example, the address 1603 Catalina... should be entered in cell F4. Also, you will need to select the range A3:D8 and use the Center Align ▤ button to center the entries. Align all other entries as shown below.

12. When you have finished, choose **File→Close** from the menu bar and **save** the workbook to your exercise diskette as **Skills Builder 1.3**.

	A	B	C	D	E	F	G	H	I	J
1				Order Tracking Sheet						
2										
3	Customer ID	Order Status	Item #	In Stock?	Order Total	Shipping Address				
4	341	S	A423	Y	100.91	1603 Catalina Avenue, Redondo Beach, CA 90277				
5	234	S	A321	Y	45.87	Will Pickup				
6	567	I	S345	N	43.23	450 Terrace Drive, Santa Clara, CA 95050				
7	879	H	D567	N	78.92	No address at this point				
8	233	I	S230	Y	23.45	23 Maple Lane, Crawfordsville, IN 47933				
9	Total Orders				292.38					

Assessment 1.1

1. Open a New workbook.

2. Use the following guidelines to create the worksheet shown below.
    *   You will need to widen some of the columns to prevent the long entries from being truncated.
    *   Use formulas to compute the Totals. Be careful because the rows and columns contain blank cells. You will need to manually override the ranges that AutoSum proposes.
    *   Align the text entries in row 3 as shown.

    Your completed worksheet should match the worksheet shown below.

3. **Click** the Print button on the Standard toolbar when you have finished.
    The Print button prints the entire worksheet. You will learn more about printing in a later lesson.

4. **Close** the workbook when you have finished and **save** it as **Assessment 1.1**.

	A	B	C	D	E	F	G
1	Diane's Café - Employee Hourly Time Log						
2							
3	Employee	Wednesday	Thursday	Friday	Saturday	Sunday	Totals
4	Mary Johnson	6.5		5	6.5	4	22
5	Cliff Packard	4	6	6.5	6.5	4	27
6	Helen Martinez	4	6	6.5	6.5		23
7	Sarah Stonestown		4	4	4		12
8	Totals	14.5	16	22	23.5	8	84

 Assessment 1.2

1. Open a New workbook.

2. Create the worksheet shown on the following page. Make sure the numbers and Totals match the worksheet as shown. Also, you will need to widen columns and align the entries as shown.

3. **Click** the Print button on the Standard toolbar when you have finished.

4. **Close** the workbook when you have finished and **save** it as **Assessment 1.2**.

Continued...

	A	B	C	D	E	F
1	Diane's Café - Monthly Expense Report - Q1					
2						
3	Item		January	February	March	Q1 Totals
4	Rent and Utilities	Rent	800	800	800	2400
5		Utilities	340	400	250	990
6		Phone	250	200	300	750
7		Insurance	350			350
8		Total	1740	1400	1350	4490
9						
10	Cost of goods sold	Produce	2500	2320	1700	6520
11		Meat	4000	3400	3700	11100
12		Grains	1000	1200	890	3090
13		Total	7500	6920	6290	20710
14						
15	Salaries	Johnson	800	780	800	2380
16		Packard	750	650	870	2270
17		Martinez	900	780	680	2360
18		Stonestown	1200	1000	990	3190
19		Total	3650	3210	3340	10200
20						
21	Other	Advertising	500	300		800
22		Uniforms		340		340
23		Janitorial	200	200	200	600
24		Miscellaneous	100	2000		2100
25		Total	800	2840	200	3840

Critical Thinking 1.1

Create a worksheet that tracks the test scores for a student. Make room in the worksheet for five subjects such as Math, History, etc. There is no need to compute Totals in this worksheet. **Close** the workbook when you have finished and **save** it as **Student Scores**.

Critical Thinking 1.2

Create a worksheet that tracks the daily schedule for a small gardening service business. The schedule should include the job location and the number of hours it took to complete the job. The type of work required should also be listed such as lawn mowing, raking, etc. **Close** the workbook when you have finished and **save** it with a descriptive name that will allow you to identify it at a later time.

Critical Thinking 1.3

Create a worksheet that will help you manage some aspect of your life. Be creative and try to think of ways that a worksheet could help you better organize your schedule and/or activities. Perhaps you have a hobby where a worksheet could be useful? Do you have investments you need to manage? You may need a worksheet to compute more complex formulas than you have learned thus far. If this is the case, then set up the structure of the worksheet now and you can always add the formulas at a later time. **Close** your workbook and **save** it with a descriptive name when you have finished.

2 Expanding on the Basics

Objectives:

- ♦ Use the Office Assistant

- ♦ Use the fill handle

- ♦ Work with formulas

- ♦ Format text and numbers

- ♦ Use the Merge and Center button

- ♦ Indent text entries

- ♦ Use the Format Painter

- ♦ Use Print Preview and the Print dialog box

The Project - Donna's Deli

In this lesson, you will help Donna Prusko develop an income and expense-tracking sheet for her new vegetarian health food business - Donna's Deli. Donna has recently given up a dead end job to pursue her dream and passion - a deli that serves delicious health-conscious food at reasonable prices. However, Donna realizes that the health of her business is just as important as the health of her customers. For this reason, she wants to develop a worksheet to track her income and expenses. The worksheet will use formulas to determine both gross and net profits and it will compute an important financial ratio. You will develop the worksheet shown below as you progress through this lesson.

	A	B	C	D	E	F
1	Donna's Deli - Income and Expense Worksheet					
2						
3		Quarterly Income				
4		Q1	Q2	Q3	Q4	
5	Dine-in Sales	21,000	23,000	28,000	42,000	
6	Take-out Sales	12,000	16,000	25,000	56,000	
7	Subtotal	$33,000	$39,000	$53,000	$98,000	
8						
9	Tips	2,500	2,700	3,000	4,500	
10	Sublease	500	500	500	500	
11	Subtotal	$3,000	$3,200	$3,500	$5,000	
12	Total Income	$36,000	$42,200	$56,500	$103,000	
13						
14		Quarterly Expenses				
15		Q1	Q2	Q3	Q4	
16	Rent	3,000	3,000	3,000	3,000	
17	Utilities	400	310	290	380	
18	Marketing	800	800	800	800	
19	Salaries	12,000	12,000	14,000	14,000	
20	Supplies	15,000	15,500	18,000	24,000	
21	Equipment	6,000	2,000	1,000	-	
22	Total Expenses	$37,200	$33,610	$37,090	$42,180	
23						
24	Gross Profit	($1,200)	$8,590	$19,410	$60,820	
25	Net Profit	($1,200)	$8,590	$16,499	$45,615	
26	Gross Profit vs. Income	-3%	20%	34%	59%	

The Office Assistant

Microsoft Office 97 has an interactive Help feature known as the Office Assistant. The Office Assistant provides tips and suggestions and it also lets you locate Help topics by typing questions in plain English. The Office Assistant monitors your activities and provides suggestions whenever it assumes you need assistance. You can display or hide the Office Assistant as discussed in the following Quick Steps.

Quick Steps: *Displaying and Hiding the Office Assistant*

To display the Office Assistant

- Click the Office Assistant 🔲 button on the Standard toolbar.

To hide the Office Assistant

- Click the Close ☒ button at the top right corner of the Office Assistant.

Hands-On 2.1 – Check out the Office Assistant

1. Start Excel.

2. **Click** the Office Assistant 🔲 button on the right end of the Standard toolbar.

    An animated paper clip or some other assistant will appear. There are several different assistants with different personalities. However, they all provide the same interactive assistance.

3. **Click** the **Tips** button on the yellow command area and a Tip of the Day will appear.

    Reading the daily tips can be an effective way to enhance your Excel skills.

4. **Click** the **Close** button at the bottom right corner of the tip.

5. Use the following steps to search for a Help topic.

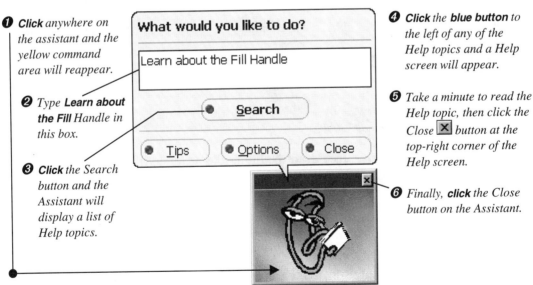

❶ **Click** *anywhere on the assistant and the yellow command area will reappear.*

❷ *Type* **Learn about the Fill** *Handle in this box.*

❸ **Click** *the Search button and the Assistant will display a list of Help topics.*

What would you like to do?

Learn about the Fill Handle

● Search

● Tips ● Options ● Close

❹ **Click** *the* **blue button** *to the left of any of the Help topics and a Help screen will appear.*

❺ *Take a minute to read the Help topic, then click the Close ☒ button at the top-right corner of the Help screen.*

❻ *Finally,* **click** *the Close button on the Assistant.*

Feel free to use the Office Assistant whenever you have a question or are unsure how to complete a procedure. The Assistant can be very helpful once you learn to use it properly. Also, you can close the Assistant at any time by clicking the Close ☒ button.

The Fill Handle

A small black square is always visible at the bottom right corner of the active cell or the active range. This square is called the **fill handle**. The fill handle can be used to copy the content of the active cell to adjacent cells. The fill handle can also be used to enter common series such as days of the week or months of the year. You can also use the fill handle to expand a repeating series of numbers such as 5, 10, 15, 20 etc.

Hands-On 2.2 – Use the fill handle to expand a series and copy cells

1. Open the workbook named **Hands-On Lesson 2** from your exercise diskette.

Use the fill handle to expand the Q1 series
2. **Click** cell **B4**.

> *Notice that cell B4 contains the heading Q1. Excel recognizes Q1 as the beginning of the series Q1 - Q4. You will expand the series by dragging the fill handle in the next step.*

3. Use the following steps to expand the Q1 - Q4 series.

❶ *Position the mouse pointer on the bottom right corner of the cell and a black cross will appear.*   ❷ **Drag** *to the right over the next three cells and a shaded rectangle will appear.*

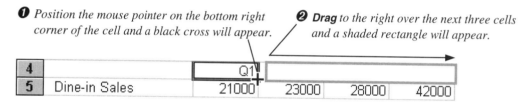

❸ *Release the mouse button and the series will be expanded to Q1 - Q4.*

> *Excel recognizes Q1 and several other entries such as a day of the week (Saturday) or a month (January) as the beginning of a series. You can always expand the series using the technique shown above. Also, notice that Excel right aligned the headings Q2 - Q4 because Q1 was right aligned.*

4. **Click** cell **B15** and use the fill handle to expand Q1 to Q1 - Q4 as you did in the previous step.

Use the fill handle to copy cells
5. **Click** cell **B7**.

6. **Click** AutoSum ⟦Σ⟧ and confirm ⟦✓⟧ the entry.
> *The Subtotal should equal 33000.*

7. Make sure cell B7 is active, then **drag** the fill handle **+** to the right until the shaded rectangle is over cells C7, D7 and E7.

8. **Release** the mouse button and the formula should be copied to those cells.

> *Notice that Excel determines whether it should copy the cell or expand a series. Excel will always copy the cell unless the cell represents the beginning of a series as explained above.*

9. **Click** cell **B11** and use **AutoSum** to compute the Subtotal.

10. Use the fill handle to copy the formula in cell B11 to cells C11, D11 and E11.

11. Use these techniques to compute the **Total Expenses** in row **22** (not Total Income in row 12).

> *Keep in mind that it would have been easier to select the four cells in these examples and use AutoSum to automatically compute the totals. However, there are times when it is beneficial to use the fill handle to copy cells as you will see in the next topic.*

Formulas

You already learned how to compute totals with the AutoSum button. The AutoSum button provides a convenient method for summing a range of numbers. The summation of a range is the most common type of formula. However, you will need to use many other types of formulas in Excel. In fact, many worksheets such as financial models require hundreds or even thousands of complex formulas! You can manually enter formulas as you will do in this section or you can use Excel's Function Wizard to assist you in creating formulas and functions.

Always begin formulas with an equal = sign

It is recommended that you always begin formulas with an equal = sign. You can also begin formulas with a plus + or minus − sign, however, it is better to adopt one method. This way, you will know that the first step in creating a formula is to always use an equal = sign.

Formulas can include cell and range references

You already used the AutoSum button to create formulas such as =SUM(C3:E3). The formula in this example contains the range reference (C3:E3). Formulas derive their power from the use of cell and range references. There are two important benefits to using references in formulas.

1. Since the formula refers to a cell or a range of cells, the formula results are automatically recalculated when the data is changed in the referenced cell(s).

2. The formula can be copied (as you did with the fill handle) to other cells.

Formulas can include arithmetic operators and spaces

Formulas can include the standard arithmetic operators shown in the following table. You can also use spaces within formulas to improve the appearance and readability of the formula. Notice that each formula in the table begins with an equal = sign. Also, keep in mind that each formula would be entered in a cell and the resulting calculation would be displayed in that cell.

Operator	Example	Comments
+ (addition)	=B7 + B11	Adds the values in cells B7 and B11.
- (subtraction)	=B7 - B11	Subtracts the value in B11 from B7.
* (multiplication)	=B7 * B11	Multiplies the values in B7 and B11.
/ (division)	=B7 / B11	Divides the value in B7 by the value in B11.
^ (exponentiation)	=B7 ^ 3	Raises the value in B7 to the third power (B7*B7*B7).
% (percent)	=B7 * 10%	Multiplies the value in B7 by 10% (.10).
( ) (calculations)	=B7 / (C4-C2)	Parentheses change the order of calculations. In this example, C2 would be subtracted from C4 and then B7 would be divided by the result. Order of calculations is discussed in detail in a later lesson.

Hands-On 2.3 – Manually enter formulas

In this exercise, you will enter two formulas in the Hands-On Lesson 2 worksheet.

Compute the Total Income in cells B12 and C12
1. **Click** cell **B12**.

2. Type **=B7+B11** and **click** the Confirm button.

   The result should be 36000. This is the summation of the two Subtotals in cells B7 and B11.

3. **Click** cell **C12**.

4. Type **=C7+C11** and **click** the Confirm ✓ button and the result should be 42200.

Relative cell references

All formulas use relative cell references unless you specifically instruct Excel to use an absolute reference (absolute references are discussed in a later lesson). Relative references make it easy to copy formulas to other cells. For example, cell C12 contains the formula =C7+C11. If this formula is copied to cell D12, then the formula in D12 will become =D7+D11. The references to cells C7 and C11 are updated to reflect the new location of the formula.

Point Mode

One potential danger that can occur when typing formulas is that you will accidentally type the wrong cell reference. This is easy to do especially if the worksheet is complex and contains large numbers of cells. **Point mode** can help you avoid this problem. With point mode, you can insert a reference in a formula by clicking or dragging the desired cell(s). You will use this technique in the following exercise.

Hands-On 2.4 – Use point mode and copy a formula with the fill handle

In this exercise, you will complete the last two formulas in row 12.

Create a formula using point mode
1. **Click** cell **D12**.

2. Type an equal **=** sign.

   Notice Excel begins building the formula by entering the equal = sign in the Formula bar.

3. **Click** cell **D7**.

   Notice that Excel adds the reference D7 to the formula in the Formula bar.

4. Type a plus **+** sign (try tapping the plus + key on the Numeric keypad).

5. **Click** cell **D11**.

   The Formula bar should contain the completed formula =D7+D11.

6. Confirm ✓ the entry and the total should be 56500.

Continued...

Copy the formula with the fill handle

7. Make sure the highlight is in cell **D12**, and then **drag** the **fill handle ✛** one cell to the right.

    The formula should be copied to cell E12 and the result should be 103000.

8. **Click** cell **E12** and notice the formula in the Formula bar.

    The formula should be =E7+E11. The references were updated to reflect the new formula location.

The Edit Formula Button and the Formula Palette

You can begin a formula by clicking the Edit Formula [=] button on the Formula bar. This has the same effect as tapping the equal = key on the Numeric keypad. Excel also displays a Formula Palette whenever the Edit Formula [=] button is clicked. The Formula Pallete can assist you in creating and editing formulas.

Hands-On 2.5 – Use the Edit Formula button to create additional formulas

1. If necessary, scroll down until rows 12 - 26 are visible.

2. **Click** cell **B24**.

    Cell B24 will contain the Gross Profit. The Gross Profit is calculated as the Total Income in cell B12 minus the Total Expenses in Cell B22.

3. **Click** the Edit Formula [=] button on the Formula bar.

    Excel will enter an equal = sign in the Formula bar and the Formula Palette will appear below the Formula bar. You will see the result of your formula in the palette as you build it using point mode.

4. **Click** cell **B12** and the Formula Palette will indicate a result of 36000.

5. Type a minus **-** sign, then **click** cell **B22**.

6. Confirm the formula by **clicking** the **OK** button on the Formula Palette.

    The Gross Profit should equal –1200 or (1200). Excel may be set-up on your computer to display negative numbers with parenthesis instead of minus signs. This is a common convention that many accountants use. As you can see, Donna's Deli is not profitable in the first quarter.

7. Copy the formula to the next three cells by **dragging** the fill handle ✛ to the right.

    The completed row should match the row shown below.

24	Gross Profit	-1200	8590	19410	60820

Calculate Net Profit by multiplying Gross Profit * Tax Rate

*You will calculate the Net Profit in the next few steps. You will use a simplified Net Profit calculation that is the Gross Profit minus income taxes. We will make the assumption that Donna will pay no taxes in Q1 and Q2 because she lost money in Q1 and her gross profit was only $8,590 in Q2. Furthermore, we will assume that Donna's tax rate will be 15% for Q3 and 25% for Q4. The formula is, Net Profit = Gross Profit * (1- Taxrate). For example, if the tax rate is 15%, then Donna will keep 85% of her Gross Profit. So the Net Profit = Gross Profit * .85.*

8. **Click** cell **B24**.

Continued...

Look at the Formula bar and notice the Gross Profit is calculated as B12 - B22. The Gross Profit and Net Profit will be the same in Q1 since Donna will not pay any income tax. In the next few steps, you will attempt to copy the gross profit formula from cell B24 to cell B25.

9. Use the following step to copy the formula from cell B24 to B25.

24	Gross Profit	($1,200)
25	Net Profit	

❶ *Drag the fill handle down to cell B25 and the Net Profit will equal 0.*

10. **Click** cell **B24** and notice the Gross Profit formula in the Formula bar is =B12-B22.

11. Now **click** cell **B25** and notice the Net Profit formula is =B13-B23.

12. Look at cells **B13** and **B23** in the worksheet and you will notice they are empty.

   The result of the formula is 0 because cells B13 and B23 are empty. This example demonstrates that you must be careful when copying formulas. Excel updated the cell references when you copied the formula. This produced an incorrect result.

13. **Click** Undo to reverse the copy procedure.

14. **Click** cell **B25** and enter the formula **=B24**.

   This simple formula makes cells B24 and B25 equal to one another.

15. **Click** cell **C25** and enter the formula **= C24**.

   Once again, the Net Profit and Gross Profit should be equal in Q2.

16. **Click** cell **D25** and enter the formula **=D24 * 85%**.

   The result should be 16498.5. We are assuming a tax rate of 15% in Q3, so Donna gets to keep 85% of her gross profit.

17. **Click** cell **E25** and enter the formula **=E24 * 75%**.

   The result should be 45615. Keep in mind that you can either type the formulas or use point mode and the Formula Palette. From this point forward, you will be instructed to enter a formula and you should use whichever method works best for you.

Calculate the ratios in row 26 by dividing the Gross Profit by the Total Income

Donna wants to determine the ratio of Gross Profit to Total Income or GP/TI. This ratio is important in determining the health of a business. This ratio is one indicator that will show Donna how fast she can grow her business by reinvesting the money she earns. This ratio will show Donna the amount of profit she will earn from each dollar of product she sells.

18. **Click** cell **B26** and enter the formula **=B24/B12**.

   The result should be -0.03333. You will convert this number to a percentage later in this lesson.

19. Use the fill handle to **copy** the formula **to** cells **C26, D26** and **E26**.

   The results should match the results shown below.

26	Gross Profit vs. Income	-0.03333	0.203555	0.34354	0.590485

20. **Click** cell **C26** and notice the formula =C24/C12.

   Once again, Excel updated the cell references when the formula was copied. In this case, it is good that the references were updated because the formula now refers to the correct Gross Profit and Total Income in cells C24 and C12.

21. **Click** the Save button to save the changes to the worksheet.

Number Formats

Excel lets you format numbers in a variety of ways. The number formats change the way numbers are displayed in the worksheet. The following table discusses the most common number formats.

Number Format	Description
General	Numbers have a General style when they are first entered. The General style does not apply any special formats to the numbers.
Comma	The Comma format inserts a comma between every third digit in the number. An optional decimal point with decimal places can also be displayed.
Currency	The Currency format is the same as the Comma format except a dollar $ sign is placed in front of the number.
Percent	A percent % sign is inserted to the right of the number. The number is multiplied by 100 and the resulting percentage is displayed in the cell.

The following table provides several examples of formatted numbers.

Number you enter	Format	How the number is displayed
1000.984	General	1000.984
1000.984	Comma with 0 decimal places Comma with 2 decimal places	1,000 1,000.98
1000.984	Currency with 0 decimal places Currency with 2 decimal places	$1,000 $1,000.98
.5366	Percent with 0 decimal places Percent with 2 decimal places	54% 53.66%

Setting Number Formats with the Formatting Toolbar

The Formatting toolbar has several buttons that let you apply the Currency, Comma and Percent number formats or styles as they are called. These are the most common types of number styles. The Formatting toolbar also has buttons that let you increase or decrease the number of decimal places. The following illustration discusses the various number formatting buttons on the Formatting toolbar.

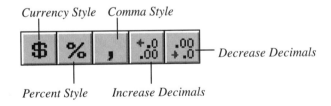

Increasing and decreasing the decimals does not change the actual number

The Increase and Decrease decimal buttons change the number of displayed decimals. For example, you could enter the number 100.37 and then format it as Currency with 0 decimal places. The number would then be displayed as $100. However, the actual number would remain 100.37. The number 100.37 would be used in any calculations that refer to that cell.

Hands-On 2.6 – Format numbers

In this exercise, you will format numbers with buttons on the Formatting toolbar.

Apply the Currency Style to the first Subtotal row

1. **Scroll up** until the top row of the worksheet is visible.

2. **Select** the **four Subtotals in row 7** (but **be careful not to use the fill handle**).

   *The fill handle is **not** used to select cells. It is only used to copy cells or to expand a series. Make sure your pointer has the thick cross ⊕ shape whenever you wish to select cells (like now).*

3. **Click** the Currency Style $ button and the cells should be formatted as shown below.

7	Subtotal	$ 33,000.00	$ 39,000.00	$ 53,000.00	$ 98,000.00

   Notice that the Currency Style adds a dollar sign in front of the number and a comma between every third digit. It also adds a decimal point with two decimal places. Excel should also have widened the columns to accommodate the additional characters and numbers. Also notice that the formatted numbers are shifted slightly to the left and do not line-up with the numbers above them. You will adjust the alignment later in this lesson.

Decrease the decimals

4. Make sure the four cells you just formatted are selected.

5. **Click** the Decrease Decimal button **twice** to remove the decimal display.

   Notice the dollar signs $ are positioned on the left side of the cells. Once again, you will adjust this alignment later in the lesson.

6. **Select** the Subtotal and Total Income cells in rows 11 and 12 as shown below.

11	Subtotal	3000	3200	3500	5000
12	Total Income	36000	42200	56500	103000

7. **Click** the Currency Style $ button, then decrease the decimals to 0.

8. Format the numbers in rows **22**, **24** and **25** as **Currency** with **0** decimals.

Apply the Comma Style

9. **Select** the numbers in rows **5** and **6**.

10. **Click** the Comma Style , button, then decrease the decimals to 0.

    Notice the Comma Style is similar to the Currency Style except a dollar sign is not displayed. Also notice that the numbers now line-up with the Currency formatted numbers in the Subtotal row.

11. Format the numbers in the ranges **B9:E10** and **B16:E21** as **Comma** with **0** decimals.

Apply the Percent Style to the last row

12. **Select** the numbers in the last row of the worksheet.

13. **Click** the Percent Style % button.

    The numbers should be formatted as Percent with 0 decimal places. The Percent Style does not display decimals because it is usually better to display percentages without decimals. You can always use the Increase Decimal button to display decimals if desired. You will learn more about number formats in the next section.

Setting Number Formats with the Format Cells Dialog Box

The Format Cells dialog box provides additional number formats that are not available on the Formatting toolbar. You can format numbers in virtually any manner by first selecting them and then using this dialog box. You can even create your own customized number formats to suit your needs.

Dollar signs $ can have a fixed or floating format

The dollar signs $ in the Hands-On Lesson 2 worksheet currently have a fixed format. In other words, they are fixed on the left side of the cells. You can use the Format Cells dialog box to change the dollar sign format to floating. The floating format positions the dollar signs just to the left of the numbers. You will use this technique in the following Hands-On exercise.

Hands-On 2.7 – Change the dollar $ signs to floating and explore the dialog box

1. **Select** the numbers with the Currency format in row 7.

2. Choose **Format→Cells...** form the menu bar.

3. Make sure the Number tab is active at the top of the dialog box.

4. Notice the Custom option is chosen at the bottom of the Category list.

   The Custom option is chosen because you modified the Currency Style when you decreased the decimal places in the previous exercises. You created a custom number format when you did this.

5. Use the following steps to format the numbers with floating dollar $ signs.

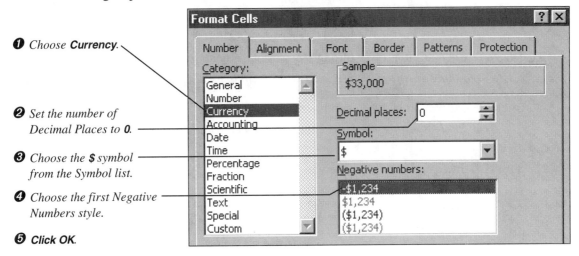

❶ Choose **Currency.**

❷ Set the number of Decimal Places to **0.**

❸ Choose the $ symbol from the Symbol list.

❹ Choose the first Negative Numbers style.

❺ Click OK.

Notice that the dollar signs are now floating just in front of the numbers. The Currency Style creates floating dollar signs. Also, notice that the numbers are now shifted slightly to the right and they no longer line-up with the numbers above them. This is because of the Negative Numbers option you set. The Negative Numbers option impacts the alignment of the numbers. You will adjust the Negative Numbers option in the next step.

Continued...

Adjust the Negative Numbers option
6. Make sure cells **B7:E7** are still selected, then choose **Format→Cells...** form the menu bar.

7. Notice the various Negative Numbers formats.

The formats that are red in color will cause negative numbers to display in red. This is a convention that many accountants like to use. Also notice that some of the formats have parenthesis around them. Once again, many accountants like negative numbers to be displayed with parenthesis instead of a minus sign as shown in the first format.

8. Choose the third Negative Numbers format **($1,234)** and **click OK**.

The numbers should now be aligned with the numbers above them. Just remember that the Negative Numbers formats determine how the numbers line-up on the right side or with the decimal points.

Check out the Accounting Style
9. Make sure cells **B7:E7** are still selected, then choose **Format→Cells...** form the menu bar.

10. Choose the **Accounting** option.

11. Make sure the Symbol type is set to **$** and the **Decimal Places** are set to **0**.

12. **Click OK** and the dollar $ signs will once again have a fixed placement on the left side of the cells.

Notice that this was how the numbers were formatted when you clicked the Currency Style button on the toolbar and decreased the decimals. The Currency Style button actually applies the Accounting Style to the numbers. The Accounting Style positions the dollar signs on the left side of the cell with a fixed format.

13. **Click** Undo [icon] to restore the Currency Style.

Check out the other number styles
14. Choose **Format→Cells...** form the menu bar.

15. Take a few minutes to browse through the various number styles in the Category list.

Feel free choose a style and then read the description that appears at the bottom of the dialog box.

16. **Click** the **Cancel** button when you have finished exploring.

Later in this lesson, you will format the other numbers that currently have dollar signs.

17. Save [icon] the changes and continue with the next topic.

Merging Cells

Excel's Merge cells option lets you merge one or more cells together. Merged cells behave as one large cell. This allows you to align text within the merged cell. You can merge cells vertically or horizontally.

The Merge and Center Button

The Merge and Center ⊞ button merges selected cells and changes the alignment of the merged cell to center. This technique is often used to center a heading across columns. The following example shows a heading that is centered across columns B through E.

The Quarterly Income heading is centered above columns B through E.

	A	B	C	D	E
3		Quarterly Income			
4		Q1	Q2	Q3	Q4

Hands-On 2.8 – Center headings across columns

1. **Select** the range **B3:E3** as shown below.

	A	B	C	D	E
1	Donna's Deli - Income and Expense Worksheet				
2					
3		Quarterly Income			

   Notice that this range includes the heading you wish to center (Quarterly Income) and the range of cells you wish to center this heading in (B3:E3).

2. **Click** the Merge and Center ⊞ button (near the middle of the Formatting toolbar).

   Notice the cells have been merged together and the Center ☰ button is depressed.

3. **Click** the Align Left ☰ button and the entry will move to the left side of the merged cell.

4. **Click** the Center ☰ button to re-center the entry.

5. Choose **Format→Cells...** from the menu bar.

6. **Click** the Alignment tab on the Format Cells dialog box.

   Notice the ☑ Merge cells box is checked. This box is checked whenever cells are merged.

7. Remove the check from the Merge cells box and **click OK**.

8. **Click** anywhere to deselect the cells and notice they are no longer merged.

9. **Click** Undo ↶ to restore the merging.

10. **Select** the range **B14:E14**.

11. **Click** the Merge and Center ⊞ button to center the Quarterly Expenses heading.

Indenting Text

The Increase Indent and Decrease Indent 📊 buttons on the Formatting toolbar let you indent text entries from the left edge of the cell. This can be useful in showing that one entry is subordinate to another.

Hands-On 2.9 – Indent text entries

1. **Click** cell **A5**.

2. **Click** the Increase Indent 📊 button **twice**.

   Notice the Dine-in Sales entry is indented slightly each time you click the button.

3. **Click** the Decrease Indent 📊 once.

4. **Click** cell **A6** and increase the indent 📊 **once**.

Indent multiple entries
5. **Select** cells **A9** and **A10**.

6. **Press & Hold** the `Ctrl` key and select the range **A16:A21**.

   The cells you should have selected are shown below.

9	Tips
10	Sublease
11	Subtotal
12	Total Income
13	
14	
15	
16	Rent
17	Utilities
18	Marketing
19	Salaries
20	Supplies
21	Equipment

7. Increase the indent 📊 **once**.

Formatting Text and Numbers

The Formatting toolbar has several buttons that let you format text and numbers. You can change the size and typeface of text. You can also change the color of text and add bold, italics and underlining to text.

Hands-On 2.10 – Formatting text and numbers

Change the typeface and size and add Bold

1. **Click** cell **A1**.

2. Use the Formatting toolbar and the following steps to format the title.

❶ *Click this drop-down button and choose a typeface. This example uses Bookman Old Style.*

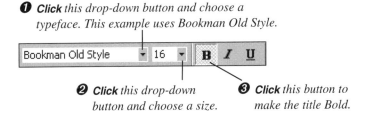

❷ *Click this drop-down button and choose a size.*   ❸ *Click this button to make the title Bold.*

Notice that the entire title is formatted. Once again, the entire title belongs to cell A1 even though it is displayed over the adjacent cells.

Change the color

3. **Click** the Font Color drop-down ![A button] button on the right end of the Formatting toolbar.

4. Choose your favorite color.

   Notice that the color you chose is now displayed on the button ![A button]. You can now apply the same color to other cells by selecting the cells and then clicking the button.

Apply the same color to another cell

5. **Click** cell **B3**.

   Cell B3 is now part of the large merged cell in the range B3:E3.

6. **Click** the Font Color ![A button] button and the same color will be applied to Quarterly Income.

7. Increase the size of Quarterly Income to **12** and make it **Bold**.

Format the Q1-Q4 headings

8. **Select** the **Q1 - Q4** headings in row 4.

9. Apply any formats you desire to Q1 – Q4.

   You will use the Format Painter to copy text and number formats in the next topic.

The Format Painter

The Format Painter button on the Standard toolbar lets you copy text and number formats from one cell to other cells. This can be an effective and efficient way to format cells. Another benefit of the Format Painter is it helps create consistent formatting throughout a workbook.

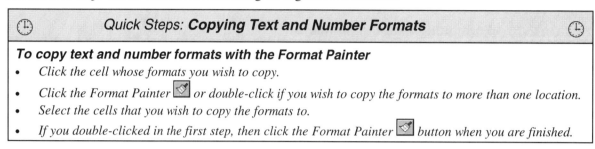

🕐 **Quick Steps: *Copying Text and Number Formats*** 🕐

To copy text and number formats with the Format Painter

- *Click the cell whose formats you wish to copy.*
- *Click the Format Painter ✎ or double-click if you wish to copy the formats to more than one location.*
- *Select the cells that you wish to copy the formats to.*
- *If you double-clicked in the first step, then click the Format Painter ✎ button when you are finished.*

Hands-On 2.11 – Copy text and number formats

In this exercise, you will use the Format Painter to copy text and number formats.

Copy text formats

1. **Click** cell **B3** (the merged cell with the Quarterly Income heading).

2. **Click** the Format Painter ✎ and the PaintBrush pointer ⬇ should appear.

3. **Click** cell **B14** (the merged cell with the Quarterly Expenses heading).

   The text formats should be copied to that heading.

4. **Click** cell **B4**.

   This cell should contain the heading Q1.

5. **Click** the Format Painter ✎.

6. **Select** the range **B15:E15** as shown below and the format will be copied to those cells.

15		Q1	Q2	Q3	Q4

Copy number formats

7. **Select** the cells that contain numbers in row 7 and add Bold **B** to the numbers.

8. **Click** cell **B7**.

   Notice that this cell (and the rest of the numbers in row 7) has a Currency Style with the dollar sign floating just in front of the number. You will use the Format Painter to copy both the number and text formats to the numbers in rows 11 and 12 and rows 22-25. Notice that these rows currently have a fixed dollar sign on the left edge of the cell.

9. **Double-click** the Format Painter ✎.

10. **Select** the range **B11:E12** as shown below and the formats will be copied to those cells.

11	Subtotal	$3,000	$3,200	$3,500	$5,000
12	Total Income	$36,000	$42,200	$56,500	$103,000

Continued...

11. **Select** the range **B22:E26** as shown below and the formats will be copied to those cells.

22	Total Expenses	$37,200	$33,610	$37,090	$42,180
23					
24	Gross Profit	($1,200)	$8,590	$19,410	$60,820
25	Net Profit	($1,200)	$8,590	$16,499	$45,615
26	Gross Profit vs. Income	($0)	$0	$0	$1

12. **Click** the Format Painter to turn it off.

Notice that you had to turn the Format Painter off this time because you double-clicked it initially. Also, notice the Percent number style in row 26 has been removed. Be careful when you are trying to copy text formats but not number formats. In this example, you wanted to copy the bold text style to row 26 but not the Currency Style. Keep in mind that the Format Painter copies both text and number formats.

13. **Select** the numbers in row 26 and use the Percent Style button to reapply the Percent Style.

14. Feel free to format the worksheet in any way that you feel looks attractive.

When formatting a worksheet, try to format the items you wish to draw attention to.

15. Turn to the second page of this lesson and take a look at the completed worksheet. The numbers and formats should match the worksheet you have developed.

16. Save the changes and continue with the next topic.

Print Preview and the Print Dialog Box

You have been printing with the Print ![] button thus far in this course. The Print button sends the entire worksheet to the printer. Excel also has a Print dialog box which provides several printing options and lets you manage your print jobs. The Print Preview feature lets you preview a worksheet prior to printing it. The worksheet appears almost exactly as it will appear when it is printed. Print Preview can save paper and wear and tear on your printer. It can also save you time and help you avoid printing worksheets that aren't quite ready to be printed.

Hands-On 2.12 – Use Print Preview and the Print dialog box

Use Print Preview

1. **Click** the Print Preview ![] button on the Standard toolbar (5th button from the left).

   The Print Preview window will appear. The colored text in your worksheet will appear in black if you do not have a color printer. You can only print colored text if you have a color printer.

2. Zoom in by **clicking** the mouse pointer (it will look like a magnifying glass) on the worksheet.

3. Use the vertical scroll bar to **scroll** up and down.

   Notice that Print Preview displays the worksheet almost exactly as it will print. Print Preview is very close to full WYSIWYG (What You See Is What You Get). Also, notice the Zoom option on the Print Preview toolbar. You just used the Zoom option by clicking on the worksheet. You will learn how to use the Setup and Margins options later in this course. Also notice the Print button. You could use this button to print the worksheet. However, we will delay printing for now.

4. **Click** anywhere on the worksheet to zoom back out.

5. **Click** the **Close** button to return to the normal worksheet view.

Check out the print range

6. If necessary, scroll to the right until you see a vertical dashed line in your worksheet.

   The line should be located between columns G and H. This line represents the right edge of the first printed page. This line appears after you use Print Preview or after you print the worksheet.

7. **Scroll** down until you see a horizontal dashed line in your worksheet.

   The line should be located around row 50. This line represents the bottom of the first page.

Continued...

Check out the Print dialog box

8. Choose **File** from the menu bar.

Notice that Print Preview can also be chosen from the File menu (but don't do it).

9. Choose **Print...** and the Print dialog box will display.

10. Take a few moments to study the following illustration.

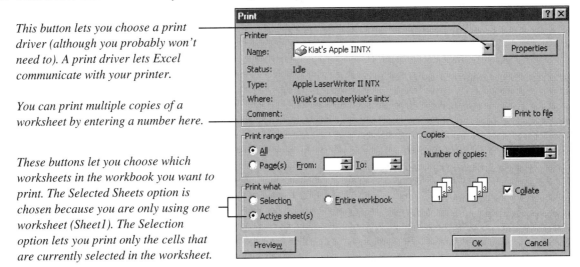

This button lets you choose a print driver (although you probably won't need to). A print driver lets Excel communicate with your printer.

You can print multiple copies of a worksheet by entering a number here.

These buttons let you choose which worksheets in the workbook you want to print. The Selected Sheets option is chosen because you are only using one worksheet (Sheet1). The Selection option lets you print only the cells that are currently selected in the worksheet.

11. Click OK to print the entire worksheet.

Keep in mind that you did not have to use the Print dialog box to print this worksheet. The Print button would have worked just fine for this worksheet. The Print dialog box becomes more useful with large worksheets or when you have special printing needs.

Print a selected range

12. Select the range **A1:E12**.

You will print just this income part of the worksheet in the next few steps.

13. Choose **File→Print...** from the menu bar.

14. Choose the Selection ⦿ Selection option and **click OK**.

15. Retrieve your printout from the printer and you will see that only the selected range was printed.

16. Feel free to experiment with the print options.

17. Close the workbook and **save** the changes when you have finished.

Now continue with the end-of-lesson questions and exercises on the following pages.

Concepts Review

True / False

1. The Office Assistant [?] button is used to display the Office Assistant.
2. The fill handle cannot be used to copy formulas.
3. The Merge and Center button can only be used with numbers.
4. Formulas must always begin with an open parenthesis (.
5. Formulas can include both cell and range references.
6. The * is used to represent multiplication in formulas.
7. Point mode can be used to insert cell and range references in formulas.
8. The Comma number style inserts a dollar sign in front of the number.
9. You can set a typeface and size for both text and numbers.
10. The Format Painter copies text formats but not number formats.

1. T   F
2. T   F
3. T   F
4. T   F
5. T   F
6. T   F
7. T   F
8. T   F
9. T   F
10. T   F

Multiple Choice

1. What should you do before clicking the Merge and Center button?
    a) Click the cell that contains the entry you wish to center.
    b) Select the cells you wish to center the entry across while making sure the entry is included in the selection.
    c) Select the entire row that contains the entry you wish to center.   ( )
    d) None of the above.

2. Which of the following symbols can be used to begin a formula?
    a) +
    b) -
    c) =
    d) All of the above.   ( )

3. Which of the following characters can be used in formulas?
    a) +
    b) %
    c) blank space
    d) All of the above.   ( )

4. How would the number 10000.367 be displayed if you format it as comma with 2 decimals?
    a) 10,000.38
    b) $10,000.38
    c) 10,000
    d) None of the above.   ( )

5. How is the dollar sign positioned with the Accounting number style?
    a) Floats to the immediate left of the number.
    b) Fixed on the left edge of the cell.
    c) The Accounting style does not place a dollar sign in front of the number.
    d) It depends on whether the number has a decimal point.   ( )

Skills Builder 2.1

In this exercise, you will open a home budget worksheet on your exercise diskette. You will format the worksheet until it matches the worksheet shown at the end of this exercise.

Open the workbook and center the title

1. **Open** the workbook named **Skills Builder 2.1** on your exercise diskette.

2. Widen column A until the text entries in that column are visible.

3. **Select** the range **A1:G1** as shown below.

1	1996 Home Budget					

4. **Click** the Merge and Center ⊞ button to center 1996 Home Budget above the worksheet.

Use the fill handle to copy headings

5. **Select** the heading **January** in cell **B3 and** the **empty cell** to the right of January.

6. **Drag** the fill handle **✛** over the **next four cells** to the right and Excel will expand the series.

    Excel assumes you want the series January - March with an empty cell between each month. This is a correct assumption and the result is shown below.

3		January		February		March

7. **Select** cells **B4** and **C4** (the Budget and Spent cells).

8. **Drag** the fill handle **✛** over the next four cells to the right and Excel will copy cells B4 and C4 to those cells.

    You should now have three sets of Budget Spent cells.

Center the month headings across columns

9. **Select** the **January** heading and the **blank cell** to the right of it.

10. **Click** Merge and Center ⊞ to center January over the Budget and Spent columns.

11. **Center** the **February** and **March** headings over their Budget and Spent columns.

12. **Select row 4** and right align ▤ the Budget and Spent headings.

Compute all three Subtotals with a single command

In the next two steps, you will use the Ctrl key to select multiple ranges.

13. **Select** the range **B9:G9** (the cells where the Subtotals in row 9 will be placed).

14. **Press & Hold** the ⌞Ctrl⌟ key while you **select** the ranges **B14:G14** and **B19:G19**.

    You should now have all three of the Subtotal ranges selected.

15. **Click** AutoSum ∑ and all three Subtotal rows will be computed.

Compute the Totals and Differences

16. **Click** cell **B21**.

17. Enter the formula **=B9+B14+B19** and confirm ✓ the entry.

    You can type the formula or use Point Mode.

Continued...

18. Use the **fill handle +** to copy the formula across the row.

19. Click cell **B22**.

This cell will contain the Difference between the January Budget and January Spent in row 21.

20. Enter the formula **=B21-C21**.

The result should be 158.

21. Compute the Differences in cells **D22** and **F22**.

The results should be 118 and -739. You may want to use some trick or shortcut to enter these formulas. For example, you may want to use the fill handle to copy the formula in cell B22 across and then delete the formulas in cells C22, E22 and G22.

Format the numbers then copy the number formats
22. Select the **Subtotal** numbers in **row 9**.

23. Click the Currency **[$]** button.

24. Click the Decrease Decimal **[.00]** button **twice** to reduce the decimals to 0.

If you want the dollar $ signs to float next to the numbers, then make sure the cells are selected and use the Format→Cells... command. Choose the Currency style and set the number of decimal places and other options as desired.

25. Click cell **B9**.

26. Double-click the Format Painter button.

27. Drag the mouse pointer over the Subtotal numbers in row 14, then row 19, and finally drag over the Total and Difference numbers in the last rows.

The Currency format should be copied to the numbers in those rows.

28. Click the Format Painter to turn it off.

Format the text
29. Click cell **A1** (the large merged cell).

30. Set the point size to **16** and use **Bold** and a color **[A]** to make the title stand out.

31. Format the headings in rows **3** and **4** in any way you feel looks attractive.

32. Format the first Subtotal row with an attractive size, color and typeface.

33. Use the Format Painter to copy the formats from the Subtotal row to the other Subtotal rows.

34. Format the Total and Differences rows with an attractive size, color and typeface.

Continued...

Change the numbers and watch the formulas recalculate

35. Click cell **G5**.

This cell contains the amount of money that was spent on the mortgage. Imagine you have an adjustable rate mortgage and the monthly payment just went up. You will change the number in cell G5 in the next step. Keep an eye on the Totals and Differences formulas at the bottom of the worksheet when you change the number. The formulas will automatically recalculate the numbers.

36. Type **1075** and Confirm ☑ the entry.

The new Total in cell G21 should be 2879 and the new difference in cell F22 should be -814.

37. Your worksheet should match the example below (although the formatting may be different). For example, your dollar signs $ may be fixed on the left edges of the cells.

38. Close the worksheet when you have finished and **save** the changes.

	A	B	C	D	E	F	G
1		1996 Home Budget					
2							
3		January		February		March	
4		Budget	Spent	Budget	Spent	Budget	Spent
5	Mortgage	1000	1000	1000	1000	1000	1075
6	Insurance	200	200	0	0	0	0
7	Phone	60	75	60	80	60	145
8	Utilities	100	78	100	120	100	95
9	**Subtotal**	**$1,360**	**$1,353**	**$1,160**	**$1,200**	**$1,160**	**$1,315**
10							
11	Clothing	100	54	100	0	100	234
12	Entertainment	120	80	120	90	120	245
13	Food	235	220	235	190	235	250
14	**Subtotal**	**$455**	**$354**	**$455**	**$280**	**$455**	**$729**
15							
16	Car Insurance	180	180	0	0	0	0
17	Car Maintenance	50	0	50	67	50	435
18	Car Payment	400	400	400	400	400	400
19	**Subtotal**	**$630**	**$580**	**$450**	**$467**	**$450**	**$835**
20							
21	**Grand Total**	**$2,445**	**$2,287**	**$2,065**	**$1,947**	**$2,065**	**$2,879**
22	**Differences**	**$158**		**$118**		**-$814**	

Skills Builder 2.2

In this exercise, you will open a worksheet on your exercise diskette. You will format the worksheet until it closely matches the worksheet shown below.

1. **Open** the workbook named **Skills Builder 2.2**.

2. **Merge and Center** [icon] the title **Corporate Budget** across columns A-E.

3. Use the fill handle **+** to expand the series Q1 to Q1 - Q4.

4. **Right align** the headings **Q1 - Q4**.

5. **Compute** the **Subtotals** and **Total**.

6. **Widen** column A until the entries in column A are visible.

7. **Format** the **numbers** as shown below.

    You will need to use the Format→Cells command to format the Subtotals and Totals as Currency with zero decimals. Format the remaining numbers as Comma with 0 decimals.

8. **Format** the **title** and **headings** with attractive text formats.

9. **Format** the **Subtotal** rows with **Italics** as shown.

10. **Format** the **Total** row with **Bold** and **Italics** as shown.

11. **Close** the workbook and **save** the changes when you have finished.

	A	B	C	D	E
1	Corporate Budget				
2					
3		**Q1**	**Q2**	**Q3**	**Q4**
4	Marketing	1,234,890	2,346,890	2,156,580	1,900,890
5	Sales	2,316,780	2,145,670	2,134,670	2,145,760
6	*Subtotal*	*$3,551,670*	*$4,492,560*	*$4,291,250*	*$4,046,650*
7					
8	Manufacturing	8,909,800	8,769,870	7,869,870	9,878,760
9	Distribution	3,456,570	3,245,670	2,314,560	3,897,860
10	*Subtotal*	*$12,366,370*	*$12,015,540*	*$10,184,430*	*$13,776,620*
11					
12	Customer Support	93,450	72,150	63,670	93,670
13	Human Resources	65,640	87,890	65,670	86,780
14	*Subtotal*	*$159,090*	*$160,040*	*$129,340*	*$180,450*
15					
16	*Total*	*$16,077,130*	*$16,668,140*	*$14,605,020*	*$18,003,720*

Skills Builder 2.3

In this exercise, you will open a workbook on your exercise diskette. You will format the worksheet until it closely matches the worksheet shown below.

1. **Open** the workbook named **Skills Builder 2.3**.

2. **Merge and Center** ⊞ the title **Q2 Sales Volume Comparison** across columns A-E.

3. Use the fill handle to expand the series Store 1 to Store 1 - Store 4 in rows 3, 8, and 13.

    As you can see, the fill handle can be used to expand many types of series.

4. **Right Align** the headings **Store 1 - Store 4.**

5. **Left Align** the **dates** in column A.

6. **Widen** column A until the entries in column A are visible.

7. **Format** the **numbers** in rows 4, 5, 9, 10, 14 and 15 as **Comma** with **0** decimals.

8. **Click** cell **B6**.

    In the next step, you will enter a formula that computes the Percentage Increase. This formula uses parenthesis to change the order of calculations. The Percentage Increase is calculated as the April 92 sales minus April 91 sales and this difference is then divided by the April 91 sales. The formula is (B5 - B4)/B4.

9. Enter the formula **=(B5 - B4)/B4**.

10. Use the fill handle to copy the formula across the row.

11. Enter similar formulas in cells **B11** and **B16** and then copy the formulas across the rows.

12. Format the numbers in the Percentage Increase rows as Percent ▣% with **2** decimals.

13. Format the worksheet in any way you feel looks attractive.

14. The completed worksheet should match the worksheet shown below.

15. **Close** the workbook and **save** the changes when you have finished.

	A	B	C	D	E
1	Q2 Sales Volume Comparison				
2					
3		Store 1	Store 2	Store 3	Store 4
4	April-91	13,234,657	34,789,564	23,000,908	65,908,456
5	April-92	14,456,900	40,987,560	28,546,905	70,987,235
6	Percentage Increase	9.24%	17.82%	24.11%	7.71%
7					
8		Store 1	Store 2	Store 3	Store 4
9	May-91	18,985,342	40,234,908	24,234,908	45,003,345
10	May-92	19,234,987	41,210,908	24,400,098	46,989,456
11	Percentage Increase	1.31%	2.43%	0.68%	4.41%
12					
13		Store 1	Store 2	Store 3	Store 4
14	Jun-91	24,234,980	65,230,980	18,230,350	51,006,983
15	Jun-92	25,235,908	66,234,908	27,908,990	58,231,900
16	Percentage Increase	4.13%	1.54%	53.09%	14.16%

Assessment 2.1

In this assessment, you will create the worksheet shown at the bottom of the page. Excel has a feature called AutoComplete that can assist you in entering data. As you are entering data in column 1, AutoComplete may propose entries in the current cell. These entries will be from cells that you have already typed in column 1. Just ignore this and continue typing your entries. You will learn more about AutoComplete in the next lesson.

1. Open a New □ workbook.

2. Use the following guidelines to create the worksheet shown below.

   • Enter the data as shown. You must create formulas in columns D and F and in rows 10, 12 and 13. The worksheet below shows the formulas in bold. The following table lists the formulas you will need to get started.

Cell	Use this formula
D4	=C4/B4
F4	=D4*E4
Row 10	Column summations (use AutoSum)
B12	=E10/B10
B13	=F10/C10

   • Format the numbers with dollar signs and percent as shown. Make sure you use the same number of decimals as shown.

   • Widen the columns and align the text entries as necessary.

   • Add bold as shown and enhance the worksheet in any other way you feel is attractive.

3. Use **Print Preview** when you have finished and **print** the worksheet when it is complete.

4. **Close** the workbook and **save** it as **Assessment 2.1**.

	A	B	C	D	E	F
1	Donna's Deli - Produce Wastage Tracking Sheet (October)					
2						
3		Lbs. Purchased	Total Purchase $	Cost per Lb.	Lbs. Wasted	Total Wastage $
4	Sweet Potatoes	350	$101.50	0.29	52	$15.08
5	Corn	220	$85.80	0.39	34	$13.26
6	Greens	180	$124.20	0.69	23	$15.87
7	Bean Sprouts	120	$22.80	0.19	34	$6.46
8	Tomatoes	290	$258.10	0.89	80	$71.20
9	Zucchini	90	$38.70	0.43	23	$9.89
10	Totals	1250	$631.10		246	$131.76
11						
12	Waste % (Lbs.)	19.68%				
13	Waste % ($)	20.88%				

Assessment 2.2

In this assessment, you will develop the worksheet shown below to track customer credit line payments.

1. Open a New ⬜ workbook.

2. Create the worksheet shown below. You must use formulas in columns D and F and row 11. Make sure the formula results match the worksheet below. Format the numbers and text as shown.

3. Use **Print Preview** when you have finished and **print** the worksheet when it is completed.

4. **Close** the workbook and **save** it as **Assessment 2.2**.

	A	B	C	D	E	F
1	**Donna's Deli - Customer Credit Lines**					
2						
3	Customer	Previous Balance	New Charges	Subtotal	Payment Amount	New Balance
4	George Lopke	100	50	150	150	0
5	Wanda Watson	230	85	315	315	0
6	Alicia Thomas	58	100	158	100	58
7	Bill Barton	60	35	95	0	95
8	Latisha Robertson	140	80	220	0	220
9	Amy Chang	200	150	350	350	0
10	Dan Long	90	65	155	100	55
11	*Total Credit*	*$878*	*$565*	*$1,443*	*$1,015*	*$428*

 Assessment 2.3

1. Create the following worksheet. You must use formulas in rows 10 and 11 and columns E and F. You will need to figure out which formulas to use to get your worksheet to match the worksheet shown below. Format the worksheet as shown.

2. **Print** the worksheet, then **close** it and **save** it as **Assessment 2.3**.

	A	B	C	D	E	F
1	**Donna's Deli - Customer Survey Results**					
2						
3	Category	January	February	March	Total	Average
4	Flavor	4.80	4.75	4.80	14.35	4.78
5	Service	4.60	4.50	4.70	13.80	4.60
6	Nutritional Value	4.95	4.95	4.83	14.73	4.91
7	Presentation	4.20	4.35	4.30	12.85	4.28
8	Price	4.20	4.20	4.45	12.85	4.28
9	Convenience	4.30	4.40	4.20	12.90	4.30
10	Total	27.05	27.15	27.28	81.48	
11	*Average*	*4.51*	*4.53*	*4.55*	*13.58*	

Critical Thinking 2.1

Create a worksheet to track the amount of money you spend each year on your automobile(s). Organize the worksheet so that certain items are grouped together with subtotals. The following list shows some groups you may want to consider.

- Fixed costs such as the monthly payment and insurance.

- Regular expenses such as gasoline and washes.

- Maintenance expenses such as oil changes, tires, and tune-ups.

Organize the worksheet so that the expenses can be totaled for each month and for each category. Include a calculation that shows the percentage of your total annual income that the automobile expenses require. **Close** the workbook when you have finished and **save** it as **Auto Expenses**.

Critical Thinking 2.2

Create a worksheet to track the amount of money you spend on gasoline and the number of gallons you use. Have the worksheet compute the number of miles per gallon your car is getting. Figure out how much you are spending on gasoline for each mile you drive. Feel free to perform other calculations as desired. **Close** the workbook when you have finished and **save** it as **MPG**.

3 Powerful Features and Automated Tools

Objectives:

- Use online Help

- Use AutoCorrect and AutoComplete

- Understand function concepts

- Create functions with the Function box

- Create functions with the Paste Function box

- Use the AVERAGE, MIN and MAX functions

- Use Cut, Copy and Paste

- Use drag & drop and drag & copy

- Add borders and colors to cells

- Use AutoFormat

- Use the Zoom Control

The Project - Centron Cellular Commission Report

In this lesson, you will develop a commission report for Centron Cellular. Centron's National Sales Manager wants statistical information on the commissions that her sales reps are receiving. You will use the AVERAGE, MIN and MAX functions to compute these numbers. You will use many other Excel features including online Help, Cut, Copy and Paste and the AutoFormat command. You will develop the following worksheet as you progress through this lesson.

	A	B	C	D	E	F	G
1	Centron Cellular						
2							
3	Region 1						
4	Sales Rep	Jan Sales	Jan Comm	Feb Sales	Feb Comm	March Sales	March Comm
5	Branston	32000	4800	32000	4800	23000	3450
6	Barton	15000	2250	32000	4800	23890	3583.5
7	Alexander	45000	6750	8900	1335	43000	6450
8	Aliotto	23000	3450	19000	2850	10900	1635
9	Chin	34000	5100	34000	5100	32000	4800
10	Total		22350		18885		19918.5
11	Average		4470		3777		3983.7
12	Maximum		6750		5100		6450
13	Minimum		2250		1335		1635
14							
15							
16	Region 2						
17	Sales Rep	Jan Sales	Jan Comm	Feb Sales	Feb Comm	March Sales	March Comm
18	Richardson	18000	2700	54000	8100	36790	5518.5
19	Thomas	12000	1800	35900	5385	45678	6851.7
20	Carter	56000	8400	34900	5235	72490	10873.5
21	Williams	39000	5850	54000	8100	21000	3150
22	Jones	23000	3450	89000	13350	38900	5835
23	Total		22200		40170		32228.7
24	Average		4440		8034		6445.74
25	Maximum		8400		13350		10873.5
26	Minimum		1800		5235		3150

Using Online Help

Excel's online Help puts a complete reference book at your fingertips. Help is available for just about any topic you can imagine. It is important that you know how to use online Help because Microsoft and other software publishers no longer provide reference manuals with their software. The reference manuals are now integrated into online Help.

The key to online Help is finding the desired Help topic

Your goal when using online Help is to locate a Help topic. The Help feature has several different methods you can use to locate topics. All Help topics have key words that identify them. For example, a Help topic that discusses copying cells can probably be located by using the key words **copying cells**. Regardless of which search method you use, the goal is to locate a topic. Once you locate the desired topic, you can display it and follow the instructions in the topic.

Help is consistent across Office applications and Windows

Online Help works the same way in Windows, Excel, Word and other Microsoft applications. The following table describes the various search methods that can be used to locate Help topics.

Search Method	Description
Contents	The Contents method is useful if you are trying to locate a topic but you aren't really sure how to describe it. The Contents method lets you navigate through a series of categories until the desired topic is located.
Index	The Index method lets you locate a topic by typing key words. An alphabetically indexed list of topics is displayed from which you can choose the desired topic. This method is most useful if you know the name of the topic or feature that you need assistance with.
Find	The Find method searches inside of the Help topics for the key words you enter. This provides an in-depth search and lets you locate topics that you may not be found using the other search methods.
Office Assistant Search	The Office Assistant Search lets you locate topics by typing questions in plain English. You used the Office Assistant Search in the previous lesson. The results are usually quite good although the Office Assistant often returns a broad range of topics.

Hands-On 3.1 – Experiment with online Help

Use an Index search

1. Start Excel and choose **Help→Contents and Index** from the menu bar.

   The Help Topics dialog box will appear. Notice the Contents, Index and Find tabs at the top of the dialog box. This dialog box lets you search for all Help topics.

2. **Click** the **Index tab** and use the steps on the next page to get help on a topic called AutoComplete.

   You will use AutoComplete and AutoCorrect in this lesson.

Continued...

❶ *Type **Auto** here. (Notice that Help displays a list of topics beginning with the word Auto. The Index is the fastest way to locate a topic if you know the name of the feature or topic you are looking for.)*

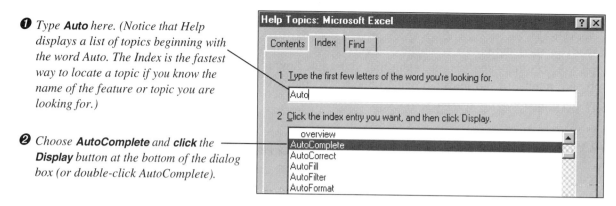

❷ *Choose **AutoComplete** and **click** the **Display** button at the bottom of the dialog box (or double-click AutoComplete).*

Excel will display a list of topics that are related to the AutoComplete feature.

3. Choose **Quickly fill in repeated entries in a column** and **click** the **Display** button.

   You could also have double-clicked the topic.

4. Take a moment to read the Help topic.

5. **Click** anywhere in the Excel worksheet area and notice the dialog box remains open.

   Help topics remain "on top" to allow you to work while reading the topic.

6. **Click** the Help Topics [Help Topics] button on the dialog box.

   The Help Topics dialog box will reappear.

7. Take 15 minutes to experiment with the Help feature. Try using the Find and Contents search method techniques. Experiment and explore until you are comfortable using Help.

8. **Close** the Help Topics dialog box when you have finished experimenting.

The What's This? Option

The What's This? option on the <u>H</u>elp menu is used to get descriptions of buttons, menu items and other screen objects. The What's This? option is useful if you are trying to figure out how a button or other object is used.

Hands-On 3.2 – Use the What's This? option

1. Choose <u>H</u>elp→What's <u>T</u>his? from the menu bar.

2. **Click** any button on the toolbars and a description will pop up.

3. **Read** the description, then **click anywhere** in the worksheet to close the description.

4. Choose <u>H</u>elp→What's <u>T</u>his?, then choose F<u>o</u>rmat→C<u>e</u>lls... from the menu bar.

   Notice that you can use What's This? to get descriptions of buttons and menu bar commands.

5. **Close** the description by clicking in the worksheet.

   Feel free to experiment with the What's This? option.

Getting Assistance with Data Entry

Excel's AutoCorrect and AutoComplete features provide assistance with entering text.

Using AutoCorrect

Excel's AutoCorrect feature can improve the speed and accuracy of entering text. AutoCorrect is most useful for replacing abbreviations with a full phrase. For example, you could set up AutoCorrect to substitute *as soon as possible* whenever you type *asap*. AutoCorrect also automatically corrects common spelling errors. For example, the word *the* is often misspelled as *teh* and the word *and* is often misspelled as *adn*. These and other common spelling mistakes are built into Excel as AutoCorrect entries. AutoCorrect also capitalizes the first letter in the names of days and it corrects words that have two initial capital letters by switching the second letter to lowercase.

Expanding AutoCorrect entries

AutoCorrect goes into action each time you type a word in a text entry and tap the Spacebar and when you complete a text entry. The word or entry you type is compared to all entries in the *AutoCorrect table*. The AutoCorrect table contains a list of words and their replacement phrases. If the word you type matches an entry in the AutoCorrect table, then a replacement phrase from the table is substituted for the word. This is known as expanding the AutoCorrect entry.

Using AutoComplete

The AutoComplete feature is useful if you want the same entry repeated more than once in a column. If the first few characters you type match another entry in the column, then AutoComplete will complete the entry for you. Of course, you can override AutoComplete by typing the remainder of the entry yourself.

Hands-On 3.3 – Use AutoCorrect and AutoComplete

In this exercise, you will open a workbook from your exercise diskette. You will experiment with AutoCorrect and AutoComplete and you will create a new AutoCorrect entry.

Use AutoCorrect to correct misspelled words

1. Open ⊞ the workbook named **Hands-On Lesson 3**.

2. **Click** cell **A1**.

3. Type **adn** (that's adn not and) and **tap** ⌈Enter⌋.

    Excel should correct the misspelling and enter the word and in the cell.

4. **Click** cell **A1**.

5. Type, **This adn that**.

    Notice that Excel corrected the misspelling again after you typed adn and tapped the Spacebar.

Create a new AutoCorrect entry

6. **Tap** ⌈Enter⌋ then choose **Tools→AutoCorrect...** from the menu bar.

Continued...

7. Use the following Hands-On Illustration to create a new AutoCorrect entry.

❶ *Notice these check boxes. These boxes instruct AutoCorrect to automatically make the specified corrections in your worksheets.*

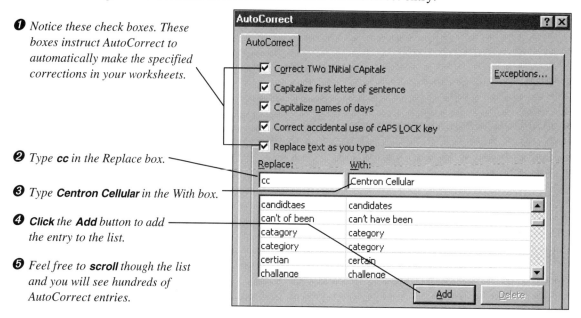

❷ *Type **cc** in the Replace box.*

❸ *Type **Centron Cellular** in the With box.*

❹ ***Click** the **Add** button to add the entry to the list.*

❺ *Feel free to **scroll** though the list and you will see hundreds of AutoCorrect entries.*

❻ **Click OK.**

8. **Click** cell **A1**.

9. Type **cc** and **tap** ⎡Enter⎤.

    AutoCorrect should replace cc with Centron Cellular. Notice that you can use AutoCorrect as a type of shorthand. AutoCorrect can replace abbreviations with phrases you use often such as your company name or address.

Delete the AutoCorrect entry
10. Choose **Tools→AutoCorrect...** from the menu bar.

11. **Scroll** through the list of AutoCorrect entries and choose the **cc, Centron Cellular** entry.

12. **Click** the **Delete** button, then **click OK**.

Use AutoComplete
13. **Click** cell **A5**.

14. Type **Branston** and **tap** ⎡Enter⎤.

15. Type the letter **B** in cell A6 and AutoComplete will display the word Branston in the cell.
    You could accept this proposal by confirming the entry, however, you will type a different entry.

16. Type **arton** (to make the entry Barton) and **tap** ⎡Enter⎤.
    AutoComplete will constantly try to assist you in completing entries. You can ignore AutoComplete and continue typing your entries or confirm the entries that AutoComplete proposes.

17. Enter the following Sales rep names into the next three cells.

7	Alexander
8	Aliotto
9	Chin

Continue with the next topic. You will continue to enhance the worksheet throughout this lesson.

Functions

Excel has over 400 built-in **functions** that perform a variety of calculations. You already used the SUM function in the previous lessons. In this lesson, you will use the MAX, MIN and AVERAGE functions.

Function Syntax

Functions must be constructed using a set of basic rules or they will not work properly. These rules are known as the syntax. The good news is that most functions have the same syntax and the syntax is very easy to use and remember. The following illustration discusses the syntax of the SUM function. This syntax also applies to the MIN, MAX and AVERAGE functions, which you are about to learn.

Always begin functions with an equal = sign unless they are embedded in a larger formula.

=SUM(B5:B9)

=SUM(A5,A10,B5:B9)

The function name always follows the equal = sign.

A set of parentheses always surrounds the argument. The argument is usually a range of cells as in this example.

If an argument has more than one parameter, then commas must separate the parameters. In this example, cells A5 and A10 would be added to the range B5:B9.

Hands-On 3.4 – Manually enter the AVERAGE function

In this exercise, you will manually enter the AVERAGE function.

Do a little detective work and use AutoSum

1. Notice the worksheet has a January Commissions column (Jan Comm).

   The commissions are calculated with a simple formula.

2. What is the commission rate that the sales reps are being paid?

   You can find this out by clicking a commission cell in Column C and checking out the formula.

3. **Click** cell **C10**.

4. **Click** AutoSum ☲ and Confirm ☑ the entry.

   The Total Commissions for January should be 20550.

5. Look at the Formula bar and notice the function =SUM(C5:C9) that AutoSum placed in the cell.

   The SUM function uses the standard function syntax discussed above.

Type the AVERAGE function

6. **Click** cell **C11**.

7. Type the function **=AVERAGE(C5:C9)** and Confirm ☑ the entry.

   The result should be 4110. This is the average of the values in the range C5:C9. Notice the syntax is the same as the SUM function except you used the function name AVERAGE instead of SUM.

The Function Box

The Function Box appears on the left end of the Formula bar whenever the Edit Formula ▣ button is clicked. The Function Box has a drop-down button that shows the 10 most recently used functions. Excel displays the Formula Palette whenever you choose one of these functions from the Function Box. The Formula palette then provides assistance in creating functions.

Hands-On 3.5 – Use the Function Box and Formula palette

In this exercise, you will use the Function Box to create the MAX and MIN functions.

Use the Function Box to create the MAX function

1. **Click** cell **C12**.

2. **Click** the Edit Formula ▣ button on the Formula bar.

3. Use the following steps to explore the Function Box.

❶ **Click** *this drop-down button and a list of the 10 most recently used functions will appear.*

❷ *Notice the most recently used function (in this case AVERAGE) appears on the face of the Function Box and at the top of the list.*

❸ *Also notice that the MAX function appears on the list shown here. It may also appear on your list. You could choose MAX at this point, however, you will choose the MAX function using the More Functions... option in the next step. This will show you how to choose a function even if it is not on the 10 most recently used functions list.*

❹ **Choose More Functions...**

The Paste Function dialog box will appear. The Paste Function dialog box provides access to all 400+ functions in Excel. This dialog box can also be displayed by clicking the Paste Function ƒx button on the Standard toolbar (but don't do it).

4. Use the following steps to choose the MAX function.

❶ *Notice the functions are organized into categories. The functions for the selected category are displayed on the right.*

❷ **Choose** *the* **Statistical** *category.*

❸ **Scroll down** *through the list of Function names and choose* **MAX**.

❹ **Click OK**.

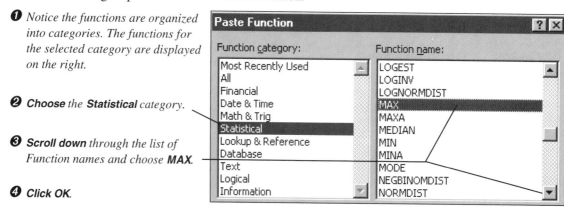

Continued...

Notice the MAX(C11) function appears in the Formula palette. This is the correct function, however, the range C11 is incorrect. You could type the correct range C5:C9 in the Formula palette or the Formula bar. However, you will use another technique in the following steps.

5. Use the following step to minimize the Formula palette so that you can see the worksheet.

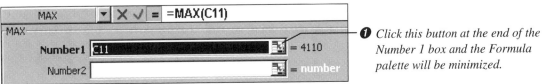

❶ *Click this button at the end of the Number 1 box and the Formula palette will be minimized.*

6. Use the following step to select the appropriate range of cells and redisplay the Formula palette.

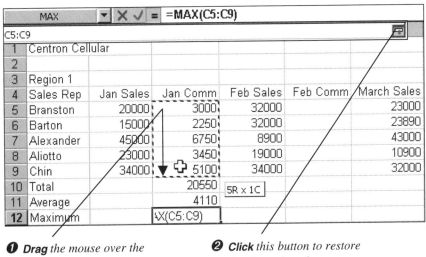

❶ **Drag** *the mouse over the range* **C5:C9** *as shown here.*

❷ **Click** *this button to restore the Formula palette.*

Take a moment to check out the formula in the Formula bar. It should be =MAX(C5:C9).

7. Complete the function by **clicking OK** on the Formula palette (the result should be 6750).

Use point mode to create the MIN function in cell C13

8. **Click** cell **C13** and type **=min(**

    You can type a function in lowercase and Excel will convert it to uppercase when you confirm the entry. Also, you must always type the opening parenthesis when entering a function in point mode.

9. **Drag** the mouse down the range **C5:C9**.

10. Type a closing parenthesis **)** and your formula should be =min(C5:C9).

11. Confirm ☑ the entry and the result should be 2250.

    In this exercise, you used three different methods to create functions. In the future, use whichever method you find easiest and which gives you the most accurate results.

Change the values and watch the formulas recalculate

You may be wondering why you used the MIN and MAX functions in this worksheet. It is easy to see which sales rep had the minimum and maximum commissions for a month. The benefit of using the functions is when the values change or when there are a large number of rows. The functions are dynamic and they will automatically recalculate the SUM, AVERAGE, MAX and MIN values.

12. **Click** cell **B5** and change the sales number from 20000 to **32000**.

    Notice how the functions recalculate the numbers. The topics on the following pages will teach you several new ways to move and copy cells.

Using Cut, Copy and Paste

Excel has several features that let you move and copy text, numbers and graphics from one location to another. You already used the fill handle to copy a cell's content to adjacent cells. The fill handle is limited in this respect because it can only be used to copy to adjacent cells. Excel also supports drag & drop, which is best for moving or copying cells a short distance within a worksheet. Cut, copy and paste is usually best for moving or copying cells a long distance within a worksheet or between worksheets or workbooks.

Cut, Copy and Paste

Cut, copy and paste is available in most Windows programs. With cut, copy and paste, you can copy cells within a worksheet, between worksheets and workbooks and even between programs.

The Windows clipboard makes it possible

The Windows clipboard is a part of the computer's memory where cut and copied objects are temporarily stored. All Windows programs have access to the clipboard. The Paste command copies the clipboard's contents into the current worksheet.

The clipboard contents are replaced with each new cut

The clipboard contents are replaced whenever new objects are cut or copied. You can paste the clipboard content over and over again as long as you do not issue a new Cut or Copy command. This is convenient if you wish to paste multiple copies of the objects.

Hands-On 3.6 – Use copy and paste

In this exercise, you will use the Copy and Paste commands to copy formulas and text.

Copy the commission formula to cell E5

1. **Click** cell **C5**.

2. Take a moment to study the formula in the formula bar.

   Your objective is to copy this formula to the February and March commission columns. This cannot be done with the fill handle because those cells are not adjacent to cell C5.

3. **Click** the Copy button on the Standard toolbar.

   Notice the flashing marquee in cell C5. This indicates the sales commission formula is on the clipboard and ready to be pasted.

4. **Click** cell **E5**.

5. **Click** the Paste button.

   The formula should be pasted and it should calculate the commission as 4800. The flashing marquee in cell C5 indicates the formula is still available for pasting into other cells.

Paste the formula into a range of cells

6. **Select** the range **E6:E9**.

7. **Click** the Paste button to paste the formula.

   You can always copy a single cell to a range of cells (as in this example).

Continued...

8. **Select** the range **G5:G9** and paste the formulas into those cells.

   Once again, you can continue to paste as long as the marquee is flashing.

9. **Tap** the (Esc) key on the keyboard and the marquee will stop flashing.

   You can always turn off the flashing marquee with the Escape key.

10. **Click** any cell that you just pasted into and notice the formula in the formula bar.

    Excel updates the references in the formulas to reflect the new formula locations.

Use the Ctrl key to paste into two separate ranges

11. **Click** cell **C10**.

12. **Click** the Copy [icon] button.

13. **Click** cell **E10**.

14. **Press & Hold** the (Ctrl) key and **click** cell **G10**.

    Both cells E10 and G10 should be selected.

15. **Click** the Paste [icon] button to paste the formula into both cells.

16. Use the preceding technique to copy the AVERAGE, MAX and MIN functions from column C to columns E and G.

Copy the heading rows for Regions 1 to Region 2

17. **Select rows 3** and **4** by dragging over the row headings as shown below.

18. **Click** the Copy [icon] button.

19. **Click** cell **A16**.

    In the next step, you will paste the range to cell A16. You should paste a large range like this to one cell (A16 in this case). When you do this, Excel will use A16 as the starting location of the pasted range. You must be careful because the pasted range will overwrite any cells that are in its way.

20. **Click** the Paste [icon] button.

    In the next exercise, you will continue to copy cells with the drag & drop technique. For now, continue with the data entry task below.

21. Enter the following Sales rep names into the range **A18:A22**.

    | 18 | Richardson |
    | 19 | Thomas |
    | 20 | Carter |
    | 21 | Williams |
    | 22 | Jones |

22. Change the heading for the second region from Region 1 to **Region 2**.

Drag & Drop

Drag & drop can be used to move or copy selected cells from one location to another. This produces the same result as cut, copy and paste. However, drag & drop may be more efficient if you are moving or copying a short distance within the same worksheet.

Use the Ctrl key to drag and copy

You drag & drop selected cells by pointing to any border of the selection and then dragging the selection to the desired location. You can make a copy of the selected cells by pressing & holding the Ctrl key while you drag & drop the selection. This is known as drag & copy. When using drag & copy, it is important to release the mouse button before the Ctrl key. Otherwise, your copy will become a move.

Hands-On 3.7 – Use drag & drop

In this exercise, you will use drag & drop to copy text and formulas in the worksheet.

Move the formula row headings to Region 2

1. Use the following Hands-On Illustration to drag & drop text entries.

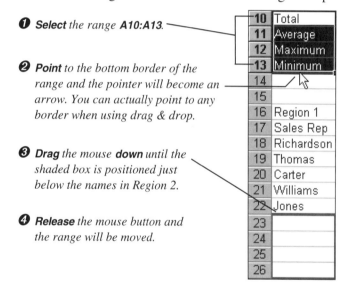

❶ **Select** the range **A10:A13.**

❷ **Point** to the bottom border of the range and the pointer will become an arrow. You can actually point to any border when using drag & drop.

❸ **Drag** the mouse **down** until the shaded box is positioned just below the names in Region 2.

❹ **Release** the mouse button and the range will be moved.

Notice how easy it was to move the cells using drag & drop. You should focus on using drag & drop if the move is a short distance within the same worksheet. Unfortunately, you should have copied the cells instead of moving them. You will correct this in the next few steps.

2. **Click** Undo 🔙 to reverse the move.

3. **Press & Hold** the ⌨Ctrl key while you drag & drop the cells as you did in the Hands-On Illustration above. **Make sure you release the mouse button first, then release Ctrl!** You will notice the mouse pointer has a plus sign attached to it to indicate a copy is being performed.

    Excel should copy the cells to the range A23:A26.

Continued...

Use drag & copy to copy the formulas

4. Use the following Hands-On Illustration to copy the January Commission formulas to Region 2.

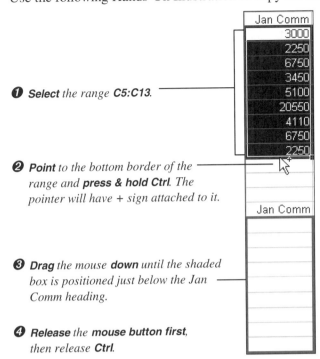

❶ *Select the range* **C5:C13**.

❷ **Point** *to the bottom border of the range and* **press & hold Ctrl**. *The pointer will have + sign attached to it.*

❸ **Drag** *the mouse* **down** *until the shaded box is positioned just below the Jan Comm heading.*

❹ **Release** *the* **mouse button first**, *then release* **Ctrl**.

5. Use drag & copy to copy the February and March commission formulas to Region 2.

6. Save ⊞ the changes.

At this point, your worksheet should match the worksheet shown below.

	A	B	C	D	E	F	G
1	Centron Cellular						
2							
3	Region 1						
4	Sales Rep	Jan Sales	Jan Comm	Feb Sales	Feb Comm	March Sales	March Comm
5	Branston	32000	4800	32000	4800	23000	3450
6	Barton	15000	2250	32000	4800	23890	3583.5
7	Alexander	45000	6750	8900	1335	43000	6450
8	Aliotto	23000	3450	19000	2850	10900	1635
9	Chin	34000	5100	34000	5100	32000	4800
10	Total		22350		18885		19918.5
11	Average		4470		3777		3983.7
12	Maximum		6750		5100		6450
13	Minimum		2250		1335		1635
14							
15							
16	Region 2						
17	Sales Rep	Jan Sales	Jan Comm	Feb Sales	Feb Comm	March Sales	March Comm
18	Richardson	18000	2700	54000	8100	36790	5518.5
19	Thomas	12000	1800	35900	5385	45678	6851.7
20	Carter	56000	8400	34900	5235	72490	10873.5
21	Williams	39000	5850	54000	8100	21000	3150
22	Jones	23000	3450	89000	13350	38900	5835
23	Total		22200		40170		32228.7
24	Average		4440		8034		6445.74
25	Maximum		8400		13350		10873.5
26	Minimum		1800		5235		3150

Adding Borders and Color to Cells

You can add borders and color to cells with the Borders and Fill Color [icon] buttons on the Formatting toolbar. Each cell has a top, bottom, left and right border. You can apply borders and color to an individual cell or to a range of cells. You can also apply borders and color by choosing Format→Cells... from the menu bar and then using the Format Cells dialog box.

Borders and color are printed when the worksheet is printed

Excel displays gridlines in the worksheet to show you the cell borders. However, the gridlines are not printed when the worksheet is printed. Borders and color, on the other hand, are printed. Keep in mind that your worksheets will print in color only if you have a color printer. If you use colors and you do not have a color printer, then the colors will print in shades of gray that are proportionate to the color density.

Hands-On 3.8 – Add borders and color

Make the title stand out

1. **Select** the range **A1:G1** in row 1 and click the Merge and Center [icon] button.

2. Make sure the range is still selected, then **click** the Borders drop-down [icon] button and the borders box will appear.

3. Use the following steps to put a thick border around the range.

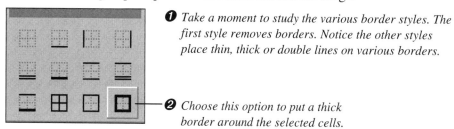

   ❶ *Take a moment to study the various border styles. The first style removes borders. Notice the other styles place thin, thick or double lines on various borders.*

   ❷ *Choose this option to put a thick border around the selected cells.*

4. Make sure the range is still selected, then **click** the Fill Color drop-down [icon] button.

5. Choose your favorite color.

6. Make sure the range is still selected, then **click** the Font Color drop-down [icon] button.

7. Choose your favorite color, then **click** outside the range and you will be able to see the formats.

   The lines on the top and left sides of the range may not be visible because the column and row headings are blocking them. Notice that the color button determined the fill color of the cells while the Font Color button determined the color of the text or numbers within the cell. Also notice that the colors and line style you chose now appear on the face of the buttons. You could now apply these same colors and line style to other selected cells by clicking the buttons.

8. **Click** the Print Preview [icon] button.

9. **Click** the mouse pointer on the worksheet to zoom in.

   You should now be able to see the lines on the top and left sides of the range. However, the colors will not be visible if you have a black and white printer. Print Preview is very accurate and it will show you the color or gray shades that will be printed.

Continued...

Add borders to all sides of all cells

10. Click the **Close** button to exit from Print Preview.

11. Select the range **A2:G26**.

   This range represents all cells in the active worksheet area except for the title row.

12. Click the Borders drop-down [icon] button.

13. Choose the All Borders [icon] style, which is the second style on the bottom row.

14. Click Print Preview [icon].

   Do you like having lines on every border of every cell? Many people find this to be busy and distracting. You will correct this by changing the pattern in the next step.

Remove the borders

15. Close the **Print Preview** window.

16. Make sure the range **A2:G26** is still selected.

17. Click the Borders drop-down [icon] button and choose the Thick Outline [icon] style.

18. Click Print Preview [icon] and you will notice the inside borders have not been removed.

19. Close the **Print Preview** window.

20. Click the Borders drop-down [icon] button and choose the No Lines [icon] button (first button).

   This will remove the lines from the selected range.

21. Click the Borders drop-down [icon] button again and choose the Thick Outline [icon] style.

22. Click Print Preview [icon] to check out the results, then **close** Print Preview.

Add color to one row and use the Format Painter to copy the format to other rows

23. Select the range **A10:G10** (all the cells in row 10).

24. Use the Fill Color [icon] button to add the color of your choice.

25. Use the Font Color [icon] button to change the font color.

26. Double-click the Format Painter [icon].

27. Paint the cells in **rows 12, 23** and **25**.

   This will format every other formula row. This way, the various formulas are clearly differentiated.

28. Click the Format Painter [icon] to turn it off.

29. Take 10 minutes to play around with the Borders, Color and Font Color buttons.

30. Save [icon] the changes and continue with the next topic.

The AutoFormat Command

The Format→AutoFormat command lets you choose from a variety of predefined formats. The predefined formats automatically apply number formats, borders, colors, font colors, font sizes and other formats. You may be pleasantly surprised when you see the professional formatting that AutoFormat can apply.

You must select a range before using AutoFormat

You must select a range or AutoFormat will not work. You may want to select all cells in the worksheet or a smaller range, as you will do in the following exercise.

Hands-On 3.9 – Use AutoFormat

Use AutoFormat on Region 1

1. **Select** the range **A3:G13** which includes all cells for Region 1.

2. Choose **Format→AutoFormat...** from the menu bar.

3. Use the following Hands-On Illustration to format the range.

    ❶ *Click the* **Options>>>** *button and check boxes will appear or disappear at the bottom of the dialog box. These boxes let you decide which formats you want AutoFormat to adjust. Make sure all the boxes are checked.*

    ❷ *Scroll through the list and choose various formats. The format you choose will display in the Sample window.*

    ❸ *Scroll to the top of the list and choose* **Classic 3**.

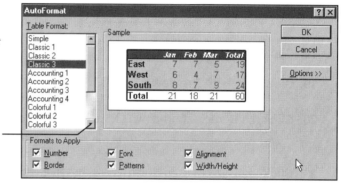

4. **Click OK** then **click** in an open part of the worksheet and check out the results.

    You will notice that AutoFormat adjusted virtually every format. Notice that AutoFormat was intelligent enough to detect the rows that have formulas and it formatted those rows in a different manner than the body and header rows. AutoFormat makes its formatting decisions by detecting which rows and columns have text, numbers and formulas.

Remove the AutoFormatting

5. **Select** the range **A3:G13** (the range you just used AutoFormat on).

6. Choose **Format→AutoFormat...** from the menu bar.

7. **Scroll** to the bottom of the Formats list and choose **None**.

8. **Click OK** and the formats will be removed.

    You can use AutoFormat to remove formats that were applied manually or with AutoFormat.

9. Experiment with AutoFormat. Format the Region 1 cells four times using a different AutoFormat each time. Finally, choose your favorite format and then apply it to Region 2.

10. Save ▣ the changes and continue with the next topic.

Using the Zoom Control

Excel's zoom control lets you change the magnification of the worksheet. Zooming changes the size of the worksheet on the screen, however, it does not affect the size of the printed worksheet. You can zoom from 10% to 400%. The following illustration shows the Hands-On Lesson 3 worksheet with a 200% zoom. Keep in mind that your worksheet may have a different number of columns and rows displayed than shown here. This is because your monitor may be a different size.

You can type a zoom percentage into this box and tap Enter, or...

you can click this button and select an option from the drop-down menu.

Notice how large the text and cells appear in this example.

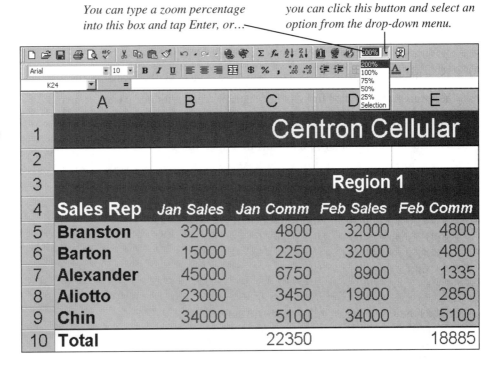

	A	B	C	D	E
1				Centron Cellular	
2					
3				Region 1	
4	Sales Rep	Jan Sales	Jan Comm	Feb Sales	Feb Comm
5	Branston	32000	4800	32000	4800
6	Barton	15000	2250	32000	4800
7	Alexander	45000	6750	8900	1335
8	Aliotto	23000	3450	19000	2850
9	Chin	34000	5100	34000	5100
10	Total		22350		18885

Hands-On 3.10 – Experiment with the Zoom Control

1. Use the following steps to adjust the Zoom Control.

    ❶ *Click in the Zoom Control box, type* **150** *and tap* **Enter***. You can zoom to any percentage between 10% and 400% by typing a number and tapping Enter.* ❷ *Click the Zoom Control button and choose* **200%.** ❸ *Zoom to 100%.*

2. **Select** the range **A4:C13**.

    Imagine that you want to analyze just the January sales numbers. You can use the Zoom Control to get a close up view of just this range.

3. **Click** the Zoom Control ⬛ button and choose **Selection**.

    Excel will zoom to the maximum percentage possible for that selection.

4. Feel free to experiment with the Zoom Control then **close** the workbook and **save** the changes.

Concepts Review

True / False

1.	An Index search is the best Help search method if you know the name of the topic or feature.	1. **T F**
2.	The Office Assistant lets you type help questions in plain English.	2. **T F**
3.	AutoCorrect entries are expanded when the Spacebar is tapped or entry is confirmed.	3. **T F**
4.	You must accept an AutoComplete entry that Excel proposes.	4. **T F**
5.	MIN and MAX are examples of functions.	5. **T F**
6.	A function's arguments are always surrounded by quotation marks "".	6. **T F**
7.	The clipboard contents are deleted whenever you click the Paste button.	7. **T F**
8.	You can paste a copied formula into multiple cells with one paste command.	8. **T F**
9.	Borders and colors are printed when the worksheet is printed.	9. **T F**
10.	The Zoom Control can zoom to a maximum of 400%.	10. **T F**

Multiple Choice

1. Which command displays the AutoCorrect dialog box?
   a) Format→AutoCorrect
   b) Tools→AutoCorrect
   c) Edit→AutoCorrect
   d) None of the above.   ( )

2. Which button is used to add borders to cells?
   a)
   b)
   c)
   d) None of the above.   ( )

3. Which key should you press if you want drag & drop to copy instead of moving?
   a) Shift
   b) Alt
   c) Ctrl
   d) None of the above.   ( )

4. Which command is used to display the AutoFormat dialog box?
   a) Tools→AutoFormat
   b) Format→AutoFormat
   c) Format→Cells
   d) None of the above.   ( )

5. Which of the following magnification ranges does the Zoom Control let you use?
   a) 10% to 400%
   b) 10% to 200%
   c) 25% to 200%
   d) 25% to 400%   ( )

Skills Builder 3.1

In this exercise, you will develop the worksheet shown at the bottom of this page.

1. Open the workbook named **Skills Builder 3.1**.

2. **Select** the range **A1:E2** as shown below.

3. **Click** the Copy ⬚ button.

4. **Click** cell **A10**, **click** the Paste ⬚ button then change 1996 in the pasted heading to **1995**.

5. **Select** the range **A3:A8** as shown below.

6. **Click** Copy ⬚, **click** cell **A12**, then **click** the Paste ⬚ button.

7. Use AutoSum ⬚ to compute the Totals in rows **7** and **16**.

8. **Click** cell **B8** and enter the function **=AVERAGE(B3:B6)**.

9. Use the Copy ⬚ and Paste ⬚ buttons to copy the AVERAGE function across rows 8 and 17.

   You can copy this function to both rows 8 and 17 because the function computes the average of a range of 4 cells and that is the formula that is required in both rows 8 and 17.

10. **Click** cell **B20** and enter the formula **=B7-B16**.

11. **Copy** this formula **across row 20**.

12. Enter a formula in cell **B21** that computes the difference between the Averages for 1996 and 1995, then copy the formula across row 20.

13. Your completed worksheet should match the worksheet shown below. **Close** the workbook and **save** the changes when you have finished.

	A	B	C	D	E
1	Quality Greeting Cards - 1996 Customer Complaints				
2		Christmas	Easter	Valentines	Thanksgiving
3	Boston	27	43	14	34
4	Los Angeles	31	47	19	39
5	New York	35	51	24	44
6	St. Louis	39	55	29	49
7	Total	132	196	86	166
8	Average	33	49	21.5	41.5
9					
10	Quality Greeting Cards - 1995 Customer Complaints				
11		Christmas	Easter	Valentines	Thanksgiving
12	Boston	19	31	16	24
13	Los Angeles	22	34	18	26
14	New York	25	37	20	28
15	St. Louis	28	40	22	30
16	Total	94	142	76	108
17	Average	23.5	35.5	19	27
18					
19	Differences Between 1996 and 1995				
20	Totals	38	54	10	58
21	Averages	9.5	13.5	2.5	14.5

Skills Builder 3.2

In this exercise, you will open a workbook on your exercise diskette. You will then use AutoFormat to apply an attractive format to the worksheet.

Use AutoFormat

1. **Open** the workbook named **Skills Builder 3.2**.

2. **Select** the range **A1:E16** which includes all cells in the worksheet.

3. Choose **Format→AutoFormat...** from the menu bar.

4. Choose the **List 2** style and **click OK**.

5. **Click** outside the worksheet and you will be able to see the format.

    The format looks good although it would be nice to have a more distinctive title row. You can format the Worksheet with AutoFormat and then add your own formatting enhancements.

Manually change the format of the title row

6. **Select** the range **A1:E1** and use Merge and Center to center the title.

7. Increase the size of the title to **14** point.

8. **Click** outside the worksheet and you will be able to see the format.

9. **Close** the workbook and **save** the changes.

Skills Builder 3.3

In this exercise, you will open a workbook and you will use copy & paste to copy text and formulas.

1. **Open** the workbook named **Skills Builder 3.3**.

2. **Select** the range **A3:E4** which includes all the text entries in rows 3 and 4.

3. Copy the cells to the clipboard.

4. **Click** cell **A10** and Paste the entries above the second set of numbers.
    Notice the text formats (including the coloring) were copied with the text.

5. **Click** cell **A17** and Paste the entries above the third set of numbers.

6. Change the headings to **February** and **March** for the second and third sets of numbers.

7. **Select** the range **A5:A8** which includes the names and word Totals in column A.

8. **Copy** the selection to the clipboard, then Paste it to cells **A12** and **A19**.

9. **Copy** the **formulas** from the Totals row below the first set of numbers and Paste them below the second and third sets of numbers.

10. **Close** the workbook when you have finished and **save** the changes.

Skills Builder 3.4

In this exercise, you will open a workbook and compute averages using three methods. You will compute the averages manually using a formula with parentheses that change the order of calculations. You will also enter AVERAGE functions with multiple parameters within the argument.

Manually compute the Average New Orders in row 18

1. **Open** the workbook named **Skills Builder 3.4**.

2. **Click** cell **B18**.

3. Type the formula **=(B4+B9+B14)/3** into cell B18 and Confirm ☑ the entry.

   The result should be 193.333... Notice the formula you entered includes parentheses ( ). The parentheses change the order of calculations. They instruct Excel to add cells B4, B9 and B14 and then divide the result of that summation by 3. Without the parentheses, Excel would first divide cell B14 by 3 and then it would add the result to B4 + B9. This would produce a very different result and you would not receive the average you are trying to compute. Keep in mind that the AVERAGE function does this work for you. This formula was entered manually to demonstrate the way an average is computed and to show how parentheses are used to change the order of calculations.

4. Use the fill handle ✛ to copy the formula across row 18.

Compute the Average Exchanges in row 19 by typing the AVERAGE function

5. **Click** cell **B19**.

6. Type the function **=average(b5,b10,b15)** and Confirm ☑ the entry.

   The result should be 23.3333. Once again, you can type the function name and arguments in lowercase and Excel will convert them to uppercase. Notice the function you entered has three parameters within the argument. In this function, the parameters are cell references and commas separate them. Most functions let you have multiple arguments within the parentheses and commas always separate the arguments. In this example, the function simply computes the average of cells b5, b10 and b15.

7. Use the fill handle ✛ to copy the formula across row 19.

Compute the Average Returns in row 20 by using point mode with the AVERAGE function

8. **Click** cell **B20**.

9. Type **=average(**

10. **Click** cell **B6**.

    The reference B6 will be added to the function in the Formula bar.

11. Type a comma **,** then **click** cell **B11**.

12. Type a comma **,** then **click** cell **B16**.

13. Type a closing parentheses **)** and Confirm ☑ the entry.

    The result should be 8.3333. Once again, using point mode is usually beneficial because it reduces errors by preventing you from typing the wrong cell reference.

14. Use the fill handle ✛ to copy the formula across row 20.

15. **Select** the cells in rows **18**, **19** and **20** and decrease the decimals ⬚ to **2**.

16. **Close** the workbook and **save** the changes.

Assessment 3.1

1. Use the following guidelines to create the worksheet shown below.

   • Use formulas to compute the Interest Charge in column E and the New Balance in Column F. The formulas are as follows.

      – Interest Charge = 1.5% * (Beginning Balance - Payments)

      – New Balance = Beginning Balance + Purchases - Payments + Interest Charge

   Notice that you must use parenthesis in the Interest Charge formula to change the order of calculations. You want Excel to subtract the Payments from the Beginning Balance and then multiply the result by 1.5%. Also, don't be confused and try to type the words Beginning Balance etc. in the formulas. You should use the appropriate cell references in the formulas.

   • Format rows 5, 10, 11 and 12 with the Currency formatting as shown.

   • Format the title and header rows as shown.

   • Compute the Totals in row 10 and use the MAX and MIN functions to compute the Highest and Lowest numbers in rows 11 and 12.

2. **Print** the worksheet when you have finished.

3. **Close** the worksheet and **save** it as **Assessment 3.1**.

	A	B	C	D	E	F
1	Bill's Hot Tubs - Accounts Receivable Report					
2						
3		Beginning			Interest	
4	Customer	Balance	Purchases	Payments	Charge	New Balance
5	Zelton	$2,000	$2,300	$1,000	$15	$3,315
6	Ranier	2450	1000	2450	0	1000
7	Worthington	5400	2190	3000	36	4626
8	Alonzo	3400	500	3400	0	500
9	Barton	100	3400	100	0	3400
10	Totals	$13,350	$9,390	$9,950	$51	$12,841
11	Highest	$5,400	$3,400	$3,400	$36	$4,626
12	Lowest	$100	$500	$100	$0	$500

Assessment 3.2

1. Use the following guidelines to create the worksheet shown at the bottom of this page.

   • Enter all the numbers and text as shown. Use the copy & paste or drag & drop techniques to copy the text or numbers whenever possible. For example, all three of the Wilson family children were paid the same allowances in all four years. Therefore, you can enter the data in row 5 and copy row 5 to rows 10 and 15.

   • Use Increase Indent [icon] to indent the Allowance, Saved and Interest Earned entries as shown.

   • Calculate the Interest Earned with the formula **Interest Earned = Saved * Interest Rate**. Use the Interest Rates shown in the following rate table. You will notice that the interest rates change from year to year.

1992	1993	1994	1995
3.5%	4.5%	6.5%	6.5%

   • Widen the columns as necessary and format the worksheet with bold, italics and the Currency format as shown.

2. You completed worksheet should match the worksheet shown below.

3. **Print** the worksheet, then **close** it and **save** it as **Assessment 3.2**.

	A	B	C	D	E	F
1	Wilson Family Allowances					
2						
3		1992	1993	1994	1995	
4	Jason					Total Interest
5	Allowance	260	300	300	340	
6	Saved	120	110	200	220	
7	*Interest Earned*	*4.2*	*4.95*	*13*	*14.3*	$ 36.45
8						
9	Cindy					
10	Allowance	260	300	300	340	
11	Saved	120	110	200	220	
12	*Interest Earned*	*4.2*	*4.95*	*13*	*14.3*	$ 36.45
13						
14	Betty					
15	Allowance	260	300	300	340	
16	Saved	130	290	280	310	
17	*Interest Earned*	*4.55*	*13.05*	*18.2*	*20.15*	$ 55.95
18						
19	Total Family Interest 1992 - 1995					$ 128.85

Assessment 3.3

1. **Open** the workbook named **Assessment 3.3**.

2. Use the **Classic3** AutoFormat style to format the worksheet as shown below.

3. **Print** the worksheet, then **close** it and **save** the changes.

	A	B	C	D	E	F	G
1			Diane's Café - Employee Hourly Time Log				
2							
3	Employee	Wednesday	Thursday	Friday	Saturday	Sunday	Totals
4	Mary Johnson	6.5		5	6.5	4	22
5	Cliff Packard	4	6	6.5	6.5	4	27
6	Helen Martinez	4	6	6.5	6.5		23
7	Sarah Stonestown		4	4	4		12
8	Totals	14.5	16	22	23.5	8	84

Critical Thinking 3.1

Open any of the Hands-On or Skills Builder worksheets that you created or modified in lessons 1 and 2. Use the Borders and Colors buttons or AutoFormat to format the worksheets. Be creative and try to choose formats that draw attention to the most important parts of the worksheet. Save the modified worksheet when you have finished.

Critical Thinking 3.2

Create a worksheet to track any investments that you may have. Enter the initial investment amount and the current value of the investment. Use a simple difference formula to compute the gain or loss. If you want a challenge, then add a formula that computes the percentage gain or loss. Create a Totals row that computes the total value of your investment portfolio. Create an AVERAGE function that computes the average gain or loss of your various investments. Feel free to save your worksheet under any name you feel is appropriate.

Critical Thinking 3.3

Create a worksheet that tracks the amount of money you spend on food. Categorize your expenditures as groceries, dining out, ordering take out and snacking or junk food. Set up the worksheet to track your expenditures on a monthly basis. Compute the total for each category. If you are really courageous, then create a formula that computes the percentage of your total food expenditures that each category consumes. You may even want to determine the percentage of each category in relation to your total income. Feel free to save your worksheet under any name you feel is appropriate.

4 Dates, Text Features and Restructuring Worksheets

Objectives:

- Work with dates

- Understand date formats

- Perform calculations on dates

- Work with multiple-line text entries

- Use cell alignment options

- Change column widths and row heights

- Insert and delete rows and columns

- Spell check worksheets

The Project - A Checkbook Register

In this lesson, you will develop a checkbook register to track checking transactions for a small home based business - Tamika's Jewelry Exchange. Tamika wants to record her checking transactions electronically, to help her manage her money more effectively. You will use dates and various text features to document the checkbook transactions. You will also learn how to restructure worksheets by inserting rows and columns. This will make the checkbook register dynamic and will allow you to change it. You will develop the following worksheet as you progress through this lesson.

	A	B	C	D	E	F	G
1	Tamika's Jewelry Exchange - Checkbook Register						
2	Today's Date		May 20, 1997				
3							
4	Date	Check Number	Transaction Description	P/B	Amount of Payment (-)	Amount of Deposit (+)	Balance Forward
5	1/1/97		Opening Balance				2000
6	1/1/97	100	Payment to Barbara Jennings for 5 pound supply of jade.	B	-400		-400
7							1600
8	1/3/97		Sales from Berkeley Telegraph Avenue outing	B		700	700
9							2300
10	1/3/97		Sale to Donna Brown of Taylor's Emporium	B		250	250
11							2550
12	1/7/97	101	Abalone shells from Pacific Abalone Supply	B	-175		-175
13							2375
14	1/9/97	102	Silver from the San Francisco Diamond and Jewelry Exchange	B	-850		-850
15							1525
16	1/14/97		Check from Mom for Christmas	P		350	350
17							1875
18	1/18/97	103	Purchased 100 jewelry boxes from Acme Packaging	B	-57		-57
19							1818
20							
21	Total days in use		139				

Working with Dates

Excel lets you work with dates in a variety of ways. You can enter dates and then use number formats to display the dates in various ways. For example, you could format a date as 12/25/97, or as December 25, 1997 or as 25-Dec-97. Excel also provides a number of date functions including the TODAY function, which inserts the current date. Dates can even be used in calculations.

Excel recognizes dates and converts them to numbers

Excel recognizes the dates you enter and it converts them to numbers. The benefit of converting dates to numbers is you can use the numbers/dates in formulas. For example, you may want to compute the number of days that an invoice is past due. This would be calculated as the difference between the current date and the original invoice date.

Excel converts dates to a number between 1 and 2,958,525. These numbers correspond to the dates January 1, 1900 through December 31, 9999. The date January 1, 1900 would be converted to the number 1. January 2, 1900 would be converted to 2, ... and December 31, 9999 would be converted to 2,958,525. In other words, there are 2,958,525 days between January 1, 1900 and December 31, 9999.

What happens when you enter a date?

Excel goes through the following steps whenever you enter a date in a cell.

1. Excel recognizes the entry as a date if you enter it using a standard date format. For example, Excel would recognize 12/25/97, or December 25, 1997 or 25-Dec-97 as dates.

2. Excel converts the date to a number between 1 and 2,958,525.

3. Excel formats the cell with a date/number format that matches the format you used when you entered the date. This displays the date exactly as you entered it.

This roundabout process is transparent to you. However, the benefit of converting dates to numbers and then formatting them with a date format is the dates can then be used in calculations.

Hands-On 4.1 – Enter dates in the checkbook register

In this exercise, you will begin developing a checkbook register. You will enter dates in column A.

Start Excel and enter a date
1. Start Excel and enter the following text entries (type the phrase Today's Date in cell A2).

	A	B	C	D	E
1	Tamika's Jewelry Exchange - Checkbook Register				
2	Today's Date				
3					
4	Date				

2. **Click** cell **A5**.

3. Type **1/1/97** and Confirm ☑ the entry.

    Notice that Excel right aligns the entry in the cell. This occurred because Excel recognized your entry as a date, it converted the date to a number and Excel always right aligns numbers.

Continued...

Verify the entry is a number by changing the number format to General

4. **Click** cell **A5** and choose **Format→Cells...** from the menu bar.

5. Make sure the Number tab is active, then choose the **General** format and **click OK**.

    The number 35431 should be displayed in the cell. This number represents the date January 1, 1997 and it can be used in formulas. This number indicates that there are 35431 days between January 1, 1900 and January 1, 1997.

Experiment with the various date formats

6. Choose **Format→Cells...** from the menu bar and choose the **Date** category.

    A variety of date formats will be displayed in the Type list. You can format a date (or any number for that matter) by choosing a format from the list. This list also shows you the types of formats Excel recognizes when you are entering a date. Excel won't recognize your entry as a date if you use a format other than the formats shown in this list.

7. Choose the **fifth format** on the list (it should be 4-Mar-97) and **click OK**.

    Your date should now be formatted with the new format but the date will still be 1-Jan-97.

8. Use the Format Cells dialog box to change the format back to 1/1/97. You will need to choose the second format from the Type list.

9. Enter the following dates into column A.

	A	B	C	D	E
1	Tamika's Jewelry Exchange - Checkbook Register				
2	Today's Date				
3					
4	Date				
5	1/1/97				
6					
7	1/3/97				
8					
9	1/3/97				
10					
11	1/7/97				
12					
13	1/9/97				

10. **Select** all of the dates and Left Align ▤ them.

11. Save 🖫 the checkbook register with the name **Hands-On Lesson 4**.

    You will continue to develop the checkbook register as you progress through this lesson.

Hands-On 4.2 – Use the TODAY function to insert the current date

The current date is often required in worksheets. This may be necessary to show the date the worksheet was created or printed. In this exercise, you will use the TODAY function to display the current date at the top of the checkbook register.

Use the Paste Function box to check out the date functions

1. **Click** cell **C2**.

2. **Click** the Paste Function *fx* button on the Standard toolbar.

    Notice Excel inserts an = sign in the Formula bar and displays the Paste Function box.

Continued...

3. **Click** the **Date & Time** category.

4. **Click** the various date functions in the Function name list and read the descriptions at the bottom of the dialog box.

   You will notice a variety of date and time functions. Many of the descriptions refer to serial numbers. A serial number is simply a number between 1 and 2,958,525 that corresponds to a date.

5. **Scroll down** and choose the **TODAY** function, then **click OK**.

   The Formula Palette and the =TODAY() function will appear. The syntax =TODAY() is the complete syntax because the TODAY function requires no argument within the parenthesis.

6. **Click OK** on the Formula Palette.

   Today's date should be inserted in cell C2.

Change the date format

7. Make sure cell C2 is active and choose **Format→Cells…** from the menu bar.

8. If necessary, scroll through the list and choose the **9th** date type (March 4, 1997).

9. **Click OK** and the new format will be applied to the date.

   These examples demonstrate that you can change the appearance of a date by formatting it. If you are entering a large number of dates, then enter the dates in whichever format is easiest for you (such as 1/1/97). Once you enter the dates, you can format them using whichever format you desire (such as January 1, 1997).

Hands-On 4.3 – Calculate the number of days the register has been in use

In this exercise, you will use a formula that subtracts the first date the checkbook register was used (January 1, 1997) from the current date. This will tell you the total number of days that the checkbook register has been in use.

1. **Click** cell **A16** and enter the phrase **Total days in use**.

2. **Click** cell **C16** and type the formula **=C2-A5**.

3. Confirm ☑ the entry and Excel will calculate the difference between the two serial numbers that represent the dates in cells C2 and A5.

   The result in cell C16 may be formatted as a date and time. In the next step, you will use the Format Painter to copy the General format from any blank cell in the workbook to cell C16. All cells in a new workbook are formatted as General. The General format will let you see the number of days the checkbook has been in use.

4. **Click** any **blank cell** in the workbook.

5. **Click** the Format Painter 🖌, then **click** cell **C16**.

   The General format should be copied to the cell. Let's assume your checkbook register has been in use from January 1, 1997 until today. How many days has your register been in use? The answer is in cell C16.

6. Save 💾 the changes and continue with the next topic.

Multiple Line Text Entries

Excel provides two methods for entering multiple lines of text within a cell. You can use the keystroke combination Alt + Enter to manually create a hard return within a cell. Excel also has a cell alignment option that forces the text to wrap within a cell as it would in a word processing document. You will use both techniques in the following exercise.

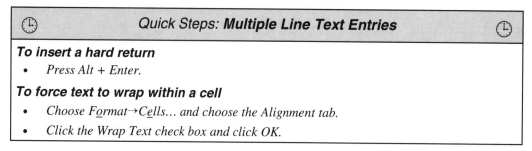

⏰	Quick Steps: *Multiple Line Text Entries*	⏰

To insert a hard return
- *Press Alt + Enter.*

To force text to wrap within a cell
- *Choose Format→Cells... and choose the Alignment tab.*
- *Click the Wrap Text check box and click OK.*

Hands-On 4.4 – Create multiple line text entries

Insert a hard return with the Alt + Enter keystroke

1. **Click** cell **B4**.

2. Type **Check** and **press** ⌨Alt + ⌨Enter.

3. Type **Number** and Confirm ✓ the entry.
   Notice Excel displays the double-line entry in the Formula bar.

4. **Click** cell **C4** and type **Transaction**.

5. **Press** ⌨Alt + ⌨Enter.

6. Type **Description** and **tap** ↦ to confirm the entry.

Use the wrap text option
7. **Click** cell **B5**.

8. Type the number **100** and **tap** ↦ to confirm the entry.

9. Choose **Format→Cells...** from the menu bar.

10. Choose the **Alignment** tab at the top of the dialog box.
    You will use the various alignment options as you progress through this lesson.

11. **Click** the Wrap Text ☑ Wrap Text check box and **click OK**.

12. Type the three-line paragraph below **without** pressing Enter or Alt+Enter and Confirm the entry.
    Keep in mind that the text may wrap differently in your cell because the column width may be different than shown here.

> Payment to Barbara
> Jennings for 5 pound
> supply of jade.

Continued...

13. **Widen Column C** until the text in cell **C5** wraps as shown at the bottom of the previous page.

    Don't be concerned if the height of row 5 is higher than the text. You will learn how to adjust the row height later in this lesson.

Have Excel automatically check the wrap text box

14. **Click** cell **D4**.

15. Choose **Format→Cells...** from the menu bar and make sure the Alignment tab is chosen.

    *Notice the Wrap Text box is **not** checked. This box must be checked if you want text to automatically wrap within cells.*

16. **Click** the **Cancel** button without checking the box.

17. Type **Amount of** and press ⎡ Alt ⎤ + ⎡ Enter ⎤.

18. Type **Payment (-)** and Confirm ☑ the entry.

    *Your last line **Payment (-)** should be too wide to fit in the cell, so Excel will wrap the line. Excel turns the Wrap Text option on whenever you use the Alt + Enter keystrokes in a cell and then type a line that is too wide for the cell.*

19. Choose **Format→Cells...** and notice the Wrap Text box is checked.

20. **Click** the **Cancel** button.

Widen column D

21. Make sure the highlight is in cell D4 (the Amount of Payment cell).

22. Try to position the mouse pointer on the column heading and you will notice it is blocked by the two-line display in the Formula bar.

23. **Click** cell **D3** (which has no entry) and the column headings will be visible.

24. **Widen** column **D** until the Payment (-) line no longer wraps.

    The first and second lines in cell D4 will remain as two lines no matter how wide the column is. This is because you used a hard return to force the second line down.

25. **Click** cell **E4** and use the **Alt + Enter** method to create the following two line entry. You will need to widen column E slightly or else the second line will wrap.

Amount of
Deposit (+)

26. Enter the phrase **Balance Forward** in cell **F4**.

    At this point, rows 1 through 5 of your worksheet should match the worksheet shown below.

	A	B	C	D	E	F	G
1	Tamika's Jewelry Exchange - Checkbook Register						
2	Today's Date		May 10, 1997				
3							
4	Date	Check Number	Transaction Description	Amount of Payment (-)	Amount of Deposit (+)	Balance Forward	
5	1/1/97	100	Payment to Barbara Jennings for 5 pound supply of jade.				

Other Cell Alignment Options

The Alignment tab on the Format Cells dialog box lets you access the Wrap Text option and several other useful options. The Vertical Alignment option lets you change the vertical positioning of text within a cell and the Orientation option lets you rotate text. You will use these options in the following exercise.

Hands-On 4.5 – Use the alignment options

Set the Vertical alignment of row 4

1. **Select** all entries in **row 4**.

   Notice how row 4 has been increased in height. This increase occurred when you used the wrap text and Alt + Enter options in the previous exercises. You will change the vertical alignment of the entries in the next few steps.

2. Choose **F**ormat→**C**ells... and **click** the **Alignment tab**.

3. Set the Vertical Alignment to **Top** [Vertical: Top] and **click OK**.

   All entries should be aligned with the top edges of the cells.

Experiment with the Orientation options

4. **Click** cell **A4** and choose **F**ormat→**C**ells.

5. Use the following steps to explore the alignment and orientation options.

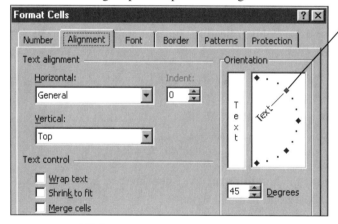

❶ *Click here to set the Orientation to 45 degrees.*

❷ *Notice the other options in this dialog box. You have already used most of these options. The only option you have not used is Shrink to fit. This option reduces the font size of an entry until it fits in the cell.*

❸ *Click OK and the entry should be at a 45-degree angle.*

6. **Click** Undo 🔙 to restore the horizontal orientation.

Hands-On 4.6 – Enter text and formulas

Enter a negative number and a formula

1. **Click** cell **D5,** type **-400** (that's negative 400) and Confirm ✓ the entry.

   This entry will be subtracted from the Balance Forward, so it is entered as a negative number. You must precede numbers with minus (hyphen) signs if you want Excel to recognize them as negatives.

2. **Click** cell **F5** and enter the formula **=D5+E5**.

   The result should be -400. This formula carries the payment or deposit into the Balance Forward column, so it can be used in a Balance Forward formula.

Continued...

Use the Format Painter to copy the Wrap Text format

3. **Click** cell **C7**.

4. Type **Sales from Berkeley Telegraph Avenue outing** and Confirm ☑ the entry.

5. **Click** cell **C5**, then **click** the Format Painter 🖌️.

6. **Click** cell **C7** and the Wrap Text formatting will be copied to that cell.

   Remember that you can use the Format Painter to copy any type of text, number or cell formats.

Copy the formula in cell F5

7. **Click** cell **F5**, then **click** the Copy 📋 button.

8. **Press & Hold** ⎡ Ctrl ⎤ while you **click** cells **F7**, **F9**, **F11** and **F13**.

   All four of these cells should be selected.

9. **Click** the Paste 📋 button to copy the formulas to these cells (the results should be 0).

10. Enter the number **700** into cell **E7**.

Enter the remaining text and numbers

11. Enter the text and numbers shown in rows 9, 11 and 13 below.

   Remember to use the Format Painter to copy the Wrap Text format from cells C5 or C7 to cells C9, C11 and C13. Your completed worksheet should match the worksheet shown below.

	A	B	C	D	E	F	G
1	Tamika's Jewelry Exchange - Checkbook Register						
2	Today's Date		May 10, 1997				
3							
4	Date	Check Number	Transaction Description	Amount of Payment (-)	Amount of Deposit (+)	Balance Forward	
5	1/1/97	100	Payment to Barbara Jennings for 5 pound supply of jade.	-400		-400	
6							
7	1/3/97		Sales from Berkeley Telegraph Avenue outing		700	700	
8							
9	1/3/97		Sale to Donna Brown of Taylor's Emporium		250	250	
10							
11	1/7/97	101	Abalone shells from Pacific Abalone Supply	-175		-175	
12							
13	1/9/97	102	Silver from the San Francisco Diamond and Jewelry Exchange	-850		-850	
14							
15							
16	Total days in use		129				

Changing Column Widths and Row Heights

So far, you have been adjusting column widths by dragging the column headings. This is the most basic technique for changing column widths and it is often the easiest and fastest method. The row heights can also be adjusted by dragging the row headings. Excel provides several other techniques for adjusting column widths and row heights. All of these techniques are discussed in this section.

Default column widths and row heights

Each column in a new worksheet has a width of 8.43 characters where the default character is Arial 10pt. Each row has a default height of 12.75 points, which is approximately equal to 1/6th inch.

The AutoFit options

Both column widths and row heights can be adjusted with the AutoFit command. AutoFit adjusts column widths to fit the widest entry in the column. Likewise, AutoFit adjusts row heights to accommodate the tallest entry in the row.

The following table summarizes the column width and row height commands. Keep in mind that you must select (or have the highlight in) the desired columns, rows or cells before using these commands.

To do this	Use this procedure
Set a precise column width	Choose Format→Column→Width and enter the desired width
Set column widths with AutoFit	Choose Format→Column→AutoFit Selection, or Double-click the right-edge of the column heading
Set a precise row height	Choose Format→Row→Height
Set row heights with AutoFit	Choose Format→Row→AutoFit, or Double-click the bottom-edge of the row heading
Manually adjust column widths and row heights	Select the desired columns or rows and drag the column or row headings

Hands-On 4.7 – Change column widths and row heights

Use AutoFit

1. **Select** the range **A1:F16** which includes all active cells in the worksheet.

2. Choose **Format→Column→AutoFit Selection**.

   Excel will widen each column to fit the largest entry in the column. Column A should be very wide because the entry in Cell A1 is quite long. Also, notice that AutoFit has no impact on the cells in column C which have the Wrap Text option turned on.

3. Undo the AutoFit, then **select** all cells in the range **A2:F16**.

   Notice that this range does not include the long entry in cell A1.

4. Choose **Format→Column→AutoFit Selection**.

Continued...

5. **Click** anywhere in the worksheet and you will see that AutoFit did a better job this time.

Manually widen column C

6. **Drag** the border between columns C and D  to the right until each entry in column C has a maximum height of two lines.

Set a precise width for column C

7. **Click** anywhere in column **C**.

8. Choose **Format→Column→Width...** from the menu bar.

9. Enter **28** in the width box and **click OK**.

Reduce the height of row 5

10. Use the following step to reduce the height of row 5.

    ❶ *Position the mouse pointer on the border between row headings 5 and 6 and* ***drag*** *the heading up slightly.*

		Payment to Barbara Jennings for
1/1/97	100	5 pound supply of jade.

    Notice this is similar to adjusting column widths.

AutoFit rows by double-clicking

11. **Double-click** the border between row headings 5 and 6.

    Excel will AutoFit the row height to fit the tallest entry in the row. You can use the double-click method to AutoFit both row heights and column widths.

12. Use the **double-click** technique to AutoFit rows **4**, **7**, **9**, **11** and **13**.

13. Take five or ten minutes to experiment with the various column width and row height options.
    Try using the double-click AutoFit technique on columns. You will need to widen the columns first, since they have already been AutoFit. Then you can use the double-click technique.

14. When you have finished, save the changes and continue with the next topic.

Inserting and Deleting Rows and Columns

Excel lets you insert and delete rows and columns. This gives you the flexibility and power to restructure your worksheets after they have been created.

Always select the rows or columns

There are a variety of ways to insert and delete rows and columns, however, it is recommended that you always select the row(s) or columns(s) you wish to insert or delete. The only exception to this rule is when you are inserting a single row or column. A single column can be inserted to the left of the column with the highlight and a single row can be inserted above the row with the highlight.

The following table discusses the various procedures that are used to insert and delete rows and columns.

To do this	Use this procedure
Insert columns	Select the number of columns you wish to insert and choose Insert→Columns. The new columns are inserted to the left of the selected columns.
Delete columns	Select the columns you wish to delete and choose Edit→Delete.
Insert rows	Select the number of rows you wish to insert and choose Insert→Rows. The new rows are inserted above the selected rows.
Delete rows	Select the rows you wish to delete and choose Edit→Delete.

Cell references are automatically updated in formulas

One of the benefits of using cell references in formulas is the references are updated when rows and columns are inserted or deleted. For example, a SUM formula such as =SUM(A1:A5) would become =SUM(A1:A7) if two rows were inserted between rows 1 and 5. This makes the formulas dynamic and allows you to restructure your worksheets as needed.

There is one important exception to the automatic updating rule!

Cell references in formulas are not updated if you try to insert rows directly above the row containing a formula. For example, imagine that cell A6 contains the formula =SUM(A1:A5). If you position the highlight in cell A6 and insert a row above A6, then the references in the formula will not be updated.

Inserting and Deleting Ranges

Excel also lets you insert and delete ranges of cells. However, this may cause values and formulas to go out of alignment in the worksheet. For this reason, it is recommended that you avoid inserting or deleting ranges and stick to inserting and deleting entire rows and columns.

Hands-On 4.8 – Insert rows and columns

You will begin this exercise by inserting a row for the opening balance.

Insert a row for the opening balance

1. **Click** cell **F5** and notice the formula in the Formula bar.

    The formula should be =D5+E5. This formula will be updated when you insert a row for the opening balance.

2. Choose **Insert→Rows** from the menu bar and a new row will be inserted above row 5.

3. **Click** cell **F6** and notice the formula has been updated to =D6+E6.

4. **Click** cell **F5** and enter the number **2000**.

    2000 represents Tamika's opening checkbook balance.

5. Enter the date **1/1/97** in cell **A5** and Left Align ▤ the entry.

6. Enter the phrase **Opening Balance** in cell **C5**.

Insert a column to differentiate personal and business expenses

Imagine that Tamika has decided to combine her personal and business expenses in one checking account. You will add a column to track whether an expense is personal or business.

7. **Click** anywhere in **column D**.

8. Choose **Insert→Columns** and a new column will be inserted to the left of column D.

    Notice the new column has the same width as column C. The cells in this new column will also have the same text and number formats as the cells to the left of them in column C.

9. **Click** cell **D4** and enter **P/B** for Personal or Business.

10. At this point all of the expenses are business related, so enter the letter **B** in cells **D6**, **D8**, **D10**, **D12** and **D14**.

AutoFit Column D and center align the entries

11. **Double-click** the border ⟨ D ↔ E ⟩ between column headings D and E.

    Excel will AutoFit Column D. The column should be just wide enough to fit the P/B entry.

12. **Select** the entire column and Center Align ▤ the entries.

13. Save ▤ the changes and continue with the next exercise.

Hands-On 4.9 – Add formulas and format the worksheet

In this exercise, you will add formulas to calculate the checkbook balance. You will also add color to improve the appearance of the checkbook register.

Add formulas to compute the balance

1. **Click** cell **G7**.

2. Enter the formula **=G5+G6**.

   The result should be 1600. Notice that Excel subtracted the number 400 in cell G6 because it was preceded by a minus - sign.

3. **Copy** the formula from cell **G7** to cells **G9**, **G11**, **G13** and **G15**.

   The balance in cell G15 should be 1525.

Format the worksheet

4. **Select** the range **A4:G4** which includes all the headings in row 4.

5. Use the Fill Color [button] button to apply a medium weight color or shade.

6. **Click** cell **G7** and apply a light Fill Color [button] to that cell.

7. Use the Format Painter [button] to copy the format from cell **G7** to cells **G9**, **G11**, **G13** and **G15**.

   This way every balance line will be highlighted with a color.

8. Feel free to format or enhance the worksheet in any way you feel is necessary.

9. Save [button] the changes and continue with the next exercise.

Hands-On 4.10 – Insert multiple rows for new transactions

In this exercise, you will insert multiple rows to allow you to enter new transactions in the register.

Insert the rows

1. **Select** rows **16** through **19** by dragging the mouse down the row headings as shown below.

16				
17	Total days in use			129
18				
19				

The rows you are about to insert will be inserted above the selected rows.

2. Choose **Insert→Rows** from the menu bar.

   Notice Excel inserts the same number of rows as you had selected.

3. **Click** anywhere in the worksheet to deselect the rows.

   Notice that Excel formatted the new rows with the same format as the row above them. In particular, the color from cell G15 should have been copied to the column G cells in the new rows.

Remove the color from two of the cells

4. **Press & Hold** the ⌐Ctrl⌐ key while you **click** cells **G16** and **G18**.

5. **Click** the Color [icon] drop-down button and choose **white** (at the bottom-right corner).

   You can always remove color from cells by applying the white color.

6. Enter the data shown below into rows 16 and 18. However, do not enter the numbers shown in column G. You should copy the balance forward formulas from previous rows to the cells in column G. Also, use the Format Painter [icon] as necessary to copy formats (such as the Wrap Text format) from the other rows.

16	1/14/97		Check from Mom for Christmas	P		350	350
17							1875
18	1/18/97	103	Purchased 100 jewelry boxes from Acme Packaging	B	-57		-57
19							1818

7. Your completed worksheet should match the worksheet shown at the beginning of this lesson.

8. Feel free to format and enhance the worksheet as desired.

9. Continue with next topic where you will spell check your worksheet.

Spell Checking

Excel's spell checker checks the spelling of text entries in a worksheet. The spell checker functions the same way as the spell checker in Microsoft Word and most other word processors.

Hands-On 4.11 – Spell check the worksheet

1. **Click** cell **A1**.

   This will force the spell checker to begin checking at the top of the worksheet.

2. **Click** the Spelling [ABC] button on the Standard toolbar.

   The Spelling dialog box will appear and the word Tamika's should be listed as Not in Dictionary.

3. Take a moment to study the Spelling dialog box options.

   The following table discusses the effect the various buttons have on the word.

Button	What the button does
Ignore	Ignores the misspelled word this time only. The speller will prompt you the next time it encounters the same misspelling.
Ignore All	Ignores the misspelled word now and for all spell checks during this Excel session.
Change	Replaces the misspelled word with the word in the Change To: box.
Change All	Replaces all occurrences of the misspelled word in this worksheet with the word in the Change To: box.
Add	Adds the misspelled word to a custom dictionary.
Suggest	Displays a full list of suggested replacement words.

4. **Click** the **Ignore** button to skip over the word Tamika's.

   Tamika's name may not be in the spell checker's dictionary but her name is spelled correctly. At this point, the spell checker may finish or it may find additional misspelled words. Use your best judgment to complete the spell check.

5. **Close** the workbook when you have finished and **save** the changes.

   Continue with the end-of-lesson questions and exercises on the following pages.

Concepts Review

True / False

1. When you enter a date, Excel converts it to a number.
2. Excel applies a date format to dates after it converts them to numbers.
3. The TODAY function returns the current time.
4. You cannot combine a hard return and automatic text wrapping in the same cell.
5. The AutoFit command changes the column width to fit the narrowest entry in the column.
6. Row heights cannot be changed.
7. The AutoFit command cannot be used to adjust row heights.
8. New columns are inserted to the left of the selected columns.
9. New rows are inserted above the selected rows.
10. A column can be deleted by selecting it and issuing the Edit→Delete command.

1. **T F**
2. **T F**
3. **T F**
4. **T F**
5. **T F**
6. **T F**
7. **T F**
8. **T F**
9. **T F**
10. **T F**

Multiple Choice

1. Which keystroke combination creates a hard return in a cell?
   a) Shift + Enter
   b) Shift + Tab
   c) Alt + Enter
   d) Ctrl + Enter.   (   )

2. Which command displays a dialog box that can be used to set the Wrap Text option?
   a) Format→Cells
   b) Edit→Cells
   c) Format→Alignment
   d) None of the above.   (   )

3. Which spell checker option skips over a word for the remainder of the spell check?
   a) Ignore
   b) Ignore All
   c) Skip
   d) Skip All   (   )

4. Which statement most accurately describes the effect that inserting a row directly above a formula would have on the formula?
   a) The formula would continue to reference the same cells.
   b) The formula references would change to include the new row.
   c) A row cannot be inserted directly above a formula.
   d) None of the above.   (   )

5. How many columns would be inserted if you had three columns selected and you issued the Insert→Columns command.
   a) 1
   b) 3
   c) 0
   d) None of the above.   (   )

Skills Builder 4.1

In this exercise, you will open a worksheet and you will modify it until it matches the worksheet on the following page.

Add two new columns

1. **Open** the workbook named **Skills Builder 4.1**.

   Look at the worksheet on the following page and notice it contains two additional columns with the headings Extra Small and Extra Large.

2. **Click** cell **E4** and notice the formula is =SUM(B4:D4).

3. **Click** anywhere in column **B**.

4. Choose **Insert→Columns** from the menu bar.

5. Now **click** in **Column F** (the Total column) and **insert** a **column**.

6. **Click** cell **G4** and notice the formula has changed to =SUM(C4:E4).

   The formula should be =SUM(B4:F4). The cell references changed to reflect the new location of cells B4:D4, which were the cells originally referenced in the formula. However, the references did not expand to include the new columns. You must be careful when inserting rows and columns. This is because Excel will not always expand the references as you desire. In this example, you inserted columns outside the range that was referenced in the original formula, so Excel did not update the formula references. Excel only updates the references if you insert columns inside the range that is referenced in the formula. You will repair the Total column formulas later in this exercise.

7. Type the headings **Extra Small** and **Extra Large** in the new columns as shown on the next page.

   Notice that both headings have the formatting of the cell to the left of them. The formatting from the column to the left was copied to the inserted columns.

8. Copy ⬛ the formatting from the **Small** heading to the headings you just typed.

Use AutoFit to adjust the column widths

9. **Select** the range **A3:G14** which includes all cells in the main part of the worksheet.

10. Choose **Format→Column→AutoFit Selection**.

Insert Subtotal rows and blank rows

   Look at the worksheet on the following page and notice it contains a Subtotal row and a blank row after each clothing group.

11. **Click** cell **G14** and notice the Total formula =SUM(G4:G13) in the Formula bar.

12. **Click** anywhere in row **6** and use the **Insert→Rows** command to insert a blank row.

13. **Click** cell **G15** and notice the Total formula has been updated to =SUM(G4:G14).

   This formula was updated because you inserted a row inside the range G4:G13 which was the original range referenced by the formula.

14. **Insert** a blank row **above** row **11**.

Continued...

15. Click cell **G16** and the Total formula should now be =SUM(G4:G15).

In the next few steps, you will insert two blank rows above row 16. The Total formula will not be updated when you do this because you will insert directly above the row containing the formula.

16. Select rows **16** and **17** by **dragging** the mouse over the row headings.

17. Choose **Insert→Rows** and two blank rows will be inserted.

18. Click cell **G18** and notice the Total formula has not been updated this time.

Excel does not update formula references when you insert rows directly above the formulas. You must be aware of this unusual convention and either design your worksheets to accommodate this or manually adjust the formulas after inserting. Notice this was the same situation that occurred when you inserted columns earlier in this exercise.

Add headings, numbers and Subtotal formulas

19. Enter the numbers shown in columns B and F and the Subtotal headings and Subtotal formulas shown in rows 6, 11, 16 and 18 below. The Total formulas in row 18 should add up the Subtotals in each column. Also, you will need to redo all the Total formulas in column G. These formulas are no longer correct because you inserted columns B and F which were outside of the columns originally referenced by the Total formulas.

20. Take a few minutes to carefully check over your worksheet when you have finished. In particular, make sure all the formulas are calculating correctly. Your completed worksheet should match the worksheet shown below.

21. Close the worksheet when you are finished and **save** the changes.

	A	B	C	D	E	F	G
1	Ricky's Clothing Store - Defective Items						
2							
3	**Shirts**	Extra Small	Small	Medium	Large	Extra Large	Total
4	Long sleeve	13	12	13	9	13	60
5	Short sleeve	8	9	8	9	8	42
6	Subtotal	21	21	21	18	21	102
7							
8	**Pants**						
9	Blue	6	5	6	4	6	27
10	Khaki	8	7	8	9	8	40
11	Subtotal	14	12	14	13	14	67
12							
13	**Shorts**						
14	White	2	3	2	4	2	13
15	Red	9	1	9	7	9	35
16	Subtotal	11	4	11	11	11	48
17							
18	Total	46	37	46	42	46	217

Skills Builder 4.2

In this exercise, you will create an accounts receivable aging report that calculates the number of days accounts are past due.

Set up the worksheet

1. If necessary, **click** the New Workbook button to open a new workbook.

2. Set up the worksheet by typing the headings and numbers shown below. Use the Alt + Enter keystroke combination to create the multi-line headings in columns C through F. You will need to widen the columns after typing the headings. Also, you may need to AutoFit Row 4 to reduce the row height.

	A	B	C	D	E	F
1	Accounts Receivable Aging Report					
2	Report Date					
3						
4	Customer	Invoice #	Invoice Date	Invoice Amount	# of days since invoice was issued	# of days past due
5	Wilson	345		123		
6	Arthur	367		980		
7	Bellmont	456		345		
8	Alexander	478		234		
9	Wilmont	489		765		
10	Barton	505		469		

Change the computer's date

Later in this exercise, you will use the TODAY () function to determine the number of days that the invoices are past due. In the next few steps, you will change your computer's internal clock so that the TODAY () function returns the same current date (6/8/97) as shown later in this exercise.

3. **Double-click** the time on the Taskbar at the bottom right corner of your screen (if it is displayed).

   or

   If the time isn't displayed on the Taskbar, then **click** the Start button, choose **Settings**, choose **Control Panel** and **double-click** the **Date and Time** icon in Control Panel.

   The Date/Time Properties dialog box should be displayed.

4. Use the dialog box controls to set the date to **June 8, 1997** and **click OK**.

   There is no need to set the time.

Insert the current date and invoice dates

5. **Click** cell **C2** and enter the function **=TODAY( )**.

   The date 6/8/97 should be displayed in the cell.

6. Enter the invoice dates shown in the third column of the worksheet on the following page (just type the dates as shown).

Continued...

	Customer	Invoice #	Invoice Date	Invoice Amount
4				
5	Wilson	345	1/20/97	123
6	Arthur	367	3/12/97	980
7	Bellmont	456	3/28/97	345
8	Alexander	478	4/4/97	234
9	Wilmont	489	4/8/97	765
10	Barton	505	4/20/97	469

Calculate the number of days since the invoices were issued

7. Click cell **E5** and enter the formula **=TODAY( )-C5**.

Enter the formula exactly as shown. Excel will format the result as a date.

8. Click any blank cell in the worksheet, then **click** the Format Painter .

9. Click cell **E5** and the General number format will be copied to that cell.

The result will be either 139 or 140 (depending upon the time of day). This is the difference between June 8, 1997 (today's date in this exercise) and the date the invoice was issued.

10. Use the fill handle **+** to **copy** the formula **down** the column.

11. Click cell **F5** and enter the formula **=E5-30**.

The result will be either 109 or 110. This number represents the number of days the invoice is past due assuming the terms are Net 30 days.

12. Copy the formula **down** the column and the worksheet should match the following worksheet.

	A	B	C	D	E	F
1	Accounts Receivable Aging Report					
2	Report Date		6/8/97			
3						
4	Customer	Invoice #	Invoice Date	Invoice Amount	# of days since invoice was issued	# of days past due
5	Wilson	345	1/20/97	123	139	109
6	Arthur	367	3/12/97	980	88	58
7	Bellmont	456	3/28/97	345	72	42
8	Alexander	478	4/4/97	234	65	35
9	Wilmont	489	4/8/97	765	61	31
10	Barton	505	4/20/97	469	49	19

Change the system date back to today's date

13. Use the technique discussed earlier in this exercise to change the system date back to today's date.

Notice the TODAY function does not display today's date in cell C2 and the dates do not change in the days past due calculations. This is because the TODAY function is refreshed only when the workbook is closed and then reopened.

14. Close the workbook and **save** it as **Skills Builder 4.2**.

15. Choose **File** from the menu bar and Skills Builder 4.2 will be displayed at the bottom of the menu.

You can open the most recently used workbooks by choosing them from the menu.

16. Choose **Skills Builder 4.2** from the File menu and the workbook will open.

Take a moment to check out the worksheet and all the formulas should be recalculated.

17. Close the workbook, **save** the changes and continue with the next exercise.

Skills Builder 4.3

In this exercise, you will open an order entry worksheet from your exercise diskette. You will modify the worksheet by removing and inserting new line items.

Open the workbook and create the formulas

1. **Open** the workbook named **Skills Builder 4.3**.

2. **Click** cell **D4** and calculate the Extended Price as the Quantity multiplied by the Unit Price.
   The result should be 239.7.

3. **Copy** the Extended Price formula down to rows **5** through **8**.

4. Use **AutoSum** to compute the Subtotal for the Extended prices in column D.

5. Calculate the Sales tax as the Subtotal multiplied by **7.75%**.

6. Calculate the Total as the Subtotal plus the Sales Tax.

7. **Select** all the numbers in columns **C** and **D** and increase the decimals to **2**.

Delete a row then insert a row

   Imagine the customer has decided to cancel his order for Electric pencil sharpeners. He also wants to add toner cartridges to his order.

8. **Select row 5** by clicking the row heading and choose **Edit**→**Delete**.
   The Subtotal, sales tax and Total should be recalculated.

9. **Click** anywhere in **row 7** and choose **Insert**→**Rows**.

10. Add the following item but make sure you use a formula in cell D7.

7	Toner cartridge	10	89.95	899.50

Insert a row and recalculate the Subtotal formula

11. **Click** anywhere in row **9** and insert a row above the Subtotal row.

12. Add the following item to the new row but make sure you use a formula in cell D9.

9	Two-line telephone	5	145.00	725.00

Make adjustments and formatting enhancements

13. **Click** cell **D10** and adjust the SUM function to account for the new row 9.

14. Do the Sales Tax and Total formulas need to be adjusted?
   The Total should be 3158.91 when you have finished.

15. Use the **TODAY** function to insert the current date in cell **E1**.

16. Format the date with the date format of your choice.

17. **Select** the range **A3:D12** and use the **AutoFit** command to adjust the column widths.

18. **Close** the workbook when you have finished and **save** the changes.

Assessment 4.1

In this assessment, you will open a worksheet on your exercise diskette. You will modify the worksheet until it matches the worksheet shown at the bottom of this page.

1. **Open** the workbook named **Assessment 4.1**.

2. Use the **TODAY** function to insert the current date in cell **C2**.

3. Format the date as shown below (although your date will be different).

4. Insert and move rows as necessary until the customer rows are reorganized in alphabetical order as shown below. You learned how to move rows in the previous lesson and you learned how to insert rows in this lesson.

5. Insert a column between columns A and B and enter the invoice numbers as shown below.

6. Compute the number of days past due in column F. Assume the terms are net 30, which means the invoice is supposed to be paid within 30 days. Your numbers will be different from the numbers shown here because your current date will be different. Your numbers should be much larger.

7. Use **AutoFormat** to format the worksheet. The example shown below uses the Classic 2 format.

8. Your completed worksheet should match the worksheet shown below. However, the # of days since invoices were issued and # of days past due will be different from the example shown here.

9. **Print** the worksheet, then **close** it and **save** the changes.

	A	B	C	D	E	F
1	Accounts Receivable Aging Report					
2	Report Date			5/10/97		
3						
4	Customer	Invoice Number	Invoice Date	Invoice amount	# of days since invoice was issued	# of days past due
5	Alexander	210	4/4/97	234	37	7
6	Arthur	155	3/12/97	980	60	30
7	Barton	246	4/20/97	469	21	-9
8	Bellmont	189	3/28/97	345	44	14
9	Wilmont	228	4/8/97	765	33	3
10	Wilson	130	1/20/97	123	111	81

Assessment 4.2

In this assessment, you will create the worksheet shown below. This worksheet computes the number of days between two test dates, the point increase in test scores, the percentage increase in test scores and the Average Number of Days and Average Percentage Increase.

1. Create the large paragraph in cells A2:C2 as follows.

    – Use the Merge and Center ⊞ button to merge cells A2:C2.

    – Turn the Wrap Text option on and set the Vertical Alignment to Top.

    – Increase the height of Row 2 as shown.

    – Type the text in the large merged cell.

2. The Percentage Increase in column H is calculated as the Point Increase in column G divided by the First Test Score in column C.

3. Format all numbers, dates and text as shown. Adjust row heights and column widths as shown.

4. **Print** the worksheet when you have finished, then **close** it and **save** it as **Assessment 4.2**.

	A	B	C	D	E	F	G	H
1	Grade 10 Performance Evaluations							
2	This worksheet computes the percentage increase in test scores for students who have been receiving special assistance. The number of days required to achieve the results is also shown.							
3								
4		First Test		Second Test				
5	Student	Date	Score	Date	Score	Number of Days Between Tests	Point Increase	Percentage Increase
6	Lisa Evans	2/3/96	78	4/30/96	87	87	9	12%
7	Clara Johnson	2/5/96	77	4/28/96	82	83	5	6%
8	Ted Thomas	2/5/96	65	5/5/96	80	90	15	23%
9	Brian Wilson	3/10/96	64	6/1/96	72	83	8	13%
10	Elizabeth Crawford	3/12/96	68	5/2/96	78	51	10	15%
11	Bernice Barton	4/1/96	72	7/10/96	88	100	16	22%
12	Average Days					82.33		
13	Average Increase							15%

Critical Thinking 4.1

Create a worksheet that calculates the number of days you have been alive. Add rows to the worksheet for either family members or friends. Of course, you will need to know their birthdays (including the year). You may even want to add a favorite pet to the worksheet although their birthdays may be a little more difficult to determine. Close the worksheet when you have finished and save it as birthdays.

Critical Thinking 4.2

Create a worksheet of any type that uses dates in calculations. Be creative and try to think of ways in which calculating dates could be helpful. Add a large paragraph to your worksheet to document the way dates are being used. Use the Wrap Text option for the paragraph and make the column wide enough to allow the paragraph to have some width. Close the worksheet when you have finished and save it under a descriptive name.

5 Working with Large Worksheets

Objectives:

- Sort worksheet rows

- Freeze header rows and columns

- Split worksheet panes

- Use the Page Setup dialog box

- Set margins in Page Setup and Print Preview

- Print titles on every page

- Create headers and footers

- Insert manual page breaks

- Use Page Break Preview

The Project - 1996 Home Budget

In this lesson, you will work with a large worksheet that tracks a personal budget and expenditures for each month in 1996. You will sort the worksheet rows and you will learn useful techniques for navigating through large worksheets. You will also learn a variety of techniques that will assist you in printing large worksheets. A partial view of the worksheet you will use is shown below.

	A	B	C	D	E	F	G	H	I	J	K
1	1996 Home Budget										
2											
3		January		February		March		April		May	
4		Budget	Spent	Budget	Spent	Budget	Spent	Budget	Spent	Budget	Spent
5	Utilities	100	78	100	120	100	95	100	78	100	120
6	Phone	60	75	60	80	60	145	60	75	60	80
7	Mortgage	1000	1000	1000	1000	1000	1075	1075	1075	1075	1075
8	Insurance	200	200	0	0	0	0	200	200	0	0
9	Subtotal	$1,360	$1,353	$1,160	$1,200	$1,160	$1,315	$1,435	$1,428	$1,235	$1,275
10											
11	Food	235	220	235	190	235	250	235	220	235	190
12	Entertainment	120	80	120	90	120	245	120	80	120	90
13	Clothing	100	54	100	0	100	234	100	54	100	0
14	Subtotal	$455	$354	$455	$280	$455	$729	$455	$354	$455	$280
15											
16	Car Payment	400	400	400	400	400	400	400	400	400	400
17	Car Maintenance	50	0	50	67	50	435	50	0	50	67
18	Car Insurance	180	180	0	0	0	0	180	180	0	0
19	Subtotal	$630	$580	$450	$467	$450	$835	$630	$580	$450	$467
20											
21	Grand Total	$2,445	$2,287	$2,065	$1,947	$2,065	$2,879	$2,520	$2,362	$2,140	$2,022
22	Differences	$158		$118		-$814		$158		$118	

Sorting

Excel has powerful sorting capabilities that let you **sort** worksheet rows or columns in a variety of ways. The most common type of sort is when entire rows are sorted based upon the text or values in a column.

Sort keys

Excel must know which rows you want to sort and which column to use as the **sort key**. Excel uses the sort key to decide how to arrange the rows. For example, imagine a worksheet has a list of names in column A. If you wanted to sort the rows according to the names, then you would specify column A as the sort key.

Always save your worksheet before sorting!

Sorting can be dangerous and it can easily render a worksheet useless. For this reason, you should always save your worksheet prior to sorting. If a problem arises, then you can close the worksheet **without** saving it. When you reopen the worksheet, it will be in the state it was in prior to sorting.

The Sort Ascending and Sort Descending buttons

The Sort Ascending ![A/Z] and Sort Descending ![Z/A] buttons let you rapidly sort **lists**. A list is a group of rows that are isolated from other rows in the worksheet. Being isolated means there is at least one empty row above and below the list. Because a list is isolated form other rows, Excel can easily determine which rows to sort when you click the Sort Ascending or Sort Descending buttons. Excel sorts all rows in the list unless it determines that the list has a **header row**.

You can always select the rows before sorting

You can always select the rows in a list before clicking the Sort Ascending and Sort Descending buttons. This may be necessary if the list contains rows that you do not want included in the sort. By selecting the rows, you are instructing Excel to sort only those rows. Excel will sort only the selected rows and it will use column A as the sort key.

Hands-On 5.1 – Use the Sort Ascending and Sort Descending buttons

In this exercise, you will open a worksheet on your exercise diskette. You will use the Sort Ascending and Sort Descending buttons to sort the rows in various ways.

Open the worksheet and check it out

1. Open ![open icon] the worksheet named **Hands-On Lesson 5**.

2. Take a few moments to browse through this worksheet.

    Notice this worksheet is very large and it contains budgetary data for all 12 months of the year. You will use this worksheet throughout this lesson.

Sort the first list based upon the column A sort key
3. **Scroll** to the top of the worksheet and **click** cell **A5**.

    Rows 5-8 constitute a list. A list is a group of rows that are isolated from other rows in the worksheet. Rows 3 and 4 are header rows. The Sort Ascending and Sort Descending buttons are designed to work with lists.

Continued...

You will sort rows 5-8 in the next few steps. When you do this, Excel will sort the entire rows. The rows will be sorted according to the text entries in column A. Keep in mind, however, that the entire rows will be sorted. Before you begin, notice that row 5 (the Utilities row) has the values 100, 78, 100, 120 etc. and row 6 (the Mortgage row) has 1000 or 1075 in each column. Also notice the rows are not in alphabetic order at this point.

4. Click the Sort Ascending ⬛ button.

Notice that the Insurance row is now on top because it is the first row in the alphabetic order. Also notice the entire rows were rearranged. For example, the Utilities row is now at the bottom of the list and the values 100, 78, 100, 120 are still part of that row.

5. Click the Sort Descending ⬛ button to reverse the sort order.

Sort the first list based upon the January Budget numbers
6. Click cell **B5**.

7. Click Sort Ascending ⬛ and the rows will now be sorted based upon the numbers in column B.

The Sort Ascending and Sort Descending buttons always use the column that contains the highlight as the sort key.

8. Click Sort Descending ⬛ to sort in descending order based upon the numbers in column B.

Sort all three lists in ascending order based upon column A
9. Click cell **A5**.

10. Click Sort Ascending ⬛.

11. Click cell **A11**.

12. Click Sort Ascending ⬛.

The rows in the second list should now be in ascending order.

13. Sort the third list (rows 16-18) in ascending order.

Add Subtotal rows
14. Click cell **A9**.

15. Enter the word **Subtotal**.

16. Enter the word **Subtotal** in cells **A14** and **A19**.

Sort the lists in Descending order
17. Click cell **A5**.

18. Click Sort Descending ⬛.

Notice that Excel includes the Subtotal row in the sort. Excel usually leaves header rows out of the sort but it is not as good at detecting Subtotal or Total rows. In situations such as this, you need to first select the rows you want to sort.

19. Click Undo ⬛ to reverse the sort.

20. Select rows **5-8** by **dragging** the mouse over the row headings.

Continued...

It is usually best to select entire rows when sorting. If you select only certain cells in the rows, then Excel will only sort those cells. This may render the entire worksheet useless. By dragging the row headings you can be certain that you have selected entire rows.

21. **Click** Sort Descending .

Excel should leave the Subtotal row out of the sort. Notice that Excel used column A as the sort key. Excel always uses column A as the sort key if you select rows prior to using the Sort Ascending or Sort Descending buttons.

22. **Sort** rows **11-13** and **16-18** in **Descending** order (you need to select the rows before sorting).

23. Save the worksheet and continue with the next topic.

The Sort Dialog Box

The Sort dialog box gives you more control over sorting than the Sort Ascending and Sort Descending buttons. The most important benefit of the Sort dialog box is it lets you specify more than one sort key.

Hands-On 5.2 – Use the Sort dialog box

1. **Click** cell **A5**.

2. Choose **Data**→**Sort...** from the menu bar.

   Notice that Excel selects rows 5-9. Excel has made an incorrect decision in determining that these rows constitute your list. The Subtotal row should not be included in the list.

3. **Click** the **Cancel** button.

4. **Select** rows **5-8**, then choose **Data**→**Sort...**

5. Use the following Hands-On Illustration to sort the rows in Ascending order.

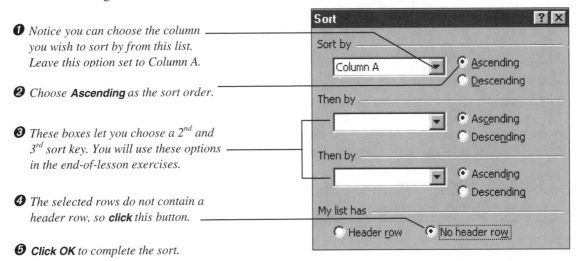

❶ *Notice you can choose the column you wish to sort by from this list. Leave this option set to Column A.*

❷ *Choose **Ascending** as the sort order.*

❸ *These boxes let you choose a 2ⁿᵈ and 3ʳᵈ sort key. You will use these options in the end-of-lesson exercises.*

❹ *The selected rows do not contain a header row, so **click** this button.*

❺ ***Click OK** to complete the sort.*

Keep in mind that this sort would have been easier to accomplish with the Sort Ascending button. This exercise was meant to be a demonstration. You will use the Sort dialog box to perform sorts using multiple sort keys in the end-of-lesson exercises.

6. **Click** Undo and continue with the next topic.

Freezing Header Rows and Columns

Header rows and columns are important because they identify the worksheet data. For example, rows 1-4 and column A in the current worksheet clearly identify the data. One problem in large worksheets is the header rows and columns scroll out of view as you move through the worksheet. Freezing the header rows and columns with the Window→Freeze Panes command can eliminate this problem.

Click in the correct cell before freezing the header rows and columns

Excel freezes all rows above the highlight and all columns to the left of the highlight when you issue the Window→Freeze Panes command. For this reason, you must click the correct cell before issuing the command. This will ensure the desired rows and columns are frozen.

Hands-On 5.3 – Freeze the header rows and columns

Scroll through the worksheet

1. **Scroll** through the worksheet until column **Y** is visible.

2. **Scroll** down until row **25** is visible.

   Notice that the row and column headings have scrolled out of view. This would make it difficult for you to edit or understand the worksheet data.

Freeze the headings and scroll again

3. **Press** ⌷Ctrl⌷ + ⌷Home⌷ to rapidly move to cell **A1**.

   You learned this keystroke combination in Lesson 1. This keystroke combination is quite useful when working with large worksheets.

4. **Click** cell **B5**.

5. Choose **Window→Freeze Panes** from the menu bar.

6. **Scroll** to column **Y**, then **scroll** down to row **25**.

   Notice that the headings in column A and rows 1-4 remain visible to allow you to identify the contents of the worksheet cells.

Unfreeze the panes

7. **Press** ⌷Ctrl⌷ + ⌷Home⌷ and notice the highlight moves to cell B5 instead of A1.

8. **Click** cell **A5** and notice you could edit this cell if desired.

   The frozen columns and rows are still available for editing.

9. Choose **Window→Unfreeze Panes**.

   Continue with the next topic.

Splitting Window Panes

The Window→Split command lets you view two sections of a worksheet at the same time. This can be useful for comparing data in two different sections of a large worksheet. As with the Freeze Panes command, you should position the highlight in the desired cell before issuing the command.

Hands-On 5.4 – Split the window panes

Scroll through the worksheet

1. **Click** cell **B5**.

2. Choose the **Window→Split** command.

    Excel will display a border that looks like the border on windowpanes.

3. **Tap** the ⬆ key on the keyboard four times.

    Notice the header rows are displayed in both the top and bottom panes. You can view any two sections of the worksheet including the same section in two different panes.

Compare the January and December budgets

4. Use the following Hands-On Illustration to adjust the vertical split bar.

    ❶ *Position the mouse pointer on the vertical split bar and drag it to the right until it is in the middle of the window.*

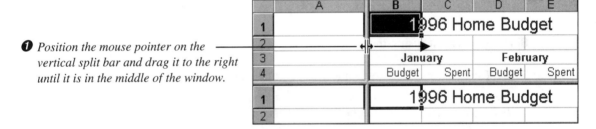

Notice this increases the amount of space that is available in the left panes. This allows you to compare two sections of the worksheet using the left and right panes.

5. **Click** in the **fourth** pane (the bottom right pane) and **scroll** to the right until **December** is visible in the fourth pane.

    Notice the left panes remain stationery as you scroll through the right panes. You can now compare the data in January and December.

6. **Click** in either of the **left** panes and scroll until December is visible in the left panes.

7. **Click** in either of the **right** panes and scroll until January is visible in the right panes.

8. Take five minutes to experiment with the **Window→Split** and **Window→Freeze Panes** commands. You may want to try splitting and freezing at the same time.

9. When you have finished experimenting, use the **Window→Remove Split** command to remove the split from the panes.

10. **Click** cell **B5** and use the **Window→Freeze Panes** command to freeze the panes.

    Continue with the next topic.

Navigating through Large Worksheets

In Lesson 1, you learned several techniques for rapidly navigating around worksheets. These techniques are reviewed in this section. You will also review selection techniques that are effective with large worksheets.

Hands-On 5.5 – Review navigating and scrolling

1. Make sure you have removed a Quick Reference Guide from the Appendix of this book.

   The Quick Reference Guide lists all of the techniques discussed in this section.

2. Use the following step to scroll to the right one screen at a time.

   ❶ *Click in an open part of the Horizontal*
   Scroll bar to scroll one screen at a time.

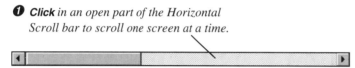

3. **Scroll one** more screen to the **right**.

4. **Scroll two** screens to the **left**.

Calculate and copy the Subtotal formulas
5. **Click** cell **B9**.

6. **Scroll** to the right (using the mouse and the scroll bar) until cell **Y9** is visible.

7. **Press & Hold** the ⌷Shift⌷ key while you **click** cell **Y9**.

   This should select the range B9:Y9 which includes all the Subtotal cells in row 9. This Shift and click technique works well in large worksheets. You may want to use this technique instead of drag-selecting because drag-selecting can be difficult to control.

8. **Click** AutoSum ⌷Σ⌷ to compute the Subtotals.

9. Use the preceding techniques to compute the Subtotals in rows **14** and **19**.

Calculate and copy the Grand Totals
10. **Click** cell **B21**.

11. Type the formula **=B9+B14+B19** and Confirm ⌷✓⌷ the entry.

12. **Click** the Copy ⌷📋⌷ button to copy the formula to the clipboard.

13. **Click** cell **C21**.

14. Use the mouse and the horizontal scroll bar (not the keyboard) to **scroll** to the right until cell **Y21** is visible.

15. **Press & Hold** the ⌷Shift⌋ key while you **click** cell **Y21**.

16. **Click** the Paste ⌷📋⌋ button.

Continued...

Calculate and copy the Differences

17. Scroll to the left until cell **B22** is visible.

18. Enter the formula **=B21-C21** and Confirm ☑ the entry.

19. Select cells **B22** and **C22** and Copy 🗒 them to the clipboard.

20. Click cell **D22**.

21. Scroll to the right until cell **Y22** is visible.

22. Press & Hold the ⎡Shift⎤ key while you **click** cell **Y22**.

23. Click the Paste 📋 button.

The Differences formula and the blank cell to the right of it should be copied across the row.

24. Save 💾 the changes and continue with the next topic.

Printing Large Worksheets

Excel has a number of options to help you print large worksheets. Most of the options are accessed through the Page Setup dialog box. The Page Setup dialog box is displayed with the *File→Page Setup* command.

The Page Setup Dialog Box

The Page Setup dialog box has many options that can be used to print large worksheets. You can adjust the page orientation, margins, headers and footers and many other options. The Page Setup dialog box is organized into four tabbed sections as shown below.

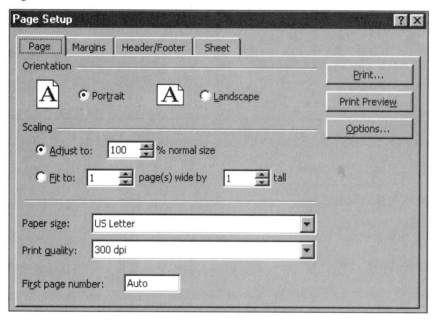

The Page Options

The Page options let you choose Portrait (vertical) or Landscape (horizontal) orientations. Landscape orientation is useful with wide worksheets like the 1996 Home Budget you are using. The Page options also provide automated features that can fit a worksheet onto the number of pages you specify.

Hands-On 5.6 – Use the Page options

Use Print Preview to check out the worksheet

1. **Click** the Print Preview ⬚ button.

2. If necessary, **zoom in** by clicking anywhere on the worksheet until the entire page is visible.

    *Notice Excel can only fit a portion of the worksheet on the page. Excel breaks the worksheet up over multiple pages if it is too large to fit on a single page. Also notice the header - **Sheet 1** at the top of the page and the footer - **Page 1** at the bottom of the page. You will learn how to create, delete and edit headers and footers later in this lesson.*

3. Use the ⬚Next⬚ button on the Print Preview toolbar to view the next two pages.

    Your worksheet should have three pages.

Continued...

4. **Use** the ⬚Previous button to move back to page 1.

5. **Zoom in** (by clicking on the worksheet) until the full page is visible.

    Notice there is a margin on the top, left and right sides of the page. You will adjust the margins later in this lesson.

6. **Click** the **Close** button to exit from Print Preview.

7. **Scroll** to the **right** and you will notice vertical dashed lines somewhere near columns I and R.

    These lines represent the page breaks and they show where one page ends and another begins.

Switch to Landscape orientation

8. **Choose** **F̲ile→Page Set̲up...** from the menu bar.

9. Make sure the Page tab is active, then **click** the Landscape ⬚A ◉ Landscape button.

10. **Click** the ⬚ Print Preview button on the right side of the dialog box.

    Print Preview and Page Setup are designed to work together, so Excel lets you access Print Preview from Page Setup and vice-versa. Notice the Landscape (horizontal) orientation.

11. **Use** the ⬚N̲ext button to view the second page.

    Your worksheet should now fit on two pages.

Use the Scaling options

12. **Click** the ⬚S̲etup... button to display the Page Setup dialog box.

    Notice the Scaling options in the middle of the dialog box. These options automatically compress or expand the printed worksheet. You can specify a compression or expansion percentage or instruct Excel to compress or expand to a specified number of pages. Excel adjusts all worksheet elements including the font size, cell size and the size of graphics and other objects. This is a convenient way to fit a worksheet on a desired number of pages.

13. **Click** the Fit To ⬚◉ F̲it to: 1 ▲▼ page(s) wide by 1 ▲▼ tall button and **click OK**.

    Excel will compress the two-page worksheet onto one page. As you can see, it wasn't such a good idea to compress a two-page worksheet onto one page. The printed worksheet will be so small that it will be unreadable. The Fit To option is most convenient when you have a few columns or rows that are spilling over to an extra page. Compressing a few rows or columns will have little impact on the font sizes and other worksheet elements.

14. **Click** the ⬚S̲etup... button.

15. **Click** the Adjust to button and change the scaling to 100% of normal as shown below.

    Setting the Adjust to percentage back to 100% turns off the Fit To option.

16. **Click OK** and Print Preview will still be displayed.

17. If necessary, zoom in until the entire worksheet is visible.

    Continue with the next topic where you will learn to adjust the margins.

The Margin Options

The Margin tab on the Page Setup dialog box lets you adjust the position of the worksheet and the headers and footers. The margins determine the distance from the edge of the page to the worksheet. The header and footer options determine the distance from the top and bottom of the page to the header and footer.

Hands-On 5.7 – Use the Margin options

The worksheet should still be in Print Preview mode from the previous exercise.

Set the margins with the Page Setup dialog box

1. Use the Previous button to move back to page 1.

    The last visible column on your worksheet will most likely be the June Budget column. The June Spent column will most likely be on the second page and the word June may be cut off and split between the two pages. You can bring the June Spent column back to the first page by reducing the left and right margins. This will create more room on the page.

2. **Click** the Setup... button.

3. **Click** the **Margins** tab in the Page Setup dialog box.

4. Use the following steps to adjust the margins.

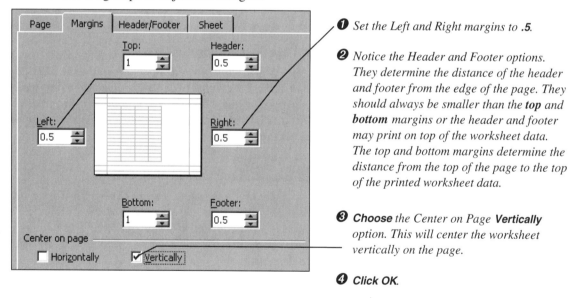

❶ *Set the Left and Right margins to .5.*

❷ *Notice the Header and Footer options. They determine the distance of the header and footer from the edge of the page. They should always be smaller than the **top** and **bottom** margins or the header and footer may print on top of the worksheet data. The top and bottom margins determine the distance from the top of the page to the top of the printed worksheet data.*

❸ **Choose** *the Center on Page **Vertically** option. This will center the worksheet vertically on the page.*

❹ **Click OK.**

Take a few moments to check out the results. The June Spent column should be on the first page.

Remove the vertical centering and adjust the header and footer positioning

5. **Click** the Setup... button.

6. Remove the check from the Vertically Vertically box.

7. Change the Header and Footer measurements to **1** and **click OK**.

    Notice both the worksheet and the header (Sheet 1) are positioned 1" down from the page. You should always make the header and footer distance smaller than the top and bottom margins. This forces the header and footer to print in the margin area.

Continued...

8. **Click** the ⬜Setup... button.

9. Change the Header and Footer measurements to **.5** and **click OK**.

Adjust the margins in the Print Preview window

10. If necessary, **zoom in** until the entire worksheet is visible.

    The entire first page should be visible.

11. **Click** the ⬜Margins button.

    Notice the horizontal and vertical lines that are displayed. These lines represent the margins and the header and footer positions. You will also notice column boundary ⊤ symbols. You can adjust the margins, header and footer positions and the width of columns by dragging the lines and column boundary symbols. Adjusting the column boundary ⊤ symbols changes the actual column widths in the worksheet.

12. Use the following steps to adjust the left margin.

    ❶ **Position** *the mouse pointer anywhere on the vertical left margin boundary and the Adjust pointer will appear.*

    ❷ **Drag** *to the right about 1" and release the mouse button.*

    1996 Home Budget

    | | January | | February | |
    | Utilities | Budget | Spent | Budget | S |
    | | 100 | 78 | 100 | |

13. **Click** the ⬜Next button on the Print Preview toolbar to view the next page.

14. If ⬜Next is still available, then **click** it again and you will notice a third page.

    Next will only be available if your worksheet has a third page.

15. **Click** the ⬜Previous button until Page 1 is visible.

16. Practice adjusting the margins, header and footer positions and the column widths ⊤. This worksheet is being used for demonstration purposes only, so don't be afraid to make mistakes.

17. **Click** the ⬜Margins button when you have finished to turn off the margin display.

Use the Page Setup dialog box to reset things

18. **Click** the ⬜Setup... button.

19. Set the various options as follows.

    - Top and bottom margins **1**
    - Left and right margins **.75**
    - Header and Footer **.5**
    - **Remove checks** from the Center on Page Horizontally and Vertically options.

    Leave the Page Setup dialog box displayed because you will continue to use it.

The Header and Footer Options

Excel provides a variety of built-in headers and footers that you can choose from. You can also create customized headers and footers to suit your particular needs. Headers print at the top of every page and footers print at the bottom of every page. You can include page numbers, dates, the workbook name and any text in a header or footer.

Choosing built-in headers and footers

Excel is quite intelligent and it provides a variety of built-in headers and footers for you to choose from. You choose built-in headers and footers in the Page Setup dialog box.

Customized headers and footers have three sections

Excel divides all headers and footers into left, center and right sections. The left section prints on the left side of the page, the center section prints in the center of the page and the right section prints on the right. You can instruct Excel to insert the current date, page number or current time in any of the sections. You can also format customized headers and footers by changing the font size and typeface.

Hands-On 5.8 – Check out the built-in headers and footers

The Page Setup dialog box should still be displayed from the previous exercise.

1. **Click** the Header/Footer tab.

   Notice the header is currently Sheet1 and the footer is Page 1. These are built-in headers and footers. The header and footer will print at the top and bottom of every page and they will be updated on each page. For example, the footer will appear as Page 2 on the second page.

2. Use the following steps to remove the header and choose a different footer.

   ❶ *Click the Header drop-down button to display a list of built-in headers.*

   ❷ *Scroll through the list and study the various headers.*

   ❸ *Scroll to the top of the list and choose (none). You can always remove a header or footer by choosing (none).*

   ❹ *Click the Footer button and choose the footer, Hands-On Lesson 5, Page 1. Excel always displays built-in headers and footers that reflect the workbook name, company name, etc.*

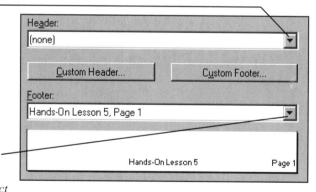

3. **Click OK** and the new footer will appear in Print Preview.

   The header will not be displayed because you chose (none).

4. Take five minutes to experiment with different built-in headers and footers. You will need to click the Setup button to return to the Page Setup dialog box. You will create a customized header and footer in the next exercise, so be brave and choose any built-in headers or footers you desire.

Hands-On 5.9 – Create a customized header and footer

1. Make sure the Page Setup dialog box is displayed and the Header/Footer tab is active.

2. **Click** the **Custom Header...** button.

3. Use the following Hands-On Illustration to create a custom header.

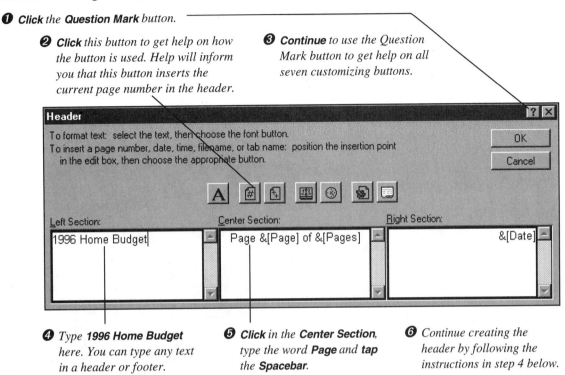

❶ **Click** *the **Question Mark** button.*

❷ **Click** *this button to get help on how the button is used. Help will inform you that this button inserts the current page number in the header.*

❸ **Continue** *to use the Question Mark button to get help on all seven customizing buttons.*

❹ *Type **1996 Home Budget** here. You can type any text in a header or footer.*

❺ **Click** *in the **Center Section**, type the word **Page** and **tap** the **Spacebar**.*

❻ *Continue creating the header by following the instructions in step 4 below.*

4. Use the following steps to complete the Center Section header.

   − **Click** the Page Number ⊞ button and the &[Page] code will be inserted.

   − **Tap** the ⟨ SpaceBar ⟩, type **of** and **tap** ⟨ SpaceBar ⟩ again.

   − **Click** the Total Pages ⊞ button and the &[Pages] code will be inserted.

5. **Click** in the **Right Section** box, then **click** the Date ⊞ button to insert the &[Date] code.

6. Take a few moments to study the header you just created. Try to understand the significance of the text and the codes. If necessary, use the Question Mark ⊞ button again to get help on the various buttons. The descriptions that appear will discuss the codes and how the buttons function.

7. **Click OK** and the customized header will be displayed in the Page Setup dialog box.

8. **Click** the footer ⊡ button, **scroll** to the top of the list and choose **(none)**.

9. **Click OK** on the Page Setup dialog box and the new header will be displayed in Print Preview.

10. **Click** the ⟨ Next ⟩ button and notice the header is also displayed on page 2.

11. Take **ten minutes** to experiment with the header and footer options.
    Continue with the next topic when you have finished experimenting.

The Sheet Options

The Sheet Options tab on the Page Setup dialog box provides a number of options that affect the entire printed worksheet. For example, you can print gridlines and column and row headings. You will instruct Excel to print gridlines and column and row headings in the following exercise. The next exercise will teach you how to print title rows and title columns. This is similar to freezing title rows and columns as you did earlier in this lesson.

Hands-On 5.10 – Use the Print and Page Order options

In this exercise, you will explore the options on the Print and Page Order sections of the Sheet tab.

1. Make sure the Page Setup dialog box is displayed.

2. Choose the **Sheet** tab.

3. Use the following Illustration to set the Gridlines and Row and Column Headings options.

❶ *Notice the Print titles option is not available. These options are not available if you display the Page Setup dialog box from the Print Preview window. You will use these options in the next exercise.*

❷ *Check the Gridlines, Black and white and Row and column headings boxes.*

❸ *Notice the Page Order option. This option determines the order in which Excel prints a multi-page worksheet.*

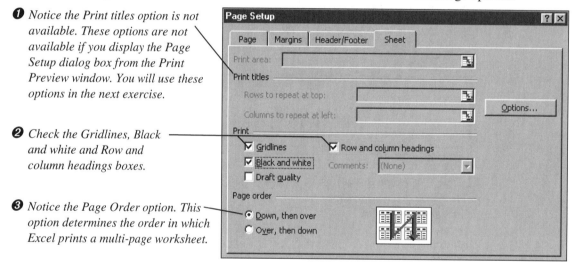

4. **Click OK** and check out the results in the Print Preview window.

   Notice the worksheet now has column and row headings and gridlines.

5. **Click** the **Close** button to exit from Print Preview.

   Continue with the next exercise where you will print title rows and columns.

Printing Title Rows and Columns

Excel lets you create title rows and columns. Title rows and columns print on every page of a printout. For example, the 1996 Budget worksheet will print on two pages. It may be difficult to understand the data on the second page because column A contains the text entries that describe the content of the various rows. This can be resolved by defining column A as a title column, which will force it to print on both pages.

You must display the Page Setup dialog box from the worksheet

The title row and title column options are not available if you display the Page Setup dialog box from the Print Preview window. To use these options, you must display the Page Setup dialog box from the worksheet itself.

Hands-On 5.11 – Set column A as a title column

The worksheet should still be displayed in the normal view (Print Preview should be closed).

1. Use the Zoom Control `75%` to zoom to 75%.

2. If necessary, scroll up or down until cells A1:A22 (all active cells in column A) are visible.

3. Choose **File→Page Setup...** from the menu bar.

4. Make sure the Sheet tab is active.

5. If necessary, drag the Page Setup dialog box to the side until column A is visible.

6. **Click** in the Columns to repeat at left `Columns to repeat at left:` box.

7. **Click** the column A heading `A` and the symbols $A:$A will appear in the Columns to repeat at left box.

8. **Remove** the **check marks** from the **Gridlines** and **Row and column headings** boxes.

9. **Click** the `Print Preview` button and notice column A on the left side of the page.

10. **Click** the `Next` button and column A will be repeated on the second page.

    Notice that it is now possible to identify the rows on both the first and second pages.

11. **Click** the `Setup...` button and notice the Print titles section is unavailable.

    Once again, you must display the Page Setup dialog box from the worksheet and not from Print Preview if you want to title rows and title columns.

12. Take 15 to 30 minutes to experiment with the options in the Page Setup dialog box.

13. When you have finished experimenting, **close** the dialog box and **close Print Preview**.

    Continue with the topic on the next page.

Page Breaks and the Page Break Preview Command

Page breaks force Excel to terminate printing on one page and begin printing on another page. Excel makes it easy to insert and remove page breaks. Excel 97 also has a new feature called Page Break Preview that lets you adjust the position of page breaks.

Hands-On 5.12 – Experiment with page breaks

Use Page Setup to restore the default margins and other print options
1. Choose **File→Page Setup...** from the menu bar.

2. **Click** the Margins tab and set the Top, Bottom, Left and Right margins to 1.

3. **Click** the Sheet tab and delete any codes or text in the Columns to repeat at left box.

4. **Click OK** to return to the worksheet.

Insert a page break
5. Use the Zoom Control to zoom to 75% or until columns L and M are visible.

   A vertical dashed line should be visible between columns L and M. This line "breaks the page" after the June Budget column.

6. **Click** cell **L1**.

   In the next step, you will insert a manual page break. This will cause the automatic page break between columns L and M to vanish. The automatic page break will be replaced by the manual page break. Also, the page break will be inserted to the left of the column with the highlight. The highlight is positioned in row 1 because you only need to break the page horizontally. Your worksheet would print on several pages if you inserted the break further down the column.

7. Choose **Insert→Page Break** from the menu bar.

   The vertical dashed line should now be to the left of column L.

8. Now choose **Insert→Remove Page Break**.

   The automatic page break should return between columns L and M.

Adjust page breaks with Page Break Preview
9. Choose **View→Page Break Preview** from the menu bar.

   You should see a dark blue page break line between columns L and M.

10. Try **dragging** the blue line to the left or right.

    Notice Excel shows you exactly which part of the worksheet will be printed on Page 1 and Page 2.

11. **Click** Print Preview and browse through the worksheet.

    Notice that Excel adjusts any parameters necessary (including font sizes) to allow the worksheet to print with the page break locations you specified.

12. **Close Print Preview** and choose **View→Normal** from the menu bar.

    Notice a vertical-dashed page break appears at the location you specified in Page Break Preview.

13. **Click** a cell to the right of the page break and choose **Insert→Remove Page Break**.

14. **Close** the workbook and **save** the changes.

Concepts Review

True / False

1. Sorting has the potential to damage worksheets, so you should always save before sorting.

2. The Sort Ascending [button image] button can only be used if you first select the desired rows.

3. The Sort dialog box allows you to specify more than one sort key.

4. The Window→Freeze Panes command lets you view two sections of the worksheet at the same time.

5. Freezing the panes makes it easier to identify data in large worksheets.

6. You can select a range of cells by clicking the first cell in the range, then pressing & holding Ctrl while you click the last cell in the range.

7. You can scroll one screen at a time by clicking an open part of the scroll bar.

8. The Page Setup dialog box provides access to many features that are useful when printing large worksheets.

9. You can set the margins in the Print Preview window.

10. Headers and footers have three sections.

1. **T F**
2. **T F**
3. **T F**
4. **T F**
5. **T F**
6. **T F**
7. **T F**
8. **T F**
9. **T F**
10. **T F**

Multiple Choice

1. Which of the following statements describes the columns and rows that are frozen when the Window→Freeze Panes command is issued?
   a) Columns to the left of the highlight and rows above the highlight.
   b) Columns to the left of the highlight and rows below the highlight.
   c) Columns to the right of the highlight and rows below the highlight.
   d) Columns to the right of the highlight and rows above the highlight.

   (   )

2. Which tab in the Page Setup dialog box lets you set the Landscape orientation?
   a) Page
   b) Margins
   c) Header/Footer
   d) Sheet

   (   )

3. Assuming the current page is 1, how will the header Page &[Page] be printed?
   a) Page 1 of 1
   b) Page 1 of 2
   c) Page 1
   d) Page 1, Current Date

   (   )

4. Which tab in the Page Setup dialog box contains an option that lets you repeat a Column on every page of a printout?
   a) Page
   b) Margins
   c) Header/Footer
   d) Sheet

   (   )

5. Which command is used to insert a manual page break?
   a) Format→Page Break
   b) Insert→Page Break
   c) Alt + Enter
   d) None of the above.

   (   )

Skills Builder 5.1

In this exercise, you will open a workbook that contains an accounts receivable aging report. You will use a formula to calculate the number of days the accounts are past due and you will sort the rows. You will also use the TODAY function.

Enter the current date and calculate the number of days past due
1. **Open** the workbook named **Skills Builder 5.1**.

2. Use the **TODAY** function to insert the current date in cell **C2**.

3. **Click** cell **E5**.

4. Type the formula **=TODAY( )-C5** and Confirm ☑ the entry.

5. Use the Format Painter 🖌 to copy the General number format from a blank cell to Cell E5.
   A whole number should be displayed in the cell.

6. Use the fill handle ✚ to copy the formula down the column.

7. **Click** cell **F5** and enter the formula **=E5-30**.

8. Use the fill handle ✚ to copy the formula down the column.

Sort the rows in various ways
   Notice the rows are currently sorted by invoice number.

9. **Click** cell **A5**.

10. **Click** the Sort Ascending 🔼 button to sort the rows by the names in column A.

11. **Click** cell **B5** and **click** the Sort Descending 🔽 button.
    The rows should be sorted in descending order by invoice number.

12. Sort the rows in **descending** order by the **invoice amount**.
    You will need to click one of the cells in column D before sorting. The largest invoice amount should be at the top of the list.

13. **Close** the worksheet and **save** the changes.

Skills Builder 5.2

In this exercise, you will use the Sort dialog box to sort worksheet rows using two sort keys.

1. **Open** the workbook named **Skills Builder 5.2**.

2. **Click** anywhere in the list of names and choose **Data→Sort...** from the menu bar.
   Excel will identify the list and select the correct rows. The header row will not be selected.

3. If necessary, set the Sort By key to **Lastname** in **Ascending** order.

4. Set the first Then By key to **Firstname** in **Ascending** order and **click OK**.
   Take a moment to study the results. Notice the rows with the same last names are grouped together. Those groups are then sorted by the first names.

Continued...

5. Choose **Data→Sort...** from the menu bar.

6. Make sure the Sort By key is set to **Lastname** in **Ascending** order.

7. Change the first Then By key to **Outstanding|Balance** and **click OK**.

   Notice the rows are still grouped by last name but the groups are now sorted according to the Outstanding Balance code in column D.

8. Sort the rows in ascending order using the Outstanding Balance in column D as the only sort key.

   There is no need to use the Sort dialog box because you are using just one sort key. Just use the Sort Ascending button. All rows with an Outstanding Balance code of N should move to the top.

9. **Close** the workbook and **save** the changes.

Skills Builder 5.3

1. **Open** the **Hands-On Lesson 5** workbook that you used throughout the Hands-On exercises in this lesson.

2. Choose **File→Page Setup...** and **click** the Header/Footer tab.

3. Remove the header by **clicking** the header button and choosing **(none)** from the top of the list.

4. **Click** the **Customize Footer** button and create a footer that looks like the following example. You will need to use the dialog box buttons to insert the &[Page] and &[Date] codes.

   Page &[Page]   **Skills Builder 5.3**   **&[Date]**

5. **Select** the **Page &[Page]** text and code in the left section and **click** the Font ⬛ button.

6. Choose **Bold Italic** from the Font Style list and **click OK**.

   You can format any header or footer with the font size and type of your choice.

7. Use the preceding technique to add Bold and Italics to the center and right sections.

8. **Click OK** and the footer should be displayed in the Page Setup dialog box.

9. **Click** the **Print Preview** button on the dialog box.

10. Use the ⬚Next⬚ button to browse though the worksheet.

11. Do whatever it takes to get this worksheet to print on two pages. You may need to go back into Setup and change the margins or some other Setup option until the worksheet fits on two pages.

12. **Close Print Preview** when you are satisfied with the results.

13. **Close** the workbook and **save** the changes.

Skills Builder 5.4

In this exercise, you will open a workbook on your exercise diskette. Your objective is to get the worksheet to print on a single page. You will accomplish this by using the Landscape orientation and Fit To options in Page Setup. You will also add a header and footer.

1. **Open** the workbook named **Skills Builder 5.4**.

2. **Click** the Print Preview [⬜] button.

   Notice the worksheet currently is in a Portrait (vertical) orientation.

3. Use the [Next] button to browse though the pages and you will notice there are three pages.

   Do you think it is possible to print this on one sheet and still be able to read it?

4. Use the [Previous] button to go back to page 1.

5. **Click** the [Setup...] button on the Print Preview toolbar.

6. Make sure the **Page** tab is active and set the orientation to **Landscape**.

7. **Click** the Fit to button and make sure it is set to 1 pages wide by 1 pages tall as shown below.

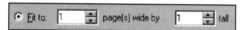

8. **Click** the Header/Footer tab.

9. Choose the built-in header **Skills Builder 5.4**.

10. Choose the built-in footer **Page 1 of ?.**

11. **Click OK** and the worksheet should fit on one page.

12. **Click** the Print [Print...] button then **click OK**.

    Check out your printed worksheet and you should see that it fits on one page. Excel can perform miracles when it comes to fitting a worksheet onto a specific number of pages. The trick is to understand the options that are available to you and to put them to good use.

13. **Close** the workbook and **save** the changes.

Assessment 5.1

In this assessment, you will sort the rows in a worksheet using three sort keys.

1. **Open** the workbook named **Assessment 5.1**.

2. Use the Zoom Control to zoom to 75% of normal.

   This will allow you to see all the worksheet rows at the same time. Notice the rows are currently sorted by 1997 Sales Volume in column D.

3. Use the Sort dialog box to sort the rows using three sort keys as follows.

   – Key 1 - Customer in Ascending order

   – Key 2 - Division in Ascending order

   – Key 3 - Key Contact in Ascending order

4. Your sorted worksheet should match the worksheet shown below.

5. **Print** the worksheet, then **close** it and **save** the changes.

	A	B	C	D
1	**1997 Orders**			
2				
3	Customer	Division	Key Contact	1997 Volume
4	Alexis	Battery Division	Frank Jordan	3303336
5	Alexis	Battery Division	Richard Warren	1605476
6	Alexis	Battery Division	Susan Christopher	1775262
7	Alexis	Battery Division	William J. Pinckerton	4831410
8	Dimension Systems	Automotive	Michael Chricton	2624192
9	Dimension Systems	Automotive	Michael Wilson	3473122
10	Dimension Systems	Automotive	Stephen Crane	2963764
11	Dimension Systems	Large Vehicle	Bill Clayton	2114834
12	Dimension Systems	Large Vehicle	Carl Bartholomew	4152266
13	Dimension Systems	Large Vehicle	Larry Alexander	4661624
14	Qualtron	Computer Technology	Bill Thompson	2454406
15	Qualtron	Computer Technology	Dick Morris	1435690
16	Qualtron	Computer Technology	Sandy Princeton	2793978
17	Qualtron	Medical Techologies	Joe Gecko	3133550
18	Qualtron	Space Systems	Bill Rogers	1945048
19	Qualtron	Space Systems	Stacey Crawford	4322052
20	Qualtron	Space Systems	Stan Barnes	1265904
21	Qualtron	Space Systems	Wanda Wilson	3812694
22	Zenex	CAD	Alice Senton	4491838
23	Zenex	CAD	Joseph Harding	3982480
24	Zenex	Semiconductor	Ben Warren	3642908
25	Zenex	Semiconductor	Lois Lane	2284620

Assessment 5.2

In this assessment, you will open a workbook from your exercise diskette. You will use the Page Setup dialog box to format the worksheet to print on one page and you will include a header and footer in the printed worksheet.

1. **Open** the workbook named **Assessment 5.2**.

2. Use the Page Setup dialog box to format the worksheet to print on one page as shown below. You will need to change the orientation, add a header and footer and change the margins or use the Fit To option.

3. Use **Print Preview** to check out the worksheet prior to printing.

4. **Print** the worksheet when you have finished, then **close** it and **save** the changes.

Mary Cook 1996 Expenses

1996 Expenses for Mary Cook

	January	February	March	April	May	June	July	August	September	October	November	December
Cell Phone	245	270	295	320	345	370	205	220	235	250	265	280
Automobile	325	345	365	385	405	425	205	240	275	310	345	380
Entertainment	150	170	190	210	230	250	15	70	125	180	235	290
Miscellaneous	105	115	125	135	145	160	165	170	175	180	185	190

Selmar Systems   Page 1 of 1   5/20/97

Critical Thinking 5.1

Create a worksheet to track your **weekly** expenditures for a 6-month period. Create one column for each week. Organize your worksheet so that related items are grouped together. For example, you may want to organize all entertainment expenses under a row heading labeled entertainment. You can indent each item under entertainment to show that they belong to that group. Create subtotals for each group and a grand total for each week. Format the worksheet so that it prints on two pages. Create a header and footer that specifies the date, page number and any other descriptive text you feel is necessary. Format the worksheet using any formatting options you desire. You may want to use AutoFormat.

6 Creating an Impact with Charts

Objectives:

- ◆ Use more than one worksheet

- ◆ Rename worksheets

- ◆ Insert a chart as a separate worksheet

- ◆ Embed a chart in a worksheet

- ◆ Create column, line and pie charts

- ◆ Edit and format charts

- ◆ Change the location of charts

- ◆ Print charts

The Project - AutoSoft Sales Report

In this lesson, you will help AutoSoft - a young and rapidly growing software company - analyze their annual sales. The executives at AutoSoft want charts that compare sales in the various quarters, a growth trend for the year and the contributions of each sales rep to the total company sales. You will create three charts that will provide an impressive solution to this request. The three charts you will create are shown below.

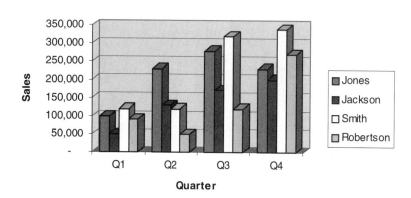

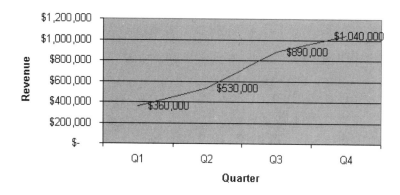

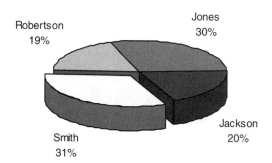

Using More than One Worksheet

Excel lets you have up to 255 worksheets in a workbook. Excel initially provides 3 worksheets in a new workbook, however, you can add additional worksheets up to the maximum of 255. A tab at the bottom of the worksheet identifies each worksheet.

Sheets can be renamed, inserted, deleted and moved

You can rename any worksheet by double-clicking the worksheet tab and typing the desired name on the tab. This lets you give meaningful names to worksheets so that you can easily identify them. You can also insert and delete worksheets and move them to different positions in the worksheet order. This gives you the flexibility to modify your workbooks as your needs change. The following table discusses the procedures that are used to rename, insert, delete, move and activate worksheets.

To	Use this procedure
Rename a worksheet	Double-click the worksheet tab and type the new name on the tab.
Insert a worksheet	Click a worksheet tab and choose Insert→Worksheet.
Delete a worksheet	Click the desired worksheet tab, choose Edit→Delete Sheet and click OK.
Move a worksheet	Drag the worksheet tab to the desired position in the worksheet order.
Activate a worksheet	Click the worksheet tab.

Hands-On 6.1 – Rename a worksheet and experiment

1. **Open** the workbook named **Hands-On Lesson 6**.

2. **Double-click** the Sheet1  tab at the bottom of the screen.

3. **Type** the name **Sales** and it will replace the name Sheet1.

4. **Click** anywhere in the worksheet to complete the renaming.

5. Position the mouse pointer on the **Sales** sheet tab. **Drag** the tab until the black triangle is to the right of the 4th sheet tab as shown below.

6. **Release** the mouse button and the Sales sheet will be repositioned.

7. **Drag** the **Sales** sheet back until it is positioned to the left of Sheet 2.

8. **Click** the **Sheet 4** tab and choose **Edit**→**Delete Sheet** from the menu bar.

9. **Click OK** to complete the deletion.

10. Try to **click** Undo and notice the sheet cannot be restored.

    Worksheets are permanently deleted when you issue the Edit→Delete Sheet command. The only way to recover a deleted sheet is to close the workbook without saving it and then reopen it.

11. **Click** the **Sales** sheet tab to make the sales sheet active and continue with the next topic.

Working with Charts

It is often easier to understand numerical data if it is presented in a chart. Excel lets you create and modify a variety of charts. Excel provides 14 major chart categories and each category has several variations to choose from. Excel literally has a chart for every occasion. The following illustration provides examples of charts you can create in Excel.

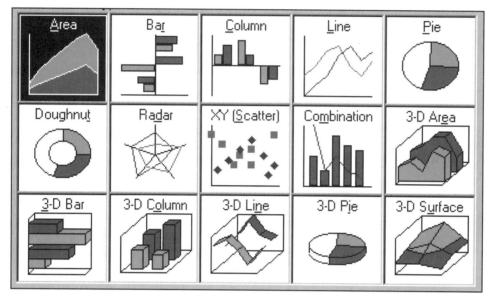

Charts can be embedded in a worksheet or placed on a separate sheet

You can place a chart on the same worksheet that contains the data the chart was created from. This is known as embedding the chart. You can also place a chart on a separate worksheet. This prevents the chart from cluttering the worksheet that contains the data and it allows you to easily print the chart. Charts are always linked to the data they were created from. A chart is automatically updated when the data changes.

Each chart type is designed for a specific purpose

Each chart type presents data in a different manner. You can present the same data in completely different ways by changing the chart type. For this reason, you should always use the chart type that most effectively conveys your data.

Creating Charts

Excel's **Chart Wizard** guides you through each step of chart creation. You can also edit and enhance a chart after it has been created.

The most important step is selecting the correct data

The first step in creating a chart is to select the data you want included in the chart. Many beginners find this step to be the most difficult. This is because they are unsure how Excel will interpret the selected data. You will receive step-by-step guidance on selecting data as you progress through this lesson.

Column and Bar Charts

Column charts compare values (numbers) by using vertical bars. Bar charts use horizontal bars. Each column or bar represents a value from the worksheet. Bar and column charts are most useful for comparing sets of values.

Column and bar charts have a category and value axis

The horizontal line that forms the base of a column or bar chart is called the **category axis**. The category axis typically measures units of time such as days, months or quarters. The vertical line on the left side of a column or bar chart is known as the **value axis**. The value axis typically measures values such as dollars. Most chart types (including column and bar charts) have a category and value axis. The following illustrations show the column chart you will create in the next few exercises. The illustrations show the objects that are present on most column charts and the corresponding data that was used to create the chart. Take a few minutes to study these illustrations carefully.

	A	B	C	D	E
1	Autosoft 1996 Quarterly Sales				
2					
3		Q1	Q2	Q3	Q4
4	Jones	100,000	230,000	280,000	230,000
5	Jackson	50,000	130,000	170,000	200,000
6	Smith	120,000	120,000	320,000	340,000
7	Robertson	90,000	50,000	120,000	270,000
8					
9	Total	$ 360,000	$ 530,000	$ 890,000	$ 1,040,000

The chart below was created using the selected data shown here. Notice the Total row was not included in the selection. The column chart compares the sales numbers for the individual quarters but it does not include the Total sales in row 9.

This is the vertical value axis. The numbering scale (0 - 350,000) was created by Excel after it determined the range of values that were included in the chart.

Notice the chart has a chart title (Sales Performance), a value axis title (Sales) and a Category axis title (Quarter). The Chart Wizard lets you specify the titles when you create the chart.

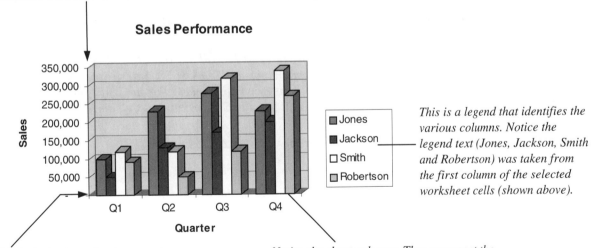

This is a legend that identifies the various columns. Notice the legend text (Jones, Jackson, Smith and Robertson) was taken from the first column of the selected worksheet cells (shown above).

This is the horizontal category axis. Notice the category axis labels (Q1, Q2, Q3 and Q4) were taken from row 3 of the selected worksheet cells (shown above).

Notice the chart columns. They represent the various data series. The first data series is the Jones' numbers in row 4. The first column in each quarter represents the Jones' numbers.

Hands-On 6.2 – Create a column chart on a separate sheet

The Hands-On Lesson 6 worksheet should still be open from the previous exercise.

Create the chart

1. **Select** the range **A3:E7** as shown on the previous page.

2. **Click** the Chart Wizard 📊 button on the Standard toolbar.

   The Chart Wizard - Step 1 of 4 dialog box will appear.

3. Use the following steps to explore the dialog box.

❶ *Check out the various chart types by clicking the options on the Chart type list.*

❷ *Choose the Column type when you have finished exploring. Also, make sure the first sub-type is chosen on the right side of the dialog box.*

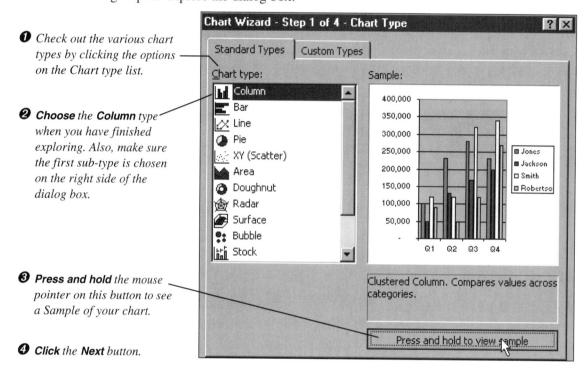

❸ *Press and hold the mouse pointer on this button to see a Sample of your chart.*

❹ *Click the Next button.*

The Chart Wizard - Step 2 of 4 box will appear. This box allows you to select a different range of cells. Notice that the range in the dialog box is =Sales!$A$3:$E$7. Sales is the worksheet name and the dollar signs indicate these are absolute cell references. For now, just ignore the dollar signs and think of the range as A3:E7. You will learn about absolute cell references soon.

4. The range Sales!$A$3:$E7 is correct, so **click** the [Next >] button.

Check out the various chart options

The Step 3 dialog box has 6 tabs that let you set various chart options. You will explore these options in the next few steps.

5. Notice the options on the Titles tab.

   You will add titles to a chart in the next exercise.

6. **Click** the **Axes tab**.

   The options on the Axes tab let you hide the labels on the category axis and value axis. You will almost always want to leave these options set to the default settings.

Continued...

7. **Click** the **Gridlines** tab.

> *Gridlines help identify the values in the chart. Your chart should have Major gridlines for the value axis displayed. These are the horizontal lines across the chart.*

8. Feel free to click the various gridlines boxes and notice how they appear in the Preview box.

9. **Click** the **Legend** tab.

> *Notice the legend on the right side of the Preview box. The Legend identifies the various columns. For example, the columns for Jones are identified by a color that also appears in the legend.*

10. **Remove** the **check** from the **Show legend box** and the legend will vanish.

11. **Click** the **Show legend box** again to redisplay the legend.

12. **Click** the **Data Labels** tab.

> *Data labels are printed at the top of the columns. They identify the exact value of the column.*

13. **Click** the **Show Value** option and values will appear at the top of each column.

> *The numbers will be very crowded in the Preview box.*

14. **Click** the **Show Label** option, then **click** the **None** option to remove the data labels.

15. **Click** the **Data Table** tab.

16. **Click** the **Show data table** check box and a table will appear below the Preview chart.

17. Take a moment to check out the data table, then **remove** the **check** from the Show data table box.

18. **Click** the `Next >` button and the Step 4 of 4 dialog box will appear.

19. **Click** the `As new sheet:` option.

> *This option instructs Excel to create the chart on a separate chart sheet.*

20. **Click** the `Finish` button.

> *Look at the sheet tabs and notice the chart has been created on a new sheet named Chart1. The Chart1 sheet is inserted immediately to the left of the Sales sheet.*

21. **Click** the Print Preview button.

> *Notice the chart occupies the entire page in a landscape orientation. Charts that are created as separate sheets are large and easy-to-view, however, they lack titles and other descriptive text.*

Delete the Chart1 sheet

22. **Click** the **Close** button on the Print Preview toolbar.

23. Choose **Edit→Delete Sheet** and **click OK**.

> *Continue with the next Hands-On exercise where you will create an embedded chart.*

Hands-On 6.3 – Create an embedded chart

In this exercise, you will use the Chart Wizard to create an embedded 3-D Column chart. An embedded chart is placed in the worksheet next to the data it is created from.

Start the Chart Wizard and define the chart area

1. Make sure the range A3:E7 is still selected.

2. **Click** the Chart Wizard ![button] button on the Standard toolbar.

3. Choose the 4th sub-type from the right side of the dialog box.

   This is the Clustered column with a 3-D visual effect as shown below.

4. **Click** the ![Next >] button, then **click** ![Next >] again on the Step 2 of 4 box.

5. **Click** the **Titles tab** and use the following steps in the Step 3 of 4 box.

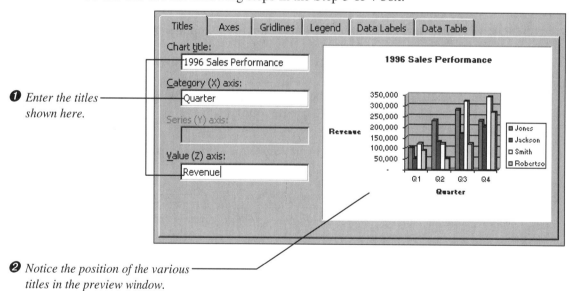

❶ *Enter the titles shown here.*

❷ *Notice the position of the various titles in the preview window.*

6. **Click** the ![Next >] button.

7. Leave the chart location set to ![● As object in:] on the Step 4 of 4 box and **click** ![Finish].

   Excel will embed the chart in your worksheet. The Chart toolbar will most likely appear as well. Continue with the next topic where you will learn how to move and size a chart.

Moving and Sizing Embedded Charts

Excel lets you move and size charts after they have been created. Excel considers the entire chart to be an object. You can easily move and resize objects using standard mouse techniques.

You must select the chart before you move or size it

You select a chart by clicking anywhere in the **Chart Area** . The Chart Area is the area just inside the border of the chart where there are no objects. Tiny squares called **sizing handles** appear on the corners and four sides of a selected chart. A chart is also automatically selected immediately after it is created. The following table discusses the move and size procedures.

To	Do this
Move a chart	Drag it to a new location.
Change the size	Drag any sizing handle.

Hands-On 6.4 – Move and size the chart

Move and size the chart

1. **Deselect** the chart by **clicking** anywhere outside of it.

   The sizing handles will vanish.

2. Use the Zoom Control to zoom to 50% 50%▾ of normal.

   This will give you plenty of room to move and size the chart.

3. Use the following steps to move and size the chart.

❶ *Click in the Chart Area (an open part of the chart) and the sizing handles will reappear.*

❷ *Position the mouse pointer in the Chart Area, then drag the chart to a new location.*

❸ *Point to a corner sizing handle and the Adjust pointer will appear.*

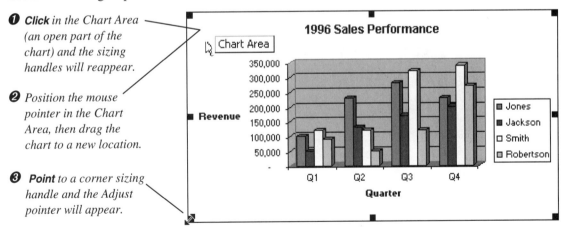

❹ *Drag the sizing handle to change both the width and height.*

❺ *Move and size the chart until both the chart and the worksheet data are visible.*

Change the data and watch the chart change

4. **Click outside the chart** to deselect it, then **Zoom** to **100%**.

5. Take a few minutes to study your chart and the worksheet data that was used to create it.

Continued...

6. **Click** cell **B4**.

7. Enter the number **300000** (that's five zeros) and watch the first column in the chart rise.

   Charts are linked to the worksheet data. They always reflect changes in the data even if they are placed in a separate chart sheet.

8. **Click** cell **B4** again and enter the number **1000000** (that's six zeros).

   Notice that 1000000 is much larger than the other numbers in the worksheet. Notice how the other columns are very small and it is difficult to determine their values in the chart. The large number changes the scale of the value axis so much, that it makes the chart difficult to interpret.

9. **Click** cell **B4** again and enter the number **100000** (that's five zeros).

10. Save 🖫 the changes and continue with the next topic.

The Chart Toolbar

The Chart toolbar has several buttons to help you format charts. The Chart toolbar can be displayed by right-clicking on any toolbar and choosing Chart from the shortcut menu. You will display the Chart toolbar in the following exercise.

Hands-On 6.5 – Use the Chart toolbar

Display the Chart toolbar

1. **Right-click** on any toolbar and a shortcut menu will appear.

    All toolbars that are currently displayed will have a check mark next to them.

2. If Chart is already checked, close the menu by clicking in the worksheet. Otherwise, choose **Chart** and the Chart toolbar will appear.

    The Chart toolbar may be anchored above the worksheet or it may float in the worksheet area.

Use the Chart Type drop-down list to choose a chart type

3. Select the chart by **clicking** anywhere in the Chart Area (an open part of the chart).

    Most of the buttons on the Chart toolbar will now become available.

4. Use the following steps to explore the Chart toolbar and change the chart type.

    ❶ *Notice the Object list and Format button. These tools are used to format chart objects. You will use these tools in the next exercise.*

    ❷ *Click the Chart Type drop-down button. This option lets you select from a variety of standard chart types.*

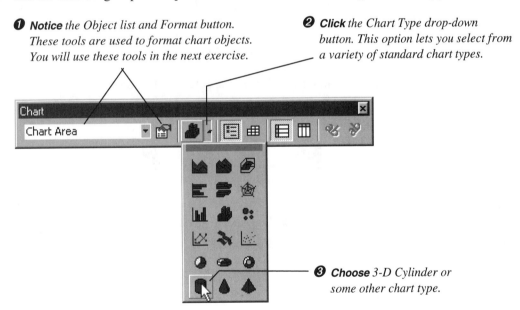

    ❸ *Choose 3-D Cylinder or some other chart type.*

5. Feel free to experiment with the options on the Chart Type drop-down list.

    However, you won't be able to choose the 3-D Column Chart that you originally had. In the next few steps, you will use another technique to choose your original 3-D Column Chart.

Use the Chart menu to choose a chart type

6. Make sure your chart is still selected, and then notice the menu bar at the top of the Excel window.

    The Menu bar should have a Chart option. The Menu bar usually has a Data menu, however, a Chart menu appears whenever a chart is selected. The Chart menu gives you access to the Chart Wizard dialog boxes. These are the same dialog boxes that appear when you create a chart with the Chart Wizard. This gives you complete control over chart properties such as the chart type.

Continued...

7. Choose **Chart**→**Chart Type...** from the menu bar.

Notice the dialog box provides access to all chart types.

8. Choose **Column** from the top of the Chart Type list and choose the **4th sub-type** on the right side of the dialog box.

9. **Click OK** to restore your original column chart.

Explore the remaining buttons on the Chart toolbar

10. **Click** the Legend 🗐 button on the Chart toolbar to turn off the legend.

11. **Click** the Legend 🗐 button again to restore the legend.

12. **Click** the Data Table ⊞ button to add a data table to the chart.

13. **Click** Data Table ⊞ again to turn off the table.

14. **Click** the By Column ▥ button (two buttons to the right of the Data Table button).

Notice Excel displays the sales rep names along the horizontal (category) axis and the Quarters in the legend box. The sales for each rep are now grouped into one set of columns. This gives you a different view of the same data.

15. **Click** the By Row ▤ button to switch to the original view.

16. **Click** anywhere on the chart title and it will become selected as shown below.

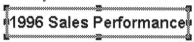

Notice the Angle Text Downward 🔖 and Angle Text Upward 🔖 buttons are now available. You can use these buttons to change the angle and appearance of certain objects such as titles.

17. Feel free to experiment with the Angle Text Downward 🔖 and Angle Text Upward 🔖 buttons.

You will proably find the angled text buttons of limited use because of the length of the title.

18. Remove the angle effect from the title by **clicking** whichever Angle Text button is currently acitve.

You will learn how to format and change the various chart objects in the following topics.

Editing and Formatting Chart Objects

Excel lets you edit and format objects within charts. You can delete or move objects, change the color of objects and perform other editing and formatting actions.

You must select the object you want to format

You select an object by clicking it or choosing it from the Objects  list. You can format the object once it is selected.

Editing and Formatting Titles

You can edit the text in any chart title. You can also change the font, size and color of titles. The following table discusses the procedures for editing and formatting chart titles.

To	Do this
Edit a title	Select the title, pause and then click the title again to position the insertion point within the title. Make the desired editing changes.
Format the font, size and color	Use the Font, Size and Font Color ![A] buttons on the Formatting toolbar.

Hands-On 6.6 – Edit and format the titles

Edit the Chart title

1. Make sure the Chart Title is selected as shown below.

2. Position the mouse pointer on the title and the pointer will have an I-Beam ^{I} shape.

3. **Click** the I-Beam ^{I} just in front of the word **Performance**.

4. Type the word **Rep** to make the title 1996 Sales Rep Performance.

    You can edit a title in the Formula bar or directly in the title box (as you just did).

Replace the Revenue title

5. **Click** the **Revenue** title (the title on the left side of the chart) and type **Sales**.

    The word Sales will appear in the Formula bar.

6. Confirm ☑ the entry and the title will become Sales.

Format the titles

7. **Click** the Chart Title (1996 Sales Rep Performance) and it will become selected.

8. Use the Formatting toolbar [Arial] [12] [**B** *I* <u>U</u>] to format the title as desired.

9. Use the Font Color [A▾] button to add color to the title.

    Be careful not to use the Fill Color [⬧▾] button. The Fill Color button will add color to the background of the title but not to the text.

10. Format the Value Axis title (Sales) and the Category Axis title (Quarter) as desired.

Hands-On 6.7 - Use the Object list and Format buttons on the Chart toolbar

Add color to the Chart Area

1. **Click** the **Chart Title** (1996 Sales Rep Performance) and it will become selected.

2. Use the following steps to further understand the Chart toolbar.

    ❶ *Notice that Chart Title appears in the Object box. The selected object name always appears in this box.*

    ❷ *Click the drop-down button and choose **Chart Area** from the list. The Chart Area will become selected. You can select objects by clicking them or choosing their name from the Object list.*

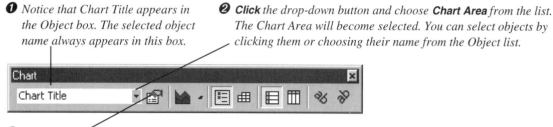

    ❸ *Click the **Format button**. A dialog box will appear with formatting options for the Chart Area.*

3. **Click** the **Patterns tab** and notice you can format either the Border or the Area.

4. **Choose any color** in the Area section and **click OK**.

    The color you chose will fill the Chart Area and provide a colored background for the chart.

Change the orientation of the value axis title

5. **Click** the value axis title (Sales) and it will become selected.

6. **Click** the Format ⬚ button on the Chart toolbar.

    A dialog box with formatting options for titles will appear.

7. **Click** the Alignment tab.

8. Use the following step to adjust the orientation.

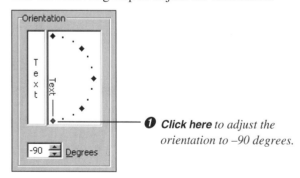

    ❶ *Click here to adjust the orientation to –90 degrees.*

9. **Click OK** and the title will have a vertical orientation.

    This will allow the chart columns to expand horizontally.

10. Feel free to edit any chart object by clicking on it and then using the Format ⬚ button on the Chart toolbar.

11. When you have finished experimenting, save the changes ⬚ and continue with the next topic.

Line Charts

Line charts are useful for comparing trends over a period of time. For example, line charts are often used to show stock market and economic activity where the upward or downward trend of the data is important.

Line charts also have a category and value axis

Line charts have a category axis and value axis, as do column charts. Most of the objects on line charts such as the legend, titles, and axis labels are used in the same way as with column charts. The illustration below shows the line chart you will create next. The chart depicts the trend in quarterly sales throughout the year. Take a moment to study the illustration and the accompanying worksheet.

3		Q1	Q2	Q3	Q4
4	Jones	100,000	230,000	280,000	230,000
5	Jackson	50,000	130,000	170,000	200,000
6	Smith	120,000	120,000	320,000	340,000
7	Robertson	90,000	50,000	120,000	270,000
8					
9	Total	$ 360,000	$ 530,000	$ 890,000	$ 1,040,000

The chart below was created using the selected data shown here. Notice the data is in two separate ranges. You will use the Ctrl key to select these non-contiguous ranges. This will let you chart just the Totals for each quarter and the Q1-Q4 labels.

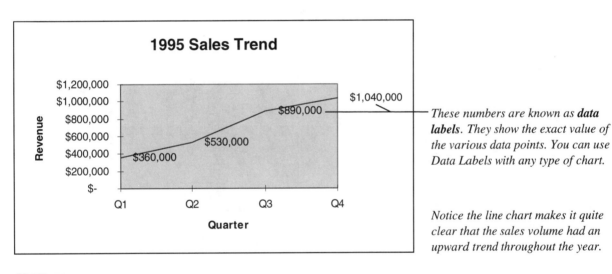

*These numbers are known as **data labels**. They show the exact value of the various data points. You can use Data Labels with any type of chart.*

Notice the line chart makes it quite clear that the sales volume had an upward trend throughout the year.

Hands-On 6.8 – Create a line chart

In this exercise, you will create a line chart in the Sales sheet. When you are finished, the Sales sheet will contain the data and both the column and line charts.

Reduce the size of the column chart to make room for the line chart

1. **Click** the column chart once to select it.

2. **Drag** a corner sizing handle until the chart is very small (approximately 1" by 1").
   You can always restore the size at a later time.

3. Move the chart to the top edge of the screen (just to the right of the worksheet data).
   You can move the chart by dragging it with the mouse.

4. **Click** outside the chart to deselect it.

Continued...

Select the data

5. Use the following Hands-On Illustration to select the data.

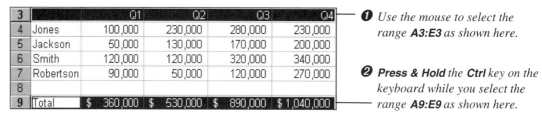

3		Q1	Q2	Q3	Q4
4	Jones	100,000	230,000	280,000	230,000
5	Jackson	50,000	130,000	170,000	200,000
6	Smith	120,000	120,000	320,000	340,000
7	Robertson	90,000	50,000	120,000	270,000
8					
9	Total	$ 360,000	$ 530,000	$ 890,000	$ 1,040,000

❶ *Use the mouse to select the range **A3:E3** as shown here.*

❷ **Press & Hold** *the **Ctrl** key on the keyboard while you select the range **A9:E9** as shown here.*

Use the Chart Wizard

6. **Click** the Chart Wizard button.

7. Choose the Line Line chart type and the 1st sub-type.

8. **Click** Next > **twice** and then enter the titles in the Step 3 of 4 box as shown below.

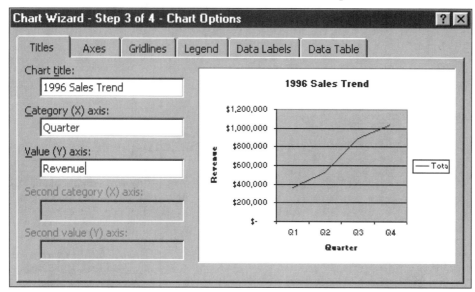

9. **Click** the Finish button.

   There was no need to click Next on the Step 4 of 4 box because we want the chart embedded in the current worksheet. Keep in mind that you can click Finish at any step in the Chart Wizard.

10. Take a few moments to study your chart, and then continue with the next topic.

Editing Charts with the Chart Wizard

The Chart Wizard can be used to edit charts after they have been created. You can set any chart option just as you would when creating a chart. Earlier in this lesson, you used the Chart option on the menu bar to display the Chart Wizard dialog boxes and edit a chart. The difference between that technique and the Chart Wizard technique, is the Chart Wizard technique guides you through the four or five steps of editing a chart just as it does when you create a new chart.

Inserting Data Labels

Excel can display **data labels** at any **data point**. Data points occur at the top of columns or at the locations where a line chart changes. Data labels display the exact values of the data points. Data labels are most effective when there are only a few data points. A chart may be cluttered if you use data labels and there are too many columns or lines.

Hands-On 6.9 – Insert data labels in the line chart

1. **Click** anywhere in the Chart Area of the line chart.

2. **Click** the Chart Wizard [button icon] button.

3. **Click** [Next >] **twice** and then **click** the **Data Labels** tab.

4. Choose the [Show value] option and **click** the [Finish] button.

   Excel displays data labels at the points that correspond to the numbers in Row 9.

5. Feel free to format the line chart in any way you desire.

6. When you have finished, **click** outside the chart to deselect it.

7. Increase the size of the column chart you created earlier and position both charts at any location you desire.

8. Save [disk icon] the changes and continue with the pie chart topic on the next page.

Pie Charts

Pie charts are useful for comparing parts of a whole. For example, pie charts are often used in budgets to show which part of the budget is being allocated for various purposes.

You typically select two sets of data when creating a pie chart. You select the values that make up the parts of the pie and labels that identify the categories. The following illustrations show a 3-D pie chart and the worksheet data you will use in the following exercises. Notice the worksheet has an extra column added to it. You will create this column in the next exercise.

3		Q1	Q2	Q3	Q4	Total
4	Jones	100,000	230,000	280,000	230,000	840,000
5	Jackson	50,000	130,000	170,000	200,000	550,000
6	Smith	120,000	120,000	320,000	340,000	900,000
7	Robertson	90,000	50,000	120,000	270,000	530,000

The names in column A will become labels on the pie slices. The numbers in column F will determine the size of the slices.

Sales Rep Contributions

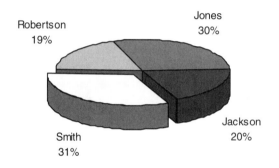

Excel calculates the percentages based upon the numbers you select. Notice that the Smith slice is "exploded" out from the pie.

Hands-On 6.10 – Create a pie chart on a separate chart sheet

In this exercise, you will create a 3-D pie chart. You will instruct Excel to insert the pie chart in a new worksheet. The Hands-On Lesson 6 workbook should still be open.

Add a Total column

1. **Click** cell **F3** and enter the word **Total** (you may need to move the column or bar chart).

2. **Select** the range **F4:F7** and use AutoSum $\boxed{\Sigma}$ to compute the Totals for column F.

    Notice these totals calculate the total annual sales for each sales rep. Your Totals should match those shown above.

Create the chart on a separate chart sheet

3. **Select** the ranges **A4:A7** and **F4:F7** as shown above (you will need to use the Ctrl key when selecting the second range).

4. **Click** the Chart Wizard ![icon] button.

5. Choose the Pie 🥧 **Pie** chart type and the 3-D 🥧 sub-type.

6. **Click** [Next >] **twice** and the Step 3 of 4 box will appear.

Continued...

7. If necessary, **click** the **Titles tab** and enter the title **Sales Rep Contributions** as the Chart title.

8. **Click** the **Legend tab** and remove the check from the box.

    The legend won't be needed because you will add data labels in the next step.

9. **Click** the **Data Labels tab** and choose the ⊙ Show label and percent option.

    Each pie slice should have the sales rep name and percentage of the total sales displayed.

10. **Click** ⌐ Next > ⌐ and the Step 4 of 4 box will appear.

11. **Click** the ⊙ As new sheet: button, and then **click** the ⌐ Finish ⌐ button.

12. Look at the sheet tabs and notice the chart has been created on a new sheet named Chart2.

13. **Double-click** the **Chart2** sheet tab and the Chart2 text will become selected.

14. Type **Pie Chart** as the new sheet name.

Exploding Pie Slices and Changing the 3-D View

You can make a pie slice stand out from the rest of the pie by **exploding** the slice. Exploding simply means to draw the slice out from the pie. Excel also lets you rotate a pie chart to draw attention to a particular part of the pie.

Hands-On 6.11 – Explode one slice and change the 3-D Rotation and Elevation

Explode the Smith slice

1. **Click** anywhere on the pie and the entire pie will become selected.

2. Now **click** once on the **Smith** slice and it will be the only selected slice.

3. Use the following step to explode the Smith slice.

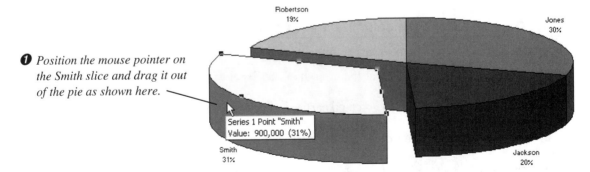

❶ *Position the mouse pointer on the Smith slice and drag it out of the pie as shown here.*

Explode all of the slices

4. **Drag** the Smith slice back into the pie until the pie is whole again.

5. **Click** outside of the pie to deselect it.

Continued...

6. **Click** anywhere on the pie and the entire pie will become selected.

7. **Drag** any slice out of the pie and all of the pie slices will become exploded.

8. **Release** the mouse button and all slices will be exploded.

9. Now explode just the Smith slice again.

   You will need to make the pie whole again by dragging a slice back to the center. All slices will move to the center when you do this. Then you can explode the Smith slice.

Change the 3-D Rotation and Elevation

10. Make sure the pie is selected, and then choose **Chart→3-D View...** from the menu bar.

11. Use the following steps to adjust the rotation and elevation.

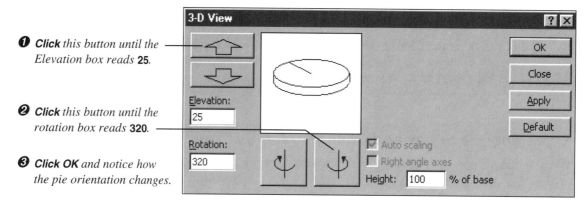

❶ **Click** *this button until the Elevation box reads* **25**.

❷ **Click** *this button until the rotation box reads* **320**.

❸ **Click OK** *and notice how the pie orientation changes.*

12. Feel free to experiment with the 3-D View and other options on the Chart menu.

13. Save your worksheet when you have finished and continue with the next topic.

Changing the Chart Location

You can move an embedded chart to a separate chart sheet and vice-versa. This is easily accomplished by selecting the chart and using the **Chart→Location...** command on the menu bar.

Hands-On 6.12 – Move the column chart to a separate chart sheet

In this exercise, you will move the column chart from the Sales sheet to a separate chart sheet.

1. **Click** the **Sales sheet tab** at the bottom of the Excel window.

2. **Click** the column chart you created earlier in this lesson.

3. Choose **Chart→Location...** from the menu bar.

4. Choose the ⊙ As new sheet: option.

5. **Click OK** and the chart will be placed on a separate chart sheet.

6. Change the name of the new sheet to **Column Chart**.

7. Feel free to experiment with charts, and then **close** the workbook and **save** the changes.

Concepts Review

True / False

1. A workbook can have a maximum of 16 worksheets.   1. **T F**
2. You can rename a worksheet by first double-clicking the sheet tab.   2. **T F**
3. Embedded charts are updated when the worksheet data changes.   3. **T F**
4. Charts on a separate chart sheet are not updated when the worksheet data changes.   4. **T F**
5. Column charts are most useful for comparing the parts of a whole.   5. **T F**
6. Column charts have a category and value axis.   6. **T F**
7. The Chart Wizard can only be used to create embedded charts.   7. **T F**
8. The Chart menu on the menu bar is only available when a chart is selected.   8. **T F**
9. You must select a chart before you can move or resize it.   9. **T F**
10. A chart has a portrait orientation when it is first created on a separate chart sheet.   10. **T F**

Multiple Choice

1. Which procedure would you use to change the position of a worksheet in the sheet order?
   a) Double-click the sheet tab then drag the tab to the desired location.
   b) Click the sheet tab and choose Edit→Move sheet from the menu bar.
   c) Drag the sheet tab to the desired location.
   d) None of the above.   (   )

2. Which command would you use to move an embedded chart to a separate sheet?
   a) Edit→Move chart
   b) Chart→Location
   c) Chart→Move
   d) This cannot be done   (   )

3. Which chart would be best for showing a trend over a period of time?
   a) Line chart
   b) Bar chart
   c) Column chart
   d) Pie chart   (   )

4. Which technique can be used to insert Data Labels after a chart has been created?
   a) Select the chart and click the Data Labels button on the Chart toolbar.
   b) Select the chart and choose the Insert→Data Labels command.
   c) Select the chart, choose Chart→Options, and then click the Data Labels tab.
   d) Data labels cannot be inserted after a chart has been created.   (   )

5. Which technique can be used to explode a single pie slice?
   a) Select the chart, click anywhere on the pie and drag the slice.
   b) Click the chart, click the pie, click the desired slice, and then drag it.
   c) Click the chart, double-click the pie and drag the slice.
   d) None of the above.   (   )

Skills Builder 6.1

In this exercise, you will use Excel's Help feature to get a description of the various chart types.

1. **Open** a New Workbook 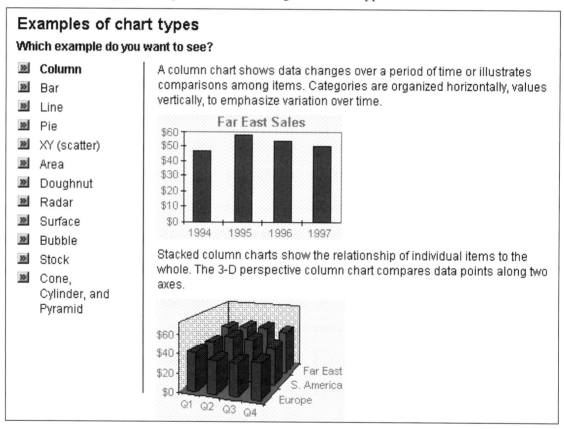.

2. Choose **Help**→**Contents and Index** from the menu bar.

3. **Click** the **Index** tab.

4. Type **charts** in the number 1 box.

5. Scroll through the list of topics under charts until you see **types of**.

6. **Double-click** the **types of** topic and the following screen will appear.

7. Take five or ten minutes to study the chart examples.

   You will need to click the ⟩⟩ *buttons on the left side of the dialog box to see the examples.*

8. **Click** the Close ⊠ button at the top-right corner of the Help dialog box when you have finished.

Skills Builder 6.2

In this exercise, you will create a column chart to display student enrollments at a university.

Enter the years in column A by expanding the series

1. **Open** the workbook named **Skills Builder 6.2**.

    Notice the enrollment data has been completed in column B but the years have not been completed in column A. Notice the first two years 1980 and 1981 form the beginning of the series 1980 - 1996. The best way to expand this series is with the fill handle.

2. **Select** cells **A4** and **A5**.

3. **Drag** the fill handle ✚ down to row 20 to expand the series.

4. Left align ▤ the years in column A.

Create the chart

5. **Select** the range **A3:B20**.

    This range includes the enrollment data and the Year and Total Enrollment labels.

6. **Click** the Chart Wizard ▦ button.

7. Choose the Column ▥ Column chart type and the first ▥ sub-type.

8. **Click** ⎡ Next > ⎤ and the Step 2 of 4 box will appear.

    Take a moment to study the step 2 dialog box and you will notice a problem. Excel is interpreting the years 1980 – 1996 as numbers and it is plotting them as a data series in the chart. The years are the short columns to the left of the tall-thin enrollment data columns. The years should actually be displayed as labels on the horizontal category axis. You will correct this in the next few steps.

9. **Click** the **Series tab** on the dialog box.

    The Series tab lets you modify the data series that are plotted in the chart.

10. Use the following step to remove the year columns.

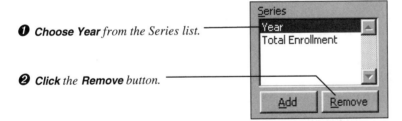

❶ *Choose Year from the Series list.*

❷ *Click the Remove button.*

    In the next few steps, you will add the years as Category axis labels.

11. **Click** in the Category (X) axis labels 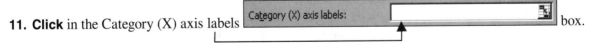 box.

12. Select the years 1980 – 1996 in the worksheet as shown on the following page.

    The Source Data dialog box will temporarily close as you select the data.

Continued...

The Category (X) axis labels box should now match the following example.

Notice that the dates are now displayed in an angled fashion on the Category axis.

13. Click [Next >] to continue with step 3 of 4.

14. Click the **Titles tab** and type the title **Student Enrollments** in the Chart title box.

15. Click the **Legend tab** and **remove** the legend.

16. Click [Finish] to complete the chart.

Take a few moments to study your worksheet and chart. Make sure you understand the relationship between the worksheet data and the chart.

Convert the chart to a line chart

Imagine you are interested in seeing only the trend in enrollments as opposed to the enrollments in individual years. You can easily convert this chart to a line chart.

17. Make sure the chart is selected.

18. Click the Chart Type [📊] button on the Chart toolbar and choose Line Chart [📈] from the list.
Your chart should be converted to a line chart.

Format the chart title
19. Click the **Student Enrollments** chart title.

20. Use the Font Color [A] button to add your color of choice to the title.

21. Feel free to format the chart and title in any other way you desire.

22. When you have finished, **close** the workbook and **save** the changes.

Skills Builder 6.3

In this exercise, you will create a chart for Holy Donuts. The chart will show the various types of donuts that make up the sales volume at Holy Donuts. What type of chart do you think you will use? Well a donut chart what else!

Create the worksheet

1. If necessary, open a New Workbook 📄 and create the worksheet shown below. Format the numbers in column B as Comma with 0 decimals.

	A	B	C
1	Holy Donuts Product Analysis		
2			
3	Type of Donut	Total Number Sold	
4	Creme Filled	12,000	
5	Frosted	10,500	
6	Nut Covered	2,300	
7	Glazed	7,000	
8	Old Fashioned	4,500	

Create the chart

Doughnut charts function much like pie charts because they are used to compare parts of a whole. Therefore, the data is selected, as it would be for a pie chart.

2. **Select** the donut data in the range **A4:B8**.

3. **Click** the Chart Wizard 📊 button.

4. Choose **Doughnut** as the Chart type and choose the **first sub-type**.

5. **Click** [Next >] **twice** and the Step 3 of 4 dialog box will appear.

6. **Click** the **Titles** tab and enter the Chart title **Donut Analysis**.

7. **Click** the **Legend tab** and remove the check from the Show Legend box.

8. **Click** the **Data Labels tab** and choose the **Show label and percent** option.

9. **Click** the [Finish] button.

Remove the border from the chart

10. Make sure the chart is selected and **click** the Format 📋 button on the Chart toolbar.

11. Make sure the Patterns tab is active and set the Border option to [● None].

12. **Click OK** and the border should be removed.

Change the color of the percentages and labels

13. **Click** any of the labels or percentages (such as Glazed 19%) and the entire group will be selected.

14. Use the Font Color [A ▾] button on the Formatting toolbar to apply a striking color such as red.

15. Feel free to modify your chart by changing the color of the donut slices or other objects. This is easily accomplished by clicking the object, clicking the Format button and choosing the desired options from the dialog box. Finally, **close** the workbook and **save** it as **Skills Builder 6.3**.

Skills Builder 6.4

In this exercise, you will create four pie charts to illustrate employee expenses for Hollywood Productions - a motion pictures production company. The pie charts will show how employee costs are divided between departments and how each department's employee costs are allocated. You will create each chart on a separate chart sheet.

Create the company pie chart

1. **Open** the workbook named **Skills Builder 6.4**.

2. Use the following Hands-On Illustration to select two ranges.

3		Marketing	Production	Finance
4	Salaries	3,400,000	4,500,000	1,200,000
5	Benefits	1,292,000	1,980,000	336,000
6	Travel	1,700,000	1,500,000	120,000
7	Total	$ 6,392,000	$ 7,980,000	$ 1,656,000

❶ *Use the mouse to select the range* **B3:D3** *as shown here.*

❷ **Press & Hold** *the* **Ctrl** *key and select the range* **B7:D7**.

3. **Click** the Chart Wizard 📊 button and create the following pie chart on a **separate chart sheet**.

    Make sure the chart type, title, and labels match the following example. Also notice the example does not have a legend.

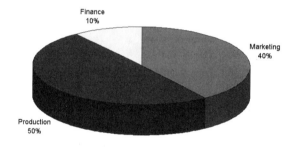

Hollywood Employee Expenses

Finance
10%

Marketing
40%

Production
50%

4. **Double-click** the **Chart1** sheet tab and change the sheet name to **Hollywood Chart**.

    Notice you can use long names when naming sheets.

5. Rename Sheet1 as **Employee Expense Data**.

Create a separate pie chart for the Marketing department

6. **Select** the range shown below.

3		Marketing	Production	Finance
4	Salaries	3,400,000	4,500,000	1,200,000
5	Benefits	1,292,000	1,980,000	336,000
6	Travel	1,700,000	1,500,000	120,000
7	Total	$ 6,392,000	$ 7,980,000	$ 1,656,000

7. **Click** the Chart Wizard 📊 button and create a pie chart on a **separate chart sheet**. Use the same chart type and labels as the previous chart but use the title **Marketing Employee Costs**.

8. Rename the sheet as **Marketing Chart**.

9. **Click** the **Employee Expense Data** sheet tab to return to that sheet.

Continued...

Create pie charts for the Production and Finance departments

10. Use the techniques in this exercise to create the same style pie charts for the Production and Finance departments. Create each chart on a separate chart sheet using the techniques in this exercise. Use the chart titles and sheet names shown in the table below. Also, you should select data for the Production department chart as shown below. You will need to decide how to select the data for the Finance department (although that should be an easy decision to make).

Chart	Use this title	Use this sheet name
Production	Production Employee Costs	Production Chart
Finance	Finance Employee Costs	Finance Chart

3		Marketing	Production	Finance
4	Salaries	3,400,000	4,500,000	1,200,000
5	Benefits	1,292,000	1,980,000	336,000
6	Travel	1,700,000	1,500,000	120,000
7	Total	$ 6,392,000	$ 7,980,000	$ 1,656,000

Rearrange the sheet tabs

11. Use the following steps to move the Employee Expense Data sheet tab.

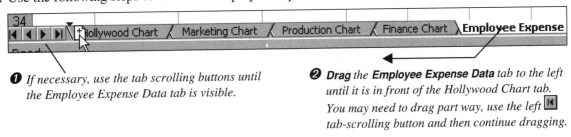

❶ *If necessary, use the tab scrolling buttons until the Employee Expense Data tab is visible.*

❷ *Drag the **Employee Expense Data** tab to the left until it is in front of the Hollywood Chart tab. You may need to drag part way, use the left* ⏮ *tab-scrolling button and then continue dragging.*

Explode the pie slices and increase the elevation

12. **Click** the **Hollywood Chart** tab to activate it.

13. **Click** once on the pie, pause, then **click** the **Production** slice (the largest slice).

14. **Drag** the slice out slightly to explode it.

15. Choose **Chart→3-D View...** from the menu bar.

16. Increase the Elevation ⬆ to **25** and **click OK**.

17. **Click** the **Marketing Chart** sheet tab.

18. **Explode** the **Salaries** slice (the largest slice) and increase the **Elevation** to **25**.

19. Explode the largest slice and increase the Elevation to **25** for the **Production** and **Finance** charts.

20. Take a few minutes to click the various sheet tabs and check out your charts.

21. Feel free to format and enhance your charts in any way.

22. **Close** the workbook when you have finished and **save** the changes.

Skills Builder 6.5

In this exercise, you will create a pie chart that shows the budget allocation for a school district. You will also learn how to print an embedded chart.

Open the workbook and create a pie chart

1. **Open** the workbook named **Skills Builder 6.5**.

2. **Select** the data shown below.

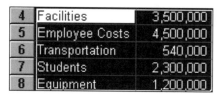

3. Use the Chart Wizard 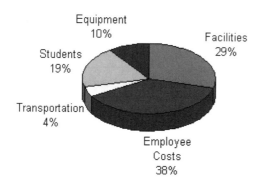 to create the **embedded** pie chart below. Make sure you include the chart title and increase the elevation as shown. Also, remove the chart border and legend as shown.

1997 Budget Allocation

Equipment 10%
Facilities 29%
Students 19%
Transportation 4%
Employee Costs 38%

Use Print Preview for the chart only

4. Make sure the chart is selected and **click** Print Preview.

   Notice the chart is displayed on a full page in landscape orientation. This is the same result as when you use Print Preview with a separate chart sheet. You can always use this technique to print embedded charts as separate objects. Just remember to select the desired chart prior to printing or using Print Preview.

5. **Close** Print Preview.

6. **Close** the workbook and **save** the changes.

Skills Builder 6.6

In this exercise, you will create a worksheet and line chart to track the trends in a stock portfolio.

1. Open a New Workbook.

2. Use the following guidelines to create the worksheet shown below.

    -   Notice that the dates in cells A4 and A5 form the beginning of a series. You can enter these dates, select them and then drag the fill handle down to cell A11 to complete the series.

    -   Columns B-D contain mixed numbers (whole numbers and fractions). Just type the numbers exactly as shown with a space between the whole numbers and the fractions.

    -   Widen columns B-D as necessary.

	A	B	C	D
1	My Stock Portfolio - 8 Week Trends			
2				
3		Silicon Technology	Dakota Mining	Anderson Diesel
4	9/6/97	58 1/2	32	45
5	9/13/97	59	31	43
6	9/20/97	56	28	45
7	9/27/97	59	30 1/8	48
8	10/4/97	63	33	49
9	10/11/97	68	34	47
10	10/18/97	70	34	42
11	10/25/97	69	36 1/2	38

3. **Select** the range **A3:D11** (all active cells except for the title).

4. Use the Chart Wizard to create the embedded line chart shown below. Make sure you have the same titles and legend as shown.

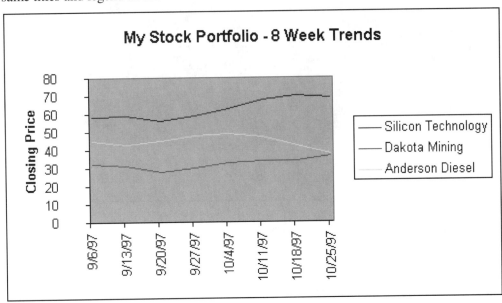

5. **Close** the workbook and **save** it as **Skills Builder 6.6**.

Assessment 6.1

1. **Click** the New Workbook [ ] button.

2. Create the worksheet shown below.

	A	B	C	D
1	SysTech 12 Month Stock Performance			
2	March 1, 1996 - February 28, 1997			
3				
4	Date	Stock Price		
5	3/1/96	78		
6	4/1/96	82.6		
7	5/1/96	83		
8	6/1/96	78.6		
9	7/1/96	72		
10	8/1/96	62		
11	9/1/96	65.8		
12	10/1/96	72.6		
13	11/1/96	85		
14	12/1/96	86		
15	1/1/97	90		
16	2/1/97	92		

3. Use the worksheet data to create the chart shown below on a **separate chart sheet**. Make sure you use the data labels and title as shown.

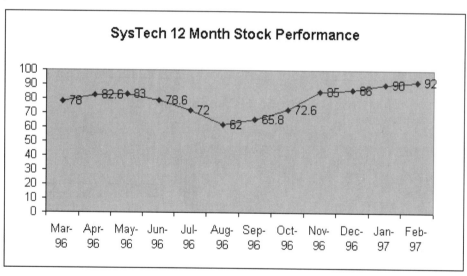

4. Rename the Chart1 sheet as **12 Month Chart**.

5. Rename the Sheet1 sheet as **12 Month Data**.

6. **Print** both the **worksheet** and **chart**.

7. **Close** the workbook and **save** it as **Assessment 6.1**.

Assessment 6.2

1. Create the worksheet and embedded column chart shown below. Notice the column chart is two-dimensional. The Differences in row 6 are simply the budget numbers minus the spent numbers. Notice the negative differences dip below the X axis in the chart.

	A	B	C	D	E	F	G	H
1	Personal Budget Analysis (January 97 - June 97)							
2								
3		Jan	Feb	Mar	Apr	May	Jun	
4	Budget	5000	5500	5000	5300	5300	5500	
5	Spent	4500	6000	4750	6200	4900	5500	
6	Difference	500	-500	250	-900	400	0	
7								

Budget Vs. Spent

(Chart: two-dimensional column chart showing Budget, Spent, and Difference series for Jan–Jun, with Y axis from -2000 to 7000.)

2. **Print** the worksheet and column chart on one page.

3. **Close** the workbook and **save** it as **Assessment 6.2**.

Assessment 6.3

1. Use the following guidelines to create the worksheet and chart shown below.

   – Type all the numbers and text entries as shown but use formulas to calculate the New Balance in column E and the Totals, Highest and Lowest in rows 9-11. The formula for New Balance is New Balance = Beginning Balance + Purchases - Payments. The Totals in row 9 can be calculated with AutoSum and the Highest and Lowest calculations in rows 10 and 11 can be accomplished with the MIN and MAX functions.

   – Format the worksheet with the AutoFormat Classic 2 style as shown.

   – Create an embedded 3-D pie chart as shown. Notice the pie chart only includes the New Balances of the customers and not the Totals or Highest and Lowest.

   – Explode the Bishop slice and adjust the chart rotation and elevation as shown.

   – Bold all of the pie slice labels as shown.

2. **Print** the worksheet and embedded chart when you have finished.

3. **Close** the workbook and **save** it as **Assessment 6.3**.

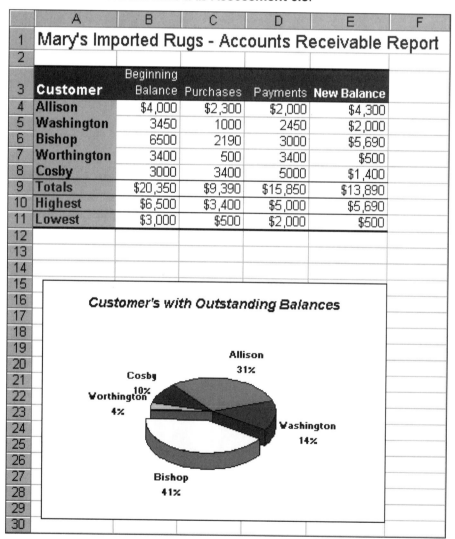

Critical Thinking 6.1

Create a worksheet to track five stocks on a weekly basis. The stocks can either be stocks you own or stocks you would like to own. You can find stock listings in the financial section of any newspaper. Include the date and the closing price of the stock on that date. Try to choose Friday as the date since this represents the end of the trading week. Create a line chart that tracks all five stocks together on the same chart. Create a descriptive title for the chart and make sure that the chart has a legend. Use Print Preview to make sure your chart and worksheet will print correctly (but don't print them). Close the workbook and save it with a descriptive name.

Critical Thinking 6.2

Create a worksheet and accompanying column chart that tracks the difference between the amount of money you spend on Christmas presents and the amount of money you receive. This is obviously very materialistic and defies the true meaning of the holiday season but then again we do live in a capitalistic society. Have your worksheet display the amount received, amount spent and the differences. Format the columns in your chart by changing the column colors to Christmas colors. Choose a green color for the amount-received columns, red for spent and some other color for the differences. Be creative and format the chart in an attractive way. Close the workbook when you have finished and save it with a descriptive name.

Critical Thinking 6.3

Create a worksheet that tracks your personal expenditures for a one-month period. Create an accompanying pie chart to show where your money is being spent. Format the pie chart in any way you feel is necessary. Try to use your worksheet on an ongoing basis to better plan your financial expenditures. Close the workbook and save it under a descriptive name.

Critical Thinking 6.4

Create a worksheet that tracks your annual income for the past 5 or 10 years. You can get the income numbers from your income tax returns. Create a column chart and a line chart to show the trends and actual income numbers. Is your income increasing, decreasing or staying the same? If your income is obtained from several sources such as a full-time job, investments, or a part-time job, then create a pie chart that shows how the income is obtained. Be creative and enhance your worksheet and charts in any way you feel is necessary. Close the workbook and save it under a descriptive name.

7 Financial Modeling and Absolute Cell References

Objectives:

- Understand absolute cell reference concepts

- Use absolute cell references

- Use mixed cell references

- Insert cell comments

- Edit and clear cell comments

- Understand financial modeling concepts

- Create financial models

- Use what-if analysis with financial models

- Display and print worksheet formulas

- Set options

The Project - Crazy Words Financial Model

In this lesson, you will develop a financial model for an exciting new business venture - The Crazy Words board game. Martin Johnson is developing a new game that is fun and helps children and adults develop language skills. Martin is an entrepreneur and he is determined to develop and market the game himself. You will develop a financial model to help Martin plan the growth and profitability of his business. You will use absolute cell references and cell comments to develop and document the model.

The model will be set up to allow you to change variables such as the selling price of the game, manufacturing costs and the commission rates of sales people. Whenever you change a variable, the model will recalculate important financial information such as the gross profit. This powerful capability will let you perform what-if analysis. For example, the model will provide answers to questions such as "What will my gross profit be if I lower my manufacturing cost to $9 per unit?" The completed model is shown below.

	A	B	C	D	E	F
1	Crazy Words Financial Model					
2						
3	Projected Units Sold	10,000	50,000	100,000	500,000	1,000,000
4	Revenue	$ 150,000	$ 750,000	$ 1,200,000	$ 4,875,000	$ 7,500,000
5	Manufacturing Cost	100,000	415,000	730,000	2,260,000	3,160,000
6	Marketing	3,000	15,000	24,000	97,500	150,000
7	Commissions	15,000	75,000	120,000	487,500	750,000
8	Office Expenses	750	3,750	6,000	24,375	37,500
9	Rent	12,000	12,000	12,000	36,000	36,000
10	Consulting Fees	5,000	5,000	5,000	15,000	15,000
11						
12	Total Costs	$ 135,750	$ 525,750	$ 897,000	$ 2,920,375	$ 4,148,500
13	Gross Profit	$ 14,250	$ 224,250	$ 303,000	$ 1,954,625	$ 3,351,500
14	Net Profit	$ 9,263	$ 145,763	$ 196,950	$ 1,270,506	$ 2,178,475
15	Gross Profit Vs. Revenue	10%	30%	25%	40%	45%
16						
17	Initial Selling Price	$15		Commission Rate		10%
18	Manufacturing Setup Cost	$10,000		Tax Rate		35%
19	Initial Manufacturing Unit Cost	$9		Office Expenses		0.50%

Absolute Cell References

Excel lets you use both **absolute** and **relative** cell references in formulas. You have been using relative references thus far in this course. Relative references are convenient because they are updated when formulas are moved or copied. However, you will encounter situations where you may not want references updated when a formula is moved or copied. You must use absolute references in these situations. Absolute references always refer to the same cell regardless of which cell the formula is moved to or copied to.

Absolute references are identified by dollar signs

You create absolute references by placing dollar signs $ in front of the column and/or row components of the reference. For example, the reference $C$1 is absolute because it has a dollar sign $ in front of both the column (C) and row (1) components. You can type the dollar signs as you type a formula or you can add the dollar signs later by editing the formula. The following illustration shows an example of how absolute references are used in formulas.

C4	▼	= =B4*$C$1
	A	B	C
1	Commission Rate		10%
2			
3		Sales	Commission
4	John	$8,500	$850
5	Ned	$10,000	
6	Ellen	$18,000	

*Cell C4 contains the formula =B4*$C$1 as shown in the Formula bar. Notice Excel lets you mix relative and absolute references in the same formula.*

*The formula becomes =B5*$C$1 when it is copied down to cell C5. The relative reference B4 is updated to B5 in the new formula but the absolute reference $C$1 continues to refer to the Commission Rate in cell C1.*

*The formula becomes =B6*$C$1 when it is copied to this cell.*

Using the F4 key to create absolute references

As mentioned above, you can create absolute references by typing dollar signs when entering a formula. Excel will also insert the dollar signs for you if you tap the F4 key on the keyboard. This is convenient if you are editing a formula. However, you must click in front of the desired reference before tapping F4.

Hands-On 7.1 – Create the Revenue formulas in row 4

In this exercise, you will open the Crazy Words workbook from your exercise diskette. You will create formulas using absolute cell references.

Enter a formula with relative references in cell B4

1. Start Excel and open 📂 the workbook named **Hands-On Lesson 7**.

    Take a few moments to study the workbook. In particular, notice that rows 4-15 will contain formulas. Many of the formulas require absolute references. The absolute references will refer to the variables in rows 17-19. When this project is finished, you will be able to play what-if analysis by quickly changing the Initial Selling Price, Manufacturing Setup Cost and other variables. The model will be recalculated each time you change a variable.

2. **Click** cell **B4**.

    The Revenue in B4 is equal to the Projected Units Sold in B3 multiplied by the Initial Selling Price in B17. In the next step, you will enter a formula that uses relative references.

3. Type the formula **=B3*B17** and Confirm ✓ the entry.

    The result should be 150,000. This is the correct number.

Continued...

4. Use the fill handle [▭] + to copy the formula one cell to the right.

    Cell C4 should display an empty result.

5. **Click** cell **C4** and notice the formula =C3*C17 in the Formula bar.

    Notice that cell C17 is empty. The formula in cell B4 uses relative references, so Excel updated the references in cell C4 when you copied the formula. This is incorrect because you want cell C4 to continue to refer to the Initial Selling Price in cell B17. In the next few steps, you will convert the reference in cell B4 to absolute.

6. **Click** Undo [↺] to reverse the copy.

Convert the reference in cell B4 to absolute and copy the formula across

7. **Click** cell **B4** and use the following steps to convert the B17 reference to absolute.

    ❶ *Click in the Formula bar just in front of the B17 reference.*　　　❷ *Tap the F4 key on the keyboard and Excel will insert dollar signs in front of the B and the 17.*

    [✕ ✓ ＝ | =B3*B17]

8. Confirm [✓] the entry and the result should still be 150,000.

9. Use the fill handle **+** to copy the formula one cell to the right.

    Cell C4 should now have the correct result of 750,000.

10. **Click** cell **C4** and notice the formula =C3*$B$17 in the Formula bar.

    Notice that the relative reference B3 was updated to C3. This is correct because the formula should refer to the Projected Units Sold in cell C3. The absolute reference $B$17, however, continues to refer to the Initial Selling Price in cell B17. This is also correct.

11. Use the fill handle **+** to **copy** the formula in cell **C4** across the row to cells **D4-F4**.

Apply a discount percentage to cells D4-F4

This model will assume that the selling price decreases as the Number of Units Sold increases. This is because Martin will need to depend upon discount distributors (such as Price-Costco and WalMart) to sell large numbers of his game. Initially, he will sell his game through small outlets at $15 per copy. However, he will need large retailers if he ever wants to sell 1,000,000 games. These discount retailers will demand large discounts.

12. **Click** cell **D4**.

13. **Click** in the Formula bar just to the right of the formula.

    Notice Excel changes the color of the cell references and the corresponding worksheet cells. This makes it easy for you to identify the cells the formula is referencing.

14. Type ***80%** to make the formula **=D3*$B$17*80%**.

    The new formula will reduce the selling price to 80% of the Initial Selling Price.

15. Confirm [✓] the entry and the result should be 1,200,000.

16. **Click** cell **E4** and use the technique in the preceding steps to multiply that formula by **65%**.

    The result should be 4,875,000.

17. Multiply the formula in cell **F4** by **50%**.

    The result should equal 7,500,000. Fifty percent is the maximum discount that Martin will give.

Hands-On 7.2 – Experiment with what-if analysis

In this exercise, you will change the Initial Selling Price in cell B17. You will watch the formulas recalculate in row 4.

1. **Click** cell **B17**.

2. Type **20** and Confirm the entry.

3. The numbers in row 4 should be recalculated as shown below.

4	Revenue	200,000	1,000,000	1,600,000	6,500,000	10,000,000

4. Change the number in **B17** to **10** and watch the numbers recalculate again.

    Notice this lets you determine the impact of Initial Selling Price on the revenue.

5. Change the number in **B17** back to **15** and continue with the next exercise.

Hands-On 7.3 – Calculate the Manufacturing Cost in row 5

The manufacturing cost of the Crazy Words game is composed of an initial setup cost and a per unit cost for each additional game manufactured. The setup cost is fixed unless Martin can find another manufacturer with lower setup fees. The per unit cost decreases as the volume increases. For example, Martin can expect to have much lower per unit manufacturing costs at 1,000,000 units sold than at 10,000 units sold. In this exercise, you will create the formulas to model this situation.

Create the formula and copy it across the row
1. **Click** cell **B5**.

2. Type **=$B$18+B3*$B$19** exactly as shown including the dollar signs.

3. Confirm [✓] the entry and the result should be 130,000.

4. Take a few moments to study the formula you just entered.

    Notice it adds the Manufacturing Setup Cost in cell B18 to the product (multiplication) of the Units Sold in B3 and the Initial Manufacturing Unit Cost in B19. Notice that both the B18 and B19 references are absolute because you will copy the formula across the row in the next few steps. You will want the copied formulas to continue to refer to those same cells.

5. Use the fill handle ✛ to copy the formula across the row to cells C5-F5.

6. Take a moment to study the results.

    Notice that Martin's Manufacturing costs are greater than his revenue when the Projected Units Sold reaches 500,000 in column E. This is because the Manufacturing Cost needs to decrease as the Projected Units Sold increases. You will apply the necessary discount percentages in the next few steps. We will assume that Martin's Initial Manufacturing Unit Cost will be reduced by 65% when the Projected Units Sold reaches 1,000,000.

Apply the discount percentages
7. **Click** cell **C5**.

Continued...

8. **Click** in the formula bar and type ***90%** at the end of the formula.

   The new formula =$B$18+C3*$B$19*90% will reduce the manufacturing cost of each unit to 90% of the initial manufacturing cost.

9. Confirm ☑ the entry and the result should be 480,000.

10. **Click** cell **D5** and use the technique in the preceding steps to multiply that formula by **80%**.

    The result should be 830,000.

11. Multiply the formula in cell **E5** by **50%** *and multiply the formula in cell* **F5** *by* **35%**.

    Row 5 should have the results shown below.

5	Manufacturing Cost	130,000	480,000	830,000	2,530,000	3,530,000

12. Save 💾 the changes and continue with the next topic.

Cell Comments

Many worksheets (such as the financial model you are developing) can become quite complex. It is important to document complex worksheets so that you (or your coworkers) can understand how the worksheets function at a later time. Excel lets you document worksheets by inserting descriptive comments.

Comments are identified by small red triangles

Excel places a small red triangle in the top-right corner of cells with comments. Comments pop up whenever you place the mouse pointer over cells that contain them. The following illustration shows the Manufacturing Cost cell with a triangle in the top-right corner and the corresponding comment.

This small triangle at the top-right corner of the cell indicates that the cell contains a comment.

The comment is displayed when the mouse pointer is positioned on the cell.

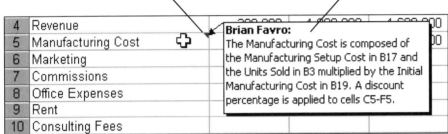

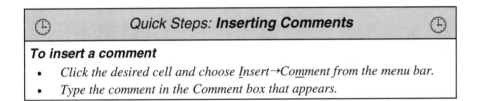

🕐	*Quick Steps:* **Inserting Comments**	🕐

To insert a comment

- *Click the desired cell and choose <u>I</u>nsert→Co<u>m</u>ment from the menu bar.*
- *Type the comment in the Comment box that appears.*

Hands-On 7.4 – Insert a comment in the Manufacturing Cost cell

In this exercise, you will insert the comment shown below into the Manufacturing Cost cell.

Insert and view a comment

1. **Click** cell **A5** and choose **<u>I</u>nsert→Comment...** from the menu bar.

   A Comment box appears. The Comment box may have a name at the top of the box such as the Brian Favro box shown below. The name is obtained from the personal information that you specify when installing Microsoft Office.

2. Type the following comment (except the name Brian Favro) into the box.

Continued...

3. **Click** anywhere outside the Comment box and the comment will be hidden.

    Notice the red triangle in the top-right corner of cell A5. This triangle indicates there is a comment in the cell.

4. Position the pointer ⬧ on cell A5 (you don't need to click) and the comment will appear.

    Only part of the comment will be visible. You will fix this by changing the size of the comment box in the next exercise.

5. Move the mouse pointer to another cell and the comment will be hidden.

Editing and Clearing Comments

Excel lets you edit and clear comments. The Edit→Clear commands let you clear comments, formats and entries from cells. You will use these commands to clear a comment in the following exercise.

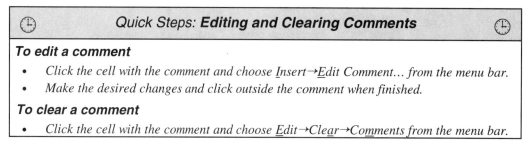

🕐   *Quick Steps: **Editing and Clearing Comments***   🕐

To edit a comment
*   *Click the cell with the comment and choose Insert→Edit Comment... from the menu bar.*
*   *Make the desired changes and click outside the comment when finished.*

To clear a comment
*   *Click the cell with the comment and choose Edit→Clear→Comments from the menu bar.*

Hands-On 7.5 – Change the dimensions of the Comment box and clear the comment

Change the dimensions of the Comment box
1. **Click** cell **A5** and choose **Insert→Edit Comment** from the menu bar.

2. Use the following step to change the dimensions of the Comment box.

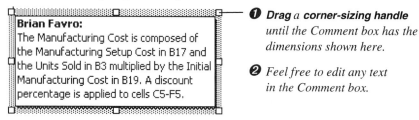

❶ *Drag a **corner-sizing handle** until the Comment box has the dimensions shown here.*

❷ *Feel free to edit any text in the Comment box.*

3. **Click** anywhere **outside the box** to complete the editing.

4. Position the pointer ⬧ on cell **A5** and notice the Comment box has the new dimensions.

Clear the comment
5. **Click** cell **A5**.

6. Choose **Edit→Clear→Comments** from the menu bar.

    The red triangle will vanish from cell A5 indicating the comment has been cleared.

7. **Click** Undo ↶ to restore the comment and continue with the next exercise.

Hands-On 7.6 – Calculate the Marketing Cost in row 6

The Marketing Cost in row 6 will include a $100,000 charge for developing an infomercial to promote Martin's game. The Marketing Cost will also include a component that is equal to 3% of the revenue. This 3% will cover the cost of running the infomercial and developing and mailing product literature.

Create the formula in cell B6

1. **Click** cell **B6**.

2. Enter the formula **=100000+B4*3%** (that's five zeros).

    The result should be 104,500. Notice there is no need to use absolute references in this formula because you are not referencing the variables in rows 17-19. In fact, you want B4 to be a relative reference because you will want it to change to B5, B6...when you copy the formula across the row.

3. Use the fill handle **+** to copy the formula to cells C6-F6.

    The completed row should match the following example.

6	Marketing	104,500	122,500	136,000	246,250	325,000

Insert a comment in cell A6

4. **Click** cell **A6**.

5. Choose **Insert→Comment** from the menu bar.

6. Type the following comment and adjust the size of the comment box until the entire comment is visible in the box.

    > Includes a $100,000 charge for developing an infomercial and a component equal to 3% of the revenue.

7. **Click** anywhere in the worksheet to complete the comment, then display the comment by positioning the mouse pointer on the cell.

8. Save the changes and continue with the next exercise.

Hands-On 7.7 – Calculate the formulas in rows 7-10

In this exercise, you will use absolute references and other techniques in rows 7-10.

Calculate the Commissions in row 7

1. **Click** cell **B7**.

2. Enter the formula **=B4*$F$17**.

    The result should be 21,000.

3. Use the fill handle **+** to copy the formula to cells C7-F7.

    The completed row should match the following example.

7	Commissions	21,000	105,000	168,000	682,500	1,050,000

Continued...

4. **Click** in each cell in row 7 and notice the formulas in the Formula bar.

    Notice how Excel updates the relative reference B4 but leaves the absolute reference $F$17 as it is.

Calculate the Office Expenses in row 8

The Office Expenses use the same type of formula as the commissions. They are simply calculated as ½% of the revenue. Once again, these are approximations and you will play what-if analysis with these percentages later in this lesson.

5. **Click** cell **B8**.

6. Enter the formula **=B4*$F$19**.

7. Copy the formula across the row to cells C8-F8.

    The completed row should match the following example.

8	Office Expenses	750	3,750	6,000	24,375	37,500

Enter the Rent and Consulting Fees in rows 9 and 10

Martin is starting his Crazy Words business out of his home and garage. He believes he can achieve a unit volume of 100,000 before opening an office and warehouse. His rent payment is $12,000 per year ($1,000/month). He assumes an office and warehouse will cost $36,000 per year. Likewise, he expects to spend $5,000 on consulting fees when his unit sales are below 100,000 and $15,000 when sales are above 100,000. In the next step, you will enter these numbers into the model in rows 9 and 10. There is no need to use formulas in rows 9 and 10.

8. Enter the numbers shown below into rows 9 and 10.

9	Rent	12,000	12,000	12,000	36,000	36,000
10	Consulting Fees	5,000	5,000	5,000	15,000	15,000

9. Save 💾 the changes and continue with the next exercise.

Hands-On 7.8 – Calculate the profit formulas in rows 12-15

Calculate the Total Costs in row 12

1. **Click** cell **B12**.

2. **Click** AutoSum **Σ** and Excel will propose the incorrect formula **=SUM(B3:B11)**.

    This formula includes the Projected Units Sold and Revenue in rows 3 and 4 which is incorrect.

3. **Select** the range **B5:B11** and Confirm ✓ the entry.

    The result should be 273,250.

4. Use the fill handle **+** to copy the formula across the row.

    The completed row should match the following example.

12	Total Costs	273,250	728,250	1,157,000	3,534,125	4,993,500

Continued...

Calculate the Gross Profit in row 13

The Gross Profit is the Revenue in row 4 minus the Total Costs in row 12.

5. **Click** cell **B13** and enter the formula **=B4-B12**.

   The result should be -123,250 or (123,250). As you can see, the model shows us that Martin won't do well if he sells only 10,000 units.

6. Use the fill handle ✛ to copy the formula across the row.

   The completed row should match the following example.

13	Gross Profit	(123,250)	21,750	43,000	1,340,875	2,506,500

Calculate the Net Profit in row 14

The Net Profit is equal to the Gross Profit minus taxes. In this model, we will assume a flat tax rate of 35% as shown in cell F18.

*The Net Profit formula is Net Profit = Gross Profit * (1-TaxRate). For example, if the tax rate is 35%, then (1-TaxRate) = 65%. Martin gets to keep 65% of the gross profit and Uncle Sam gets 35%. You will use absolute references in the Net Profit formula when referencing the Tax Rate in cell F18. You will also use parentheses to change the order of calculations.*

7. **Click** cell **B14** and enter the formula **=B13*(1-$F$18)** exactly as shown.

   The result should be -80,113 or (80,113). This result makes no sense because Martin won't pay taxes if he loses money. However, we will leave it as it is for now. Notice the parentheses were required in the formula you just entered. You want Excel to subtract the Tax Rate in F18 from the number 1 first, then multiply the result by cell B13. The parentheses instruct Excel to perform that calculation first.

8. Use the fill handle ✛ to copy the formula across the row.

   The completed row should match the following example.

14	Net Profit	(80,113)	14,138	27,950	871,569	1,629,225

Calculate the Gross Profit vs. Revenue in row 15

In a previous lesson, you learned that the Gross Profit vs. Revenue ratio can be an important ratio in determining the health of a business. You will calculate this ratio in the following steps.

9. **Click** cell **B15** and enter the formula **=B13/B4**.

   The result should be -1 or (1). Notice there is no need to use absolute references in this formula.

10. Use the fill handle ✛ to copy the formula across the row.

    Cells C15 - F15 should have zeros in them. This is because the ratio returns a number between 0 and 1 and you must format the cells as percent in order to see the correct percentage.

11. **Select** cells **B15:F15**.

12. Use the Percent Style ⧆ button to format the numbers as percent.

    The completed row should match the following example.

15	Gross Profit Vs. Revenue	-82%	3%	4%	28%	33%

13. Save ⧆ the changes and continue with the next exercise.

Hands-On 7.9 – Format the numbers

1. Use the Currency Style button and the Decrease Decimal button to format rows **4** and **12-14** as currency with 0 decimals.

2. Add **bold** to the numbers in row **3**.

3. Use the Fill Color button to add color to rows **13** and **15**.

   The Gross Profit and Gross Profit vs. Revenue are important so we want them to stand out.

4. Format the worksheet in any other way you feel is necessary.

   At this point, your worksheet should match the worksheet shown below.

	A	B	C	D	E	F
1	**Crazy Words Financial Model**					
2						
3	Projected Units Sold	**10,000**	**50,000**	**100,000**	**500,000**	**1,000,000**
4	Revenue	$ 150,000	$ 750,000	$ 1,200,000	$ 4,875,000	$ 7,500,000
5	Manufacturing Cost	130,000	480,000	830,000	2,530,000	3,530,000
6	Marketing	104,500	122,500	136,000	246,250	325,000
7	Commissions	21,000	105,000	168,000	682,500	1,050,000
8	Office Expenses	750	3,750	6,000	24,375	37,500
9	Rent	12,000	12,000	12,000	36,000	36,000
10	Consulting Fees	5,000	5,000	5,000	15,000	15,000
11						
12	Total Costs	$ 273,250	$ 728,250	$ 1,157,000	$ 3,534,125	$ 4,993,500
13	Gross Profit	$ (123,250)	$ 21,750	$ 43,000	$ 1,340,875	$ 2,506,500
14	Net Profit	$ (80,113)	$ 14,138	$ 27,950	$ 871,569	$ 1,629,225
15	Gross Profit vs. Revenue	-82%	3%	4%	28%	33%
16						
17	Initial Selling Price	$15		Commission Rate		14%
18	Manufacturing Setup Cost	$30,000		Tax Rate		35%
19	Initial Manufacturing Unit Cost	$10		Office Expenses		0.50%

5. Save the changes and continue with the next exercise.

Hands-On 7.10 – Analyze the results and play what-if analysis

Analyze the model

1. Take a close look at the Gross Profit in row 13 and the Gross Profit vs. Revenue in row 15. Can you draw any conclusions from the numbers? Will Martin's business be healthy if the Projected Units Sold are less than 100,000?

   After analyzing the model, Martin realizes he will be quite wealthy if everything goes right and he sells 500,000 units or more. However, he also realizes this may not happen and he needs to protect his downside. He needs to make the business profitable even if only 10,000 units are sold. His goal is a Gross Profit vs. Revenue ratio of 10% at 10,000 units sold and 20% at 50,000 units and above.

Continued...

2. Take a moment to study the model.

Are there any ways that Martin can reduce his expenses and increase his profit? You may find an answer to this question by studying the model (including the comments in the Manufacturing Cost and Marketing cells).

Eliminate the infomercial expense from the Marketing cost
3. **Click** cell **B6**.

Look at the Formula bar and notice the 100,000 cost for developing the infomercial. Martin realizes the $100,000 infomercial is a bad idea. He decides to cancel the infomercial and concentrate on hiring sales people. You will make the necessary adjustments in the next few steps.

4. Type the new formula **=B4*2%** in the cell and confirm ✅ the entry.

The result should be 3,000. You reduced the percentage from 3% to 2% because Martin no longer needs to air the infomercial.

5. Use the fill handle **+** to copy the formula across the row.

Notice that eliminating the $100,000 infomercial has a huge impact on the Gross Profit and Gross Profit vs. Revenue. This is especially true when the units sold are 100,000 or less. However, the Gross Profit vs. Revenue is still less than 20% when the units sold are less than 100,000. You will find other ways to trim costs later in this exercise.

Edit the comment in cell A6
6. **Click** cell **A6** and choose **Insert**→**Edit Comment** from the menu bar.

7. **Select** all the text in the Comment box.

8. Type the phrase **Is equal to 2% of the revenue** and it will replace the selected text.

9. **Click** anywhere in the worksheet to confirm the change.

Perform what-if analysis

Martin realizes that the Manufacturing Setup Cost in cell B18 is prohibitively high. Also, the initial Manufacturing Unit Cost of $10 is high especially when the Units Sold are small. Martin decides to locate another manufacturer to help reduce these costs.

10. **Click** cell **B18**.

11. Enter the number **15000** and watch the impact this change has on the model.

Notice the entire model is recalculated. Pay close attention to the numbers in rows 13 and 15.

12. Now enter the number **10000** and notice the impact this change has.

13. Change the Initial Manufacturing Cost in cell **B19** from $10 to **$9**.

This should have a huge impact on the profitability of the business. As you can see, the model has shown us that keeping the manufacturing cost low is extremely important.

14. **Click** cell **F17** and change the commission rate from 14% to **10%**.

What kind of impact does this change have? Will reducing the commission rate have an impact on the number of units sold? As you can see, many of the variables are interdependent. However, the model shows us the impact of changing one or more variables.

15. Take 15 minutes to experiment with the model.

Try changing the variables in rows 17 - 19. Feel free to add comments to any cells and make any other changes you desire. Continue with the next topic when you have finished.

Displaying Formulas

Excel normally displays the results of formulas in worksheet cells. However, you may need to display the actual formulas from time-to-time. Displaying the formulas can be helpful especially in complex worksheets like the Crazy Words financial model. Displaying the formulas can help you understand how a worksheet functions. It can also be used to "debug" or locate problems.

Setting Options in Excel

The Tools→Options command displays the Options dialog box. The Options dialog box is used to display formulas and set other global options.

Hands-On 7.11 – Display formulas

Display the formulas and use Print Preview

1. Choose **Tools→Options...** from the menu bar.

2. Make sure the **View** tab is active on the dialog box.

3. Take a moment to study the options in the dialog box.

4. **Click** the ☑ Formulas check box and **click OK**.

    Excel will widen the worksheet columns and display the formulas.

5. Feel free to browse through the worksheet and check out the formulas.

    Notice how useful this technique could be if you wanted to understand how a worksheet functions. This technique is also useful for locating problems in formulas.

6. **Click** the Print Preview button.

7. Feel free to use the Next and Previous buttons to browse through the pages.

    Notice you could print the formulas if you needed to.

8. **Click** the **Close** button to exit from Print Preview.

Reset the options

9. Choose **Tools→Options...** from the menu bar.

10. Remove the check from the Formulas ☐ Formulas box and **click OK**.

    Your worksheet should be back to normal.

11. **Close** the workbook and **save** the changes.

    Continue with the end-of-lesson questions and exercises on the following pages.

Concepts Review

True / False

1. Absolute references continue to refer to the same cell even if the formula that contains them is moved.   1. **T F**

2. Formulas containing absolute references cannot be copied.   2. **T F**

3. Absolute references are identified by dollar signs.   3. **T F**

4. Absolute and relative references can be combined in the same formula.   4. **T F**

5. Cell comments are identified by a red triangle in the top-right corner of the cell.   5. **T F**

6. You must click a cell that contains a comment to make the comment pop up.   6. **T F**

7. Comments cannot be cleared.   7. **T F**

Multiple Choice

1. Which keystroke is used to convert a relative reference to an absolute reference?
    a) F1
    b) F2
    c) F4
    d) F8   (   )

2. Which command is used to create a new comment?
    a) Insert→Comment
    b) Format→Comment
    c) Edit→Comment
    d) None of the above.   (   )

3. Which command is used to edit a comment?
    a) Insert→Edit Comment
    b) Format→Comment
    c) Edit→Comment
    d) None of the above.   (   )

Skills Builder 7.1

In this exercise, you will create a worksheet that calculates commissions as Total Sales * Commission Rate. You will change the Commission Rate to see the impact the change has on the Total Sales. You will use an absolute reference when referencing the commission rate.

Set up the worksheet

1. **Click** the New Workbook ⬜ button.

2. Create the worksheet shown below.

    Type the Total Sales and Commission Rate as shown. You will also need to widen the columns.

	A	B	C
1	January Commission Report		
2			
3	Commission Rate		10%
4			
5		Total Sales	Commission
6	John	42000	
7	Ned	38000	
8	Ellen	65000	
9	Hellen	18000	
10	Bill	29000	

Create the Commission formula

3. **Click** cell **C6**.

4. Enter the formula **=B6*$C$3**.

    The result should be 4200. Do you understand why cell C3 must be referenced using an absolute reference? Once again, this is because you will copy the formula down the column and the copied formulas must refer to cell C3.

5. Use the fill handle ✛ to copy the formula down the column to cells C7-C10.

Adjust the commission rate

6. **Click** cell **C3** and change the percentage to **15%**.

    *By this time, you should see the benefit of setting up variables (such as the commission rate) and then referencing them in formulas. This gives you the ability to perform what-if analysis. Keep in mind that you will almost always need to use absolute references when referencing variables in this manner. Absolute references are necessary whenever you **copy** a formula that references a variable in a fixed location.*

7. Change the commission percentage back to **10%**.

8. **Close** the workbook and **save** it as **Skills Builder 7.1**.

Skills Builder 7.2

In this exercise, you will open a workbook from your exercise diskette. You will create a formula that uses a mixed cell reference. The column component of the reference will be relative but the row component will be absolute.

Enter the initial formula

1. Open the workbook named **Skills Builder 7.2**.

2. Take a moment to study the worksheet.

   The goal of this exercise is to create a formula in cell B6 that can be copied across rows 6, 9, 12 and 15. The formula in cell B6 will divide the Eastern Region's Q1 sales in cell B5 by the Q1 goal in cell B3. The general form of the formula will be =B5/B3. However, an absolute reference will be needed to allow you to copy the formula.

3. **Click** cell **B6** and enter the formula **=B5/B3**.

   The result should be 75%. The formula returned the correct result. However, you won't be able to copy the formula to other rows as you will see in the next few steps. Also notice cell B6 (and the other cells) have already been formatted with the proper currency and percent formats.

Try coping the formula without using absolute references

4. Make sure cell **B6** is active, then **click** the Copy button.

5. **Click** cell **B9** and **click** the Paste button.

   The result should be a huge percentage. This is obviously an incorrect result.

6. Look at the Formula bar and notice the formula in cell B9 is =B8/B6.

   Look at cells B8 and B6 and you will notice that B8 is the correct reference but B6 in incorrect. You must use an absolute reference if you want to copy the formula from cell B6.

7. **Click** Undo to reverse the copy.

Convert the reference in cell B6 to absolute
8. **Click** cell **B6**.

9. **Click** in the Formula bar just in front of the number **3** in the reference B3.

10. Type a dollar sign **$** in front of the number 3 to make the formula **=B5/B$3**.

11. Confirm the entry.

    Notice that only the row component ($3) of the B$3 reference is absolute. When you copy the formula across the row or to other rows, the reference to column B will be updated to C, D etc. This way, the formula will refer to the correct goal in row 3. The absolute reference to row 3, however, will not change because you used the dollar sign. This way, you can copy the formula to any row and the B$3 reference will refer to the correct cell in row 3.

Copy the formula across the rows

12. **Click** the Copy button.

13. **Select** cells **C6** through **E6** in row 6.

Continued...

14. Click the Paste button.

15. Notice the marquee is still flashing in cell B6.

You can continue to paste the formula as long as the marquee is flashing.

16. Select cells **B9:E9** in row 9.

17. Click the Paste button.

18. Paste the formula into the cells in rows **12** and **15**.

All you need to do is select the cells and click the Paste button.

19. Tap the Esc key to turn off the flashing marquee.

20. The completed worksheet is shown below.

	A	B	C	D	E
1	Regional Sales Results				
2		Q1	Q2	Q3	Q4
3	Goal	$1,000,000	$1,250,000	$1,500,000	$2,000,000
4					
5	Eastern Region	$750,000	$825,000	$1,400,000	$1,800,000
6	Percent of Goal	75%	66%	93%	90%
7					
8	Southern Region	$900,000	$1,100,000	$1,600,000	$1,950,000
9	Percent of Goal	90%	88%	107%	98%
10					
11	Central Region	$1,200,000	$1,300,000	$2,300,000	$1,800,000
12	Percent of Goal	120%	104%	153%	90%
13					
14	Western Region	$500,000	$1,250,000	$2,200,000	$3,000,000
15	Percent of Goal	50%	100%	147%	150%

Analyze the copied formulas and the absolute references

21. Take a moment to study the percentages shown above and notice they reflect the percentage of the goal (in row 3) that each region achieved.

22. Click cell **C9** and the formula =C8/C$3 should appear in the Formula bar.

Notice the C8 reference refers to the cell immediately above the formula. The C$3 reference is mixed. The C component refers to column C and the $3 component is absolute, so it will always refer to row 3. This mixed reference lets you copy the formula to any row and still have the reference refer to the proper goal in row 3.

23. Take as much time as necessary to study the worksheet and understand the importance of the absolute cell references.

24. Close the workbook when you have finished and **save** the changes.

Skills Builder 7.3

In this exercise, you will create a worksheet that calculates interest payments on a loan. You will set up the interest rate and loan amount as variables. This will allow you to easily adapt the worksheet for use with various loans. You will also create a pie chart to show the percentage of the payments that are applied to interest and the percentage that are applied to the principal.

Set up the worksheet

1. **Click** the New Workbook button.

2. Create the worksheet shown below.

   Just type in the Opening Balance and Interest Rate percentage as shown. Use the Alt + Enter keystroke combination to create the entries in cells B6 and C6. Widen the columns as needed.

	A	B	C	D
1	Loan Analysis			
2				
3	Opening Balance		10000	
4	Interest Rate		10%	
5				
6	Payment	Interest Paid	Principal Paid	Balance

Enter the formulas

3. **Click** cell **D7** and enter the formula **=C3**.

   This assignment formula sets up the opening balance for the loan. This way you can change the opening balance in cell C3 and create a whole new loan scenario.

4. **Click** cell **A8** and enter **500** as the first payment.

5. **Click** cell **B8**.

6. Type the formula **=D7*$C$4/12** and Confirm the entry.

   The result should be 83.3333... Notice this formula computes the interest. It multiplies the opening balance in D7 by the interest rate in C4. The result is divided by 12 because cell C4 contains an annual rate and the payments are monthly. Once again, the reference to cell C4 is absolute because you want the formula to continue to refer to this cell when it is copied down the column.

7. **Click** cell **C8** and enter the formula **=A8-B8**.

   The result should be 416.666...

8. **Click** cell **D8** and enter the formula **=D7-C8**.

   The result should be 9583.33. Notice this formula deducts the current payment's principle from the previous balance.

9. Use the Comma Style button to format row 8 as Comma with two decimals.

Copy the formulas down the columns and create totals

10. Use the Zoom Control to zoom to **75%** of normal.

    If necessary, adjust the zoom control until you can see 25 rows.

11. **Click** cell **A8**.

Continued...

12. Use the fill handle to **copy** the number **500** down to row **20**.

Cells A8:A20 should now have the number 500 in them.

13. Use the fill handle to copy the formulas in cells **B8**, **C8** and **D8** down to row 20.

You will need to complete all three columns before the formulas will calculate correctly.

14. Click cell **A22** and enter the word **Totals**.

15. Click cell **B22** and use AutoSum Σ to calculate the total Interest Paid.

The result should be 804.05. The AutoSum formula should be =SUM(B8:B21).

16. Use AutoSum Σ to calculate the total Principal Paid in cell **C22**.

The result should be 5,695.95.

17. Format cells **B22** and **C22** as Currency with **2** decimals and widen the columns if necessary.

Create an embedded pie chart
18. Select the **Interest Paid** and **Principal Paid** headings in cells **B6** and **C6**.

19. Press & Hold Ctrl while you **select** the total interest and principle in cells **B22** and **C22**.

20. Click the Chart Wizard button.

21. Choose the Pie Pie chart type and the 3-D sub-type.

22. Click Next > **twice** and the Step 3 of 4 box will appear.

23. If necessary, **click** the **Titles tab** and enter the title **Interest vs. Principal** as the Chart title.

24. Click the **Legend tab** and remove the check from the Show legend box.

The legend won't be needed because you will add data labels in the next step.

25. Click the **Data Labels tab** and choose the Show label and percent option.

26. Click the Finish button.

The Interest should equal 12% of the pie. This represents 12% of the total payments.

Play what-if analysis
27. Click cell **C4**.

28. Enter **15%** as the interest rate and watch the worksheet and chart change.

29. Click cell **C3** and enter **20000** as the opening balance.

30. Take a few minutes to experiment with your loan worksheet.

Try changing the opening balance in cell C3 and the interest rate in cell C4. Try entering new payment amounts in column A.

31. Close the workbook when you have finished and **save** it as **Skills Builder 7.3**.

Assessment 7.1

1. Use the following guidelines to create the worksheet shown below.

   – Type the text entries as shown in the worksheet below. Type the numbers in column B and the percentage in cell B3.

   – Use a formula to compute the discounted price in cell C6. Use an absolute reference when referring to the discount rate in cell B3. Remember that you are trying to calculate the discounted price, which means your formula must subtract the discount rate in B3 from 1. The generic formula is Discounted Price = Original Price * (1 - Discount Rate).

   – Copy the formula in cell C6 down the column.

2. Format the cells with the Currency format shown.

3. Sort the worksheet rows so they are in ascending order by column A.

4. Change the percentage in cell B3 to 10% and watch the worksheet recalculate.

5. Change the percentage in cell B3 to 15% and watch the worksheet recalculate.

6. The completed worksheet is shown below (although your worksheet rows will be sorted and the percentage in cell B3 will be 15%).

7. **Print** the worksheet when you have finished.

8. **Close** the workbook and **save** it as **Assessment 7.1**.

	A	B	C
1	Price Change Worksheet - January		
2			
3	January Discount Rate	20%	
4			
5	Item	Original Price	Discounted Price
6	Track & Walk Footwear	$34.50	$27.60
7	Action Aerobics Wear	$19.00	$15.20
8	Designer Jeans	$50.00	$40.00
9	Sherman Cowboy Boots	$67.95	$54.36
10	Jensen Back Packs	$34.55	$27.64
11	Rain n Shine Coats	$45.00	$36.00
12	Diamond Back Socks	$2.95	$2.36
13	Steck-Harman Shirts	$19.95	$15.96
14	Back Country Jeans	$24.95	$19.96

Assessment 7.2

1. Open the workbook named **Assessment 7.2**.

2. Insert the following comment into cell **A3**.

> This table includes the commission rates and bonuses for all sales reps in all quarters. All sales reps listed here were paid the same commission rates and bonuses in 1996.

3. Use the following guidelines to calculate the compensation in rows 9, 13, 17 and 21.

    - Create the compensation formula **=B8*B4+B5** in cell B9. Notice the compensation is calculated as the Sales * Commission Rate + Bonus.

    - Take a few minutes to study the formula and try to understand what will happen when you copy the formula to another row or cell. The references are relative, so they will continue to refer to cells in the same location relative to the original formula.

    - Edit the formula in the Formula bar and turn the row components of both the B4 and B5 references into absolute references. This is the same technique you used in Skills Builder 7.2.

    - Copy the formula across row 9, 13, 17 and 21. The results are shown in the worksheet below.

    - Use the Format Painter to copy the currency style from any cell in the Sales rows to the Compensation rows. You can copy from one cell to all four rows if you double-click the Format Painter initially.

4. Create the Total Sales and Total Compensation rows shown in the worksheet below.

5. **Print** the worksheet when you have finished, then **close** it and **save** the changes.

	A	B	C	D	E
1	Sales Rep Compensation Worksheet - 1996				
2					
3		Q1	Q2	Q3	Q4
4	Commission Rates	8%	10%	12%	15%
5	Bonuses	$2,000	$3,000	$5,000	$10,000
6					
7	Bev Hart				
8	Sales	$85,000	$56,000	$35,000	$127,000
9	Compensation	$8,800	$8,600	$9,200	$29,050
10					
11	Liz Davidson				
12	Sales	$45,000	$67,000	$87,000	$34,000
13	Compensation	$5,600	$9,700	$15,440	$15,100
14					
15	Milton Jones				
16	Sales	$56,000	$23,000	$87,900	$65,780
17	Compensation	$6,480	$5,300	$15,548	$19,867
18					
19	Alex Sheraton				
20	Sales	$45,000	$78,000	$62,890	$65,900
21	Compensation	$5,600	$10,800	$12,547	$19,885
22					
23	Total Sales	$231,000	$224,000	$272,790	$292,680
24	Total Compensation	$26,480	$34,400	$52,735	$83,902

Assessment 7.3

1. Use the following guidelines to create the financial model shown below.

   – Type the headings, labels and numbers shown in column A and rows 1-4.

   – Use formulas to calculate the numbers in rows 6-9. The formulas should multiply the revenue in row 4 by the variables in rows 15-19. For example, the employee costs in cell B6 are calculated as the Revenue in cell B4 multiplied by the percentage in cell B15. Use absolute references in these formulas when referring to the variables, so that you can copy the formulas across the rows. You must use absolute references in order to get full credit for this assessment!

   – Use AutoSum to calculate the Total Costs in row 10.

   – Calculate the Gross Profit in row 12 as the Revenue - Total Costs.

   – Calculate the Net Profit in row 13 as the Gross Profit * (1 - Tax Rate). Once again, use absolute references when referring to the Tax Rate in cell B19.

   – Format the numbers and text entries as shown.

2. Play what-if analysis with your model by changing the variable percentages in rows 15-19. You may want to demonstrate this to your instructor. Make sure the model recalculates correctly when the variables are changed.

3. **Print** your model when you have finished, then **close** it and **save** it as **Assessment 7.3**.

	A	B	C	D	E
1	1997 Projected Income				
2					
3		Q1	Q2	Q3	Q4
4	Revenue	$345,000	$390,000	$480,000	$500,000
5					
6	Employee Costs	62,100	70,200	86,400	90,000
7	Capital Expenditures	75,900	85,800	105,600	110,000
8	Manufacturing	58,650	66,300	81,600	85,000
9	Marketing & Sales	55,200	62,400	76,800	80,000
10	Total Costs	$251,850	$284,700	$350,400	$365,000
11					
12	Gross Profit	$93,150	$105,300	$129,600	$135,000
13	**Net Profit**	**$55,890**	**$63,180**	**$77,760**	**$81,000**
14					
15	Employee Costs	18%			
16	Capital Expenditures	22%			
17	Manufacturing	17%			
18	Marketing & Sales	16%			
19	Tax Rate	40%			

Critical Thinking 7.1

David is a graduating high school senior who will be entering college in the fall. Create a worksheet that determines how much additional money David will need from his parents each year while he is attending college. David will receive $6,500 per year in grants, $2,500 in scholarships and $1,000 for work-study. David also anticipates having a summer job but he is unsure how much it will pay. David's expenses include $10,500 per year tuition, $5,000 for room and board, $1,250 for books and supplies and $1,800 for personal expenses. David expects his annual expenses to increase by 5% per year. Your worksheet should compute the amount his parents will need to contribute in each of the next four years. Include a variable field for David's first year summer employment income. Assume his summer employment income will increase by 10% per year after the first year. The worksheet should recalculate his parent's contributions each time you change the estimated income from his first summer's employment.

Critical Thinking 7.2

Create a financial model for Berkeley Bicycles – a retailer of racing and mountain bicycles. Your model should calculate the projected gross profit, net profit and gross profit vs. revenue for each quarter of 1998. Use the following guidelines when creating your model.

- **Revenue** – Assume Berkeley Bicycles receives revenue from bicycle sales and accessory sales. List these revenue sources as separate items in the worksheet. You are responsible for approximating the revenue in each quarter.

- **Expenses** – Expenses include employees, building, insurance, inventory, advertising and any other items you feel should be added to the model. You are responsible for approximating the expenses in each quarter.

- **Variables** – Your model should recalculate the gross profit, net profit and gross profit vs. revenue whenever certain variables change. The variables you should use are tax rate and advertising as a percentage of revenue. The tax rate should be used in the calculation of net profit and advertising is an expense. Also, build a factor into the model that assumes a new employee will be added when revenues reach a certain threshold. You should determine both the employee costs and the revenue thresholds.

- **Absolute References** – Use absolute references whenever possible so that formulas can be copied.

Close the workbook when you have finished and save it with a descriptive name.

Critical Thinking 7.3

Use Excel to create an important date calculator for use at home or the office. Your calculator should calculate the number of days until important events occur. Important events can be dates such as your birthday, the arrival of a new baby, Christmas etc. The calculator should automatically calculate and display the number of days until each important event whenever the calculator worksheet is opened. Make sure you include at least five important dates/events. You will need to use the TODAY() function at some place in the calculator. Insert the TODAY function in one cell and then reference that cell in the formulas that calculate the number of days to the event(s). Use an absolute reference when referencing the TODAY function so that you can copy the formula to other cells.

8 Working with Multiple Sheet Workbooks

Objectives:

- ◆ Create links between cells in different worksheets

- ◆ Create linking formulas

- ◆ Make copies of a worksheet

- ◆ Copy text and number formats between worksheets

- ◆ Create and use cell names

- ◆ Use the Name list to go to a named cell

- ◆ Change and delete cell names

- ◆ Protect worksheets and workbooks

- ◆ Unlock cells in protected worksheets

- ◆ Use 3-D selecting and formatting techniques

- ◆ Print multiple sheet workbooks

The Project - Folsom Technical College Budget Tracking

In this lesson, you will help the Folsom Technical College track their 1996 Federal grant and budget allocations. The school receives an annual federal grant, which is then allocated to various budget categories. Janice Milton, the school's director, wants a workbook that tracks the year-to-date expenditures and consolidates the information on a master worksheet. The master sheet will provide summary information and it will give Janice an instant overview of how their expenditures compare to their budget allocations. The workbook will be dynamic. The master sheet will be linked to detail sheets where all the necessary detail information will be stored. The illustration below shows the master sheet and three detail sheets that you will create in this lesson.

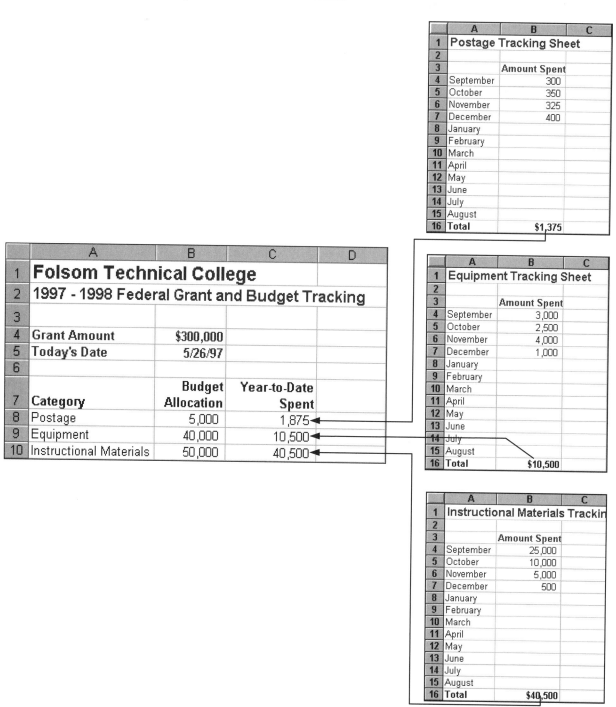

Linking Cells

Excel lets you link cells between different worksheets and between different workbooks. Linking lets you reflect values from a "source" worksheet into a "destination" worksheet. This powerful capability is the glue that binds worksheets together.

Linking lets you set up summary and detail worksheets

Linking is often used to feed totals from detail worksheets into a summary or master worksheet. This way, you can keep detailed information in the detail sheets and see the totals or the "big picture" in the summary sheet. This capability reflects the needs of many organizations. For example, top level managers are usually interested in seeing the "big picture" whereas detailed information is needed at the departmental level. The illustration on the previous page shows three detail sheets feeding data into a master sheet. Notice the Totals on the detail sheets are reflected in the master sheet.

Linking Formulas

You link cells together by inserting linking formulas in the destination worksheet. Linking formulas specify which cells in the source worksheet the data should be taken from. You must use the correct syntax when creating linking formulas. The following illustrations show examples of linking formulas between cells in the same workbook and between cells in different workbooks.

This formula is inserted into a cell in a destination worksheet. The exclamation point ! separates the sheet name Postage from the cell name B16. The number in cell B16 of the Postage sheet will be reflected into the cell in the destination sheet that contains this formula.

=Postage!B16

This formula also specifies a filename (which is surrounded by square brackets). This type of formula lets you link cells between different workbooks.

='[Federal Grant - 95.xls]Postage'!B16

You can type linking formulas or create them using point mode

You can type linking formulas or use the mouse to create them in point mode. You have been creating formulas with point mode throughout this text. The exercises in this lesson will show you how to type linking formulas and how to create them using point mode.

Hands-On 8.1 – Open a workbook and check it out

In this exercise, you will open a workbook that contains a master sheet and a detail sheet.

1. Open ☑ the workbook named **Hands-On Lesson 8**.

2. **Click** cell **B4** and notice this cell contains the number $300,000.

   This is the amount of the Federal grant that Folsom Technical College was awarded for the 1997 - 1998 school year. Their objective is to allocate this grant to several budget categories and then track their actual expenditures throughout the year. The Director Janice Milton, wants up-to-date information on how their expenditures compare to their budget forecasts.

3. **Click** cell **B5** and notice this cell contains the TODAY function.

   This cell will always display the current date.

4. Notice the categories in column A and the budget allocations in column B.

   The budget allocations add up to $300,000 as shown in cell B19. As you can see, the budgets are equal to the total grant of $300,000.

5. Notice the cells in column C will contain the Year-to-Date Spent numbers.

   The detail sheets will track the year-to-date expenditures for each category. The cells in column C will be linked to the year-to-date expenditure totals in the detail sheets.

6. Notice column D.

   The Available Balance in column D will be the difference between the Budget Allocation in column B and the Year-to-Date Spent numbers in column C. Column D will show how much budget is available for each category.

7. **Click** the **Postage** sheet tab.

   Each month the total amount spent on postage will be entered into a cell in column B. Cell B16 will contain a SUM function that will sum up all cells in the column. Cell B16 will be linked to cell C8 in the Master sheet.

8. **Click** the **Master** sheet tab.

   Notice cell C8 will contain the Year-to-Date Spent amount for postage. Once again, this cell will be linked to cell B16 in the Postage sheet.

9. Feel free to study this workbook more closely, then continue with the next exercise.

Hands-On 8.2 – Create a link to the Postage sheet

Enter data and a SUM formula in the Postage sheet

1. **Click** the **Postage** sheet tab.

2. Enter the three numbers shown below into column B.

	A	B
1	Postage Tracking Sheet	
2		
3		Amount Spent
4	September	300
5	October	350
6	November	325

3. **Click** cell **B16** and use AutoSum Σ to compute the column total.

   The total should be 975. You want AutoSum to sum the entire range B4:B15. This way, AutoSum will keep a running total as you enter data throughout the year.

Type the linking formula

4. **Click** the **Master** sheet tab.

5. **Click** cell **C8**.

6. Type the formula **=Postage!B16** and Confirm ✔ the entry.

   Make sure you type the formula exactly as shown including the exclamation mark!. The number 975 should appear in cell C8. Notice the formula instructs Excel to link to cell B16 in the Postage sheet. The exclamation mark simply separates the two arguments.

Add the December postage and watch the linked cell update

7. **Click** the **Postage** tab.

8. **Click** cell **B7**.

9. Enter the number **400** and the SUM formula in cell B16 should display the number 1,375.

10. **Click** the **Master** sheet tab and cell C8 should now display 1375.

    Links are dynamic and the cell that contains the link (the destination cell) will always reflect the current value from the source cell. In the next exercise, you will format cell C8 with a comma style.

11. Take a few moments to study the worksheets before continuing.

Hands-On 8.3 – Delete the link and recreate it using point mode

Delete the link

1. **Click** the **Master** sheet tab.

2. **Click** cell **C8** and **tap** the ⎡Delete⎤ key to remove the linking formula.

    You can delete linking formulas just as you delete any other formula.

3. Make sure the highlight is in cell C8.

Recreate the link using point mode

4. Type an equal = sign.

    Excel will display the equal sign in the Formula bar.

5. **Click** the **Postage** sheet tab.

    Excel will display the Postage sheet and the sheet name Postage will appear in the Formula bar followed by an exclamation point.

6. **Click** cell **B16** and the completed linking formula =Postage!B16 will appear in the Formula bar.

7. Confirm ✅ the entry and Excel will display the Master sheet with the completed link in cell C8.

    Once again, the result should be 1375. Notice that point mode works the same way with linking formulas as it does with other formulas. Excel understands that you want to create a linking formula the moment you click the sheet tab after typing an equal sign.

Calculate the Available Balance in cell D8 and format cell C8

8. **Click** cell **D8** and enter the formula **=B8-C8**.

    The result should be 3,625.

9. **Click** cell **B8** and use the Format Painter 🖌 to copy the Comma style to cell **C8**.

10. Save 💾 the changes and continue with the next topic.

Working with Multiple Sheet Workbooks

Copying Worksheets

The Folsom grant and budget workbook will eventually have several worksheets with the same structure as the Postage sheet. For example, each sheet will have a title in cell A1 and monthly totals for September through August will be entered in column B. Excel makes it easy to copy entire worksheets. You can then modify the titles and data in the copied sheet while leaving the formulas and overall structure intact.

Copying a sheet with the Select All button and the Copy and Paste buttons

The easiest way to copy a worksheet is to click the Select All button at the top-left corner of the worksheet. You can then use the Copy and Paste commands to copy and paste the sheet.

Hands-On 8.4 – Make three copies of the Postage sheet

In this exercise, you will make three copies of the Postage worksheet. The copies will become three new sheets named Equipment, Instructional Materials and Mileage.

Create the Equipment sheet
1. **Click** the **Postage** sheet tab.

2. **Click** the Select All button at the top-left corner of the worksheet.
   The entire worksheet will become selected.

3. **Click** the Copy button.

4. **Click** the **Sheet3** sheet tab.

5. Make sure the highlight is in cell A1, then **click** the Paste button.
   The entire Postage sheet should be copied to Sheet3.

6. **Double-click** the **Sheet3** tab and rename the sheet **Equipment**.

Edit the title and numbers in the Equipment sheet
7. **Double-click** cell **A1** and the insertion point will be positioned in the cell.
   You learned how to do in-cell editing in an earlier lesson.

8. Use the Delete and/or BackSpace keys to remove the word **Postage**.

9. Type the word **Equipment** and Confirm the change.
   The title should now read Equipment Tracking Sheet.

10. Change the numbers in cells B4:B7 as shown below.

	A	B
1	Equipment Tracking Sheet	
2		
3		Amount Spent
4	September	3,000
5	October	2,500
6	November	4,000
7	December	1,000

Continued...

197

Create both the Instructional Materials and Mileage sheets.

11. **Click** the Select All [ ] button on the Equipment sheet.

12. **Click** the Copy [ ] button.

13. **Click** the **Sheet4** sheet tab.

14. **Click** the Paste [ ] button.

15. **Click** the **Sheet5** sheet tab.

16. **Click** the Paste [ ] button.

   Notice you can paste multiple copies of a sheet once it has been copied to the clipboard.

Rename the sheets and edit the contents

17. Rename **Sheet4** as **Instructional Materials** and rename **Sheet5** as **Mileage**.

18. Edit the titles and numbers in the Instructional Materials and Mileage sheets as shown below.

	A	B	C
1	Instructional Materials Tracking Sheet		
2			
3		Amount Spent	
4	September	25,000	
5	October	10,000	
6	November	5,000	
7	December	500	

	A	B
1	Mileage Tracking Sheet	
2		
3		Amount Spent
4	September	2,000
5	October	1,700
6	November	1,280
7	December	1,000

19. Save [ ] the changes and continue with the next exercise.

Copying Formats Between Worksheets

The Format Painter can be used to copy text and number formats between worksheets. This technique creates consistent formatting between worksheets. You can copy the formats from one cell or a range of cells to another worksheet. You can also copy the formats of an entire worksheet. This technique is useful provided the sheets have the same structure.

Hands-On 8.5 – Format the Postage sheet and copy the formats to other sheets

In this exercise, you will format the text and number entries in the Postage sheet. You will use the Format Painter to copy the formats to the three worksheets you just created.

Copy individual formats from the Master sheet to the Postage sheet

1. **Click** the **Master** sheet tab.

2. **Click** cell **A2**.

    You will copy the text formats from this subheading to the heading in the Postage sheet.

3. **Click** the Format Painter.

4. **Click** the **Postage** sheet tab.

5. **Click** cell **A1** and the formats will be copied to that cell.

    Cell A1 should have the same dark blue color and size as the subheading in the Master sheet. Notice you can switch to any sheet after the Format Painter has been activated.

6. **Click** the **Master** sheet tab, then **click** cell **A4**.

7. **Click** the Format Painter, then **click** the **Postage** sheet tab.

8. **Click** cell **B3** to copy the formats to that cell.

9. **Click** the **Master** sheet tab and **select** cells **A19** and **B19** as shown below.

10. **Click** the Format Painter.

11. **Click** the **Postage** sheet tab and **select** cells **A16** and **B16** as shown below.

    The bold formatting and the Currency number format should be copied to the cells.

Copy all formats from the Postage sheet to the Equipment sheet

The Postage, Equipment, Instructional Supplies and Mileage sheets all have an identical structure and format. This common structure enables you to use the Format Painter to copy all formats from one sheet to another. The Format Painter will copy all text and number formats and it will even copy column widths and row heights to the other sheets.

12. Make sure the Postage sheet is active, then **click** the Select All button.

    The entire Postage sheet should be selected.

13. **Click** the Format Painter.

Continued...

14. Click the **Equipment** sheet tab.

15. Click the Select All [ ] button (even though it appears to be depressed).

16. Click anywhere in the worksheet to deselect it.

The entire sheet should have the same formatting as the Postage sheet. Notice how this technique creates consistent formatting between worksheets (provided they have an identical structure).

Copy all formats from the Equipment sheet to the Instructional Materials and Mileage sheets

17. Click the Select All [ ] button on the Equipment sheet.

18. Double-click the Format Painter [ ].

Double-clicking the Format Painter lets you copy the formats as many times as desired.

19. Click the **Instructional Materials** sheet tab, then **click** the Select All [ ] button.

Notice the Format Painter is still active.

20. Click the **Mileage** sheet tab, then **click** the Select All [ ] button.

21. Click the Format Painter [ ] to deactivate it.

22. Click anywhere in the worksheet to deselect it.

Take a few moments to check out the various sheets and the formatting should be consistent.

Edit the Mileage sheet
23. Click the **Mileage** sheet tab.

24. Click cell **B3**, change the heading to **Mileage**, and then **click** Align Right [ ].

The numbers in column B are the number of miles that have been driven in a given month. You will add another column to compute the actual Mileage Expense. The Mileage Expense is calculated as the number of miles multiplied by a cost of 32 cents per mile.

25. Click cell **C3** and enter the heading **Mileage Expense**.

26. Click cell **C4** and enter the formula **=B4*.32**.

The result should be 640.

27. Use the fill handle ✚ to copy the formula down the column as far as row 15.

Some of the cells will display a 0 because column B is not yet complete.

28. Use AutoSum [Σ] to compute the total mileage in cell **C16**.

Format the Mileage sheet

29. Use the Format Painter [ ] to copy the formats from cell **B3** to **C3** and from **B16** to **C16**.

You may need to widen column C after copying the formats.

30. Use the Format Painter [ ] to copy the Comma format from cell **B4** to cell **B16**.

*Notice the Total Mileage should **not** have a Currency format.*

31. Now add Bold [B] to cell **B16**.

Your next task will be to link the Master sheet with the three worksheets you just created and formatted. You will learn how to name cells and use the names to simplify the linking formulas.

Cell Names

Excel lets you assign a name to any cell or range of cells. For example, you could assign the name **Postage** to cell B16 in the Postage sheet. Cell names can be used in a variety of ways, as you will learn on the following pages.

Cell names can be used in formulas

Cell names can be used in formulas in place of cell references. For example, cell B16 in the Postage sheet contains the linking formula =Postage!B16 (where Postage is the sheet name and B16 is the cell reference). If you assigned the name PostageTotal to cell B16, then you could use the linking formula =PostageTotal instead of the more complicated formula =Postage!B16.

Cell names are available throughout the workbook

You can use cell names anywhere in a workbook. This is convenient because you can assign a name in one sheet and then use the name in any other sheet. You will use this technique to create linking formulas throughout the Folsom Technical College workbook.

Creating Names with the Name Box

The Name box is located on the left end of the Formula bar. The Name box usually displays the reference of the active cell. When the cell has been assigned a name, however, the name is displayed in the Name box. You can easily name a cell by clicking in the Name box and typing the desired name. The name is assigned when you tap the Enter key.

Rules for creating cell names

Cell names can have up to 255 characters although you will want to keep your names much shorter than that. Also, cell names cannot contain spaces. If necessary, use the underscore _ character as a substitute for spaces. For example, use the name **Instructional_Materials** as opposed to **Instructional Materials**.

Hands-On 8.6 – Name the Total cells in the detail sheets

In this exercise, you will create descriptive names for the Totals in the detail sheets. You will use the names to create linking formulas in the next exercise.

Name the Total cell in the Equipment sheet

1. **Click** the **Equipment** sheet tab, then **click** cell **B16**.

2. Use the following Hands-On Illustration to name the cell.

    ❶ *Click in the Name box at the left end of the Formula bar and the B16 reference will become selected.*

    ❷ *Type the name **Equipment** (it will replace B16) and tap **Enter**.*

    | B16 | ▼ | = | =SUM(B4:B15) |

3. **Click** anywhere in the worksheet (other than cell B16).

4. **Click** cell **B16** and the name Equipment will appear in the Name box.

    The Name box displays the cell name or reference of the current cell.

Continued...

Name the Total cells in the Instructional Materials and Mileage sheets

5. **Click** the **Instructional Materials** sheet tab, then **click** cell **B16.**

6. **Click** in the **Name** box.

7. Type **Instructional_Materials** (be careful not to use a space) and **tap** ⎣Enter⎦.

   The underscore _ character is inserted by pressing Shift and tapping the hyphen - key. Don't use a blank space because Excel won't accept it.

8. **Click** the **Mileage** sheet tab, then **click** cell **C16**.

9. **Click** in the Name box and enter the name **Mileage**.

Using the Name List

The drop-down button on the right-side of the Name box displays the Name list. The Name list displays all cell names in the workbook. You can rapidly move the highlight to a named cell by choosing the name from the list.

Hands-On 8.7 – Go to a named cell

1. Use the following steps to go to the cell named Equipment.

   ❶ **Click** *the Name List button.* ———

   ❷ *Choose* **Equipment**. ———

   Notice Excel displays the Equipment sheet and positions the highlight in the Equipment cell.

2. Use the steps shown above to go to the cell named **Instructional_Materials**.

Hands-On 8.8 – Use cell names to create linking formulas

Create a linking formula by typing the cell name

1. **Click** the **Master** sheet tab, and then **click** cell **C8**.

   Notice this cell contains the linking formula =Postage!B16. You created this link in an earlier exercise. In the remainder of this exercise, you will create links to the Totals in the other three sheets. However, you will use cell names in the linking formulas instead of using sheet names and cell references as you did in cell C8.

2. **Click** cell **C9**.

3. Type the formula **=Equipment** and Confirm ☑ the entry.

   The number 10500 should appear. This is the total from cell B16 of the Equipment sheet.

   Continued...

4. **Click** the Name List ▾ button and choose **Equipment**.

   Excel will position the highlight in cell B16 of the Equipment sheet. Notice the total is 10500.

Create a linking formula using point mode
5. **Click** the **Master** sheet tab.

6. **Click** cell **C10**.

7. Type an equal = sign.

8. **Click** the **Instructional Materials** sheet tab.

9. **Click** cell **B16** and confirm ✓ the entry.

   The formula =Instructional_Materials appears in the Formula bar. The result should be 40500.

Create the last linking formula
10. **Click** cell **C11**.

11. Type **=Mileage** and confirm ✓ the entry.

    The result should be 1913.6. Keep in mind that these links are dynamic. If the totals change in the detail sheets, then the Master sheet will change as well.

Format cells C9:C11 and copy the Available Balance formula
12. **Click** cell **C8**, then **click** the Format Painter 🖌.

13. **Select** cells **C9:C11** to copy the Comma style to those cells.

14. Use the fill handle to copy the Available Balance formula from cell **D8** to cells **D9:D11**.

Changing and Deleting Cell Names

You can change and delete cell names after they have been created. However, formulas that use the cell names will not work after the names have been changed or deleted. You will need to recreate any linking formulas that used the changed or deleted names. For this reason, you should choose cell names carefully when you create them. Cell names are changed and deleted with the **Insert→Name→Define...** command.

Hands-On 8.9 – Change the Instructional_Materials name

In this exercise, you will change the Instructional_Materials cell name to Instructional. You will also recreate the linking formula that used the Instructional_Materials cell name.

Rename the Instructional_Materials cell

1. Make sure the Master sheet is active.

2. **Click** the Name List button and choose **Instructional_Materials**.

3. Choose **Insert→Name→Define...** from the menu bar.

4. Use the following step to add the name Instructional and delete the name Instructional_Materials.

❶ *Choose* **Instructional_Materials** *and it will appear in the Names in Workbook box.*

❷ *Click in this box and use the Delete and/or Backspace keys to delete the text* _Materials*. Only the word Instructional should remain as shown here.*

❸ *Click the Add button to add Instructional to the list.*

❹ *Choose* **Instructional_Materials** *from the list and click the Delete button.*

❺ *Click OK.*

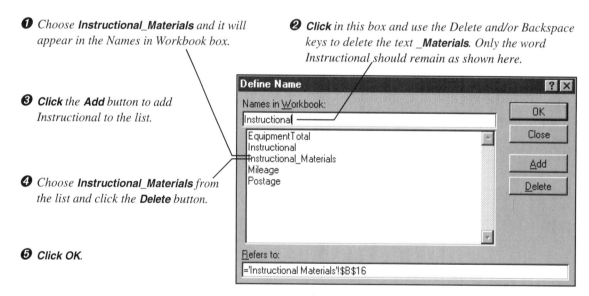

5. **Click** the Name List button and notice the name Instructional is now assigned to cell B16.

   Also notice the name Instructional_Materials is no longer available. You must always use the technique demonstrated in step 4 if you want to change a cell name.

Repair the formula in the Master sheet
6. **Click** the **Master** sheet tab.

7. Notice a #NAME? message appears in cells C10 and D10.

   This message indicates that a formula is referencing a cell name that no longer exists. You will correct this by replacing the formula in cell C10.

8. **Click** cell **C10** and enter the formula **=Instructional**.

   The result should once again be 40,500. The formula in D10 is dependent on C10, so it will return the correct result (9,500) once the formula in C10 is corrected.

Hands-On 8.10 – Create a Salaries sheet

In this exercise, you will create a new worksheet to track employee salaries. You will create cell names that will eventually be used to link the year-to-date salaries into the Master sheet.

Copy the Postage sheet to the Salaries sheet

1. **Double-click** the **Sheet6** tab and rename the sheet as **Salaries**.

2. **Click** the **Postage** sheet tab.

   You will copy the Postage sheet to the Salaries sheet in the next few steps. This will form the structure of the Salaries sheet, which you will then modify.

3. **Click** the Select All ▭ button at the top-left corner of the Postage sheet.

4. **Click** the Copy 🗐 button.

5. **Click** the **Salaries** sheet tab, then **click** cell **A1**.

   The highlight must be in cell A1 if you wish to paste an entire sheet.

6. **Click** the Paste 🗐 button to paste the Postage sheet.

7. **Click** anywhere in the sheet to deselect it.

Edit the Salaries sheet

8. Use the following guidelines to edit the Salaries sheet as shown below.

   – *Edit the text entries including the title and add new columns and numbers as shown.*

   – *Copy the SUM formula from cell B16 across the row to cells C16:F16.*

   – *Use the Format→Column→Width... command to widen columns B-F to 10.*

   – *Use the Format Painter to copy the text and comma formats from column B to columns C-F.*

	A	B	C	D	E	F
1	Salary Tracking Sheet					
2						
3		Connie	Alicia	Thomas	Mildred	Burt
4	September	3,500	2,750	3,400	4,250	4,200
5	October	3,750	3,250	3,450	3,850	3,450
6	November	4,200	3,800	3,400	2,900	3,480
7	December	4,000	3,750	3,400	3,450	3,490
8	January					
9	February					
10	March					
11	April					
12	May					
13	June					
14	July					
15	August					
16	Total	$15,450	$13,550	$13,650	$14,450	$14,620

9. Save 🖫 the changes and continue with the next exercise.

Hands-On 8.11 – Name the cells in the Salaries sheet and create linking formulas

Name the cells

1. Make sure the Salaries sheet is active, then **click** cell **B16**.

2. Use the following steps to name cell B16.

   ❶ **Click** *in the Name box and the*   ❷ *Type the name* **Connie_Salary** *and tap* **Enter**.
   reference B16 will become selected.

   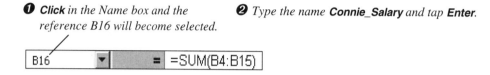

3. Name cells C16:F16 as shown in the following table.

Cell	Use this name
C16	Alicia_Salary
D16	Thomas_Salary
E16	Mildred_Salary
F16	Burt_Salary

Create links in the Master sheet

4. **Click** the **Master** sheet tab.

5. **Click** cell **C14**.

   Cell C14 needs to be linked to the Connie_Salary cell.

6. Enter the formula **=Connie_Salary** and the result should be 15450.

7. Use the names you just created to link cells C15, C16, C17 and C18 to the Salaries sheet.

8. Use the Format Painter [icon] to copy the Comma style format from cell **C11** to cells **C14:C18**.

Copy the Available Balance formula to rows 14-18

9. **Click** cell **D11**.

10. **Click** the Copy [icon] button.

11. **Select** cells **D14:D18** and **click** the Paste [icon] button.

12. Now use the fill handle to copy the Total formula from cell **B19** to cells **C19** and **D19**.

   The completed Master sheet should match the example on the following page (except for the date).

Continued...

	A	B	C	D
1	**Folsom Technical College**			
2	**1997 - 1998 Federal Grant and Budget Tracking**			
3				
4	Grant Amount	$300,000		
5	Today's Date	5/25/97		
6				
7	Category	Budget Allocation	Year-to-Date Spent	Available Balance
8	Postage	5,000	1,375	3,625
9	Equipment	40,000	10,500	29,500
10	Instructional Materials	50,000	40,500	9,500
11	Mileage	5,000	1,914	3,086
12				
13	Salaries			
14	Connie	42,000	15,450	26,550
15	Alicia	40,000	13,550	26,450
16	Thomas	40,000	13,650	26,350
17	Mildred	38,000	14,450	23,550
18	Burt	40,000	14,620	25,380
19	Total	$300,000	$126,009	$173,991

Take a few minutes to study the work you have completed thus far in this lesson. In particular, try to understand how the Master sheet functions. The number in cell C19 reflects the total expenditures year-to-date. The number in cell D19 shows how much of the $300,000 grant is still available. All the numbers in the Year-to-Date Spent column are linked to the detail sheets.

13. Feel free to add additional data to the January, February etc. rows in the detail sheets.

The Master sheet will reflect the updated expenditures and Totals.

You will continue to enhance the workbook throughout this lesson.

Using Row and Column Titles to Create Cell Names

You can rapidly name a group of cells using existing row and/or column titles as the names. You accomplish this by selecting both the titles and the cells that you wish to assign the names to. These cells will normally be adjacent to the title cells. You then use the **Insert→Names→Create...** command to create the names. You will use this technique in the following exercise.

Hands-On 8.12 – Assign names to the budgeted amounts in the Master sheet

In this exercise, you will assign names to each of the budgeted amounts for the employees in column B of the Master sheet. You will use these names to create linking formulas in the Salaries sheet. The linking formulas will reflect the budgets from column B of the Master sheet.

Create names for the employee budgets

1. Make sure the Master sheet is active.

2. **Select** the range **A14:B18** as shown below.

    You will use the Name Create command to assign the employee names to cells B14:B18.

14	Connie	42,000
15	Alicia	40,000
16	Thomas	40,000
17	Mildred	38,000
18	Burt	40,000

3. Choose **Insert→Name→Create...** from the menu bar.

    The Create Names dialog box appears. The check boxes let you specify which cells should be used for the names. In this example, the cells in the Left Column (column A) will be used to name the cells in column B. For this reason, the Left Column box should be checked.

4. Make sure the Left Column ☑ Left Column box is checked and **click OK**.

5. **Click** cell **B14** and notice the word Connie appears in the Name box.

    This cell was assigned the name Connie.

6. **Click** the Name List ▼ button and notice the names Alicia, Thomas, Mildred and Burt now appear on the list (although you may need to scroll to see them).

7. **Click** cell **B15** and notice this cell has been assigned the name Alicia.

Insert links in the Salaries sheet

8. **Click** the **Salaries** sheet tab.

9. **Click** cell **A17** and enter the word **Budget**.

10. **Click** cell **B17** and enter the formula **=Connie**.

    The number 42000 should appear. This is the budget amount for Connie from the Master sheet.

11. Enter the formula **=Alicia** in cell **C17**.

12. Create the same type of linking formulas in cells **D17**, **E17** and **F17**.

13. Save 🖫 the changes and continue with the next topic.

Protection Options

Excel lets you protect the structure of workbooks and the contents of cells. Protecting a workbook prevents structural changes from being made such as the deletion of worksheets. Likewise, protected cells cannot be edited or formatted. The protection options prevent your workbooks from being accidentally or intentionally modified. Protection is often applied to complex workbooks that would be difficult to recreate.

Protecting Worksheets and Workbooks

You can protect individual worksheets or entire workbooks with the **Tools**→**Protection** commands. Excel lets you use a password when protecting worksheets or workbooks. The password prevents others from removing the protection. You must be careful when using a password because you will not be able to remove the protection yourself if you forget the password.

Hands-On 8.13 – Protect the Master sheet

In this exercise, you will protect the Master sheet. The Master sheet can be protected because there is no need to modify it or enter data into it. The Master sheet also contains important data and formulas such as the grant and budget numbers which you will want to prevent others from changing.

1. **Click** the **Master** sheet tab.

2. Make sure the Master sheet is complete and it is functioning properly.

    You should always make sure a sheet is completed before protecting it. This way you won't need to unprotect and re-protect it if you need to change it at a later time.

3. Choose **Tools**→**Protection**→**Protect Sheet...** from the menu bar.

4. Take a moment to check out the Protect Sheet dialog box.

    Notice you could enter a password (although you will not use a password in this exercise). There are also several options in the dialog box, which are not discussed at this time.

5. **Click OK**.

6. **Click** any cell in the worksheet and try typing in a new number.

    Excel will display a message box indicating the cell can't be changed.

7. **Click OK** to close the message box.

Unprotect the sheet
8. Choose **Tools**→**Protection**→**Unprotect Sheet...** from the menu bar.

    The Unprotect option appears on the Protection menu after a sheet has been protected.

9. **Click** any empty cell in the worksheet and enter any number or text.

    Notice the unprotected sheet can be edited once again.

10. **Click** Undo 🔄 to reverse the editing change.

11. Use the **Tools**→**Protection**→**Protect Sheet...** command to reprotect the sheet.

12. Save 💾 the changes and continue with the next topic.

Unlocking Cells in a Protected Worksheet

Excel lets you unlock or unprotect specific cells within a protected worksheet. Unlocked cells can be edited even though the overall worksheet is protected. This way, you can protect important formulas and the structure of the sheet while allowing data entry in less important parts of the sheet. You must unlock the cells before protecting the worksheet.

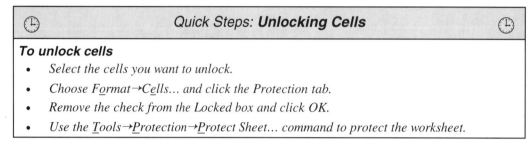

*Quick Steps: **Unlocking Cells***

To unlock cells
- *Select the cells you want to unlock.*
- *Choose Format→Cells... and click the Protection tab.*
- *Remove the check from the Locked box and click OK.*
- *Use the Tools→Protection→Protect Sheet... command to protect the worksheet.*

Hands-On 8.14 – Unlock cells in the Postage and Salaries sheets

In this exercise, you will unlock several cells in the Postage and Salaries sheets. Finally, you will protect the sheets to prevent the formulas and overall structure from being changed.

Unlock cells in the Postage sheet
1. **Click** the **Postage** sheet tab.

2. **Select** the range **B4:B15.**

    This range includes all cells in column B between the Amount Spent heading and cell B16.

3. Choose **Format→Cells...** from the menu bar and **click** the **Protection** tab.

4. Remove the check from the Locked ☐ Locked box and **click OK**.

    This action will have no effect on your sheet until you protect it in the next step.

Protect the sheet and enter data
5. Use the **Tools→Protection→Protect Sheet...** command to protect the sheet.

6. **Click** cell **B16** and try typing in the cell.

    A message box will appear because this cell is protected.

7. **Click OK** to close the message box.

8. **Click** cell **B8** and enter any number.

    Excel lets you enter the number because you unlocked the cell prior to protecting the sheet.

Unlock cells and protect the Salaries sheet
9. **Click** the **Salaries** sheet tab and **select** the range **B4:F15.**

10. Choose **Format→Cells...** from the menu bar.

11. Remove the check from the Locked box and **click OK**.

12. Protect the worksheet.

    All cells in this sheet will now be protected except for the data entry cells in the range B4:F15.

13. Save 🖫 the changes and continue with the next topic where you will protect the last three sheets.

3-D Selecting and Formatting

Excel provides a number of commands and techniques to let you modify more than one worksheet at the same time. These commands and techniques are known as 3-D (three-dimensional) because worksheets are stacked on top of one another in a 3-D format. 3-D commands are most effective when all the affected worksheets have the same structure. For example, the Equipment, Instructional Materials and Mileage worksheets all have the same structure. The key to using 3-D commands is to select all the desired worksheets before issuing a command. This way, all the selected worksheets are affected when the command is issued. You select multiple worksheets by pressing the ⌐Ctrl⌐ key and clicking the sheet tabs of the desired sheets. You will use this technique in the following exercise.

Hands-On 8.15 – Unlock the same range of cells in the three remaining sheets

1. **Click** the **Equipment** sheet tab.

2. **Press & Hold** the ⌐Ctrl⌐ key while you **click** the **Instructional Materials** sheet tab.

    Both the Equipment and Instructional Materials tabs will appear white in color.

3. Continue to hold ⌐Ctrl⌐ while you click the **Mileage** sheet tab.

    Now all three tabs will be white, which indicates they are all selected. Any commands you issue in the Equipment sheet will be applied to the same range of cells in the other two sheets.

4. **Release** the ⌐Ctrl⌐ key, then **select** the range **B4:B15** in the Equipment sheet.

    You will unlock the cells in the next step.

5. **Click** the **Instructional Materials** sheet tab, then **click** the **Mileage** sheet tab and notice the range B4:B15 is selected in those sheets as well.

6. Use the **F**ormat→**C**ells... command to Unlock the cells.

    The three sheets should still be selected.

7. Choose **T**ools→**P**rotection from the menu bar and the Protect Sheet option will be ghosted out.

    The 3-D selection techniques let you issue commands that affect ranges of cells. However, some commands such as Protect Sheet are not available when multiple sheets are selected.

8. **Click** anywhere in the worksheet to close the menu.

9. **Click** the **Postage** sheet tab and the three sheets will no longer be selected.

10. **Click** the **Equipment** sheet tab and use the **T**ools→**P**rotection→**P**rotect Sheet... command to protect just that sheet.

11. Protect the **Instructional Materials** sheet and then protect the **Mileage** sheet.

12. Try entering data in the Equipment, Instructional Supplies and Mileage sheets and you will notice the cells in the range B4:B15 of each sheet are unlocked.

    All other cells in the sheets will be locked.

13. Take as much time as necessary to study the work you have done in this workbook.

    You will learn how to print multiple sheet workbooks on the following pages. This has been a long project and a good review of the techniques we have covered thus far, will serve you well.

Printing Multiple Sheet Workbooks

In an earlier lesson, you used the Page Setup commands to adjust the margins, headers and footers, page orientation and other elements of a printed worksheet. The Page Setup options only impact the selected worksheet(s). You can apply the Page Setup options to multiple worksheets but you must select the desired sheets first. In the previous topic, you learned how to select multiple sheets with the Ctrl key.

Deciding Which Sheets to Print

Excel prints only the current sheet or the selected sheets when you click the Print button. If you want to print more than one sheet, then you should use the Ctrl key to select the desired sheets before clicking the Print button. You can also print all sheets by choosing File→Print... from the menu bar. You can then choose the Entire Workbook option in the Print dialog box.

Hands-On 8.16 – Use Print Preview to check out the printing options

Display only the Master sheet in Print Preview

1. **Click** the **Master** sheet tab.

2. **Click** Print Preview.

   Notice the Next button is unavailable. Excel only displays the selected sheet(s) in Print Preview.

3. **Close** the **Print Preview** window.

Select all six sheets and display them in Print Preview

4. **Press & Hold** the Ctrl key, then **click** the **Postage** sheet tab.

   Both the Master and Postage sheets should be selected.

5. Continue to hold Ctrl while you **click** the other four sheet tabs.

   All six sheets should be selected.

6. **Click** Print Preview.

7. Use the Next button to browse through the worksheets.

   Notice that all six sheets are available because you selected them prior to clicking Print Preview.

   These same sheets would be printed if you had clicked the Print button instead of Print Preview. Also notice the header and footer on the sheets. The name of each sheet is included in the header and the page number is included in the footer. You could create a new header or footer and it would impact all six sheets (because they are selected).

Check out the Print dialog box

8. **Click** the Print... button.

   Notice the Active Sheets option is chosen. You can also use the Entire Workbook option to print all sheets in a workbook.

9. **Click** the **Cancel** button to exit from the Print dialog box.

   You will print multiple page workbooks in the exercises on the following pages.

10. **Close** the workbook and **save** the changes.

Concepts Review

True / False

1. Linking formulas are inserted in the source worksheet.

2. Linking formulas can be typed or created using point mode.

3. The Format Painter can be used to copy formats between worksheets.

4. The Select All ▢ button can be used to select an entire worksheet.

5. It is OK to use spaces in cell names.

6. It is OK to use the underscore _ character in cell names.

7. Cell names can only be used in the worksheet they were created in.

8. Linking formulas begin with an equal = sign.

9. You can go to a named cell by choosing the name from the Name list.

10. You must unlock cells after a worksheet has been protected if you want to be able to edit those cells.

1. **T   F**
2. **T   F**
3. **T   F**
4. **T   F**
5. **T   F**
6. **T   F**
7. **T   F**
8. **T   F**
9. **T   F**
10. **T   F**

Multiple Choice

1. Which of the following procedures can be used to create a cell name?
   a) Click the desired cell, click in the Name box, type the desired name and tap Enter.
   b) Click the desired cell and type the desired name.
   c) Click the desired cell, click in the Name box, type the desired name and click the Confirm ✓ button.
   d) None of the above.

   (   )

2. How many characters can be used in a cell name?
   a) Up to 35
   b) Up to 255
   c) Up to 18
   d) None of the above.

   (   )

3. Which command is used to change or delete a cell name?
   a) Insert→Name→Create
   b) Tools→Name→Create
   c) Insert→Name→Define
   d) None of the above.

   (   )

4. Which command is used to create cell names from existing column or row titles?
   a) Insert→Name→Create
   b) Tools→Name→Create
   c) Insert→Name→Define
   d) None of the above.

   (   )

5. Which key must be held down if you want to select multiple worksheets?
   a) Shift
   b) Ctrl
   c) Alt
   d) None of the above.

   (   )

Skills Builder 8.1

In this exercise, you will open a workbook that contains one worksheet. You will copy the worksheet twice to create three identical worksheets. You will then format the worksheets and use the Format Painter to ensure consistent formatting between the sheets.

Copy the worksheet and rename and edit the sheets

1. **Open** the workbook named **Skills Builder 8.1**.

2. **Click** cell **B10** and use the following steps to compute the average for column B.

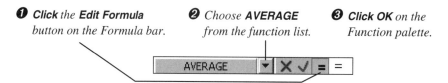

❶ **Click** *the* **Edit Formula**   ❷ *Choose* **AVERAGE**   ❸ **Click OK** *on the*
    button on the Formula bar.   *from the function list.*   *Function palette.*

3. **Copy** the formula across the row.

4. **Click** the Select All button, then Copy the sheet to the clipboard.

5. **Click** the **Sheet2** tab and Paste the sheet.

6. **Paste** the sheet into **Sheet3**.

7. Rename the sheets as **Test1**, **Test2** and **Test3**.

8. Change the headings in row 3 of the Test2 and Test3 sheets to **Test 2** and **Test 3**.

9. Change a few of the numbers in the Test2 and Test3 sheets so the sheets contain different data.

Format the Test1 sheet and copy the formats

10. **Click** the **Test1** tab, then **click** cell **A1**.

11. Increase the font size to **14** and apply a color to the text.

12. **Click** cell **A3**, increase the size to **12** and apply the same color as in the previous steps.

13. Format the Average row in any way you desire.

14. **Click** the Select All button to select the entire sheet.

15. **Double-click** the Format Painter.

16. **Click** the **Test2** sheet tab.

17. **Click** the Select All button to copy the formats to that sheet.
    Once again, you were able to copy the formats in this manner because the sheets are identical.

18. **Click** the **Test3** sheet tab and **click** Select All to copy the formats to that sheet.

19. Turn the Format Painter off by **clicking** it.

20. **Close** the workbook and **save** the changes.

Skills Builder 8.2

In this exercise, you will create a workbook that contains four worksheets. The master sheet will be linked to three source sheets. You will also create two charts in the main sheet.

Create the master sheet

1. Open a New ⬜ workbook.

2. Create the worksheet shown below and widen columns **A-E** to **15**. You can widen the columns by selecting them and then using the **Format→Column→Width...** command.

	A	B	C	D	E
1	1996 Sales - Consolidated Systems, Inc.				
2					
3		Q1	Q2	Q3	Q4
4	Eastern Region				
5	Central Region				
6	Western Region				
7	Total Sales				

3. Rename the sheet as **National**.

Create the first source sheet

4. **Rename** Sheet2 as **Eastern Region** and create the worksheet shown below. Type the numbers shown in rows 4-7 and use AutoSum to compute the Total Sales in row 8. Make sure you format the cells as shown and widen the columns to **15**.

	A	B	C	D	E
1	1996 Sales - Eastern Region				
2					
3		Q1	Q2	Q3	Q4
4	Boston	500,000	350,000	340,000	300,000
5	New York	560,000	450,000	280,000	700,000
6	Atlanta	700,000	325,000	450,000	650,000
7	Miami	650,000	600,000	200,000	230,000
8	Total Sales	$2,410,000	$1,725,000	$1,270,000	$1,880,000

5. Save 💾 the workbook as **Skills Builder 8.2** and continue with the next step.

Copy the Eastern Region sheet to sheets 4 and 3

6. **Click** the **Sheet3** tab and choose **Insert→Worksheet** from the menu bar.

   A new worksheet named Sheet4 will appear.

7. **Click** the **Eastern Region** sheet tab.

8. **Click** the Select All ⬜ button and Copy 📋 the sheet to the clipboard.

9. **Click** the **Sheet4** tab and Paste 📋 the copied sheet.

10. **Click** the **Sheet3** tab and Paste 📋 the sheet again.

11. Rename Sheet4 as **Central Region** and rename Sheet3 as **Western Region**.

Continued...

Edit the Central Region and Western Region sheets

12. **Click** the **Central Region** sheet tab.

13. Change the title to **1996 Sales - Central Region**.

14. Change the city names to **Chicago, Dallas, St. Louis** and **Denver**.

15. Change all the numbers in row 4 to **500,000** by **clicking** in cell **B4** and **dragging** the fill handle three cells to the right.

    This will make the numbers slightly different from those in the Eastern Region sheet.

16. **Click** the **Western Region** sheet tab.

17. Change the title to **1996 Sales - Western Region** and change the city names to **Los Angeles, San Francisco, Phoenix** and **Seattle**.

18. Enter the number **800,000** in cell **B4**, then use the fill handle to copy the number to the next three cells to the right.

Name the cells in the detail sheets

19. **Click** the **Eastern Region** sheet tab, then **click** cell **B8**.

20. **Click** in the Name box on the left end of the Formula bar.

21. Type the name **Eastern_Q1** and **tap** ⌷Enter⌷.

22. Assign names to the Total Sales cells in the Eastern, Central and Western sheets. Use the same naming convention as in the previous step. For example, use the name Eastern_Q2 for cell C8 in the Eastern sheet and Central_Q1 for cell B8 in the Central sheet.

Create linking formulas in the National sheet

23. **Click** the **National** sheet tab, then **click** cell **B4**.

24. Enter the linking formula **=Eastern_Q1**.

    The number 2410000 should appear in cell B4.

25. Create links in rows 4, 5 and 6 to the three detail sheets. You may want to copy the formula in cell B4 across the row and then edit the formula in each cell by simply changing the Q1 to Q2 etc.

Complete the National sheet

26. Use AutoSum Σ to compute the Total Sales in row 7 of the National sheet.

27. Format the numbers in rows 4 - 6 as Comma with 0 decimals and format the totals in row 7 as Currency with 0 decimals. You may want to use the Format Painter 🖌 to copy the formats from one of the detail sheets.

Create a column chart and pie chart in the National sheet

28. Create the column and pie charts shown on the next page.

    Notice the column chart compares each region's numbers in the various quarters. The pie chart compares the contributions of each region to the total sales for the year. To create the pie chart, you will need to add column F as shown on the next page.

Continued...

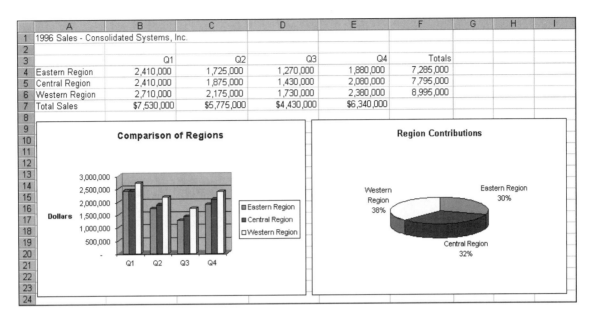

	A	B	C	D	E	F	G	H	I
1	1996 Sales - Consolidated Systems, Inc.								
2									
3		Q1	Q2	Q3	Q4	Totals			
4	Eastern Region	2,410,000	1,725,000	1,270,000	1,880,000	7,285,000			
5	Central Region	2,410,000	1,875,000	1,430,000	2,080,000	7,795,000			
6	Western Region	2,710,000	2,175,000	1,730,000	2,380,000	8,995,000			
7	Total Sales	$7,530,000	$5,775,000	$4,430,000	$6,340,000				
8									
9									

Change numbers in the Eastern Region sheet and watch the charts change

Notice the Eastern Region percentage in the pie chart is currently 30%. This number will change when you change numbers in the Eastern detail sheet in the next few steps.

29. Click the **Eastern Region** sheet tab and **click** cell **B4**.

30. Enter the number **1,000,000** and **copy** it across the row.

This will make the Eastern numbers substantially larger than they were.

31. Click the **National** sheet tab and notice how the Eastern Region pie chart percentage is now 37%.

Format the National sheet and copy the formats to the other sheets

32. Format the title in row 1, the headings in row 3 and the Total Sales in row 7 of the National sheet. Use whichever font sizes, colors and/or borders you feel are attractive.

33. Select rows **1-3** of the Master sheet by dragging the mouse pointer ⇩ down the row headings.

34. Double-click the Format Painter 🖌.

35. Click the **Eastern Region** sheet tab then **select** rows **1-3** by dragging the mouse pointer ⇩ down the row headings.

The formats from the National sheet should be copied to rows 1-3. Notice you were able to copy the formats because rows 1-3 have the same structure in the two sheets.

36. Click the **Central Region** sheet tab and **paint** the formats to rows 1-3 of that sheet.

37. Paint the formats to rows 1-3 of the Western Region sheet.

38. Paint 🖌 the formats from row **7** of the National sheet to row **8** of the detail sheets.

39. Feel free to modify and format the worksheets in any way you desire.

Continued...

Select all four sheets and add a header

In the next few steps, you will create a header on all four sheets. You will display the Page Setup dialog box directly from the worksheet with the File→Page Setup command. You must display the Page Setup dialog box from the worksheet if you want the Page Setup options to impact all the selected sheets. The Page Setup options will not impact all the selected sheets if you display the dialog box from Print Preview.

40. **Press & Hold** Ctrl and **click all four sheet tabs** (National - Western Region).

41. Choose **File→Page Setup...** from the menu bar.

42. **Click** the **Header/Footer** tab, then **click** the **Custom Header** button.

43. Type the text **Folsom Technical College** in the Left Section box.

44. **Click** in the **Center Section** box and **click** the Sheet Name button.

    The &[Tab] code will appear. This code places the sheet name in the header.

45. **Click** in the **Right Section** box and **click** the Date button.

    The &[Date] code will appear. This code places the date in the header.

46. **Click OK** to complete the header, then **click** the Print Preview button on the dialog box.

47. Use the Next button to browse through the pages.

    Notice the National sheet is split by a page break. You will correct this soon. Also notice the header appears on all pages.

48. **Close** the **Print Preview** window.

Change the National sheet to Landscape orientation
49. **Click** the **National** sheet tab.

    The other sheet tabs will be deselected.

50. Choose **File→Page Setup...** from the menu bar.

51. **Click** the **Page** tab.

52. Set the orientation to **Landscape** and **click OK**.

Use Print Preview
53. **Select** all four sheet tabs (you will need to use the Ctrl key).

54. **Click** Print Preview.

55. Use the Next button to browse through the pages.

    The National sheet should be the only sheet with a Landscape orientation. This is because it was the only sheet tab selected when you set the Landscape orientation.

56. **Close** the **Print Preview** window.

57. Feel free to modify the worksheet in any way you desire. Try experimenting with the print options in the Page Setup dialog box.

58. **Close** the workbook when you have finished and **save** the changes.

Assessment 8.1

1. Use the following guidelines to create a new workbook with the three worksheets shown below.
   - Enter the numbers and data shown into three separate sheets. However, do not enter the numbers in rows 6 and 7 of the master sheet because you will insert linking formulas in those cells. Use AutoSum to compute the Totals in all three sheets.
   - Name the master sheet **Both Stores** and name the detail sheets **Eastside Store** and **Westside Store**.
   - Create cell names for each Total in row 11 of the detail sheets. Name the Totals in the Eastside sheet Eastside_January, Eastside_February and Eastside_March. Use a similar naming convention for the Westside sheet.
   - Create links in rows 6 and 7 of the master sheet to the Totals in the detail sheets.
   - Format the titles, headings and numbers as shown. Make sure you use consistent formatting across the worksheets. You can use the Format Painter to ensure consistent formatting. Use whichever font color you desire.
   - Your completed worksheets should match the worksheets shown below.

	A	B	C	D
1	**Jane's Collectibles**			
2				
3	**January - March Sales**			
4				
5		January	February	March
6	Eastside Store	18,250	16,050	16,800
7	Westside Store	23,450	19,000	21,900
8	**Totals**	**$ 41,700**	**$ 35,050**	**$ 38,700**

	A	B	C	D	E
1	**Jane's Collectibles - Eastside Store**				
2					
3	**January - March Sales**				
4					
5		January	February	March	
6	Dolls	5000	3450	4500	
7	Spoons	1,500	3,400	3,700	
8	Figurines	2,750	2,000	2,300	
9	Antiques	5,600	4,500	3,400	
10	Crystal	3,400	2,700	2,900	
11	**Totals**	**$ 18,250**	**$ 16,050**	**$ 16,800**	

	A	B	C	D	E
1	**Jane's Collectibles - Westside Store**				
2					
3	**January - March Sales**				
4					
5		January	February	March	
6	Dolls	7,500	4,000	6,000	
7	Spoons	2,000	4,000	5,000	
8	Figurines	2,950	3,000	3,700	
9	Antiques	6,000	5,000	4,000	
10	Crystal	5,000	3,000	3,200	
11	**Totals**	**$ 23,450**	**$ 19,000**	**$ 21,900**	

2. You may want to demonstrate the linking formulas to your instructor by changing a number in one of the detail sheets and watching the numbers change in the master sheet.

3. **Print** all three sheets when you have finished.

4. **Close** the workbook and **save** it as **Assessment 8.1**.

Assessment 8.2

1. Use the following guidelines to create a new workbook with the four worksheets shown below.

   – Enter the numbers and data shown below into four separate sheets. You will need to insert one new worksheet. However, don't enter the Transactions in column D of the summary worksheet. These Transaction numbers will be linked to the monthly transaction sheets.

   – Use AutoSum to compute the Totals in all four sheets.

   – Name the master sheet **Transaction Summary** and name the detail sheets **January**, **February** and **March**.

   – Create cell names for each Total in cell C10 of the detail sheets. Name the Total in cell C10 of the January sheet January_Total. Likewise, name the Totals in the February and March sheets February_Total and March_Total.

   – Create links in column D of the summary sheet to the Totals in the detail sheets. Use the cell names from the detail sheets in the linking formulas.

   – Format the titles, headings and numbers as shown. Make sure you use consistent formatting across the detail worksheets. You can use the Format Painter to ensure consistent formatting. Use whichever font color you desire.

   – Your completed worksheets should match the worksheets shown below.

	A	B	C	D
1	1997 Visa Card Transaction Summary			
2				
3	Month	Finance charge	Payment	Transactions
4	January	120	900	315.55
5	February	85	100	431.30
6	March	90	100	275.90
7	April			
8	May			
9	June			
10	July			
11	August			
12	September			
13	October			
14	November			
15	December			
16	Total	$295.00	$1,100.00	$1,022.75

	A	B	C
1	January Transactions		
2			
3	Date	Description	Amount
4	1/2/97	BayView Health Club	35.00
5	1/7/97	Bob's Pizza	14.90
6	1/9/87	Century Cinemas	34.90
7	1/14/97	William's AutoCare	230.75
8			
9			
10	Total		$315.55

	A	B	C
1	February Transactions		
2			
3	Date	Description	Amount
4	2/2/97	BayView Health Club	35.00
5	2/4/97	Southeast Airlines	230.00
6	2/8/97	Western Dental	120.50
7	2/16/97	Mel's Diner	45.80
8			
9			
10	Total		$431.30

	A	B	C
1	March Transactions		
2			
3	Date	Description	Amount
4	3/2/97	BayView Health Club	35.00
5	3/6/97	Home Depot	40.90
6	3/23/97	Aetna Insurance	200.00
7			
8			
9			
10	Total		$275.90

2. You may want to demonstrate the linking formulas to your instructor by changing a number in one of the detail sheets and watching the numbers change in the summary sheet.

3. **Print** all four sheets when you have finished.

4. **Close** the workbook and **save** it as **Assessment 8.2**.

 **Templates and Graphics**

Objectives:

- Understand template concepts

- Create templates from existing workbooks

- Use templates as the basis for new workbooks

- Understand template organization

- Use clip art

- Move and size clip art

- Use drawing objects

The Project – Tradewinds Race Results Template

In this lesson, you will help Tom Davidson, Manager of the Tradewinds Sailing Club, develop an Excel template. The template will form the basis of new workbooks for reporting race results. Tom wants all race result reports to have a common look and feel. He wants the company logo and other formatting enhancements to appear at the top of all reports. The best way to achieve this is to use a template as the basis for new workbooks. You will create the template and workbook shown below. You will use Excel's drawing objects to enhance the workbook as shown below.

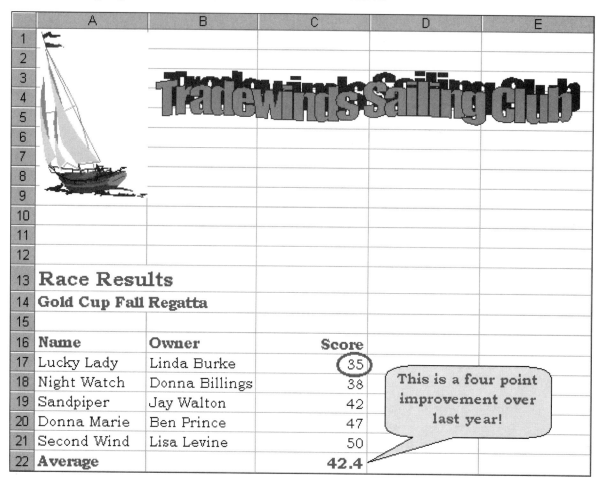

Templates

Templates form the basis of new workbooks. Templates can include text, numbers, formulas, macros and virtually any formatting you desire. Excel provides several ready-to-use templates. You can also create your own customized templates. Customized templates can be very useful because you can create a template with the formatting and features you use most often.

Templates are used as the basis for new workbooks

You can use a template as the basis for a new workbook. The template remains unchanged when the workbook is modified and saved. This lets you use a template over-and-over as a basis for new workbooks.

Creating and editing templates

You create new templates by creating a workbook with the formatting and features you desire and then saving the workbook as a template. Excel also lets you edit existing templates. You can edit both the ready-to-use templates provided by Excel and the customized templates you have created. This way, you can continually modify a template until it precisely meets your needs.

Hands-On 9.1 – Set up the Tradewinds race results template

In this exercise, you will begin creating a workbook that will form the basis of the Tradewinds race results template. The workbook will contain a picture, WordArt, text and several formatting options.

Change the default font and column widths

Tom Davidson, Manager of the Tradewinds Sailing Club, wants race result worksheets to have wider columns and a different font than the default settings Excel normally uses. In the next few steps, you will widen the columns and change the default font for the entire workbook.

1. Start Excel or use the New Workbook ⬚ button to open a new workbook.

2. **Click** the Select All ⬚ button to select the entire worksheet.

3. Use the Formatting toolbar to set the font to **Bookman Old Style** size **11** as shown below.

   Use another font if Bookman Old Style is unavailable.

4. Use the **F**ormat→**C**olumn→**W**idth... command to set the width to **16** for the entire worksheet.

   Continue with the next topic where you will add WordArt and a picture to the workbook.

Using Clip Art

Excel lets you insert clip art anywhere in a worksheet. You can use clip art that is provided with Microsoft Office or you can insert your own clip art (such as a company logo). Clip art is inserted with the **Insert→Picture** command.

Microsoft Office Clip Gallery

Microsoft provides a number of clip art images with Microsoft Office. These clip art images are installed as part of Office 97. All Office 97 programs (including Excel) can use the clip art. Office 97 also has a Clip Gallery feature, which makes it easy to manage the clip art and other graphics on your system. You will use Clip Gallery to insert clip art in the following exercise.

Hands-On 9.2 – Insert clip art

Tom wants the sailing club's logo to appear in the template. In this exercise, you will insert and size a clip art image. The clip art you will insert should be in the Clip Gallery. If it isn't, then you will need to install it with the Microsoft Office installation CD ROM.

1. **Click** cell **A1**.

2. Choose **Insert→Picture...** from the menu bar.

    Notice the Clip Art and From File options. The Clip Art option displays the Clip Gallery dialog box. The Clip Gallery is a convenient way to organize and manage your clip art. The From File option lets you insert pictures that are located on any disk drive on your system.

3. Choose **Clip Art...** and use the following steps to insert an image.

    ❶ *Notice the dialog box tabs. The Clip Gallery lets you organize Clip Art, Pictures (such as scanned in pictures), Sound and Video. You can use any of these elements in Office 97 documents. Make sure the Clip Art tab is chosen.*

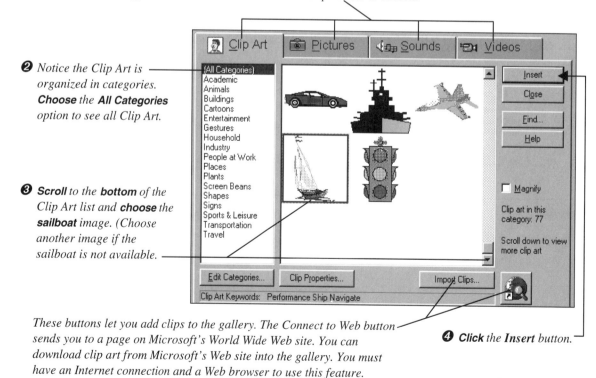

❷ *Notice the Clip Art is organized in categories.* **Choose** the **All Categories** *option to see all Clip Art.*

❸ **Scroll** *to the* **bottom** *of the Clip Art list and* **choose** *the* **sailboat** *image. (Choose another image if the sailboat is not available.*

❹ **Click** *the* **Insert** *button.*

These buttons let you add clips to the gallery. The Connect to Web button sends you to a page on Microsoft's World Wide Web site. You can download clip art from Microsoft's Web site into the gallery. You must have an Internet connection and a Web browser to use this feature.

Continued...

Excel will insert the picture and the Picture toolbar will appear. If the picture toolbar didn't appear, then you can display it with the Vīew→Toolbars command.

Reduce the size of the picture

Notice the picture has sizing handles (small squares) on its edges. You change the size of pictures by dragging the sizing handles. This is the same technique you used to change the size of charts. Sizing handles appear whenever you click a picture.

4. Use the following step to reduce the size of the picture.

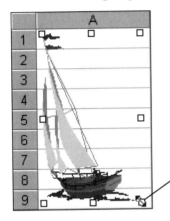

❶ *Drag this **sizing handle** up and left until the picture fits in the range A1:A9 as shown here. (You may need to drag the Picture toolbar out of your way.)*

5. **Click** outside the picture and it will be deselected.

The Picture toolbar will also close.

6. **Click** the **picture** and the Picture toolbar will reappear.

Remove the border from the picture

Your picture may have a border surrounding it. You will remove the border in the following steps.

7. **Click** the Line Style ▤ button on the Picture toolbar.

8. Choose **More Lines...** from the bottom of the menu.

The Format Picture dialog box appears. This dialog box lets you adjust a variety of picture options.

9. **Click** the Colors and Lines tab and use the following steps to remove the line.

❶ *Click the **Color** button in the Line section of the dialog box.*

❷ *Choose **No Line** and **click OK.***

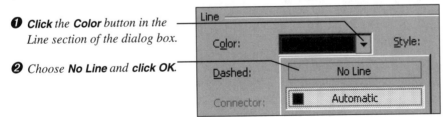

10. Feel free to experiment with the buttons on the Picture toolbar.

You can adjust the contrast, brightness and other aspects of the picture.

11. When you have finished experimenting, feel free to **click** the Reset Picture 🖼 button on the right-end of the Picture toolbar.

This will restore the original settings of the picture. You will need to reduce the size of the picture as shown above if you use the Reset Picture button.

Drawing Objects

Excel has an excellent set of drawing objects that let you create lines, arrows, rectangles, callouts, WordArt and many other objects. These objects are easy-to-use and a lot of fun! The drawing objects are particularly useful for emphasizing areas of interest on worksheets and charts.

Working with drawing objects

You create drawing objects by choosing the desired object from the Drawing toolbar and then dragging the mouse in the document. Drawing objects can also be edited and formatted after they have been created.

Hands-On 9.3 – Use WordArt

In this exercise, you will use WordArt. WordArt lets you create stylized text in a variety of shapes, colors and formats.

1. Locate the Drawing button on the Standard toolbar. This button displays or hides the Drawing toolbar that is shown below. The Drawing toolbar is usually docked at the bottom of the screen. If necessary, click the Drawing button to display the drawing toolbar. The following illustration discusses the layout of the Drawing toolbar.

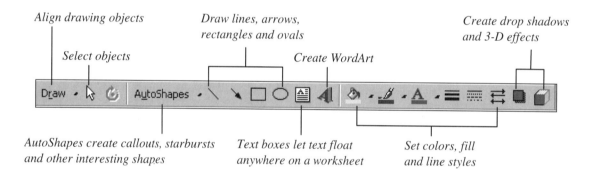

2. **Click** the WordArt button on the Drawing toolbar.

   The WordArt Gallery dialog box appears.

3. Choose a WordArt style (the examples in this book uses the style in the fourth-column, fourth-row) and **click OK**.

   The Edit WordArt text dialog box appears. This box lets you type the desired WordArt text and it lets you change the typeface and point size of the text.

4. **Type** the phrase **Tradewinds Sailing Club.**

5. Feel free to choose a typeface (the example in this book uses Impact) and **click OK**.

   The WordArt object is inserted in your worksheet and the WordArt toolbar appears. Be aware that your WordArt text may look different from the example in this book if you changed the typeface.

Continued...

6. Use the following steps to position and size the object.

❶ Reduce the size of the image by dragging a corner-sizing handle.

❷ Position the mouse pointer on the image and drag it to the top of the worksheet.

❸ Continue to position and size the image until it fits between columns B and E as shown above.

❹ Feel free to experiment with the WordArt toolbar. The WordArt must be selected (with sizing handles) in order to edit it. Use UnDo to reverse any action.

7. Now enter and format the text shown in rows 13 and 16 below.

Use the font color, point size and typeface of your choice. Your completed worksheet should closely match the worksheet below. You will save the workbook as a template in the next exercise.

Saving a Workbook as a Template

You save a workbook as a template by issuing the Save or Save As commands. However, you must set the Save as Type to Template when the Save As dialog box appears. The template is then available for use.

How templates are organized

Templates are used with all Microsoft Office programs including Word, Excel, PowerPoint and Access. Office templates are organized in subfolders of the C:\Program Files\Microsoft Office\Templates folder. You can store templates in either the Templates folder or the subfolders. The Office programs display the Templates folder and the subfolders whenever you open a template or save a workbook as a template.

Hands-On 9.4 – Save the workbook as a template

1. **Click** the Save button and the Save As dialog box will appear.

2. Use the following steps to save the workbook as a template.

❶ *Type* **Tradewinds Race Results** *in the Filename box.*

❷ *Choose* **Template** *from the Save as Type list. This instructs Excel to save the workbook as a template. Notice the Templates folder appears at the top of the dialog box. You will save your template in the Templates folder, so there is no need to choose a subfolder.*

❸ **Click** *the* **Save** *button and if necessary, click Yes to replace the template if it already exists.*

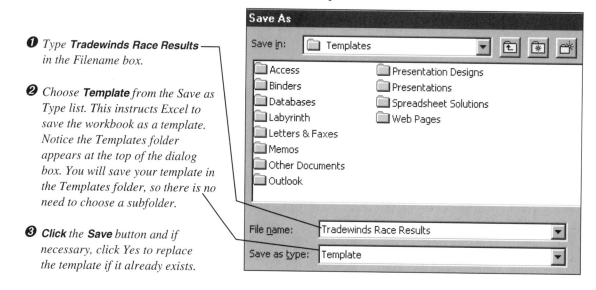

3. Choose **File→Close** from the menu bar to close the template.

Basing a New Workbook on a Template

You can use a template as the basis for a new Workbook. This is accomplished by issuing the **File→New...** command. You can then develop the workbook and save it when you are finished. The original template remains unchanged, so you can continue to use the template to create new workbooks.

Hands-On 9.5 – Use the template to create a new workbook

1. Choose **File→New...** from the menu bar.

2. Use the following steps to create a new workbook from the Tradewinds template.

❶ *Notice these tabs. The Tradewinds template should be under the General tab.*

❷ *Click the* **Spreadsheet Solutions** *tab. The Spreadsheet Solutions tab contains a sophisticated Invoice template and a template for Village Software. Village Software is a company that provides sophisticated templates for Excel users. You can find out information about Village Software by opening the template (but don't do it). You will use the Invoice template at the end of this lesson.*

❸ *Click the* **General** *tab.*

❹ *Choose* **Tradewinds Race Results** *and* **click OK**.

A new workbook appears with the same graphics and formatting as the Tradewinds template.

3. Continue with the next exercise where you will modify and save the workbook.

Hands-On 9.6 – Modify the workbook and use drawing objects

In this exercise, you will modify and then save the new workbook. The Tradewinds Race Results template will remain unchanged. This way, you can use the template over-and-over.

1. Add the text, numbers and AVERAGE function (in Cell C22) shown in rows 14 and 17-22 below.

   Feel free to format the entries with color and other formatting options.

	A	B	C
12			
13	**Race Results**		
14	**Gold Cup Fall Regatta**		
15			
16	Name	Owner	Score
17	Lucky Lady	Linda Burke	35
18	Night Watch	Donna Billings	38
19	Sandpiper	Jay Walton	42
20	Donna Marie	Ben Prince	47
21	Second Wind	Lisa Levine	50
22	Average		42.4

Continued...

In the next few steps, you will use drawing objects to enhance the worksheet.

Add an oval to emphasize the best score

2. **Click** the Oval [⬭] button on the Drawing toolbar.

3. Use the following steps to draw an oval in cell C17.

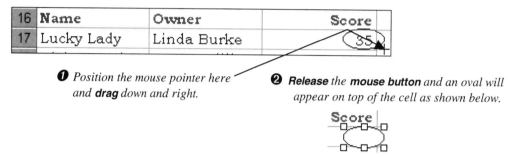

❶ *Position the mouse pointer here and* **drag** *down and right.*

❷ **Release** *the* **mouse button** *and an oval will appear on top of the cell as shown below.*

Remove the fill color to give the oval a see-through appearance

You can change the properties of objects including the fill color, line style etc. In the next few steps, you will set the oval's fill color to none. This will create a see-through appearance.

4. Make sure the oval is selected and **click** the Fill Color drop-down [⬛] button (not the big button).

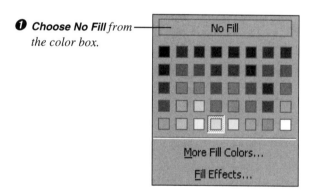

❶ **Choose No Fill** *from the color box.*

The oval should now have a see-through appearance.

5. Now use the Line Color [✎] button to change the line color of the oval.

6. Feel free to adjust the size or position of the oval by dragging the sizing handles or the oval itself.

7. Feel free to change thickness of the oval with the Line Style [≡] button.

Use an AutoShape to create a callout

Office 97's AutoShapes let you create a number of fun shapes to enhance your worksheets. In the following steps, you will use an AutoShape to create a callout.

8. **Click** the [AutoShapes ▾] button on the Drawing toolbar.

9. Use the steps on the following page to choose a callout.

Continued...

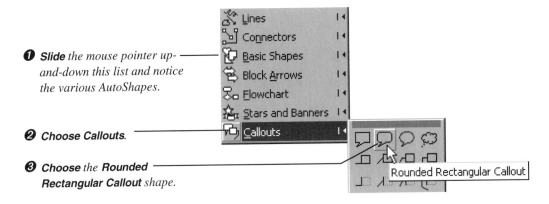

❶ **Slide** *the mouse pointer up-*
and-down this list and notice
the various AutoShapes.

❷ **Choose Callouts.**

❸ **Choose** *the* **Rounded**
Rectangular Callout *shape.*

---

10. Use the following steps to create the callout.

Owner	Score	
Linda Burke	(35)	
Donna Billings	38	
Jay Walton	42	
Ben Prince	47	
Lisa Levine	50	
	42.4	

❶ *Position the mouse pointer to the right of the*
42.4 average and **Drag up to the right** *until*
the callout has approximately this shape.

❷ **Release** *the mouse button and the callout*
will be created. You will change the shape
and position in the following steps.

Enter and format text in the callout

11. Now type the text shown below into the callout.

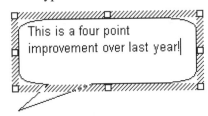

This is a four point
improvement over last year!

12. **Select** the text in the callout by dragging the mouse over it.

13. Format the text with a **Bookman Old Style 11** point **Bold** font.

14. Add color to the text using the Font Color [A] button and Center Align [≣] it.

Change the position, size and fill

15. **Click** anywhere outside the callout to deselect it.

16. Use the following steps to format the callout.

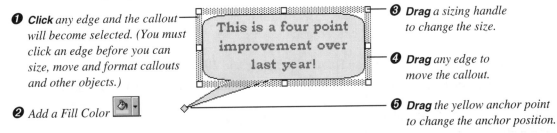

❶ **Click** *any edge and the callout*
will become selected. (You must
click an edge before you can
size, move and format callouts
and other objects.)

❷ *Add a Fill Color* [🪣]

This is a four point
improvement over
last year!

❸ **Drag** *a sizing handle*
to change the size.

❹ **Drag** *any edge to*
move the callout.

❺ **Drag** *the yellow anchor point*
to change the anchor position.

Continued...

17. If necessary, continue to format your callout until it has the shape and position shown below.

Your completed worksheet should closely match the worksheet shown below.

	A	B	C	D	E
1					
2					
3		Tradewinds Sailing Club			
4					
5					
6					
7					
8					
9					
10					
11					
12					
13	**Race Results**				
14	**Gold Cup Fall Regatta**				
15					
16	**Name**	**Owner**	**Score**		
17	Lucky Lady	Linda Burke	35		
18	Night Watch	Donna Billings	38	This is a four point	
19	Sandpiper	Jay Walton	42	improvement over	
20	Donna Marie	Ben Prince	47	last year!	
21	Second Wind	Lisa Levine	50		
22	**Average**		**42.4**		

Hands-On 9.7 – Save the workbook

You have been working on a workbook that is based upon the Tradewinds Race Results template. In this exercise, you will save the workbook. The Tradewinds template will remain unchanged.

1. Click the Save [icon] button.

Excel displays the Save As dialog box. Notice the Save As Type is set to Microsoft Excel Workbook. This saves your work as a workbook leaving the original template unchanged.

2. Type the name **Hands-On Lesson 9** in the File name box and **click** the **Save** button.

Close the workbook and use the template again

3. Close the workbook with the **File→Close** command.

4. Choose **File→New...** from the menu bar.

5. Choose the **Tradewinds Race Results** template and **click OK**.

Notice the template is intact and it doesn't contain the data and graphics you added in rows 17-22.

6. Choose **File→Close** and continue with the next topic.

Additional Drawing Object Techniques

The following table lists a variety of techniques you can use with drawing objects.

Technique	How to do it
Float text anywhere on the worksheet	Use the Text Box ▣ tool.
Select multiple objects	Click Select Objects ▣ and drag over the desired objects.
Use the keyboard to select multiple objects	Press the ⌷Shift⌷ key and click the desired objects.
Draw perfect horizontal, vertical or 45 degree lines	Press the ⌷Shift⌷ key while drawing a line or arrow line.
Draw perfect squares	Press the ⌷Shift⌷ key while using the Rectangle ▣ tool.
Draw perfect circles	Press the ⌷Shift⌷ key while using the Oval ▣ tool.
Copy objects using the mouse and keyboard	Press the ⌷Ctrl⌷ key while dragging the objects
Format objects	Right-click the object and choose the desired Format command from the menu.

Hands-On 9.8 – Experiment with drawing objects

1. Take a few minutes to experiment with the drawing objects.

    Try using the techniques in the table above. Also, experiment with the various buttons on the Drawing toolbar especially the AutoShapes. You will almost certainly find AutoShapes fun and interesting to use.

2. **Close** the workbook when you have finished without **saving** the changes.

Concepts Review

True / False

1. A template is updated and changed each time you save a workbook that is based upon the template.

2. You can change the size of pictures after they have been inserted.

3. The Save As dialog box is used to save a workbook as a template.

4. The Drawing ![button] button displays and hides the Drawing toolbar.

5. You cannot format text within a callout box.

6. The Select Objects ![tool] tool lets you select multiple drawing objects.

1. **T   F**

2. **T   F**

3. **T   F**

4. **T   F**

5. **T   F**

6. **T   F**

Multiple Choice

1. Which command opens a template for use as a new workbook?
    a) Format→Template
    b) File→New
    c) Insert→Template
    d) None of the above.   (   )

2. Which command is used to insert a picture?
    a) Insert→Picture
    b) Format→Picture
    c) Insert→Clip Art
    d) None of the above.   (   )

3. Which folder are Microsoft Office templates usually stored in?
    a) C:\Program Files\Microsoft Office\Templates
    b) C:\Templates
    c) C:\Excel\Templates
    d) None of the above.   (   )

4. Which keyboard key is used to draw horizontal, vertical or 45 degree lines?
    a) Shift
    b) Alt
    c) Ctrl
    d) None of the above.   (   )

5. Which keyboard key is used to select multiple drawing objects?
    a) Shift
    b) Alt
    c) Ctrl
    d) None of the above.   (   )

Skills Builder 9.1

In this exercise, you will use an Excel Spreadsheet Solutions template called Invoice. The Invoice Spreadsheet Solution lets you set up a customized invoice for your business or home use. Your instructor will need to install the template if it is not already installed on your computer system.

Open the template and check out the workbook

1. Choose **F̲ile→N̲ew...** from the menu bar and **click** the **Spreadsheet Solutions** tab.

2. Choose **Invoice** and **click OK**.

    Excel should display a workbook with an Invoice sheet and a Customize Your Invoice sheet. This is a sophisticated template that contains a customized toolbar and other options.

Customize the Invoice

3. **Click** the **Customize Your Invoice** sheet tab.

4. Enter the following information into the Type Company Information Here section of the worksheet.

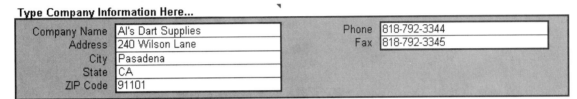

    The next section of the worksheet lets you set Default Invoice Information. We will skip this section. The bottom section displays a sample of the formatted text that will appear in the invoice. It also lets you choose a logo for your invoice. You will choose a logo using Office clip art.

5. **Scroll to** the **bottom** of the worksheet and **click** the **Select Logo** button.

6. Use the following steps to choose a logo.

    ❶ *Use the Look In list to* **navigate** *to C:\Program Files\Microsoft Office \Clipart\Popular as shown here. This folder should contain the clip art.*

    ❷ **Scroll** *through the clip art list and* **choose Darts** *(or another if Darts isn't listed).*

    ❸ **Click** *the* **Insert** *button.*

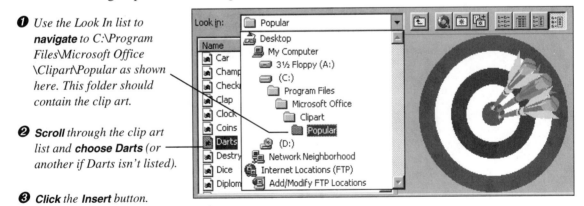

    The Formatted Information at the bottom of the worksheet should have the following appearance. This information will be used in the Invoice template.

Continued...

7. **Click** the **Invoice tab** and the Customize Your Invoice sheet will vanish.

8. The logo and company information will be visible at the top of the invoice (although you may need to move the Invoice toolbar).

9. Take ten minutes to explore the invoice.

   The invoice contains cell comments, formulas and various types of controls. Keep in mind that this invoice is a worksheet. It just happens to be a sophisticated worksheet with a lot of customization.

10. Try entering a fictitious customer and product order in the invoice.

11. Do a little detective work to determine how the SubTotal, Total and other calculations are set up.

    Some of the formulas use functions you may not be familiar with yet.

12. **Close** the workbook but **do not** save it because it will occupy too much space on your diskette.

13. Feel free to open the Village Software Spreadsheet Solutions template.

    That template contains information on how to contact Village Software. Village Software provides customized Excel 97 templates for a variety of purposes.

Skills Builder 9.2

In this exercise, you will modify the Tradewinds template.

Open the template

1. Choose **F̲ile**→**N̲ew...** from the menu bar and **click** the **General** tab.

2. **Double-click** the **Tradewinds Race Results** template.

   A new workbook that is based upon the template will appear.

3. Change the text in cell A13 from Race Results to **Regatta Results**.

4. **Click** the Save button.

5. Set the Save as type to **Template** and the filename to **Tradewinds Race Results** as shown below.

   You will need to change the name in the File name box. It is probably set to Tradewinds Race Results1 or some similar name.

6. **Click** the **Save** button and then **click Yes** to replace the template.

   You can always edit an existing template using the steps above.

7. Choose **F̲ile**→**C̲lose** to close the template.

Use F̲ile→N̲ew to base a new workbook on the template

8. Choose **F̲ile**→**N̲ew...** from the menu bar.

9. **Double-click** the **Tradewinds Race Results** template.

   The new workbook should contain the modified text.

10. **Close** the workbook **without** saving the changes.

Skills Builder 9.3

In this exercise, you will insert a picture, use drawing objects and then copy the objects.

Insert and size a picture

1. **Click** the New Workbook ⬜ button to open a new workbook.

2. **Click** cell **B2**.

   This is where the first picture will be inserted.

3. Choose **Insert**→**Picture** →**Clip Art...** from the menu bar.

4. If necessary, scroll through the Clip Art and choose the turtle 🐢 (or any other image).

5. **Click** the **Insert** button.

6. Use the following step to widen the turtle image.

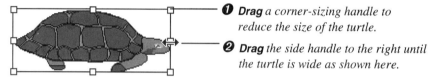

   ❶ **Drag** *a corner-sizing handle to reduce the size of the turtle.*

   ❷ **Drag** *the side handle to the right until the turtle is wide as shown here.*

Create a text box and draw a horizontal arrow

7. Use the following step to create a text box and draw a perfect horizontal line.

   Text boxes let you place "floating" text anywhere on the worksheet.

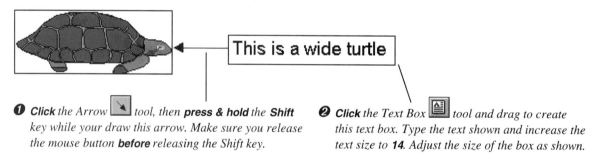

   This is a wide turtle

   ❶ **Click** *the Arrow* 🔲 *tool, then* **press & hold** *the* **Shift** *key while your draw this arrow. Make sure you release the mouse button* **before** *releasing the Shift key.*

   ❷ **Click** *the Text Box* 🔲 *tool and drag to create this text box. Type the text shown and increase the text size to* **14**. *Adjust the size of the box as shown.*

Select the objects

8. **Click** the Select Objects 🔲 tool.

9. **Drag** the mouse pointer ⬚ until all three objects are enclosed in the selection box.

10. **Release** the mouse button and all three objects will have sizing handles.

11. **Click** the Drawing Selection 🔲 tool to deactivate it.

Copy the objects with drag & copy

12. Position the mouse pointer ⬚ on the turtle (but don't click).

13. **Press & Hold** the ⬚ Ctrl ⬚ key and the mouse pointer will have a plus + sign attached to it.

   The plus sign indicates the object is about to be copied as opposed to being moved.

Continued...

14. Continue to hold ⌐Ctrl⌐ while you **drag** the mouse down about three inches.

15. Release the mouse button **first**, then **release** ⌐Ctrl⌐.

You should have an exact duplicate of the objects. Remember to use this technique when you want to copy any objects including charts, pictures or drawing objects.

16. Use the preceding steps to make a third copy of the objects.

Experiment

17. Experiment by inserting various pictures and drawing various objects.

18. Try deleting objects by selecting them and tapping the ⌐Delete⌐ key.

19. Try copying objects with the drag & copy technique.

20. When you have finished experimenting, **close** the workbook without saving the changes.

Skills Builder 9.4

In this exercise, you will create a template that will be used for quarterly forecasts at Zephron Industries. All Zephron sales reps will use the template as a basis for quarterly sales forecasts. The template will include three worksheets: A data sheet; a column chart sheet; and a pie chart sheet. You will create the charts and data sheet as part of the template. This way, the charts will already be created for the sales reps. The sales reps will simply need to type in the forecast data on a quarterly basis.

Create the data sheet using dummy data

You will create a data sheet in the next few steps. You will include dummy data in the data sheet to help you test the template. You will delete the data prior to saving the template.

1. **Click** the New Workbook [ ] button.

2. **Click** the Select All [ ] button.

3. Use the **Format→Column→Width...** command to set the column widths to **12**.

4. Use the following guidelines to create the worksheet shown below.

   - Enter the data shown below. The text entries in row 2 and 4 are Merged and Centered [ ] across columns A-G. Also, you will need to use a SUM formula in cell C14.

   - Apply the shading and borders shown. This example shows the text reversed out (white text on a dark background). You can accomplish this by selecting the desired range and applying a dark background color with the Fill Color [ ] button. Then apply a white color to the text with the Font Color [ ] button.

   - Format the numbers with the Comma and Currency styles shown.

     The completed sheet should match the sheet shown below.

	A	B	C	D	E	F	G
1							
2			Zephron Quarterly Sales Forecast				
3							
4			Sales Rep - Donna Wilson				
5							
6							
7							
8							
9	Product	Forecast Units	Forecast Dollars				
10	Cell Phones	230	21,900				
11	Pagers	560	24,000				
12	GPS Systems	725	65,000				
13	PC's	120	190,000				
14	Total		$ 300,900				

5. Rename Sheet1 as **Data Sheet**.

Create a bar chart on a separate sheet

6. Use [Ctrl] and the mouse to **select** the ranges **A10:A13** and **C10:C13** as shown on the next page.

Continued...

Select these cells

10	Cell Phones	230	21,900
11	Pagers	560	24,000
12	GPS Systems	725	65,000
13	PC's	120	190,000

7. Use the Chart Wizard to create the chart shown below **as a new sheet**.

The As a new sheet option is chosen in the last step of the wizard. Use your best judgment when determining the chart type and the various chart options. Keep in mind that the data is already selected, so you only need to be concerned with the various chart-formatting options.

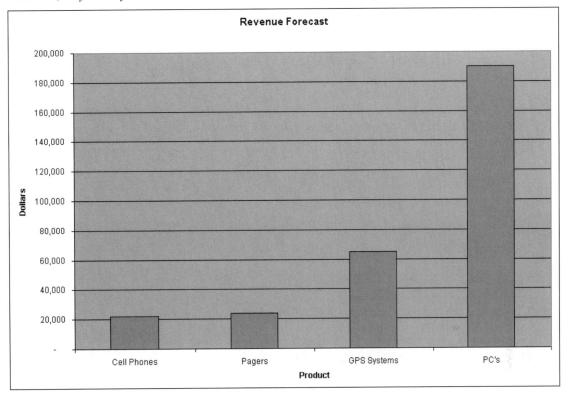

8. Rename the Chart1 sheet as **Revenue Chart**.

Create a pie chart on a separate sheet

9. Insert the pie chart shown on the following page as a new sheet. You must decide which data to select and all other chart options. Hint: Look at the pie chart and notice the labels on the slices. Also notice there are only four slices, so only four sets of data should be included in the selection.

Continued...

Revenue Percentage by Product

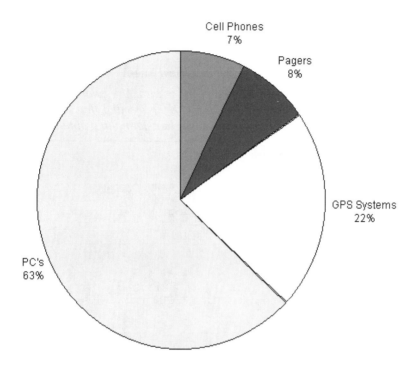

10. Rename the pie chart sheet as **Product Chart**.

11. **Click** the **Data Sheet** tab to make it active.

12. Change the order of the sheet tabs by **dragging** the Data Sheet tab to the left of the chart tabs.

Delete the dummy data and save the workbook as a template

13. **Select** the data in the Data Sheet as shown below.

10	Cell Phones	230	21,900
11	Pagers	560	24,000
12	GPS Systems	725	65,000
13	PC's	120	190,000

14. **Tap** Delete to delete the data.

   The Total in cell C14 will be zero (or a dashed line). However, the formula in C14 is still intact, so the Total will recalculate when new data is entered in the cells. The Revenue chart and Contributions chart will also be meaningless until data is entered in the Data Sheet.

15. **Click** the Save 🖫 button.

16. Set the **Save as type** to **Template**.

17. Change the File name to **Zephron** and **click** the **Save** button. If necessary, **click Yes** to replace the existing Zephron template.

   The workbook will be saved as a template.

18. Choose **File→Close** from the menu bar to close the template.

   You will use the template to create a new workbook in the next exercise.

Skills Builder 9.5

In this exercise, you will use the template you created in the previous exercise.

Use the template and change the data
1. Choose **File→New...** from the menu bar.

2. **Double-click** the **Zephron** template.

3. Enter the data in the 2ⁿᵈ and 3ʳᵈ columns shown below into the Data Sheet.

10	Cell Phones	100	12,500
11	Pagers	200	10,000
12	GPS Systems	450	85,000
13	PC's	250	350,000

The Total should be calculated as $457,500. The data will also be formatted with the Comma and Currency style formats you set in the template.

Check out the workbook then save it
4. **Click** the **Revenue Chart** and **Product Chart** sheet tabs.

   Notice the charts have been recreated.

5. **Click** the button and the Save As dialog box will appear.

6. Choose **3 ½ Floppy** from the Save in list and make sure the Save as Type option is set to **Microsoft Excel Workbook**.

7. Type the name **Skills Builder 9.5** in the File name box and **click** the **Save** button.

   The workbook has been saved and the template is ready to be used again.

Close the workbook and check out the template
8. Choose **File→Close** to close the workbook.

9. Choose **File→New...** and **double-click** the **Zephron** template.

   Notice the template is unchanged. As you can see, this powerful template contains text, formatting, formulas and charts. This type of template is especially useful when provided to inexperienced users who are interested only in entering data. You can also use the protection techniques discussed in the previous lesson to protect a template. This way, inexperienced users won't accidentally damage a workbook that is based upon the template.

10. **Close** the workbook **without** saving it and continue with the Assessment exercises.

Assessment 9.1

1. **Create** the workbook shown below. You will need to create the chart as shown and use the drawing tools to create the Text box and Arrow line. Use the chart style shown here and notice the chart has data labels on top of each column. Also, draw the arrow as a perfect horizontal line.

2. **Print** the worksheet on one page. You may need to reduce the size of your chart as shown here.

3. **Close** the workbook and **save** it as **Assessment 9.1**.

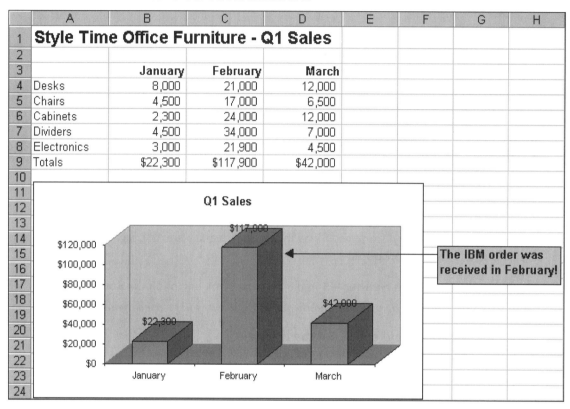

Assessment 9.2

In this assessment, you will create a template for the Redmont school district. Each school within the district will use the template to create a budget workbook and accompanying chart.

1. Create the workbook and chart shown below using the dummy data shown below.

2. Use the **File→Page Setup** command and create a footer that displays only the filename in the center section of the footer.

3. **Delete** the dummy data in cells **B4:B8** and **save** the workbook as a **template** named **Redmont**.

   If necessary, replace the existing Redmont template.

	A	B	C	D	E	F
1	Redmont School District					
2						
3	Item	Budget				
4	Facilities	$1,000,000				
5	Employee Costs	1,000,000				
6	Transportation	1,000,000				
7	Students	1,000,000				
8	Equipment	1,000,000				
9						

1997 Budget Allocation

Equipment 20%
Facilities 20%
Students 20%
Employee Costs 20%
Transportation 20%

4. **Close** the template.

5. Use the **File→New...** command to create a new workbook that is based upon the Redmont template. You may want to demonstrate this to your instructor.

6. Add the phrase **- Barrett School** to the title in cell A1.

7. Change the data in cells **B4:B8** as shown on the following page.

Continued...

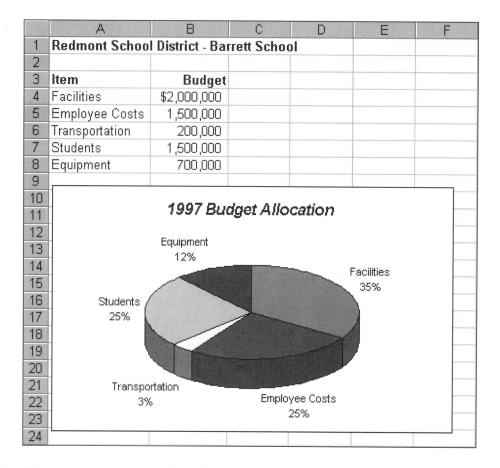

8. The chart in your new workbook should match the chart shown above.

9. **Save** the new workbook as **Assessment 9.2**.

10. **Print** the workbook and then **close** it when you have finished.

Critical Thinking 9.1

Make a list of the ways templates can benefit you.

1. _____

2 _____

3. _____

4. _____

Critical Thinking 9.2

Open any workbook you have used in this course that you would like to use as a template. Choose a workbook that could be useful to you on an ongoing basis. Delete any dummy data from the workbook and save it as a template under the name My Template. You may even want to save it to your exercise diskette, so that you can copy it into the template folder on your own computer system.

10 The IF Function and Lookup Functions

Objectives:

♦ Use the IF function

♦ Use the VLOOKUP and HLOOKUP functions

♦ Assign names to ranges

The Project - Paper Plus Commission Report

In this lesson, you will help Wanda Richardson, the Accounting Manager at a wholesale paper distributor named Paper Plus, calculate monthly commissions for the Paper Plus sales force. The commission rate of each sales person is dependent upon the total sales that person made for the month. You will begin by using the IF function to calculate commission rates for the Paper Plus telemarketing sales force. You will use the VLOOKUP function for the more complex calculations that are required for the direct sales force. The worksheet you will develop is shown below.

	A	B	C	D	E
1	**Paper Plus Monthly Commission Calculations**				
2	**November 1997 Report**				
3	*Prepared by Wanda Richardson*		*11/30/97*		
4					
5	**Telemarketing Sales**	**November Sales**	**Commission Rate**	**Total Commission**	**Above or Below Quota?**
6	Bill Evans	11,000	10%	1,100	Above Quota
7	Dorothy Simms	12,500	10%	1,250	Above Quota
8	Ted Long	8,000	5%	400	Below Quota
9	Elsie Green	4,500	5%	225	Below Quota
10					
11					
12	**Direct Sales**	**November Sales**	**Commission Rate**	**Total Commission**	**Above or Below Quota?**
13	Ned Greenfield	19,500	10%	1,950	Below Quota
14	Vincent Coleman	21,000	15%	3,150	Above Quota
15	Richard Medford	9,500	0%	-	Under Achiever
16	Donna Brownlow	52,000	25%	13,000	Over Achiever
17	Alonzo Cortez	24,500	15%	3,675	Above Quota
18	Bill Peterson	12,500	10%	1,250	Below Quota
19	Willie Wilson	4,000	0%	-	Under Achiever
20	Denise Barns	75,000	25%	18,750	Over Achiever
21					
22					
23			Sales Volume	Commission Rate	Message
24			-	0%	Under Achiever
25			10,000	10%	Below Quota
26			20,000	15%	Above Quota
27			30,000	20%	Above Quota
28			50,000	25%	Over Achiever

The IF Function

Excel's IF function uses a logical operator such as greater than > or less than < to compare two **expressions**. An expression can be a number, text, a cell reference or a formula. If the comparison is true, then the IF function enters a value in the cell (the cell that contains the IF function). If the comparison is false, it enters a different value in the cell. The general syntax of the IF function is discussed below.

Syntax	Discussion
IF(Logical Comparison,True,False)	The Logical Comparison compares two numbers, cells or other elements using standard logical operators such as less than <, greater than > and equal to =. The True and False components can be numbers, cell references or text entries.

The following illustration provides a practical example of the IF function syntax.

Take a few moments to study the IF function shown here. This function is entered into cell C2. The logical comparison, IF B2>=10000 is True because cell B2 contains the number 11,000. The IF function returns the value 10% because 10% is in the True section of the formula as shown in the generic IF function syntax above.

C2	▼	= =IF(B2>=10000,10%,5%)
	A	B	C
1	**Telemarketing Sales**	**November Sales**	**Commission Rate**
2	Bill Evans	11,000	10%
3	Dorothy Simms	6,500	5%

This cell contains the same IF function except it references cell B3 instead of B2. The value 5% is returned because 6,500 is less than 10000.

The following table shows the logical operators that can be used in IF functions.

Logical Operator	Description
=	Equal
<	Less than
>	Greater than
>=	Greater than or equal to
<=	Less than or equal to
<>	Not equal to

Hands-On 10.1 – Use the IF function to determine commission rates

In this exercise, you will open a workbook on your exercise diskette. You will use an IF function to determine whether a telemarketing sales representative should receive a 5% or 10% commission rate for the month. The commission rate will be determined by the IF function after the function determines whether or not the sales rep achieved the monthly quota of $10,000.

Enter an IF formula
1. **Open** the workbook named **Hands-On Lesson 10**.

2. **Click** cell **C6**.

Continued...

Take a moment to study the worksheet. The sales person in row 6 should have a commission rate of 10% if his sales are greater than or equal to $10,000 and 5% if his sales are less than $10,000. The IF function you are about to enter will return 5% because cell B6 (6,500) is below $10,000.

3. Type the following function **=IF(B6>=10000,10%,5%)**

4. Confirm [✓] the entry and the number .05 should appear in the cell.

Format the cell as percent and change the number in cell B6

5. Format the cell as Percent Style [%] to display the number as 5%.

6. Take a few moments to study the function you just entered and try to understand the logic.

7. **Click** cell **B6** and change the number to **11,000**.

    Cell C6 should now display 10% because the sales rep exceeded the $10,000 quota.

Enter another IF formula in cell C7

8. **Click** cell **C7** and enter the formula **=IF(B7>=10000,10%,5%)**

    The result should be .01.

9. Format cell **C7** with the Percent Style [%].

Copy the formulas with the fill handle and compute the commissions

10. **Click** cell **C7**.

11. Use the fill handle **+** to copy the IF function down to cells **C8** and **C9**.

12. **Click** cell **D6**.

13. Enter the formula **=B6*C6**.

    *The result should be 1,100. The commission is equal to the Sales * Commission Rate.*

14. Use the fill handle **+** to copy the formula in D6 down to cells D7, D8 and D9.

15. Save [💾] the changes and continue with the next topic.

Returning Text Entries with the IF Function

Thus far, you have used the IF function to return percentage rates. You can return many other values with the IF function including text entries. For example, in the next exercise, the IF function will return the phrase **Below Quota** if sales are less than 10,000 or **Above Quota** if sales are greater than or equal to 10,000. You must enclose text in quotation marks if you use it as the True or False value in an IF function. For example, the function you will enter in cell E6 is =IF(B6>=10000,"Above Quota","Below Quota"). The text that is used for the True and False values is surrounded by quotation marks.

Returning null values with the IF function

A null value is the same as an empty cell or nothing. You may want the IF function to return a null value in some situations. For example, you may want the function to enter a phrase in a cell if the IF statement is true and nothing if the statement is false. You create a null value by typing an opening and closing parenthesis "" with nothing between them. The null value can be used in either the true or false arguments of the IF function.

Hands-On 10.2 – Use the IF function to return quota status messages

1. **Click** cell **E6**.

2. Type **=IF(B6>=10000,"Above Quota","Below Quota")** and Confirm ☑ the entry.

    Make sure you type the formula exactly as shown. It is especially important that you type the commas, quotations and parenthesis correctly. The phrase Above Quota should be entered in cell E6 because the sales were 11,000 which is greater than 10,000.

3. Use the fill handle **+** to copy the IF formula you just entered down to cells E7, E8 and E9.

4. Right Align ☰ cells **E6:E9** (the cells with the Above Quota and Below Quota results).

5. At this point, rows 1-9 of your worksheet should match the example below.

	A	B	C	D	E
1	**Paper Plus Monthly Commission Calculations**				
2	**November 1997 Report**				
3	*Prepared by Wanda Richardson*		*11/30/97*		
4					
5	**Telemarketing Sales**	**November Sales**	**Commission Rate**	**Total Commission**	**Above or Below Quota?**
6	Bill Evans	11,000	10%	1,100	Above Quota
7	Dorothy Simms	12,500	10%	1,250	Above Quota
8	Ted Long	8,000	5%	400	Below Quota
9	Elsie Green	4,500	5%	225	Below Quota

6. Save 💾 the changes and continue with the next topic.

Lookup Functions

Excel's VLOOKUP (Vertical Lookup) and HLOOKUP (Horizontal Lookup) functions look up values in tax tables, commission rate tables and other types of "lookup" tables. The VLOOKUP function is used most often, so it is discussed in this section. The generic syntax of the VLOOKUP function and a discussion of the function's arguments are shown below.

VLOOKUP(search argument, lookup table, column number)

The following table discusses the three arguments in the VLOOKUP function. The table uses the illustration below as an example. Also, you will notice the table discusses the lookup table argument (the second argument in the function) before it discusses the search argument (the first argument). As you read the table and the illustration below the table, make sure you refer to the formula that is shown in the formula bar of the illustration (=VLOOKUP(B13,Comm_Table,2).

Argument	Discussion
lookup table	This is the name or range reference of a lookup table. In the illustration below, the lookup table is in the range A17:C22 and it has been given the name Comm_Table.
search argument	The lookup function searches down the left column of the lookup table for the search argument. The search argument is usually a number or a reference to a cell that contains a number. In the illustration below, the function searches down the left column of the lookup table looking for the number 19500 (19500 is the search argument in cell B13).
column number	After VLOOKUP locates the search argument in the left column of the lookup table, it moves across the table to the specified column number. In the illustration below, the number 2 is used in the VLOOKUP function, so the function moves to the second column in the lookup table.

The following illustration provides additional details on the VLOOKUP function shown in the Formula bar.

	A	B	C	D
11				
12	Direct Sales	November Sales	Commission Rate	Above or Below Quota?
13	Ned Greenfield	19,500	10%	Below Quota
14				
15				
16				
17		Sales Volume	Commission Rate	Message
18		0	0%	Under Achiever
19		10,000	10%	Below Quota
20		20,000	15%	Above Quota
21		30,000	20%	Above Quota
22		50,000	25%	Over Achiever

This VLOOKUP function is in cell C13.

The lookup table is in the range A17:C22 and it has been given the name Comm_Table. You can name ranges just like you name cells. The range names can be used in functions like VLOOKUP.

The search argument is B13. VLOOKUP searches down the left column of the lookup table for the number 19500 (the number that is in cell B13). VLOOKUP doesn't need to find an exact match in the table. It just needs to locate the range that 19500 falls in. It chooses row 19. The reason for this is discussed in detail below.

This is the lookup table. It has been given the range name Comm_Table. Range names can be used in formulas and functions the same way a cell name can be used in a linking formula. The range name identifies the table as occupying the range A17:C22.

The third argument in the function is 2. This instructs the lookup function to move across row 19 to the second column in the table. This is cell B19 which contains the number 10%. 10% is returned and entered into cell C13 which contains the VLOOKUP function.

More details on how VLOOKUP works

VLOOKUP searches **down** the left column of the lookup table for the search argument. VLOOKUP is searching for the number 19500 in the example on the previous page. The function doesn't need to find the exact number 19500. As soon it locates a number that is greater than the search argument (19500), it stops and chooses the previous table row. In the example above, it stops when it finds 20000 and then chooses the previous row which is row 19. The function then goes to the column number specified in the third parameter of the function (2 in this example). The cell it goes to is then returned. In the example on the previous page, the function goes to row 19 and the 2nd column of the table. This is cell B19, so the number 10% is returned.

The entries in the left column of the lookup table must be in ascending order

The VLOOKUP function searches down the left column and stops when it finds the first value that is greater than or equal to the search argument. For this reason, the rows in the lookup table must be sorted in ascending order on the first column. This way, you can be assured that VLOOKUP will stop at the proper row and return the correct value.

Hands-On 10.3 – Create the lookup table and give it a range name

In this exercise, you will create the lookup table shown below. You will also assign a range name to the table. The range name will be used in the VLOOKUP function in the next exercise.

Create the lookup table

1. If necessary, use the zoom control until you can see at least 25 rows in your worksheet.

2. **Click** cell **C20**.

3. Enter the phrase **Sales Volume**.

4. Complete the lookup table by entering the text and numbers shown below.

   Keep in mind that this illustration only shows rows 19-25 of the worksheet. Rows 1-18 are not shown here simply to conserve space in the illustration.

	A	B	C	D	E
19					
20			Sales Volume	Commission Rate	Message
21			0	5%	Below Quota
22			10,000	10%	Below Quota
23			20,000	15%	Above Quota
24			30,000	20%	Above Quota
25			50,000	25%	Over Achiever

Continued...

Assign a range name to the table

In the next few steps, you will assign a range name to the table. You will be able to reference the table in the VLOOKUP function by using the range name.

5. Use the following steps to create the range name.

❶ **Select** *the table you just created as shown below.*   ❷ **Click** *in the Name box and type the name* **Comm_Table**.   ❸ *Tap* **Enter** *to complete the name.*

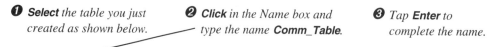

Comm_Table	▼	=	Sales Volume			
	A	B	C	D	E	F
19						
20			Sales Volume	Commission Rate	Message	
21			0	5%	Below Quota	
22			10,000	10%	Below Quota	
23			20,000	15%	Above Quota	
24			30,000	20%	Above Quota	
25			50,000	25%	Over Achiever	
26						

6. **Click** any cell in the table and the table will be deselected.

    Notice the range name is no longer displayed in the Name box. You must select all cells in the table (or any named range) in order for the range name to appear in the name box.

7. **Select** the entire table (cells C20:E25) and the name Comm_Table will appear in the Name box.

8. Save 💾 the changes to the workbook and continue with the next exercise.

Hands-On 10.4 – Create a VLOOKUP function

In this exercise, you will use the VLOOKUP function to calculate the commission rates in cells C13:C18. These commission rates cannot be calculated with the IF function. This is because there are five different commission levels that the direct sales people can achieve depending upon their sales volume. The IF function can only handle two levels because of its True / False limitations.

Enter a VLOOKUP function in cell C13

1. **Click** cell **C13**.

2. Enter the function **=VLOOKUP(B13,Comm_Table,2)** into the cell.

    Excel should return the number .1 (10%).

3. Take a few moments to study the function you just entered and understand how it works.

    Keep in mind that you are trying to determine the commission rate that Ned Greenfield should be paid. The function looks for Ned's sales number 19,500 in the left column of the lookup table. It stops when it gets to 20,000 (cell C23) and then backs up one row because Ned's sales are between 10,000 and 20,000. The function then moves across row 22 to the second column in the lookup table, which is column D. This makes sense because column D contains the commission rates. Cell D22 contains the 10% rate that Ned should be paid. The number .1 (10%) is then returned and inserted into cell C13.

Enter a VLOOKUP function in cell C14

4. **Click** cell **C14**.

Continued...

5. Enter the function **=VLOOKUP(B14,Comm_Table,2)**.

    The number .15 (15%) should be returned. Notice that all arguments were the same for this function except you told VLOOKUP to lookup the number in cell B14 instead of B13.

Copy the formula
6. **Click** cell **C14**.

7. Use the fill handle ➕ to copy the VLOOKUP function down to cells C15:C18.

8. **Click** cell **C15** and notice the VLOOKUP function has been updated in the Formula bar.

    The relative cell reference C14 is updated to C15, C16 etc. as the function is copied down. This is correct because you want the function to lookup the number to the left of the function.

Calculate the commissions in column D and copy the cell formats
9. **Click** cell **D13**.

10. Enter the formula **=B13*C13**.

    The result should be 1,950.

11. Use the fill handle ➕ to copy the formula in D13 down to cells D14:D18.

12. Apply the Percent Style 🔲 to cells **C13:C18**.

Use VLOOKUP to determine the messages in column E
13. **Click** cell **E13**.

14. Enter the function **=VLOOKUP(B13,Comm_Table,3)**.

    The message Below Quota should be returned. Notice you used the same arguments for this function as you did with the function in cell C13 except the last argument is 3 instead of 2. This instructs VLOOKUP to return the value from column 3 of the lookup table instead of column 2.

15. Use the fill handle ➕ to copy the VLOOKUP function from cell E13 down to cells E14:E18.

16. Right Align 🔲 cells **E13:E18** (the cells with the Above Quota and Below Quota results).

17. Rows 12 through 25 of the worksheet should match the following illustration.

	A	B	C	D	E
11					
12	Direct Sales	November Sales	Commission Rate	Total Commission	Above or Below Quota?
13	Ned Greenfield	19,500	10%	1,950	Below Quota
14	Vincent Coleman	21,000	15%	3,150	Above Quota
15	Richard Medford	9,500	5%	475	Below Quota
16	Donna Brownlow	52,000	25%	13,000	Over Achiever
17	Alonzo Cortez	24,500	15%	3,675	Above Quota
18	Bill Peterson	12,500	10%	1,250	Below Quota
19					
20			Sales Volume	Commission Rate	Message
21			0	5%	Below Quota
22			10,000	10%	Below Quota
23			20,000	15%	Above Quota
24			30,000	20%	Above Quota
25			50,000	25%	Over Achiever

Continued...

Change the values in the lookup table and watch the functions recalculate

18. Click cell **D21** and change the number in that cell to **0%**.

Cell C15 should have a rate of 0% and the corresponding commission in cell D15 will also be null.

19. Click cell **E21** and change the message to **Under Achiever**.

The Under Achiever message will appear in cell E15.

Move the lookup table and add two more sales reps

Imagine that two new sales reps are hired. The lookup table currently occupies Row 20. For this reason, you must move the table before adding the new sales reps. This is easy to do because you assigned the range name (Comm_Table) to the table. You can move a table with a range name and the VLOOKUP functions will continue to refer to the correct cells in the new table location.

20. Click the Name box button and choose Comm_Table from the list.

Excel will select the Comm_Table range, which happens to be your lookup table. In the previous lesson, you learned how to go to any cell in the workbook by choosing the cell name from the Name list. Likewise, you can select any named range by choosing the range name from the list.

21. Use the following step to move the table down three rows.

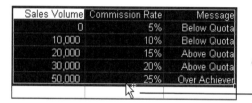

❶ *Position the mouse pointer on the bottom edge of the selected range and drag the range down three rows.*

22. Create rows 19 and 20 as shown below.

You will need to enter the data shown in cells A19, B19, A20 and B20. You can copy the formulas from row 18 down to the other cells in rows 19 and 20. The completed workbook is shown below.

	A	B	C	D	E
1	**Paper Plus Monthly Commission Calculations**				
2	November 1997 Report				
3	*Prepared by Wanda Richardson*		11/30/97		
4					
5	**Telemarketing Sales**	**November Sales**	**Commission Rate**	**Total Commission**	**Above or Below Quota?**
6	Bill Evans	11,000	10%	1,100	Above Quota
7	Dorothy Simms	12,500	10%	1,250	Above Quota
8	Ted Long	8,000	5%	400	Below Quota
9	Elsie Green	4,500	5%	225	Below Quota
10					
11					
12	**Direct Sales**	**November Sales**	**Commission Rate**	**Total Commission**	**Above or Below Quota?**
13	Ned Greenfield	19,500	10%	1,950	Below Quota
14	Vincent Coleman	21,000	15%	3,150	Above Quota
15	Richard Medford	9,500	0%	-	Under Achiever
16	Donna Brownlow	52,000	25%	13,000	Over Achiever
17	Alonzo Cortez	24,500	15%	3,675	Above Quota
18	Bill Peterson	12,500	10%	1,250	Below Quota
19	Willie Wilson	4,000	0%	-	Under Achiever
20	Denise Barns	75,000	25%	18,750	Over Achiever
21					
22					
23			Sales Volume	Commission Rate	Message
24			-	0%	Under Achiever
25			10,000	10%	Below Quota
26			20,000	15%	Above Quota
27			30,000	20%	Above Quota
28			50,000	25%	Over Achiever

23. Close the workbook, **save** the changes and continue with the end-of-lesson exercises.

Concepts Review

True / False

1. The IF function determines whether a comparison is true or false.

2. The second argument in an IF function is the False argument.

3. The VLOOKUP function searches down the left column of the lookup table.

4. The VLOOKUP function stops searching when it finds a value that is less than the search argument.

5. A lookup table cannot be moved once it has been created.

6. The last argument in a VLOOKUP function specifies the column which the entry or number should be taken from.

7. The entries in the left column of the lookup table should be in descending order.

8. The VLOOKUP function cannot return text entries.

1. **T   F**

2. **T   F**

3. **T   F**

4. **T   F**

5. **T   F**

6. **T   F**

7. **T   F**

8. **T   F**

Multiple Choice

1. Which of the following IF functions has proper syntax?
   a)   =IF(B2>>10000,10%,5%)
   b)   IF(B2+35,10%,5%)
   c)   =IF(B2<>150,10%,5%)
   d)   None of the above.

   (   )

2. Which of the following logical operators can be used in IF functions?
   a)   >=
   b)   <=
   c)   =
   d)   All of the above.

   (   )

3. If an IF statement is entered into cell B5 and the condition evaluates to true, then which cell will receive the number that is returned by the IF function?
   a)   B5
   b)   B6
   c)   A5
   d)   None of the above.

   (   )

4. If an IF statement is entered into cell B5 and the condition evaluates to false, then which cell will receive the number that is returned by the IF function?
   a)   B5
   b)   B6
   c)   A5
   d)   None of the above.

   (   )

5. Which characters must surround text if you want an IF function to enter the text in a cell?
   a)   ( )
   b)   " "
   c)   [ ]
   d)   None of the above.

   (   )

Skills Builder 10.1

In this exercise, you will set up the commission analysis worksheet shown on the following page. You will use an IF function in the commission rate column. The IF function's arguments will reference the Quota and commission rates in cells C3, C4 and C5. You will use absolute values in the IF function to allow you to copy the function to other cells.

Create an IF function and copy it down the column

1. Open ![icon] the workbook named **Skills Builder 10.1**.

2. **Click** cell **C9**.

3. Type the function **=IF(B9 >=C3,C4,C5)** and Confirm ![icon] the entry.

   The result should be .05. Take a moment to study the function you just entered. Notice the IF statement compares the sales in cell B9 to the quota in cell C3. The $700,000 sales are not greater than or equal to the $725,000 quota, so the expression is false. The False part of the IF function references cell C5 which contains the number 5% or .05. This is why .05 is entered into cell C9.

4. Use the fill handle **+** to copy the IF function down to cells C10, C11, C12 and C13.

   Your objective is to have a commission rate of .05 or .1 entered into the cells. You will get the wrong results in all cells other than cell C10. Can you figure out why you got incorrect results? The next few steps in this exercise will explain why this happened.

Figure out why the function did not copy correctly

5. **Click** cell **C11**.

   Look at the Formula bar and the formula should be =IF(B11>=C5,C6,C7). Notice the B11 reference is referring to the correct cell. Are the C5, C6 and C7 references correct? The B11>=C5 argument should be comparing the sales in cell B11 to the Quota in cell C3. Likewise, the references to cells C6 and C7 should actually be referring to the commission rates in cells C4 and C5. Do you understand what the problem is? The problem is that you should have used absolute cell references for the C3, C4 and C5 references in the original IF formula in cell C9. You want the IF formulas in cells C10, C11, C12 and C13 to continue to reference those cells. You will correct this in the next few steps.

6. **Click** Undo ![icon] to reverse the copy.

7. **Click** cell **C9**.

8. **Click** in the Formula bar just in front of the **C3** reference.

9. **Tap** the ⌐F4⌐ key and Excel will insert dollar signs $ in front of the C and the 3.

   This converts the reference to absolute.

10. **Click** just in front of the **C4** reference in the Formula bar and **tap** ⌐F4⌐ again.

11. Convert the **C5** reference to absolute.

12. Confirm ![icon] the entry.

   The result should still be .05.

Continued...

Copy the formula again

13. Use the fill handle to copy the formula down to cells C10, C11, C12 and C13.

This time the IF functions should return the correct percentages of .05 and .1.

14. **Click** any of the cells and check out the Formula in the formula bar.

Try to understand how the IF function works and how the absolute values let you copy the function.

15. Format cells **C9:C13** with the Percent %️ style.

16. Calculate the Commissions Paid in column D.

*The Commissions Paid = Sales * Commission Rate.*

17. Calculate the Total Commissions Paid in cell **D14**.

The completed worksheet should match the worksheet shown below.

Play what-if analysis

In the next few steps, you will change the quota in cell C3 and the commission rates in cells C4 and C5. The IF functions and the Commissions Paid formulas will be recalculated. This will let you determine the impact that changing the quota and commission rates has on the Total Commissions Paid in cell D14.

18. **Click** cell **C3**.

19. Change the quota to **$500,000**.

Notice that all the sales reps are now paid 10% and the commissions paid increases substantially.

20. Change the Above Quota commission rate to **8%** and notice the impact this has on the Total Commission Paid.

21. Feel free to continue playing what-if analysis.

22. When you have finished, **close** the workbook and **save** the changes.

	A	B	C	D
1	**Commission Analysis Worksheet**			
2				
3	Quota		$725,000	
4	Above Quota		10%	
5	Below Quota		5%	
6				
7				
8		May Sales	Commission Rate	Commissions Paid
9	Wellington	$700,000	5%	$35,000
10	Banks	$550,000	5%	$27,500
11	Burnett	$650,000	5%	$32,500
12	Johnson	$900,000	10%	$90,000
13	Curtin	$800,000	10%	$80,000
14	**Total Commission Paid**			$265,000

Skills Builder 10.2

In this exercise, you will use an IF function to determine whether or not sales reps should receive a bonus for their quarterly sales.

1. **Open** the workbook named **Skills Builder 10.2.**

2. Use AutoSum ▣Σ in column E to calculate the Total Sales for July, August and September.

   The results should match the worksheet below (although your totals may have a Currency format).

3. Calculate the **commissions** in column F.

   The Commissions are calculated as the Total Sales in column E multiplied by the Commission Rate in cell B4. There is no need to use an IF function because there is just one commission rate. However, you will need to use an absolute reference to cell B4 if you want to copy the formula down the column.

4. **Click** cell **G7** and type the function **=IF(E7 >=70000,$B$3,0)**

   Study the function for a few moments before confirming the entry and try to determine what the result will be. Try to answer the following questions? How much must the sales rep sell in order to receive a bonus? How much is the bonus? What bonus is paid if the sales do not meet the objective specified in the IF function?

5. Confirm ✓ the entry and the result will be 0.

6. **Copy** the formula down the column.

7. Calculate the **Total Compensation** in column H as the Commission plus the Bonus.

8. **Format** the cells as shown below.

9. **Close** the workbook and **save** the changes when you have finished.

	A	B	C	D	E	F	G	H
1	Sales Rep Compensation Report							
2								
3	Bonus	2,000						
4	Commission Rate	16%						
5								
6		July	August	September	Total Sales	Commission	Bonus	Total Compensation
7	Sales Rep	$14,000	$23,000	$21,000	$58,000	$9,280	$0	$9,280
8	Larson	12,000	29,000	45,000	86,000	13,760	2,000	15,760
9	Jackson	10,000	21,000	54,000	85,000	13,600	2,000	15,600
10	Tate	23,000	12,000	34,000	69,000	11,040	-	11,040
11	Belum	32,000	32,000	21,000	85,000	13,600	2,000	15,600
12	Davidson	12,000	23,000	21,000	56,000	8,960	-	8,960
13	Winston	43,000	32,000	12,000	87,000	13,920	2,000	15,920

Skills Builder 10.3

In this exercise, you will create the worksheet shown below. You will use IF functions in columns D and E to determine which items need to be reordered and the quantity to reorder.

1. Start a New Workbook 📄 and enter the data shown in rows 1-3 and columns A-C below.

    You will need to widen the columns as shown.

2. **Click** cell **D4**.

    In the next step, you will enter an IF function in cell D4. The IF function will display a Reorder message if the Current Inventory is less than the Reorder Point. The IF function will leave the cell empty if the Current Inventory is greater than the Reorder Point. You leave a cell empty by entering an open and closed parenthesis "".

3. Enter the function **=IF(C4<B4,"Reorder","")** and the cell should remain empty.

    Type the function exactly as shown with the quotation marks in the correct positions. The Current Inventory is 40, which is greater than the Reorder Point, so there is no need to reorder.

4. Copy the function down the column and you should receive the results shown below.

5. **Click** cell **E4**.

6. Enter the function **=IF(D4="Reorder",B4-C4+20,"")** and the cell should remain empty.

    Notice this function checks cell D4 to see if the word Reorder has been entered in that cell. If Reorder has been entered in the cell, then the function subtracts the Current Inventory from the Reorder Point to determine the difference. It then adds 20 to that number and the resulting number becomes the Quantity to Reorder. In other words, you want to reorder up to the reorder point plus 20 additional products. If column D does not contain the Reorder message, then the open and closed parenthesis "" return a null value and the cell remains empty.

7. **Copy** the formula down the column to get the completed worksheet shown below.

8. **Close** the workbook when you have finished and **save** it as **Skills Builder 10.3**.

	A	B	C	D	E
1	Inventory Order Worksheet				
2					
3	Item	Reorder Point	Current Inventory	Reorder?	Reorder Quantity
4	Walton Dinnerware	25	40		
5	Sterling China	30	28	Reorder	22
6	Biltmore Tea Service	45	40	Reorder	25
7	Walthington Silverware	50	55		
8	Stewart Crystal	25	50		
9	Oakley Pots	80	65	Reorder	35
10	Barnsworth Skillets	120	85	Reorder	55

Skills Builder 10.4

In this exercise, you will use a lookup table and a VLOOKUP function to assign the letter grades A - F to students based upon their test scores. The completed worksheet will match the worksheet below.

Create the worksheet and lookup table

1. Start a New Workbook ⬜ and enter the data shown in rows 1-3 and columns A and B below.

   You will use a lookup function to determine the letter grades in column C.

2. Type the data shown in the lookup table in columns E and F.

3. **Select** the data in the lookup table as shown below.

Test Scores	Letter Grade
0	F
65	D
70	C
80	B
90	A

4. **Click** in the Name box on the left end of the Formula bar and type the name **Grade_Table**.

5. **Tap** [Enter] and the name **Grade_Table** will be assigned to the lookup table.

   Once again, you should always assign a name to a lookup table and use that name in the VLOOKUP function.

Enter the VLOOKUP functions
6. **Click** cell **C4**.

7. Enter the function **=VLOOKUP(B4,Grade_Table,2)**.

   The result should be B. Take a few moments to study this function and understand how it works. Once again, the VLOOKUP function will search down the left column of the lookup table for the search argument 87 (the value in cell B4). It will stop at 90, which is the first number larger than 87 and it will move up to the previous row. It will then go to the second column in the lookup table and return the letter grade B that is in cell F8.

8. Use the fill handle to copy the function down the column.

   The completed worksheet should match the worksheet shown below.

9. **Close** the workbook when you have finished and **save** it as **Skills Builder 10.4**.

	A	B	C	D	E	F
1	**Final Grade Calculations**					
2						
3	**Student**	**Test Scores**	**Letter Grade**		**Grade Table**	
4	Mildred Thomas	87	B		Test Scores	Letter Grade
5	Alicia Kim	95	A		0	F
6	Susan Savant	34	F		65	D
7	Ralph Reed	67	D		70	C
8	Bill Bickerson	82	B		80	B
9	Ruth Ashley	91	A		90	A
10	Tim Thompson	94	A			
11	Bernice Brown	78	C			

Skills Builder 10.5

In this exercise, you will create a simple financial model that uses tax rates from a lookup table to compute the Net Profit. The tax rate calculations in this model have been simplified to make the problem easy to understand.

Calculate the five-year growth using percentages

1. Open ⬚ the workbook named **Skills Builder 10.5**.

   In the first part of this exercise, you will calculate five-year projections for Projected Sales, Employee Costs, Capital Expenditures etc. by multiplying the numbers in column B by a percentage. These formulas will be inserted in column C and then copied across the rows.

2. **Click** cell **C4**.

   The owner of King's bakery is projecting sales growth of 27% for each of the next five years. You will model this in cell C4.

3. Enter the formula **=B4*1.27**

   The result should be 508000. Multiplying by 1.27 is equivalent to adding 27% of 400000 to 400000. In the next step, you will copy this formula across the row. This will show growth of 27% for each year.

4. Use the fill handle to copy the formula in cell C4 across the row.

5. Use the preceding steps to calculate the growth for the items in rows 5-9. The growth rates are shown in the table below. Make sure you copy the formulas across the rows after you enter them and make sure you add 1 to the growth rates. For example, the growth rate of employee costs is 15% but you should use the number 1.15 in the formula.

Item	Growth Rate
Employee Costs	15%
Capital Expenditures	15%
Operating Costs	25%
Cost of Goods Sold	12%
Marketing and Advertising	20%

6. Format the cells with the Currency and Comma formats shown on the following page.

   Make sure your numbers match the numbers on the following page.

Calculate the Gross Profit

   The Gross Profit is equal to the Projected Sales in row 4 minus the expenses in rows 5-9. You will calculate the Gross Profit with a formula that uses the SUM function to sum the expenses and then subtracts the result from the Projected Sales.

7. **Click** cell **B10**.

8. Enter the formula **=B4-SUM(B5:B9)**

   The result should be $15,000. Take a moment to study the formula and notice the SUM function is just like any other SUM function. You can include functions like SUM or IF inside other formulas.

9. Use the fill handle to copy the formula across the row.

Continued...

Calculate the Total Taxes using the VLOOKUP function

10. Click the Name list button on the left side of the Formula bar and choose **Tax_Table** from the list.

The Tax Table at the bottom of the worksheet will become selected. This lookup table was assigned the name Tax_Table before the workbook was copied to your exercise diskette.

11. Click cell **B11**.

12. Enter the formula **=B10*VLOOKUP(B10,Tax_Table,2)** into the cell.

The result should be 1500. Once again, you can embed functions like VLOOKUP in larger formulas. In this example, the Total Taxes are calculated as the Gross Profit in cell B10 multiplied by the Tax Rate that is returned by the VLOOKUP function.

13. Copy the formula across the row.

Calculate the Net Profit and format all cells

14. Click cell **B12**.

15. Enter a formula to calculate the Net Profit as the Gross Profit - Total Taxes.

The result should be $13,500.

16. Copy the formula across the row.

17. Format all cells with the Currency and Comma formats shown below.

18. Format cells **B10:F12** with **bold** as shown.

Your completed worksheet should match the worksheet shown below.

19. Close the workbook when you have finished and **save** the changes.

	A	B	C	D	E	F
1	King's Bakery Five-Year Financial Projections (1997 - 2001)					
2						
3		1997	1998	1999	2000	2001
4	Projected Sales	$400,000	$508,000	$645,160	$819,353	$1,040,579
5	Exployee Costs	185,000	212,750	244,663	281,362	323,566
6	Capital Expenditures	30,000	34,500	39,675	45,626	52,470
7	Operating Costs	50,000	62,500	78,125	97,656	122,070
8	Cost of goods sold	95,000	106,400	119,168	133,468	149,484
9	Marketing and Advertising	25,000	30,000	36,000	43,200	51,840
10	Gross Profit	$15,000	$61,850	$127,530	$218,041	$341,148
11	Total Taxes	$1,500	$15,463	$47,186	$85,036	$133,048
12	Net Profit	$13,500	$46,388	$80,344	$133,005	$208,100
13						
14						
15			Tax Table			
16		Income	Tax Rate			
17		-	0			
18		10,000	10%			
19		20,000	15%			
20		30,000	25%			
21		65,000	32%			
22		100,000	37%			
23		150,000	39%			

Assessment 10.1

In this exercise, you will use two IF functions to create the worksheet shown below. The IF function in column D will assign bonus points if a certain number of homework assignments have been turned in. The IF function in column F will return a letter grade of A or B depending on the Total Points earned in column E.

1. Start a New Workbook and enter the data shown in rows 1-3 and columns A-C below.

   You will need to use the Alt + Enter keystroke combination to create the double-line entries in row 3. You will also need to widen the columns as shown.

2. Use an IF function to calculate the Bonus Points in column D.

   A Bonus of 15 points is given if the Total Homework Assignments Turned In is greater than or equal to 12, otherwise, no bonus points are given.

3. Calculate the Total Points in column E as the Total Test Points for Semester in column B plus the Bonus Points in column D.

4. Use an IF function to calculate the Final Grade in column F.

   A grade of A is given if the Total Points is greater than or equal to 450, otherwise, a grade of B is given. Remember that the IF function will only return text arguments (such as A or B) if the argument is enclosed in parenthesis " " within the IF function.

5. Your completed worksheet should match the worksheet shown below.

6. **Print** the workbook, then **close** it and **save** it as **Assessment 10.1**.

	A	B	C	D	E	F
1	Final Grade Report					
2						
3	Student	Total Test Points for Semester	Total Homework Assignments Turned In	Bonus Points	Total Points	Final Grade
4	Cathy Wilson	425	10	0	425	B
5	Lisa Johnson	454	13	15	469	A
6	Steven Chang	410	8	0	410	B
7	Jill Downey	490	15	15	505	A
8	Carlos Martinez	475	15	15	490	A
9	Jermaine Green	495	15	15	510	A
10	Marty Austin	440	15	15	455	A

Assessment 10.2

In this exercise, you will use IF functions and VLOOKUP functions to create the worksheet below. The IF functions in column C will determine if the customer qualifies for the Free Rental program. The VLOOKUP functions in column D will determine how many free rentals the customer receives.

1. Start a New Workbook and enter the data shown in rows 1-3 and columns A and B below.

2. Use IF functions in column C to determine if a customer qualifies for the frequent renter program. Customers qualify if they have 5 or more frequent renter points in column B. The IF function should return the message **Free Rentals** if they qualify and nothing "" if they don't qualify.

3. Create the lookup table located at the bottom of the worksheet and name it **Free_Rentals_Table**.

4. Use VLOOKUP functions in column D to determine the number of free rentals each customer should receive. The function should use the Frequent Renter Points Earned in column B as the search argument and it should search the Free_Rentals_Table for the correct # of free rentals.

5. Your completed worksheet should match the worksheet shown below.

6. **Print** the workbook, then **close** it and **save** it as **Assessment 10.2**.

	A	B	C	D
1	Julie's Videos Frequent Renter Awards			
2				
3	Customer	Frequent Renter Points Earned	Qualify for Free Rentals?	# of Free Rentals
4	Dale Smith	6	Free Rentals	1
5	Sue Jackson	17	Free Rentals	3
6	Liz Johnson	3		0
7	Al Chase	22	Free Rentals	4
8	Bruce Pique	11	Free Rentals	2
9	Benny Jones	4		0
10	Tim Taylor	14	Free Rentals	2
11				
12				
13				
14			Free Rentals Table	
15			Number of Rentals	Free Rentals
16			0	0
17			5	1
18			10	2
19			15	3
20			20	4
21			25	5

Critical Thinking 10.1

Create a worksheet that tracks stock investments. Create cells for the purchase price and current value of each investment. Create a formula that calculates the gain or loss and another formula to calculate the percentage gain or loss. Create a lookup function in another cell that reports whether the return on investment is Poor, Average, Good or Excellent. You will need to set up a lookup table and determine the thresholds for the Poor, Average, Good and Excellent messages.

11

Financial Functions and Goal Seeking

Objectives:

- ◆ Understand financial function concepts

- ◆ Use the Payment (PMT) function

- ◆ Use the Future Value (FV) function

- ◆ Use the Goal Seeker

The Project - Purchasing a New Automobile

In this lesson, you will learn to use financial functions to help you make wise financial decisions. You will use the Payment function to determine the monthly payment for a shiny new Oldsmobile Aurora automobile. You will adjust the purchase price, down payment, interest rate and other variables to see the impact these changes have on the monthly payment. You will also use the Goal Seeker to determine the down payment that is required to achieve the monthly payment you desire. The completed worksheet is shown below.

	A	B	C	D
1	**Car Loan Analysis for Jane Evans**			
2				
3	Make and Model	97 Olds Aurora		
4	Purchase Price	35,000		
5	Down Payment	8,000		
6	Loan Amount	27,000		
7	Interest Rate	8%		
8	Number of Months	60		
9	Monthly Payment	$550.00		
10	Total Interest	$6,000.00		
11	Total Cost of Car	$41,000.00		
12				
13				
14	**Interest vs. Purchase Price**			
15				
16				
17	Total Interest			
18	15%			
19				
20				
21				
22	Purchase			
23	Price			
24	85%			
25				
26				

Financial Functions

Excel provides a variety of financial functions to help you answer financial questions and make intelligent financial decisions. The financial functions can be used to determine monthly payments on loans, the total interest paid on loans, the future value of an investment and other related questions. Excel also has advanced financial functions for calculating depreciation of assets, internal rates of return and other more advanced topics. In this lesson, you will use the PMT (Payment) and FV (Future Value) functions. These are the most useful financial functions for the average Excel user.

Syntax of financial functions

Like all functions, financial functions have a syntax that must be followed. You can construct financial functions with the Function box or you can enter them manually. The generic syntax of the PMT and FV functions is shown in the following table.

Function	Syntax
PMT (Payment)	PMT(rate, periods, loan amount)
FV (Future Value)	FV(rate, periods, payment)

The PMT and FV functions work with annuities

An annuity is a series of equal payments made over a period of time. For example, most car loans or fixed rate mortgages are annuities because the payment amounts remain constant throughout the term of the loan. The PMT and FV functions can only be used with annuities where the payment amount remains constant. The various arguments in the PMT and FV functions are discussed in the following table.

Argument	Description
periods	This is the number of periods in an annuity. Most annuities (such as loans) have a monthly payment period. For this reason, you should specify the number of months in the function as opposed to the number of years. For example, you should use 60 as the number of periods for a five year auto loan (5 years * 12 months per year).
rate	This is the interest rate for each period in an annuity. Most annuities have a monthly period, so the monthly interest rate should be specified. For example, you should use 1% as the interest rate for a loan with a 12% annual rate (1% per month).
payment	This is the payment amount for each period in the annuity. The payment must be the same for each period.
loan amount	Opening balance or amount borrowed for a loan.

Hands-On 11.1 – Create the auto loan worksheet

In this exercise, you will create a loan worksheet that will calculate the monthly payment on a car loan. The payment will be calculated with the PMT function. You will set up the purchase price, down payment and interest rate as variables. This way, you will be able to change these parameters and see the impact the changes have on the payment.

Set up the worksheet

1. Start Excel or start a new ⬜ worksheet.

2. Enter the data shown below. Format the text and numbers and widen columns A and B as shown.

	A	B
1	Car Loan Analysis for Jane Evans	
2		
3	Make and Model	97 Olds Aurora
4	Purchase Price	35,000
5	Down Payment	8,000
6	Loan Amount	
7	Interest Rate	
8	Number of Months	
9	Monthly Payment	
10	Total Interest	
11	Total Cost of Car	

Calculate the Loan Amount

The Loan Amount is the Purchase Price - Down Payment. The PMT function will use the Loan Amount as one of its arguments.

3. **Click** cell **B6**.

4. Enter the formula **=B4-B5**.

   The result should be 27,000.

5. Type an interest rate of **12%** in cell **B7** and confirm ✅ the entry.

6. Type **60** as the Number of Months in cell **B8** and confirm ✅ the entry.

Calculate the Monthly Payment with the PMT function
7. **Click** cell **B9**.

8. Type the formula **=PMT(B7,B8,B6)** and confirm ✅ the entry.

   The result should be ($3,243.61). The generic Payment function syntax is =PMT(rate, periods, loan amount). Notice how the references you used in the formula correspond to the generic syntax.

   Notice Excel formats the payment with the Currency format. Also notice the payment is red in color and surrounded by parenthesis. The red color and parenthesis indicate this is a negative number. Excel treats payments as debits (money you are paying), so they are assigned a negative number. This is a convention that bankers and other financial professionals use. You will convert this number to a positive number in the following steps.

Continued...

Also notice that $3,243.61 is a very large payment. This is because the interest rate in cell B7 is an annual rate of 12%. These financial functions have monthly periods, so you are paying 12% interest per month! The interest rate must be divided by 12 (the number of months in a year) in order to use a monthly interest rate in the function. You will do this in the following steps.

9. **Click** in the Formula bar and edit the formula as follows:
   - Type a minus sign **-** between the equal sign **=** and function name PMT.
   - Divide the B7 reference by 12. The completed formula is shown below.

   ### = - PMT(B7**/12**,B8,B6)

10. **Confirm** ☑ the entry and the new payment should be $600.60.

    This payment will certainly be more affordable! The minus sign converts the number to a positive and the B7/12 argument creates a 1% per month rate.

Calculate the Total Interest

The Total Interest can be calculated by first multiplying the Monthly Payment * Number of Months to determine the total payments. The Loan Amount in cell B6 can then be subtracted from the total payments to determine the Total Interest.

11. **Click** cell **B10** and enter the formula **=B9*B8-B6**.

    The Total Interest in cell B10 should be $9,036.01.

Calculate the Total Cost of Car

The Total Cost of Car is simply the total payments plus the down payment.

12. **Click** cell **B11** and enter the formula **=B9*B8+B5**.

    The result should be $44,036.01. As you can see, the Purchase Price of $35,000 plus the Total Interest of $9,036.01 add up to $44,036.01 (the Total Cost of Car).

13. The completed worksheet is shown below (although the example below also shows selected data, which will be used to create a chart in the next few steps).

	A	B
1	Car Loan Analysis for Jane Evans	
2		
3	Make and Model	97 Olds Aurora
4	Purchase Price	35,000
5	Down Payment	8,000
6	Loan Amount	27,000
7	Interest Rate	12%
8	Number of Months	60
9	Monthly Payment	$600.60
10	Total Interest	$9,036.01
11	Total Cost of Car	$44,036.01

Create a pie chart to compare the Total Interest to the Purchase Price

14. **Select** cells **A4:B4** and **A10:B10** as shown above (you must use the Ctrl key).

    This selection will allow the pie chart to compare the Total Interest to the Purchase Price.

Continued...

15. Click the Chart Wizard 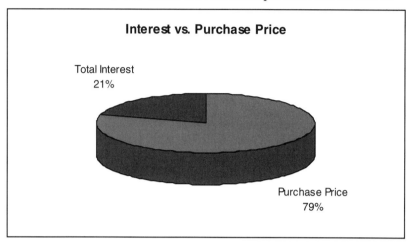 button.

16. Use the Chart Wizard to create the embedded pie chart shown below.

Interest vs. Purchase Price

Total Interest
21%

Purchase Price
79%

17. Save 🖫 the workbook as **Hands-On Lesson 11** and continue with the next topic.

Goal Seeking

Excel provides several tools to let you perform advanced what-if analysis. In this section, you will use the Goal Seeker tool. The Goal Seeker lets you set a goal for a cell that contains a formula. For example, you will set a goal of $550 for the Monthly Payment in cell B9. The Goal Seeker lets you choose another cell whose contents the Goal Seeker will change. The cell with the formula must be dependent on the second cell. For example, you will let the Goal Seeker adjust the Down Payment in order to achieve the $550 Monthly Payment.

🕐	*Quick Steps: **Goal Seeking***	🕐

To use the Goal Seeker
- *Develop and test the worksheet until it is functioning properly.*
- *Click the cell that you want to set a goal for. The cell must contain a formula.*
- *Choose Tools→Goal Seek... from the menu bar.*
- *Type the desired goal (number) in the To Value box.*
- *Click the By changing Cell box and specify the cell whose value you want the Goal Seeker to adjust.*
- *Click OK, then click OK again if you wish to confirm the change.*

Hands-On 11.2 – Use the Goal Seeker

1. Click cell **B9**.

> *It is usually a good idea to click the cell you want to set a goal for prior to starting the goal seeker. This way, the first option in the Goal Seeker will already be set when you start the goal seeker. Also, this will ensure you are setting a goal for the correct cell.*

2. Choose **Tools→Goal Seek...** from the menu bar.

Continued...

3. Use the following Hands-On Illustration to set the Goal Seek parameters.

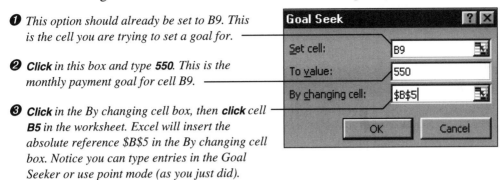

❶ *This option should already be set to B9. This is the cell you are trying to set a goal for.*

❷ **Click** *in this box and type* **550**. *This is the monthly payment goal for cell B9.*

❸ **Click** *in the By changing cell box, then* **click** *cell* **B5** *in the worksheet. Excel will insert the absolute reference $B$5 in the By changing cell box. Notice you can type entries in the Goal Seeker or use point mode (as you just did).*

4. **Click OK** and the Goal Seeker should indicate it has found a solution to the goal.

    Notice the Down Payment in the worksheet has been adjusted to 10,275.

5. **Click OK** on the Goal Seek Status dialog box to confirm the change to the Down Payment.

    As you can see, you will need a larger down payment if you want a $550 Monthly Payment.

Set a new Monthly Payment goal but adjust the interest rate this time

6. **Click** Undo ⟲ to reverse the change to the Down Payment.

7. **Click** cell **B9** and choose **Tools→Goal Seek...** from the menu bar.

8. Type **550** in the To Value box.

9. **Click** in the **By changing cell** box, then **click** cell **B7** in the worksheet (the Interest Rate cell).

10. **Click OK** and an interest rate of 8% will appear in the worksheet.

11. **Click OK** again to confirm the change to the Interest Rate.

    Notice the impact this change has on the chart. The Total Interest (in the chart) has decreased to 15%.

Play what-if analysis

    You can also play what-if analysis manually by changing the Interest Rate, Down Payment, Purchase Price and other values.

12. **Click** cell **B4** and change the Purchase Price to **$20,000**.

    What impact does this change have on the other variables and the chart?

13. Feel free to experiment with this worksheet and play what-if analysis.

14. **Close** the workbook when you have finished and **save** the changes.

Concepts Review

True / False

1. The PMT function can only be used if the payment amount is the same for each payment period.

1. **T   F**

2. Most loans and other annuities have a yearly payment period.

2. **T   F**

3. The cell you are seeking a goal for must contain a formula.

3. **T   F**

Multiple Choice

1. Which command is used to initiate the Goal Seeker?
   a) Edit→Goal Seek
   b) Format→Goak Seek
   c) Tools→Goal Seek
   d) None of the above.

   (   )

2. Which of the following PMT formulas has the arguments in the correct positions?
   a) =PMT(rate, periods, loan amount)
   b) =PMT(rate, loan amount, periods)
   c) =PMT(periods, rate, loan amount)
   d) None of the above.

   (   )

Skills Builder 11.1

In this exercise, you will use the PMT function to calculate mortgage payments on a 30-year fixed mortgage. You will multiply the 30 years by 12 within the PMT function to determine the total number of periods in the loan. The generic syntax of the PMT function is repeated below for your convenience.

Payment Function Syntax   **=PMT(rate, periods, loan amount)**

Set up the worksheet

1. Start a New Workbook [□] and create the following worksheet.

> *Make sure you use a formula to calculate the Loan Amount in cell B5 as the Purchase Price - Down Payment.*

	A	B
1	30-Year Mortgage Worksheet	
2		
3	Purchase Price	260,000
4	Down Payment	25,000
5	Loan Amount	235,000
6	Interest Rate	9%
7	Number of Years	30
8	Monthly Payment	
9	Total Interest	
10	Total Cost of Home	

2. **Click** cell **B8** and enter the formula **= - PMT(B6/12,B7*12,B5)**

> *The result should be $1,890.86. Notice the formula has a minus sign between the equal = sign and the PMT function. Also, the first argument **divides** the Interest Rate in cell B6 by 12 because the argument requires the monthly rate. Likewise, the second argument **multiplies** the Number of Years in cell B7 by 12 because the argument requires the number of months. Excel also formats the result with the Currency style because you used the PMT function.*

3. **Click** cell **B9** and use the formula **=B8*B7*12-B5** to calculate the Total Interest.

> *The result should be $445,710.73. Take a few moments to study the formula and notice it calculates the total payments over the term of the loan and subtracts the Loan Amount. Also notice the number of months was determined by multiplying the number of years in cell B7 by 12.*

4. **Click** cell **B10** and use the formula **=B9+B3** to calculate the Total Cost of Home.

Create a pie chart

5. **Select** cells **A3:B3** and **A9:B9** as shown below.

> *This selection will allow the pie chart to compare the Total Interest to the Purchase Price.*

	A	B
1	30-Year Mortgage Worksheet	
2		
3	Purchase Price	260,000
4	Down Payment	25,000
5	Loan Amount	235,000
6	Interest Rate	9%
7	Number of Years	30
8	Monthly Payment	$1,890.86
9	Total Interest	$445,710.73
10	Total Cost of Home	$705,710.73

Continued...

6. **Click** the Chart Wizard 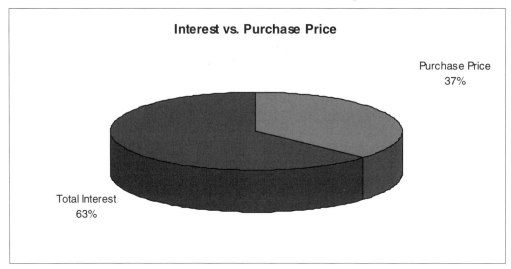 button and create the embedded pie chart shown below.

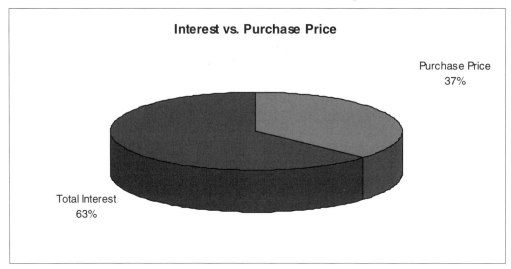

Interest vs. Purchase Price

Purchase Price
37%

Total Interest
63%

Play what-if analysis

7. **Click** cell **B6**.

   Notice the Monthly Payment in cell B8 is approximately 1,890.

8. Change the Interest Rate to **8%** and notice the impact it has on the Monthly Payment.

9. Experiment with various interest rates. Also, try changing the down payment and see the impact it has on the Monthly Payment.

10. **Close** the workbook when you have finished and **save** it as **Skills Builder 11.1**.

Skills Builder 11.2

In this exercise, you will use the Future Value (FV) function to determine the future value of a college fund. This could be important if you are planning on saving for a college education. This worksheet can be used to determine the future value of nearly any investment that has constant payments or contributions. The generic syntax of the FV function is repeated below for your convenience.

Future Value Function Syntax   **=FV(rate, periods, payment)**

Set up the worksheet

1. Start a New Workbook ⬜ and create the following worksheet.

	A	B
1	Ted's College Fund	
2		
3	Interest Rate	8%
4	Number of years	18
5	Monthly Contribution	200
6	Future Value	

2. Change the width of column B to **14** as shown above.

3. **Click** cell **B6** and type the function **=FV(B3/12,B4*12,B5)**.

   *Notice the Interest Rate in cell B3 is **divided** by 12 to give a monthly rate. The Number of Years in cell B4 is multiplied by 12 to give the total number of monthly payments.*

4. Confirm ✅ the entry and the result should be ($96,017.23).

   Notice the FV function returns a negative number, as did the PMT function.

Convert the result to a positive number

5. **Click** in the Formula bar and insert a minus sign between the = sign and the FV.

6. Confirm ✅ the entry and the result should be positive.

Use the Goal Seeker to determine the required Interest rate for a $200,000 future value

7. **Click** cell **B5** and change the Monthly Contribution to **$300**.

   Notice this increases the Future Value of the investment to approximately $144,000. In the next few steps, you will use the Goal Seeker to determine the interest rate necessary to have a Future Value of $200,000 with a Monthly Contribution of $300.

8. **Click** cell **B6** and choose **Tools→Goal Seek...** from the menu bar.

9. Set the **To Value** option to **$200,000**.

10. Set the **By changing cell** option to **B3** (the Interest Rate cell).

11. **Click OK** and notice an 11% Interest Rate is required.

12. **Click Cancel** on the Goal Seek Results dialog box to cancel the change to the interest rate.

13. Use the Goal Seeker to determine the Interest Rate that is required to achieve a $275,000 Future Value with a $325 Monthly Contribution.

14. **Close** the workbook when you have finished and **save** it as **Skills Builder 11.2**.

Assessment 11.1

1. Create the worksheet below using the FV function to calculate the future value in cell B7.

	A	B
1	Investment Projections	
2		
3	Account	Utilities Mutual Fund
4	Projected Annual Rate of Return	11%
5	Number of Years	20
6	Monthly Contribution	$800
7	Future Value	$692,510

2. Format all cells as shown and adjust the width of columns A and B to **19**.

3. **Print** the worksheet, then **close** the workbook and **save** it as **Assessment 11.1**.

 Assessment 11.2

1. Create the worksheet below using the PMT function to calculate the monthly payment in cell B7.

	A	B
1	Home Equity Loan Analysis	
2		
3	Lender	Wells Fargo
4	Interest Rate	10.50%
5	Number of Years	10
6	Loan Amount	$15,000
7	Monthly Payment	$202

2. Format all cells as shown and adjust the width of column A to **24** and column B to **11**.

3. **Print** the worksheet, then **close** the workbook and **save** it as **Assessment 11.2**.

Critical Thinking 11.1

1. **Open** the **Assessment 11.1** workbook.

2. Use the **File→Save As...** command to save the workbook as **Critical Thinking 11.1**.

    This will create a copy of the workbook.

3. Use the Goal Seeker to answer the following questions. Write your answers in the space provided.

    –   If the Rate of Return is 11% and the Number of Years is 20, then what must the Monthly Contribution be in order to have a Future Value of $1,000,000?   _____

    –   If the Rate of Return is 11% and the Monthly Contribution is $800, then what must the Number of Years be in order to have a Future Value of $1,000,000?   _____

    –   If the Number of Years is 20 and the Monthly Contribution is $800, then what must the Rate of Return be in order to have a Future Value of $1,000,000?   _____

Critical Thinking 11.2

1. **Open** the **Assessment 11.2** workbook.

2. Use the **File→Save As...** command to save the workbook as **Critical Thinking 11.2**.

    This will create a copy of the workbook.

3. Use the Goal Seeker to answer the following questions. Write your answers in the space provided.

    –   If the Interest Rate is 10.5% and the Number of Years is 10, then what must the Loan Amount be in order to have a Monthly Payment of $175?   _____

    –   If the Interest Rate is 11% and the Loan Amount is $15,000, then what must the Number of Years be in order to have a Monthly Payment of $175?   _____

    –   If the Number of Years is 10 and the Loan Amount is $15,000, then what must the Interest Rate be in order to have a Monthly Payment of $175?   _____

Critical Thinking 11.3

Create a worksheet that determines the future value of accumulated interest on a new credit card. Assume the card has an annual interest rate of 19.6%. In addition, assume that $200 per month of charges are incurred and a payment of $125 is made each month. Set up the worksheet so that the future value of the accumulated interest can be determined by changing the number of months that this spending pattern continues for. The accumulated interest will continue to grow because the monthly payment is less than the amount being purchased.

12 Macros

Objectives:

- Understand macro concepts

- Record macros

- Run macros

- Assign macros to buttons and shortcut keys

- Create global macros with the Personal Macro workbook

- Create buttons in worksheets

- Create customized toolbar buttons

- Hide and unhide worksheets and workbooks

- Display the Personal Macro workbook

- Deleting macros, buttons and customized toolbar buttons

The Project - West County Vocational Training Student Roster

In this lesson, you will develop a worksheet to track student enrollments at the West County Vocational Training center. Tina Johnston, the Administrative Secretary, wants to add new students to a student roster. Tina wants to sort the roster in three different ways. You will develop macros and customized buttons to automate these tasks for Tina. The worksheet and customized macro buttons you will create are shown below.

	A	B	C	D	E	F	G
1	**West County Vocational Training Student Roster**						
2							
3	Instructor	Student	Section	Starting Date			
4	Allison	Ames, Jason	1	1/1/97			
5	Allison	Ames, Donna	1	1/8/97			
6	Allison	Williams, Cora-Lee	1	3/6/97			
7	Allison	Leno, Jane	1	10/23/97			
8	Dawes	Brown, Lisa	1	6/8/97			
9	Dawes	Jackson, Mary	1	8/9/97			
10	Smith	Sorrell, Barbara	1	9/12/97			
11	Smith	Wilson, Wanda	1	10/22/97			
12	Allison	Ames, Alice	2	1/4/97			
13	Allison	Turner, Ted	2	6/6/97			
14	Allison	Zobe, Wayne	2	10/10/97			
15	Dawes	Jones, Al	2	3/4/97			
16	Dawes	Davis, Ted	2	3/11/97			
17	Dawes	Carlson, Michael	2	10/20/97			
18	Smith	Tomei, Mel	2	2/23/97			
19	Smith	Norman, Will	2	3/2/97	Sort by Starting Date		
20	Smith	Ames, Donald	2	8/9/97			
21	Allison	Yee, Donese	3	3/3/97	Sort by Section		
22	Dawes	Brown, Carl	3	2/10/97			
23	Dawes	Almore, Brian	3	10/11/97	Sort by Instructor		
24	Smith	Ellsworth, Sid	3	3/17/97			
25	Smith	Carey, Mary	3	5/5/97			
26	Smith	Carey, Harry	3	6/6/97			

What are Macros?

Macros are automated procedures you can play back at any time. Macros are useful for automating routine tasks especially when those tasks are performed often.

Macros can be written with Visual Basic or recorded

You can use the Microsoft Visual Basic programming language to create macros to accomplish just about any task. However, Visual Basic is beyond the scope of this text and only the concepts will be discussed here. Excel also has a macro recording feature which can record the keystrokes and commands you issue. You can then play back these recorded macros at a later time. This is similar to the automatic redial feature on telephones. The redial feature records commonly used phone numbers that you can redial by pressing one or two keys. Similarly, macros can easily play back recorded keystrokes and commands.

Macros can be assigned to buttons, menus or shortcut keys

Macros should be designed to save time and help you become more productive. In order for this to occur, macros must be easy to run especially if you use the same macro over-and-over again. Excel lets you assign macros to toolbar buttons, menus, shortcut keys and to buttons in a worksheet. You can then run a macro by clicking a button, choosing a menu option or pressing a shortcut key.

Creating Macros for the Current Workbook Only

Macros are only available in the workbook you create them in unless you assign them to the Personal Macro Workbook. The Personal Macro Workbook makes macros available in all workbooks on your computer system. This is useful if the macro can be used in various workbooks. For example, you may want a macro to format headings with a format you are particularly fond of. You could create a macro to accomplish this and then make the macro available to all workbooks. You will assign macros to the Personal Macro Workbook later in this lesson. Some macros, however, can only be used in the workbook they are designed for. For example, in the first part of this lesson, you will develop a macro to sort worksheet rows in a specific way. The macro will only be useful in the workbook you create it in.

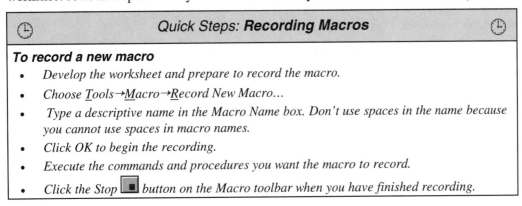

🕐	*Quick Steps:* ***Recording Macros***	🕐

To record a new macro
- *Develop the worksheet and prepare to record the macro.*
- *Choose Tools→Macro→Record New Macro...*
- *Type a descriptive name in the Macro Name box. Don't use spaces in the name because you cannot use spaces in macro names.*
- *Click OK to begin the recording.*
- *Execute the commands and procedures you want the macro to record.*
- *Click the Stop ▪ button on the Macro toolbar when you have finished recording.*

Hands-On 12.1 – Open a workbook and record a macro

Open the workbook and start the recording

1. **Open** the workbook named **Hands-On Lesson 12**.

2. If necessary, use the Zoom Control until you can see 25 rows in the worksheet.

   Take a moment to study the worksheet. Notice it contains a list of students. Each student has been assigned to an instructor. Also notice the list isn't sorted in any particular way. The goal of the next few exercises is to be able to add new students to the bottom of the list. The list will then be sorted and the new students will move to the appropriate locations in the list. You will create macros to automate the sorting process.

   Keep in mind that it is usually best to practice the procedure you want a macro to record before you actually record the macro. This will help you avoid mistakes while recording the macro. In this exercise, you will skip the practice steps because you will be guided step-by-step through the recording process.

3. Choose **Tools→Macro→Record New Macro...** form the menu bar.

   The Record Macro dialog box appears.

4. Use the following steps to name the macro and begin the recording process.

   ❶ *Type* **Sort_by_Instructor** *here. Use the underscore character between words instead of spaces. Spaces are not allowed in macro names.*

   ❷ *Notice the macro will be stored in* **This Workbook** *only. It would be available in all workbooks if Personal Macro Workbook were chosen.*

   ❸ *Type the description shown here.*

Record Macro	? X
Macro name:	
Sort_by_Instructor	OK
Shortcut key: Store macro in:	Cancel
Ctrl+ This Workbook	
Description:	
Sorts the list first by Instructor, then by Student and then by Section	

5. **Click OK** and the macro will begin recording your actions.

   The Stop Recording ▣ button and toolbar should appear somewhere in the worksheet. If it doesn't appear, then display it by using the View→Toolbars→Stop Recording command.

6. **Click** cell **A5**.

   The purpose of this action is to position the highlight somewhere in the list. You learned in an earlier lesson that Excel selects all rows in a list when you use the Sort command. By positioning the highlight in cell A5, you can be certain that Excel will select the list prior to sorting it. This action has been recorded by the macro and the highlight will move to cell A5 when the macro runs.

7. Choose **Data→Sort...** from the menu bar.

   This action has also been recorded by the macro.

Continued...

8. Use the following steps to set the Sort parameters.

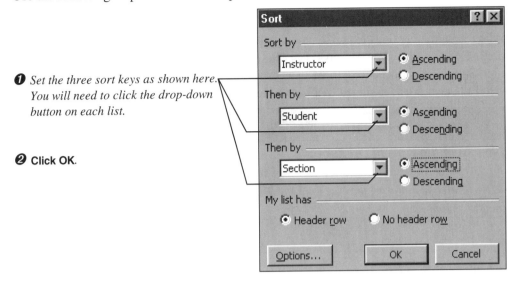

❶ *Set the three sort keys as shown here. You will need to click the drop-down button on each list.*

❷ **Click OK**.

The list will be sorted as shown below. Keep in mind that the macro recorded this sort sequence.

	A	B	C	D
1	West County Vocational Training Student Roster			
2				
3	Instructor	Student	Section	Starting Date
4	Allison	Ames, Alice	2	1/4/97
5	Allison	Ames, Donna	1	1/8/97
6	Allison	Ames, Jason	1	1/1/97
7	Allison	Turner, Ted	2	6/6/97
8	Allison	Williams, Cora-Lee	1	3/6/97
9	Allison	Yee, Donese	3	3/3/97
10	Dawes	Brown, Carl	3	2/10/97
11	Dawes	Brown, Lisa	1	6/8/97
12	Dawes	Davis, Ted	2	3/11/97
13	Dawes	Jackson, Mary	1	8/9/97
14	Dawes	Jones, Al	2	3/4/97
15	Smith	Ames, Donald	2	8/9/97
16	Smith	Carey, Harry	3	6/6/97
17	Smith	Carey, Mary	3	5/5/97
18	Smith	Ellsworth, Sid	3	3/17/97
19	Smith	Norman, Will	2	3/2/97
20	Smith	Sorrell, Barbara	1	9/12/97
21	Smith	Tomei, Mel	2	2/23/97

9. Click the Stop Recording ▣ button to turn off the recording process.

The macro is now ready to be played back.

Running Macros

Macros can be run in a variety of ways. The method you use depends upon how you assigned the macro prior to recording it. In the previous exercise, you created a macro without assigning it to a button, toolbar or shortcut key. For this reason, you must run the macro with the standard procedure shown in the following Quick Steps. This procedure can be used to run any macro that has been recorded in the current workbook even if the macro was assigned to a button, toolbar or shortcut key.

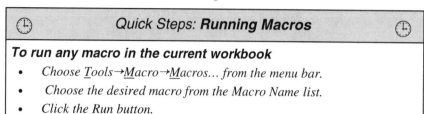

⏱	*Quick Steps: **Running Macros***	⏱

To run any macro in the current workbook

• *Choose Tools→Macro→Macros... from the menu bar.*

• *Choose the desired macro from the Macro Name list.*

• *Click the Run button.*

Hands-On 12.2 – Add new students and use the macro to sort the list

Add a student

1. **Click** cell **A22**.

    Students will always be added to the end of this list.

2. Add the following student to the list.

22	Allison	Zobe, Wayne	2	10/10/97

Run the macro

3. Choose **Tools→Macro→Macros...** from the menu bar.

    The Sort_by_Instructor macro should be the only macro on the list. However, there may be one or more macros that are preceded by the phrase PERSONAL.XLS. If you see a personal macro, then that means there are personal workbook macros on your system. Personal workbook macros are available to all workbooks. You will work with personal workbook macros later in this lesson.

4. Choose **Sort_by_Instructor** and **click** the **Run** button.

    The list should be sorted and Zobe, Wayne should move to row 10 and become the last of Instructor Allison's students.

Add another student and run the macro

5. **Click** cell **A23** and add the following student to the list.

23	Dawes	Almore, Brian	3	10/11/97

6. Use steps 3 and 4 above to run the macro.

    Keep in mind that you can have the highlight anywhere in the worksheet when you run the macro. This is because the first step in the macro moves the highlight to cell A5. The list is then sorted correctly because cell A5 is within the list.

7. Save 🖫 the changes to the workbook and continue with the next topic.

    The macro is saved with the workbook, so it will be available the next time you use the workbook.

Assigning a Macro to a Button

Excel has a Forms toolbar with buttons to assist you in creating **online forms**. Online forms can have various types of controls to assist users in data entry, decision making and other tasks.

The Button 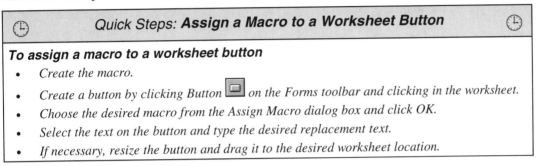 control lets you create a button and assign a macro to it. The assigned macro runs whenever the button is clicked. The button can be placed at any location in the worksheet. The button can also have descriptive text to identify the assigned macro.

🕐   *Quick Steps:* ***Assign a Macro to a Worksheet Button***   🕐

To assign a macro to a worksheet button

- *Create the macro.*
- *Create a button by clicking Button* *on the Forms toolbar and clicking in the worksheet.*
- *Choose the desired macro from the Assign Macro dialog box and click OK.*
- *Select the text on the button and type the desired replacement text.*
- *If necessary, resize the button and drag it to the desired worksheet location.*

Hands-On 12.3 – Create a button and assign the Sort_by_Instructor macro

Create the button

1. Choose **View**→**Toolbars** from the menu bar and choose **Forms**.

    This will display the Forms toolbar.

2. **Click** the Button ⬛ button.

3. **Click** the mouse pointer ✛ in an open part of the worksheet.

    A button will be created and the Assign Macro dialog box will appear.

4. Choose **Sort_by_Instructor** from the list and **click OK**.

Widen the button and move it

5. Use the following step to widen the button.

❶ **Drag** *a side-sizing handle until the button is approximately this wide.*

6. Use the following step to move the button.

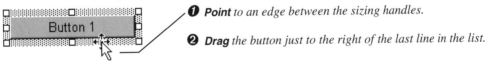
❶ **Point** *to an edge between the sizing handles.*

❷ **Drag** *the button just to the right of the last line in the list.*

Change the button text

7. **Drag** the mouse pointer over the Button 1 text and it will become selected as shown below.

8. Type the phrase **Sort by Instructor** and it will replace the Button 1 text.

Continued...

287

9. **Click** outside the button and it should have the appearance and size shown below.

Sort by Instructor

10. **Right-click** on the button.

    The button will become selected and a shortcut menu will pop up. You can always move, size and edit a button by first right-clicking on it.

11. **Click** outside the button to deselect it.

Add a student and run the macro by clicking the button

12. Add the following student in row 24.

| 24 | Dawes | Carlson, Michael | 2 | 10/20/97 |

13. **Click** the ⟨Sort by Instructor⟩ button to run the macro.

    The new record should be sorted into the list.

14. Add the following two students to the bottom of the list.

| 25 | Smith | Wilson, Wanda | 1 | 10/22/97 |
| 26 | Allison | Leno, Jane | 1 | 10/23/97 |

15. **Click** the ⟨Sort by Instructor⟩ button to sort the students into the list.

16. Save 💾 the changes and continue with the next exercise.

Hands-On 12.4 – Record two more sort macros and assign them to buttons

Record the next macro

1. Choose **Tools→Macro→Record New Macro...** from the menu bar.

2. Type **Sort_by_Section** in the Macro name box.

    There is no need to type a description for this macro.

3. **Click OK** to begin the recording process.

4. **Click** cell **A5** to position the highlight within the list.

    You want the macro to sort the worksheet on column A, so it is important to have the highlight in the column.

5. Choose **Data→Sort...** from the menu bar.

6. Set the first two sort fields as shown on the next page and set the third field to (none).

Continued...

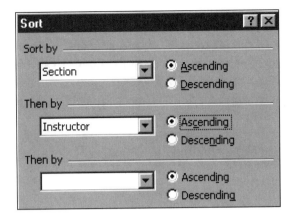

7. **Click OK** to complete the sort.

8. **Click** the Stop Recording ■ button to stop the recording process.

   Take a few moments to make sure the worksheet is sorted correctly.

Assign the macro to a button

9. **Click** Button ▢ on the Forms toolbar and **click** in the worksheet to create a button.

10. Choose **Sort_by_Section** from the Assign Macro box and **click OK**.

11. **Widen** the button until it is the same width as the Sort by Instructor button.

12. **Drag** the button to a position just above the Sort by Instructor button.

13. **Select** the **Button 2** text and type the phrase **Sort by Section**.

Create a third sort macro and button

14. Use the techniques you have just learned to create another macro named **Sort_by_Starting_Date** that sorts the list first by the **Starting Date** and then by the **Section**. Make sure you click somewhere in the list as the first step in the recording process.

15. Assign the macro to a new button with the text **Sort by Starting Date** on the button.

16. Size and position the button above the Sort by Section button.

Run the macros

17. **Click** any of the buttons to change the way the list is sorted.

18. **Click** each button several times to make sure the macros are functioning correctly.

    Keep in mind that the macros in this worksheet will probably be useful only in this worksheet. You can use macros to automate any routine task (like sorting). However, macros like those you just created are only useful if the worksheet is used on an ongoing basis. In the following sections, you will create macros that can be used with a variety of workbooks.

19. Save 🖫 the changes and continue with the next topic.

Creating Macros for Use with All Workbooks

As mentioned earlier, macros are only available in the workbook they are created in unless you assign them to the Personal Macro Workbook. Macros in the Personal Macro Workbook are available to all workbooks on your computer system. The Personal Macro Workbook contains only macros that have been assigned to it. This workbook is usually **hidden** and is not visible to you. Later in this lesson, you will learn to unhide the Personal Macro Workbook to enable you to delete macros from it.

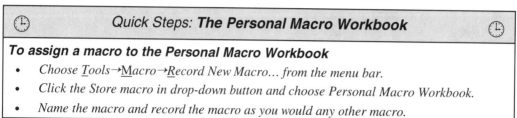

*Quick Steps: **The Personal Macro Workbook***

To assign a macro to the Personal Macro Workbook

- *Choose Tools→Macro→Record New Macro... from the menu bar.*
- *Click the Store macro in drop-down button and choose Personal Macro Workbook.*
- *Name the macro and record the macro as you would any other macro.*

Hands-On 12.5 – Create a formatting macro

In this exercise, you will create a macro that formats text. This macro will be available in all workbooks because you will assign it to the Personal Macro Workbook. Formatting macros are good candidates for the Personal Macro Workbook because they can help ensure consistent and rapid formatting across workbooks.

Select the title cell and begin recording

1. **Click** cell **A1**.

   You normally want to select cells prior to recording a formatting macro. You will also need to select the cells you wish to format prior to running the macro. In this example, only cell A1 needs to be selected because we are interested in formatting only this title.

2. Choose **Tools→Macro→Record New Macro...** from the menu bar.

3. Type **FormatTitle** as the macro name.

4. **Click** the **Store macro in** button and choose **Personal Macro Workbook** as shown below.

   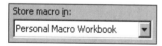

5. **Click OK** to begin the recording (click Yes to replace the macro if Excel tells you it already exists).

Format the title while the macro records your commands

6. Set the font size to **14** and **click** the Bold **B** button.

7. Use the Font Color **A** button to choose your favorite color.

8. **Click** the Stop Recording **■** button to turn off the recording process.

Use the macro in another workbook

9. **Click** the New button to open a new workbook.

10. Enter the phrase **This is a test heading** in cell **A1**.

Continued...

11. Make sure the highlight is in cell A1, then choose **Tools→Macro→Macros...** form the menu bar.

12. Take a few moments to study the names in the Macro Name list.

    Notice the macros you recorded in the other workbook have a Hands-On Lesson 12 prefix. These macros are only available in the Hands-On Lesson 12 workbook because they were not assigned to the Personal Macro Workbook. Also notice the macro named PERSONAL.XLS!FormatTitle. Personal Macro Workbook macros are always preceded by the PERSONAL.XLS! prefix and they can be used in all workbooks.

13. Choose **PERSONAL.XLS!FormatTitle** and **click** the **Run** button.

    The heading should be formatted exactly as in the other workbook.

14. Leave the workbook open because you will continue to use it.

Assigning a Macro to a Shortcut Key

Excel lets you assign a macro to a shortcut key. You can then run the macro by pressing the shortcut key. You can use this technique to run Personal Workbook Macros in any workbook. You must use the Ctrl key or the Ctrl + Shift combination as part of the shortcut. The following Quick Steps show you how to assign a macro to a shortcut key.

🕐   *Quick Steps:* **Assigning a Macro to a Shortcut Key**   🕐

To assign a macro to a Shortcut Key
- *Choose Tools→Macro→Record New Macro... from the menu bar.*
- *Click the Shortcut Key box and enter the desired keystroke.*

Hands-On 12.6 – Assign a macro to a shortcut key

In this exercise, you will create another macro that formats the list headings. You will assign the macro to the Personal Macro Workbook and you will assign it a shortcut key.

Switch to the Hands-On Lesson 12 workbook and begin recording

1. Choose **Window** from the menu bar.

    The Hands-On Lesson 12 workbook will be listed on the menu. The Windows menu always lists all open workbooks.

2. Choose **Hands-On Lesson 12** from the menu to switch to that workbook.

    You can always switch between open workbooks with this technique.

3. **Select** the list headings in row 3 as shown below.

4. Choose **Tools→Macro→Record New Macro...** from the menu bar.

5. Type **FormatHeadings** as the Macro Name.

    *Notice the **Store macro in** option is set to Personal Macro Workbook. The most recent **Store macro in** setting remains in effect until it is changed again.*

Continued...

6. Use the following step to assign the shortcut key.

❶ *Click in the Shortcut key box and type a lower case **f**. (This assigns the shortcut key Ctrl + f to the macro. You could also press the Shift key while typing the f to assign the Ctrl + Shift + f keystroke combination.)*

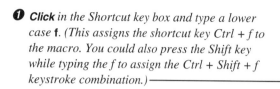

7. **Click OK** to begin recording the macro.

Format the headings

8. **Click** the Bold button and **click** the face of the Font Color button.

This will apply the same color that was applied to the title.

9. Use the Fill Color button to apply a background color to the cells.

If you chose a poor color combination, then feel free to choose another. The macro will record (and later play back) all these actions but the end result will be the desired combination.

10. **Click** the Stop Recording button to turn off the recording process.

This macro will now be available in all workbooks on your computer system.

Switch to the new workbook and type a heading line

11. Choose **Window** from the menu bar.

The new workbook you opened in the previous exercise will be listed on the menu as Book2 or some similar name.

12. Choose Book2 (or the similar name) from the menu to switch to that workbook.

13. Type the following headings in row 3.

Run the macro and close the workbook

14. **Select** the headings you just typed.

15. **Press & Hold** the ⌈Ctrl⌉ key while you **tap** the letter ⌈F⌉ on your keyboard.

The macro will format the headings with the same formatting you applied in the other workbook. You can now use this macro to format headings in any workbook.

Notice how the shortcut keys are fast and easy to use, however, they must be memorized. A shortcut key works well if you use the macro often and you can memorize the shortcut key. In the next topic, you will assign a macro to a toolbar button that will also be available to all workbooks.

16. Choose **File→Close** and choose **No** when Excel asks if you want to save the workbook.

This will close the new workbook and return you to the Hands-On Lesson 12 workbook. Leave the Hands-On Lesson 12 workbook open because you will continue to use it.

Assigning Macros to Toolbar Buttons

Earlier in this lesson, you assigned macros to buttons within a worksheet. Unfortunately, worksheet buttons are only available in the worksheet they were created in. With Excel, however, you can add new buttons to the toolbars and assign macros to those buttons. You can even create your own customized toolbars. Toolbars are available in all workbooks, so you can use customized toolbar buttons to run Personal Workbook Macros. Assigning macros to toolbars is convenient because there is no need to remember shortcut keystrokes.

Quick Steps: *Assign a macro to a toolbar button*

To assign a macro to a toolbar button

- *Right-click any toolbar and choose Customize... from the shortcut menu.*
- *Click the Commands tab.*
- *Scroll through the Categories list and choose Macros.*
- *Drag the smiley face Custom Button from the dialog box to any toolbar.*
- *Right-click on the new button and choose Assign Macro from the pop up menu.*
- *Choose the desired macro and click OK.*

Hands-On 12.7 – Assign the FormatTitle macro to a new toolbar button

In a previous exercise, you created the FormatTitle macro. In this exercise, you will assign this Personal Workbook Macro to a toolbar button.

1. Use the following steps to display the Customize dialog box.

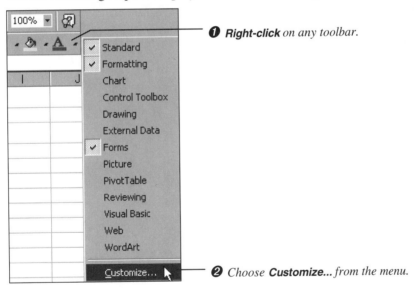

❶ *Right-click on any toolbar.*

❷ *Choose **Customize...** from the menu.*

The Customize dialog box will appear.

2. **Click** the **Commands** tab.

3. **Scroll** through the Categories list and choose **Macros**.

The Custom Button smiley face will appear on the Commands list.

Continued...

4. Use the following steps to add a button to the Formatting toolbar.

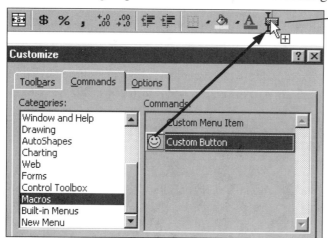

❶ *Drag the **Smiling Face** from the dialog box to the right end of the Formatting toolbar as shown here (but don't release the mouse button just yet).*

❷ *Notice the vertical I-beam shape shown here is just inside the last button on the toolbar. This will cause the new button to be added to the end of the toolbar. You must place a new button somewhere on an existing toolbar. Don't be concerned if a color palette or some other object pops up.*

❸ ***Release** the mouse button to place the smiley face button on the toolbar.*

Assign a macro to the button

5. Use the following steps to assign a macro to the button.

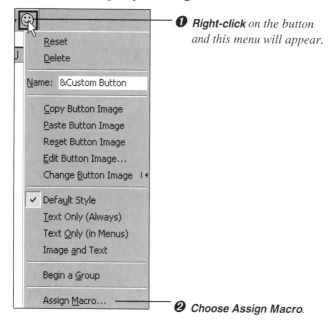

❶ ***Right-click** on the button and this menu will appear.*

❷ *Choose Assign Macro.*

6. Choose the **PERSONAL.XLS!FormatTitle** macro and **click OK**.

The macro has been assigned to the button. Leave the dialog box open because you will continue to use it in the next topic.

Using Descriptive Text on Toolbar Buttons

Excel 97 makes it easy to use descriptive text (such as a macro name) on a customized button. This makes it easy to identify the macro that is assigned to a button. You will use this technique to replace the smiley face with text in the following exercise.

| | Quick Steps: **Add text to a toolbar button** | |

To add text to a toolbar button
- *Right-click any toolbar and choose Customize... from the shortcut menu.*
- *Right-click on the desired button.*
- *Type the desired text in the Name box of the shortcut menu.*
- *Choose **Text only** from the shortcut menu and close the Customize box.*

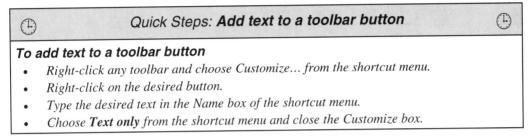

Hands-On 12.8 – Add text to the button

The Customize dialog box should still be open from the previous exercise.

1. Right-click the smiley face button on the toolbar and the shortcut menu will appear.

2. Use the following steps to add text to the button.

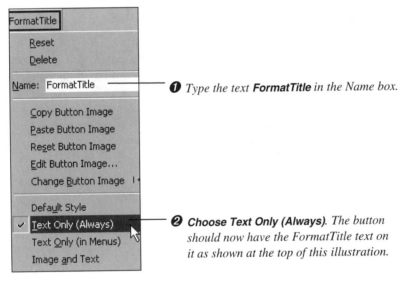

❶ *Type the text **FormatTitle** in the Name box.*

❷ *Choose **Text Only (Always)**. The button should now have the FormatTitle text on it as shown at the top of this illustration.*

3. Now **Close** the **Customize** dialog box.

Open a new workbook and use the button to run the macro

4. **Click** the New [ ] button.

5. Enter the phrase **This is a test** in cell **A1** and Confirm [✓] the entry.

6. Make sure the highlight is in cell A1, and then **click** the [FormatTitle] button on the toolbar.

   The macro should run and format cell A1 with the formatting options discussed earlier in this lesson. Once again, this toolbar button and the corresponding macro are now available to all workbooks on this computer system.

7. Choose **File→Close** and then choose **No** to close the workbook without saving the changes.

   Leave the Hands-On Lesson 12 workbook open because you will continue to use it.

Deleting Macros

You can delete macros after you have recorded them. However, any shortcut keys or buttons that have been assigned the macros will no longer function.

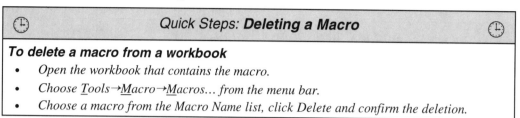

⏰	*Quick Steps:* **Deleting a Macro**	⏰

To delete a macro from a workbook
- *Open the workbook that contains the macro.*
- *Choose Tools→Macro→Macros... from the menu bar.*
- *Choose a macro from the Macro Name list, click Delete and confirm the deletion.*

Deleting Macros from the Personal Macro Workbook

Excel stores Personal Workbook Macros in the Personal Macro Workbook. The Personal Macro Workbook is always open, however, it is usually hidden from view. In order to delete macros from the Personal Macro Workbook, you must first unhide the workbook. The macros can then be deleted using the procedure in the Quick Steps above. When you are finished, you should hide the Personal Macro Workbook using the Quick Steps described below.

Hiding and Unhiding Worksheets and Workbooks

Excel lets you hide rows, columns, worksheets and entire workbooks from view. This is done for a variety of reasons. For example, you may want to hide an important sheet in a workbook to prevent inexperienced users from damaging it. The Quick Steps below describe how to hide and unhide rows, columns, worksheets and workbooks.

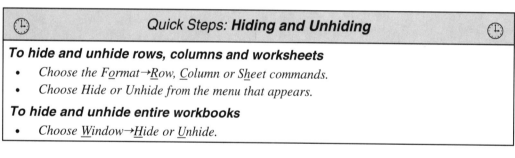

⏰	*Quick Steps:* **Hiding and Unhiding**	⏰

To hide and unhide rows, columns and worksheets
- *Choose the Format→Row, Column or Sheet commands.*
- *Choose Hide or Unhide from the menu that appears.*

To hide and unhide entire workbooks
- *Choose Window→Hide or Unhide.*

Hands-On 12.9 – Delete Macros

Delete the Sort by Starting Date macro

1. Choose **Tools→Macro→Macros...** from the menu bar.

2. Choose the **Sort_by_Starting_Date** macro.

3. **Click** the **Delete** button and then **click Yes** to confirm the deletion.

Unhide the Personal Macro Workbook

4. Choose **Window→Unhide...** from the menu bar.

   The Unhide dialog box lists all hidden workbooks. The Personal workbook will usually be the only workbook displayed in this dialog box.

Continued...

5. Choose **Personal** and **click OK**.

    Excel will display the Personal Macro Workbook although it will appear to be empty. Even though this workbook appears to be empty, you must still have it open if you want to delete Personal Macro Workbook macros.

Delete the FormatHeadings macro

6. Choose **Tools→Macro→Macros...** from the menu bar.

7. Choose the **FormatHeadings** macro.

8. **Click** the **Delete** button and then **click Yes** to confirm the deletion.

    Keep in mind that you could not have deleted this macro if you had displayed the Macro dialog box from the Hands-On Lesson 12 workbook. The macro would have been displayed in the Macro dialog box but Excel would not have let you delete it. You can only delete Personal Macro Workbook macros by unhiding the Personal Macro Workbook as in this exercise.

Hide the Personal Macro Workbook

9. Choose **Window→Hide** to hide the Personal Macro Workbook.

    You should always hide the Personal Macro Workbook after deleting macros from it.

10. Save 🖫 the changes to Hands-On Lesson 12 and continue with the next topic.

Deleting Worksheet Buttons and Toolbar Buttons

A worksheet button is easily deleted by right-clicking the button and choosing Cut from the shortcut menu. Toolbar buttons can be deleted by displaying the Customized dialog box and dragging the desired button from the toolbar into the dialog box. It doesn't matter where in the dialog box the button is dropped.

Hands-On 12.10 – Delete a worksheet button and the FormatTitle button

Delete the Sort by Starting Date button

1. **Right-click** on the **Sort by Starting Date button** and the shortcut menu will appear.

2. Choose **Cut** from the menu and the button will be deleted.

Delete the FormatTitle button

3. **Right-click** the FormatTitle button and choose **Customize...** from the shortcut menu.

4. **Drag** the FormatTitle button from the Formatting toolbar into the dialog box.

5. **Drop** the button anywhere in the dialog box and it will vanish.

    You can always use this technique to remove customized buttons from a toolbar.

6. **Close** the Customized dialog box.

7. Choose **File→Exit** and save the changes to the **Personal Macro Workbook** and the **Hands-On Lesson 12** workbook.

    You have to save changes to the Personal Macro Workbook like any other workbook. Now continue with the end-of-lesson questions and exercises on the following pages.

Concepts Review

True / False

1. Personal Workbook Macros are only available in the workbook they are created in.   1. **T   F**

2. Excel lets you create macros by recording your keystrokes and commands.   2. **T   F**

3. Macro names cannot contain spaces.   3. **T   F**

4. You use the Tools→Macro→Macros… command to record a new macro.   4. **T   F**

5. The Button ▣ button is located on the Drawing toolbar.   5. **T   F**

6. The Personal Macro Workbook is always open but it is normally hidden from view.   6. **T   F**

7. The **Store macro in** option on the Record Macro dialog box lets you store a macro in the Personal Macro Workbook.   7. **T   F**

8. Macros can be assigned to shortcut keys.   8. **T   F**

9. The Customize dialog box is used to assign macros to a customized toolbar button.   9. **T   F**

10. The Customize dialog box can be displayed by right-clicking in the worksheet and choosing Customize… from the shortcut menu.   10. **T   F**

Multiple Choice

1. Which of the following commands is used to record a new macro?
   a) Tools→Record New Macro…
   b) Tools→Macro→Macros…
   c) Tools→Macro→Record New Macro…
   d) None of the above.   (   )

2. Which of the following commands can be used to run a macro?
   a) Tools→Macro→Run Macro
   b) Tools→Macro→Macros…
   c) Tools→Record Macro→Run
   d) None of the above.   (   )

3. Which of the following techniques can be used to run a macro?
   a) Click a toolbar button that has been assigned a macro.
   b) Use a shortcut key.
   c) Use the Tools→Macro→Macros… command.
   d) All of the above.   (   )

4. Which of the following buttons do you use to create a new button in a worksheet?
   a) ▣
   b) ☺
   c) 🗺
   d) None of the above.   (   )

5. Which command is used to unhide the Personal Macro Workbook?
   a) Tools→Macro→Unhide
   b) Window→Unhide
   c) Format→Workbook→Unhide
   d) None of the above.   (   )

Skills Builder 12.1

In this exercise, you will create a macro that selects an entire worksheet, widens the columns and formats all cells with bold. You will assign the macro to the Personal Macro Workbook.

Begin recording the macro

1.   Start a new  workbook.

2.   Choose **Tools→Macro→Record New Macro...** from the menu bar.

3.   Type the macro name **FormatSheet** in the Record Macro dialog box.

4.   Set the **Store macro in** option to **Personal Macro Workbook**.

5.   **Click OK** (replace the macro if it already exists) to begin the recording process.

Set the desired formats

6.   **Click** the Select All button.

7.   **Click** Bold to bold all cells.

8.   Choose **Format→Column→Width...** from the menu bar.

9.   Type **12** in the Column Width box and **click OK**.

Stop the recording then play back the macro

10. **Click** the Stop button.

11. Choose **File→Close** and choose **No** when Excel asks if you want to save the workbook.

12. Start a new workbook.

13. Choose **Tools→Macro→Macros...** to display the Macro dialog box.

14. Choose the **PERSONAL.XLS!FormatSheet** macro and **click** the **Run** button.

     The column and text formats will be set. Keep in mind that you can apply virtually any cell, column, text or number format with a macro. Only your needs and creativity limit you.

Delete the macro from the Personal Macro Workbook

15. Choose **Window→Unhide...** from the menu bar.

16. Choose **Personal** from the Unhide box and **click OK**.

     The Personal Macro Workbook will display.

17. Choose **Tools→Macro→Macros...** from the menu bar.

18. Choose the **FormatSheet** macro from the list.

19. **Click** the **Delete** button, and then **click Yes** to confirm the deletion.

20. Choose **Window→Hide...** to hide the Personal Macro Workbook.

     In this exercise, you deleted the macro to keep the computer system "clean". Normally, you would leave Personal Macro Workbook macros on the system, so they could be used in all workbooks.

21. **Close** the empty workbook **without** saving the changes.

Skills Builder 12.2

In this exercise, you will create a print macro that maximizes the print area by switching the orientation to Landscape and reducing the margins. The macro will also change the default header and footer. You will store the macro in the Personal Macro Workbook to make it available to all workbooks.

Begin recording the macro

1. Start a new 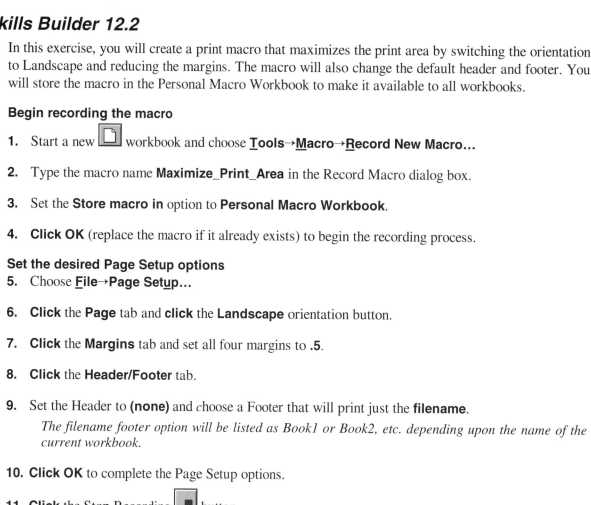 workbook and choose **Tools**→**Macro**→**Record New Macro...**

2. Type the macro name **Maximize_Print_Area** in the Record Macro dialog box.

3. Set the **Store macro in** option to **Personal Macro Workbook**.

4. **Click OK** (replace the macro if it already exists) to begin the recording process.

Set the desired Page Setup options

5. Choose **File**→**Page Setup...**

6. **Click** the **Page** tab and **click** the **Landscape** orientation button.

7. **Click** the **Margins** tab and set all four margins to **.5**.

8. **Click** the **Header/Footer** tab.

9. Set the Header to **(none)** and *c*hoose a Footer that will print just the **filename**.

    The filename footer option will be listed as Book1 or Book2, etc. depending upon the name of the current workbook.

10. **Click OK** to complete the Page Setup options.

11. **Click** the Stop Recording ▪ button.

Make sure the Page Setup settings are correct

12. Enter the phrase, **This is a test** into cell A1.

13. **Click** the Print Preview button.

    Notice the orientation, margins and header and footer. Are they set according to the specifications in this exercise? If they aren't, then you should record the macro again.

14. **Close Print Preview**, then **close** the workbook **without** saving the changes.

Run the macro

15. Start a New Workbook and enter the phrase, **This is a test** into cell **A1**.

16. Choose **Tools**→**Macro**→**Macros...**

17. Choose the **PERSONAL.XLS!Maximize_Print_Area** macro and **click** the **Run** button.

    Your screen will probably flash while the macro sets up the page. This will take a few moments.

18. **Click** the Print Preview button and the page should have the landscape orientation and other Page Setup options you recorded in the macro.

    Keep in mind that you could assign this (and any other Personal Macro Workbook macro) to a shortcut key or to a customized toolbar button.

19. **Close Print Preview**, then **close** the workbook **without** saving the changes.

Skills Builder 12.3

In this exercise, you will create a macro that formats numbers with a floating currency format. Many people prefer this format to the fixed dollar sign format that is applied by the Currency $ button. The floating format is a good candidate for a macro. This is because you normally have to apply this format with the Format Cells dialog box which can be time consuming and cumbersome.

Begin recording the macro

1. Start a new workbook and enter the number **100000** in cell **A1**.

    You will format this number while recording the macro. This way, you can be certain the proper format has been applied to the number.

2. Make sure the highlight is in cell A1, then choose **Tools**→**Macro**→**Record New Macro.**

3. Type the name **Floating_Currency_Format**.

4. Make sure the **Store macro in** option is set to **Personal Macro Workbook**.

5. **Click** the Shortcut key **check box** and **type** a lower case **c** as shown below.

    This will set the shortcut key to Ctrl + c.

    Shortcut key:
    Ctrl+ c

6. **Click OK** (replace the macro if it already exists) to begin the recording process.

Set the currency format

7. Choose **Format**→**Cells** and click the **Number** tab.

8. Choose **Currency** from the Category list and *set* the Decimal Places to **0**.

9. Make sure the Symbol box is set to dollar sign $.

10. Leave the Negative Numbers format as it is and **click OK**.

    The number should be formatted with the floating currency format $100,000.

11. **Click** the Stop Recording ■ button.

Use the macro in a worksheet

12. **Close** the workbook **without** saving the changes.

13. Open the workbook named **Skills Builder 12.3**.

14. **Select** cells **B6:E6** in row 6 as shown below.

| 6 | Subtotal | 3,551,670 | 4,492,560 | 4,291,250 | 4,046,650 |

15. Press Ctrl + C and the floating currency format should be applied to the cells.

    Remember that Ctrl + c was the shortcut key you assigned to your macro.

16. Use your macro to apply the floating currency format to the Subtotals in rows 10 and 14 and the Totals in row 16. You will need to select the cells first and then press Ctrl + c. Once again, this macro can be used in any workbook because you assigned it to the Personal Macro Workbook.

17. **Close** the workbook when you have finished and **save** the changes.

Skills Builder 12.4

In this exercise, you will open a workbook from your diskette. You will create a macro that deletes rows from the workbook. You will copy one of the existing buttons in the worksheet and then assign the macro to the new button.

Begin recording the macro

1. Open 📂 the workbook named **Skills Builder 12.4**.

    Notice this workbook is a duplicate of the Hands-On Lesson 12 workbook you used throughout the Hands-On exercises in this lesson. Now you will add a button to delete students from the list.

2. **Click** cell **A8**.

    You will delete Ted Turner from the list and have the macro record this action.

3. Choose **Tools→Macro→Record New Macro...**

4. Type the name **Delete_Students**.

5. Set the **Store macro in** option to **This Workbook**.

    We want this macro to be restricted for use in this workbook only.

6. **Click OK** to begin the recording process.

Delete the row

7. Choose **Edit→Delete...** from the menu bar.

8. Choose the Entire Row ⦿ Entire Row option and **click OK**.

    The row will be deleted.

9. **Click** the Stop Recording ■ button.

Copy a button and assign a new macro to the copied button

10. **Right-click** the **Sort by Section** button and choose **Copy** from the shortcut menu.

11. **Click** outside the button to deselect it.

12. **Right-click** the button again and choose **Paste** from the shortcut menu.

    Excel will paste a copy of the button slightly off of the original button.

13. **Drag** the copied button up and **drop** it just above the Sort by Section button.

14. **Select** the **text** on the copied button and change it to **Delete Students**.

15. **Click** outside the button to deselect it.

16. **Right-click** the **Delete Students** button again and choose **Assign Macro...** from the menu.

17. Choose the **Delete_Students** macro and **click OK**.

Move the buttons to the top of the worksheet

    In the next few steps, you will move the buttons to the top of the worksheet. The buttons are currently in the rows you will delete. They would be deleted with the rows if you were to leave them there. For this reason, you will move them to the top of the worksheet.

Continued...

18. **Click** cell **A2**.

19. Choose **Insert**→**Rows** from the menu bar.

    You will position the buttons in rows 2 and 3 between the title and headings.

20. **Right-click** the **Delete Students** button and it will become selected.

    The button must be selected in order to move it.

21. **Drag** the button to the top of the worksheet just below the title.

    The button should be somewhere in rows 2 and 3.

22. **Drag** the other buttons to the locations shown below.

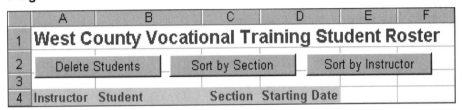

Freeze the header rows

In the next two steps, you will freeze rows 1-4 with the Window→Freeze Panes command. This way, the heading row and the buttons will always be visible.

23. **Click** cell **A5**.

24. Choose **Window**→**Freeze Panes** from the menu bar.

Use the button to delete several rows
25. **Click** cell **A18**.

    The Al Jones row needs to be deleted.

26. **Click** the **Delete Students** button and the row should be deleted.

27. Use your new button to delete row 20 (the Mary Carey row).

    You will need to click in the row first and then click the Delete Students button.

28. **Select** rows **5** and **6** as shown below.

29. **Click** the **Delete Students** button.

    Both Alice Ames and Donna Ames should be deleted.

30. Feel free to delete additional rows or add students to the bottom of the list. Use the Sort by Section and Sort by Instructor buttons to sort the list. These buttons have the same sorting macros assigned to them as you created earlier in this lesson.

31. **Close** the workbook when you have finished and **save** the changes.

Assessment 12.1

In this assessment, you will create a macro that inserts the phrase Today's Date in cell A1 and the TODAY() function in cell A2. The macro will also format the two cells. You will assign the macro to the current workbook only.

Create the macro

1. Start a new ⬜ workbook.

2. Begin recording a new macro. Give the macro the name **Assessment_12_1**, set the **Store macro in** option to **This Workbook** and assign the shortcut keystroke **Ctrl + d** to the macro. Your macro should record all of the actions in the next few steps.

3. Enter the phrase **Today's Date** into cell **A1**.

4. Format cell A1 with an **Arial 16 Bold Italic** font and use the Font Color ⬛ button to apply a color to the text.

5. Use the *=TODAY( )* function to enter the current date in cell **A2**.

6. Left Align ⬛ the date in cell A2.

7. Format cell A2 with an **Arial 12 Bold Italic** font and use the Font Color ⬛ button to apply the same color you used in cell A1.

8. Set the width of column A to **20**.

9. Stop the macro recording.

Undo the changes and test the macro

10. Use Undo ⬛ to Undo all the actions the macro recorded.

    The worksheet should be back in the original state it was in prior to recording the macro. However, the macro has been saved and can be used to restore the changes at any time.

11. Run the macro.

    If your macro does not insert and format the text and widen column A as discussed above, then you will need to record it again.

12. Once your macro is functioning correctly, delete the contents of cells A1 and A2 and restore their formatting to the default settings. You can use the Format Painter ⬛ to copy the formats from any empty cell to cells A1 and A2.

13. Set the width of column A to **8.43** (the default width).

    Your worksheet should look like a new worksheet.

14. **Click** the Save ⬛ button and save the workbook as **Assessment 12.1**.

Demonstrate the macro

15. Demonstrate the macro to your instructor by using the Ctrl + d keystroke combination.

16. After demonstrating the macro, **close** the workbook and **save** the changes.

    This will preserve the data entry, formatting and column width adjustments the macro has made.

Assessment 12.2

In this assessment, you will create the macro buttons and corresponding macros shown below.

1. **Open** the workbook named **Assessment 12.2**.

2. Create three macros for use in **this workbook only** and assign them to buttons as shown below. The following table describes the button text, macro names and macro function for each button.

Button text	Macro name	Macro function
Sort by Patron	Sort_by_Patron	Sort the list in ascending order based upon the patron names in column A.
Sort by Details	Sort_by_Details	Sort the list in ascending order based upon the details in column C.
Currency Format	Currency_Format	Format the current cell (or selected cells) with a floating currency format with 0 decimals. The floating currency format must be set with the Format Cells dialog box. This macro will be used to format the detail entries in Column C.

3. Test your macros until they function correctly.

4. Remove the Currency format from all entries in Column C in preparation for demonstrating the macros to your instructor.

Demonstrate the macros

5. **Demonstrate** the sort buttons to your instructor.

6. Use Sort by Details as the final sort demonstration.

7. **Demonstrate** the Currency Format button by formatting all number entries in column C with the Floating Currency format.

8. When you have finished demonstrating, your worksheet should have the appearance shown below.

9. **Close** the workbook and **save** the changes.

	A	B	C	D	E
1	Annual Holiday Donation Drive				
2					
3	Patron	Type of Donation	Details		
4	Sato, Michael	Money	$5		
5	Turner, Jane	Money	$10		
6	Townsend, Brian	Money	$25		
7	Bixby, Bill	Money	$50		
8	Sinhg, Ricky	Money	$65	Sort by Patron	
9	Carlson, Wanda	Money	$100		
10	Leonard, Leroy	Food	Canned Goods	Sort by Details	
11	Williams, Bernice	Food	Canned Goods		
12	Kester, Glenn	Food	Dried Goods	Currency Format	
13	Williams, John	Food	Turkey		

Critical Thinking 12.1

Create two Personal Workbook Macros. The first macro should format subtotal rows with a format that allows them to stand out in worksheets. The second macro should format the total rows in worksheets. Feel free to use any formatting options you have learned. This includes text formats, number formats and cell formats such as shading and borders. Try to create some consistency between the formats you use for the subtotal and total formats. The formats and macros should be designed so that they can be used in a wide range of worksheets. Also, assign the macros to shortcut keys that are easy to remember. This will make it easy to run the macros.

Critical Thinking 12.2

Open the Skills Builder 2.1 and Skills Builder 2.2 workbooks that you created earlier in this course. Use the macros you created in Critical Thinking exercise 12.1 to format the Subtotal and Total rows in these worksheets. Use the File→Save As command to save Skills Builder 2.1 as Critical Thinking 12.2a and Skills Builder 2.2 as Critical Thinking 12.2b. Close all open workbook when you have finished.

Critical Thinking 12.3

Think of five ways that macros could be useful in worksheets. Be creative and understand that you can automate just about any procedure with a macro. Write your ideas in the spaces provided below.

Five useful ways to use macros

1. _____

   _____

2. _____

   _____

3. _____

   _____

4. _____

   _____

5. _____

   _____

Critical Thinking 12.4

Choose one of the useful ways to use macros that you described above and create a worksheet that uses a macro as you describe. Test your macro to make sure it functions properly and demonstrate your ideas to your instructor. Save you workbook with a descriptive name when you have finished.

13 Databases and PivotTables

Objectives:

- Understand database concepts

- Set up a database

- Use data forms to enter, edit and delete records

- Use automatic subtotaling

- Use AutoFilter

- Understand PivotTable concepts

- Create PivotTables

- Rotate row and column headings in PivotTables

The Project - National Computing Solutions Sales Rep Database

In this lesson, you will develop a database for National Computing Solutions, a nationwide provider of customized hardware and software solutions for businesses. Donna Boyer, the National Sales Manager, wants to track and analyze the sales performance of her sales representatives. You will develop a database that lets Donna analyze the data with subtotals, filters and PivotTables. The database is shown below along with the PivotTable you will create.

	A	B	C	D	E	F	G	H	I
1	National Computing Solutions								
2	1997 Sales Database								
3									
4	Name	Years Employed	Position	Region	State	SW Sales	HW Sales		
5	Alvizo, Alex	7	Senior Sales Rep	Western	CA	450,000	340,000		
6	Zain, Beth	7	Senior Sales Rep	Western	CA	340,000	800,000		
7	Brown, Bill	3	Telemarketer	Western	CA	546,000	120,000		
8	Smith, Bob	3	Sales Rep	Western	CA	200,000	180,000		
9	Hubbs, Daniel	4	Telemarketer	Eastern	FL	340,000	230,000		
10	Martinez, Carlos	4	Senior Sales Rep	Eastern	FL	450,000	450,000		
11	Williams, Michael	3	Sales Rep	Eastern	FL	120,000	340,000		
12	Cain, Mary	5	Senior Sales Rep	Central	IL	234,000	560,000		
13	Thomas, Will	2	Sales Rep	Central	IL	230,000	120,000		
14	Wilson, Bernie	1	Sales Rep	Central	IL	120,000	170,000		
15	Watson, Tom	8	Sales Rep	Eastern	MA	230,000	340,000		
16	Smith, Michael	5	Telemarketer	Eastern	MA	123,000	230,000		
17	Cray, Zip	6	Telemarketer	Western	WA	900,000	780,000		
18	Richards, Paul	4	Telemarketer	Western	WA	234,000	546,000		
19									
20			State						
21	Region	Data	CA	FL	IL	MA	WA	Grand Total	
22	Central	Sum of SW Sales			584000			584000	
23		Sum of HW Sales			850000			850000	
24	Eastern	Sum of SW Sales		910000		353000		1263000	
25		Sum of HW Sales		1020000		570000		1590000	
26	Western	Sum of SW Sales	1536000				1134000	2670000	
27		Sum of HW Sales	1440000				1326000	2766000	
28	Total Sum of SW Sales		1536000	910000	584000	353000	1134000	4517000	
29	Total Sum of HW Sales		1440000	1020000	850000	570000	1326000	5206000	
30									

What is a Database?

Databases let you store and manage sets of related data. For example, in this lesson, you will create a database that holds sales data for sales representatives. The database will store and manage all the information for the sales representatives. The database will also let you analyze the sales data in a variety of ways using automatic subtotaling, AutoFilter and PivotTables.

Databases are composed of records

Databases are composed of records where each record contains the same type of data. For example, your sales representative database will have one record for each sales representative. In Excel, each row in the database is a record.

Records are divided into fields

Each record in a database is divided into fields. Records can have many fields. For example, your sales representative database will have fields for the sales representative's name, position, length of employment and sales results. In Excel, each column in the database is a field.

What can you do with a database?

Excel provides a number of features that are designed specifically to work with databases. For example, Excel automatically creates a data entry form to make it easy to enter records into the database. You can easily sort databases, find records, create subtotals and analyze the data with PivotTables and other analysis tools.

Setting up a New Database

You create a database as you would create any other worksheet. However, there are three rules you should follow when setting up a new database. These rules are described in the following illustration.

Rule 1 - *Always give the database the name Database as shown here. Many of Excel's tools will identify a range named Database as a database.*

	A	B	C	D	E	F	G	H
1	National Computing Solutions							
2	1996 Sales Database							
3								
4	Name	Years Employed	Position		Region	State	SW Sales	HW Sales
5								
6								

Rule 2 - *Always use column headings for the first row in the database. These column headings become the field names that identify the fields in the database.*

Rule 3 - *Always select the column headings and one blank row when naming the database. The blank row lets you use the data form to enter new records in the database.*

Hands-On 13.1 – Set up the database

Adjust column widths and enter the data

You can widen the columns in a database and format the text and numbers as in any other worksheet. In this exercise, you will set up a database and format the first empty row in the new database. This way, all records in the database will have the number formats you specify.

1. Start Excel or **click** the New Workbook ⬜ button.

2. Make sure the highlight is somewhere in column A and choose **Format→Column→Width...** from the menu bar.

3. Set the width to **17** and **click OK**.

4. Adjust the column widths as shown in the following table.

Columns	Use this width
B and C	15
D and E	Leave as is
F and G	11

5. Enter the data shown below.

	A	B	C	D	E	F	G
1	National Computing Solutions						
2	1997 Sales Database						
3							
4	Name	Years Employed	Position	Region	State	SW Sales	HW Sales

Name the database

6. Use the following steps to name the database.

   ❶ *Select the range **A4:G5** as shown below. Make sure you select the empty cells in row 5 as shown. Also, select only the cells shown (not the entire rows).*

   ❷ **Click** *in the Name box, type* **Database** *and* **tap Enter**.

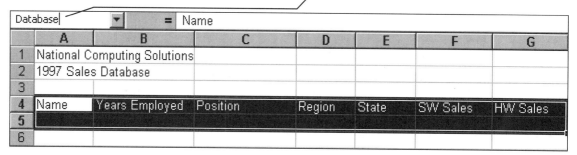

You should always name a database using the technique above. Including the blank cells in the selection allows Excel's data form tool to identify the location where new rows are to be added. It is also important to use the name Database. The data form tool easily identifies this name as do many of Excel's other database tools.

Continued...

Format the cells and numbers

7. Use the following steps to format several cells.

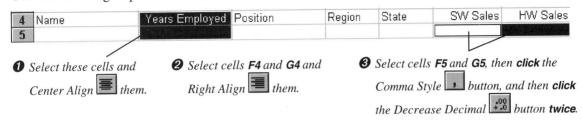

❶ *Select these cells and Center Align* ☰ *them.*

❷ *Select cells* **F4** *and* **G4** *and Right Align* ☰ *them.*

❸ *Select cells* **F5** *and* **G5**, *then* **click** *the Comma Style* ▮ *button, and then* **click** *the Decrease Decimal* ▮ *button* **twice***.*

> *You won't be able to see the Comma Style in cells F5 and G5 until you enter numbers in those cells. All the formats you just set will be carried to each new record you add to the database.*

8. Save ▣ your database to your exercise diskette as **Hands-On Lesson 13**.

Using Data Forms

The **Data→Form...** command displays the Data Form dialog box. The Data Form makes it easy to enter, edit and locate records in a database. When you issue the **Data→Form** command, Excel automatically identifies a database that has been given the name **Database** and displays a record in the data form.

Hands-On 13.2 – Use the data form to enter records

1. Choose **Data→Form...** from the menu bar.

> *Excel will identify your database (because you named it Database) and display the form below.*

2. Use the following steps to enter the first record.

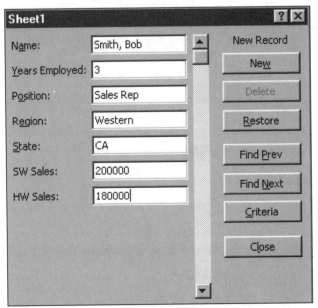

❶ *Notice Excel uses the field names from your database as the labels for the boxes in the data form.*

❷ *Type the name* **Smith, Bob** *in the Name box, then* **tap** *the* **Tab** *key on the keyboard to move to the Years Employed field.*

❸ **Enter** *the* **data** *in the rest of the form as shown here. Use Tab to complete each entry and move to the next field.*

❹ *When you have finished entering the data in this record,* **click** *the* New *button to insert the record in the database and to prepare to enter another record.*

3. If necessary, **drag** the Data Form dialog box slightly until you can see your database.

> *Notice the record is entered below the heading row. Also notice the numbers in cells F5 and G5 have the Comma Style you set in the previous steps.*

Continued...

4. Enter the following 13 records into the database.

You will need to click the [New] *button after typing the data for each record. Make sure you enter all the records because you will need the data throughout this lesson.*

Name	Years Employed	Position	Region	State	SW Sales	HW Sales
Hubbs, Daniel	4	Telemarketer	Eastern	FL	340,000	230,000
Smith, Michael	5	Telemarketer	Eastern	MA	123,000	230,000
Watson, Tom	8	Sales Rep	Eastern	MA	230,000	340,000
Williams, Michael	3	Sales Rep	Eastern	FL	120,000	340,000
Martinez, Carlos	4	Senior Sales Rep	Eastern	FL	450,000	450,000
Wilson, Bernie	1	Sales Rep	Central	IL	120,000	170,000
Thomas, Will	2	Sales Rep	Central	IL	230,000	120,000
Cain, Mary	5	Senior Sales Rep	Central	IL	234,000	560,000
Zain, Beth	7	Senior Sales Rep	Western	CA	340,000	800,000
Alvizo, Alex	9	Senior Sales Rep	Western	CA	450,000	340,000
Brown, Bill	3	Telemarketer	Western	CA	546,000	120,000
Richards, Paul	4	Telemarketer	Western	WA	234,000	546,000
Cray, Zip	6	Telemarketer	Western	WA	900,000	780,000

5. Make sure you **click** the [New] button after entering the last record.

This button inserts the record in the database. This step is necessary because you will use the form to browse through and edit the records in the next few steps. You would lose the last record if you browsed prior to using the New button.

6. **Click** the Find Previous [Find Prev] button until the **Alvizo, Alex** record is displayed.

7. **Click** in the **Years Employed** field and change the 9 to a **7**.

8. Use the vertical scroll bar in the data form dialog box to scroll through the records.

9. Try **dragging** the scroll box [ ] up or down and notice the record number (such as 6 of 14) is displayed at the top right corner of the data from box.

10. Move to record **4**, then move to record **10**.

11. Notice the Delete and Restore buttons on the data form.

The Delete button permanently deletes a record and Restore lets you reverse your last action such as an editing change. However, Restore will not let you recover a deleted record.

12. Click the [Close] button to return to the database.

13. Save [ ] the changes to your database and continue with the next topic.

Using Criteria to Find Records

The Data Form has a Criteria button that lets you locate records by specifying logical search criteria. For example, you may want to find a record where the **Name = Smith, Bob** or you may want to find the next record where **SW Sales >700000**. You can use the same logical operators (< > =) with search criteria as you used with the IF function earlier in this book. You can also use the asterisk * wildcard character with search criteria. This character is convenient if you know only the first part of the name or word you are searching for. For example, you could search for Smith* in the Name field and Excel would locate the first record with a last name of Smith. Search criteria are most useful in large databases with many records.

Hands-On 13.3 – Use criteria to locate records

1. Choose **Data→Form...** and the data form will be displayed.

2. **Click** the [Criteria] button and all the field boxes will appear empty.

3. **Click** in the Name box and type **=Watson, Tom**.

4. **Click** the [Find Next] button (or tap Enter) and the Watson, Tom record should appear.

5. **Click** the [Criteria] button and type **=Brown***.

6. **Click** the [Find Next] button and the Brown, Bill record will appear.

7. Take 5 minutes to practice locating records using various criteria. Try entering criteria in other boxes but make sure you click the Criteria button before entering each search criteria. Also, Excel may "beep" when you try to locate a record. If this happens, you will need to search in the opposite direction. For example, if you use the [Find Next] button and Excel "beeps", then try using the [Find Prev] button.

8. **Close** the data form when you have finished.

Sorting a Database

You learned how to sort a list in Lesson 5. A database is a type of list, so the Sort Ascending [A/Z↓], Sort Descending [Z/A↓] and Sort dialog box commands can be used in databases.

Hands-On 13.4 – Sort the database

1. **Click** cell **A5**.

2. **Click** the Sort Ascending [A/Z↓] button to sort the database based upon the names in column A.

3. **Click** cell **B5**, then **click** Sort Descending [Z/A↓] to sort by Years Employed in descending order.

4. Sort the database by State (column E) in ascending order.
    The CA records should be listed first followed by FL etc.

Displaying Automatic Subtotals

Excel can automatically display subtotals and grand totals for numeric fields in your database. You can rapidly display subtotals to analyze your database and then remove them just as easily. The following illustration shows the Hands-On Lesson 13 database with subtotals displayed.

Excel displays an outline bar to let you increase or decrease the amount of information displayed in the subtotaled database.

The database is sorted on the State field and a subtotal is inserted each time the State field changes. Excel automatically inserts the subtotals and Grand Total and formats the worksheet as shown.

	A	B	C	D	E	F	G
1	National Computing Solutions						
2	1997 Sales Database						
3							
4	Name	Years Employed	Position	Region	State	SW Sales	HW Sales
5	Alivzo, Alex	7	Senior Sales Rep	Western	CA	450,000	340,000
6	Zain, Beth	7	Senior Sales Rep	Western	CA	340,000	800,000
7	Brown, Bill	3	Telemarketer	Western	CA	546,000	120,000
8	Smith, Bob	3	Sales Rep	Western	CA	200,000	180,000
9					**CA Total**	1,536,000	1,440,000
10	Hubbs, Daniel	4	Telemarketer	Eastern	FL	340,000	230,000
11	Martinez, Carlos	4	Senior Sales Rep	Eastern	FL	450,000	450,000
12	Williams, Michael	3	Sales Rep	Eastern	FL	120,000	340,000
13					**FL Total**	910,000	1,020,000
14	Cain, Mary	5	Senior Sales Rep	Central	IL	234,000	560,000
15	Thomas, Will	2	Sales Rep	Central	IL	230,000	120,000
16	Wilson, Bernie	1	Sales Rep	Central	IL	120,000	170,000
17					**IL Total**	584,000	850,000
18	Watson, Tom	8	Sales Rep	Eastern	MA	230,000	340,000
19	Smith, Michael	5	Telemarketer	Eastern	MA	123,000	230,000
20					**MA Total**	353,000	570,000
21	Cray, Zip	6	Telemarketer	Western	WA	900,000	780,000
22	Richards, Paul	4	Telemarketer	Western	WA	234,000	546,000
23					**WA Total**	1,134,000	1,326,000
24					**Grand Total**	4,517,000	5,206,000

Quick Steps: *Displaying and Removing Subtotals*

To display subtotals

- *Sort the database on the field that you want subtotals to be based. For example, sort on the State field if you want subtotals to appear each time the state field changes.*
- *Choose Data→Subtotals...*
- *Set the At Each Change In field to the same field you sorted on.*
- *Choose the desired function from the Use Function box. This will normally be SUM.*
- *Choose the numeric fields you want subtotaled in the Add Subtotal box and click OK.*

To remove subtotals

- *Choose Data→Subtotals...*
- *Click the Remove All button*

Hands-On 13.5 – Experiment with subtotals

Display subtotals

1. Make sure the database is sorted in ascending order by the State field.

Continued...

The CA records should appear first followed by FL etc. In the next few steps, you will subtotal the database. The SW Sales and HW Sales will be subtotaled each time the state field changes (from CA to FL etc). The database should always be sorted on the field that controls the subtotals.

2.   Choose **Data→Subtotals...** from the menu bar.

3.   Use the following steps to set the subtotal parameters.

❶ *Make sure this option is set to **State**. A subtotal will appear each time the State field changes.*

❷ *Leave this option set to Sum. You can use a variety of functions for subtotals but Sum is most often used.*

❸ ***Scroll** through this list of field names and **check** **SW Sales** and **HW Sales**. These fields will be subtotaled each time the State field changes.*

❹ ***Click OK** and the subtotals will appear.*

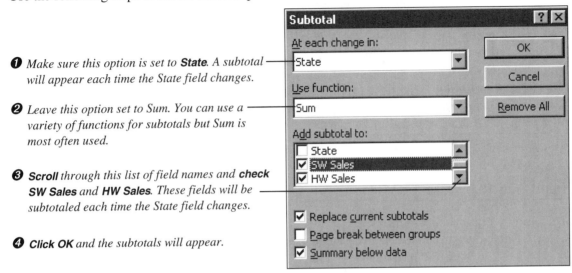

Take a few moments to study the subtotals before continuing.

Use the outline options

4.   Use the following steps to experiment with the outline options on the left side of the worksheet.

❶ ***Click** the **1** button and only the Grand Total will be displayed.*

❷ ***Click** the **2** button to display the subtotals and Grand Total.*

❸ ***Click** the **3** button to display the complete database again including the subtotals and Grand Total.*

❹ *Experiment with these buttons. They will remove or restore one set of data such as the CA or FL records.*

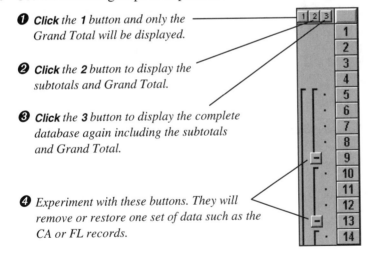

Remove the subtotals

5.   Make sure the highlight is somewhere in the database and choose **Data→Subtotals...**

6.   **Click** the **Remove All** button.

As you can see, subtotals are easy to display and remove. The key to subtotals is to sort the database on the field that the subtotals will be based upon. In this example, the control field was State, so subtotals were displayed each time the State field changed.

AutoFilter

Excel's AutoFilter command lets you display certain records in the database while hiding others. This is known as filtering the records. For example, you could use AutoFilter to display only those records where the State is equal to CA.

Quick Steps: *AutoFilter*

To use AutoFilter to filter records

- *Click anywhere in the database and choose Data→Filter→AutoFilter.*
- *Click the drop-down arrow next to the field(s) you want to filter and choose the item you wish to filter on.*

To remove AutoFilter

- *Choose Data→Filter→Show All to display all records or Data→Filter→AutoFilter to remove the AutoFilter drop-down buttons.*

Hands-On 13.6 – Use AutoFilter

Display only the CA records

1. **Click** anywhere in the database and choose **Data**→**Filter**→**AutoFilter**.

    Drop-down ▼ *buttons will appear next to each field name.*

2. **Click** the button ▼ to the right of the **State** field and choose **CA** from the list.

    Only the CA records should be displayed. The other records are still in the database but they are not displayed at the moment.

3. **Click** the button ▼ to the right of the **Position** field and choose **Senior Sales Rep** from the list.

    Only records with a State field equal to CA and a Position field equal to Senior Sales Rep will be displayed. There should only be two records displayed. As you can see, the second AutoFilter choice created a subset of the first choice.

Remove AutoFilter

4. Choose **Data**→**Filter**→**Show All**.

    Notice that all records are displayed and the drop-down buttons remain.

5. Choose **Data**→**Filter**→**AutoFilter** to remove the drop-down buttons.

6. Take 10 minutes to experiment with AutoFilter and subtotals. Try to understand the differences between these two features and visualize ways you could use these features.

7. Remove all AutoFiltering and subtotals when you have finished experimenting.

8. Save 💾 the changes to your database and continue with the next topic.

Pivot Tables

PivotTables are one of the most powerful analytical tools in Excel. You create PivotTables using data from a database. PivotTables let you view the data in a variety of ways. This ability to view the same data in a variety of ways is what makes PivotTables so powerful.

PivotTables automatically summarize the data

When you create a PivotTable, you specify the database fields you want included in the PivotTable. You will always include one or more numeric fields (such as SW Sales and HW Sales). Excel automatically summarizes the numeric fields and computes subtotals and totals based upon the other fields you include in the PivotTable. For example, in the next exercise, you will create a PivotTable that includes the Region and State fields along with the SW and HW Sales numbers. The PivotTable will display SW and HW subtotals for the Regions and States. This is similar to the Subtotals command you used earlier in this lesson. However, PivotTables let you easily change the way the data is presented thus giving you different views of the same data.

Hands-On 13.7 – Create a PivotTable

In this exercise, you will use the PivotTable wizard to create a PivotTable in the current worksheet. The Hands-On Lesson 13 database should still be open. Also, make sure you have removed subtotals and AutoFilter from the database as you were instructed to do in the previous exercise.

Start the PivotTable wizard

1. Use the Zoom Control to zoom in until you can see at least 30 rows on your screen.

   You will need the extra space for the PivotTable.

2. **Click** anywhere in the database and choose **Data→PivotTable Report....** from the menu bar.

3. Take a moment to read the opening dialog box for the PivotTable Wizard.

   Notice you can create PivotTables from a variety of sources including Microsoft Excel databases and external data sources such as a Microsoft Access database.

4. **Click** [Next >] to accept the Microsoft Excel database setting.

   The next step in the wizard will automatically recognize your database.

5. **Click** [Next >] again to accept your Database as the data source.

6. Take a moment to read the step 3 dialog box.

   This dialog box is where you set up a PivotTable. You set up a PivotTable by dragging field buttons from the right side of the dialog box to the white areas labeled PAGE, ROW, COLUMN and DATA.

Continued...

7. Use the following steps to set up the PivotTable.

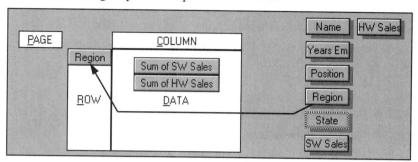

❶ **Drag** *the* **Region** *button from the right side to the top of the* **ROW** *section as shown above.*

❷ **Drag** *the* **SW Sales** *button to the* **DATA** *area. Excel will label the button Sum of SW Sales as shown above.*

❸ **Drag** *the* **HW Sales** *button to the* **DATA** *area.*

8. Take a few moments to study the dialog box.

When Excel creates the PivotTable, it will list the regions (Eastern, Central and Western) as row headings on the left side of the PivotTable. Then Excel will summarize the SW Sales and HW Sales for each region and display them in the data area to the right of the region row headings.

9. Click [Next >] when your Step 3 dialog box matches the one shown above.

The Step 4 dialog box will appear. It lets you specify where the PivotTable should be inserted in the worksheet and it lets you set several options.

10. Choose the [⦿ Existing worksheet] option.

11. Click cell **A20** in the worksheet (you may need to move the dialog box).

The dialog box will have the sheet and cell reference shown below.

⦿ Existing worksheet
Sheet1!$A$20

12. Click [Finish] and Excel will create the PivotTable shown below.

20	Region	Data	Total
21	Central	Sum of SW Sales	584000
22		Sum of HW Sales	850000
23	Eastern	Sum of SW Sales	1263000
24		Sum of HW Sales	1590000
25	Western	Sum of SW Sales	2670000
26		Sum of HW Sales	2766000
27	Total Sum of SW Sales		4517000
28	Total Sum of HW Sales		5206000

Take a moment to study the PivotTable and notice it automatically creates sums of the SW Sales and HW Sales for the various regions. For example, the Western region SW Sales is the sum of all SW Sales in CA and WA including the Sales Rep, Telemarketing and Senior Sales Rep sales.

Keep in mind that this PivotTable is very basic. You could display the same subtotals and totals with the subtotals command that you learned earlier in this lesson. However, your PivotTable will become more useful as you continue to enhance it.

Continued...

Modify the PivotTable

13. The PivotTable toolbar should have appeared when you created the PivotTable. If it didn't appear, then display it with the **View**→**Toolbars**→**PivotTable** command.

14. **Click** anywhere on the PivotTable, and then **click** the PivotTable Wizard [image] button on the PivotTable toolbar.

    Step 3 of the PivotTable Wizard will reappear.

15. **Drag** the **State** button from the right side of the dialog box to the COLUMN area as shown below.

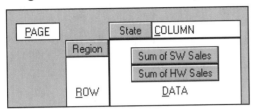

16. **Click** the Finish button.

17. Use the following illustration to get a better understanding of the PivotTable you just created.

❶ *Notice the SW Sales and HW Sales are summarized for each state. These sales are the sums of the Sales Rep, Telemarketer and Senior Sales Rep sales for each state.*

❷ *Also notice the Grand Totals in this column. The Grand Totals show the SW Sales and HW Sales totals for each region.*

20			State					
21	Region	Data	CA	FL	IL	MA	WA	Grand Total
22	Central	Sum of SW Sales			584000			584000
23		Sum of HW Sales			850000			850000
24	Eastern	Sum of SW Sales		910000		353000		1263000
25		Sum of HW Sales		1020000		570000		1590000
26	Western	Sum of SW Sales	1536000				1134000	2670000
27		Sum of HW Sales	1440000				1326000	2766000
28	Total Sum of SW Sales		1536000	910000	584000	353000	1134000	4517000
29	Total Sum of HW Sales		1440000	1020000	850000	570000	1326000	5206000

❸ *The Total Sum of SW Sales and Total Sum of HW Sales in rows 28 and 29 show the totals for each state.*

18. The Step 3 PivotTable dialog box is shown below to let you compare the dialog box to the PivotTable that was created. Take a few moments to study the PivotTable above and the dialog box below and try to understand how the PivotTable was formed.

    Notice how Excel does a lot of work for you when it creates a PivotTable. Excel adds all the subtotals, grand totals and formatting to create the sophisticated PivotTable shown above.

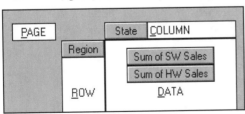

As you can see, the PivotTable gives you a variety of ways to analyze the data. This one PivotTable lets you instantly see the SW and HW sales for the Regions, States and entire company. However, you will discover the true power of PivotTables in the next topic.

Rotating the Row and Column Headings

PivotTables derive their name from the fact that you can rotate or **pivot** the row and column headings around the data. This produces a different view of the same data. For example, in the PivotTable you just created, the Regions are used as the row headings and the States are used as the column headings. However, by rotating the State and Region headings around the data you can create different views of the data as shown in the following examples.

20			Region			
21	State	Data	Central	Eastern	Western	Grand Total
22	CA	Sum of SW Sales			1536000	1536000
23		Sum of HW Sales			1440000	1440000
24	FL	Sum of SW Sales		910000		910000
25		Sum of HW Sales		1020000		1020000
26	IL	Sum of SW Sales	584000			584000
27		Sum of HW Sales	850000			850000
28	MA	Sum of SW Sales		353000		353000
29		Sum of HW Sales		570000		570000
30	WA	Sum of SW Sales			1134000	1134000
31		Sum of HW Sales			1326000	1326000
32	Total Sum of SW Sales		584000	1263000	2670000	4517000
33	Total Sum of HW Sales		850000	1590000	2766000	5206000

In this example, the State field is used as the row heading and the Region field is the column heading. This gives a different view of the same data.

20			Region			
21	Data	State	Central	Eastern	Western	Grand Total
22	Sum of SW Sales	CA			1536000	1536000
23		FL		910000		910000
24		IL	584000			584000
25		MA		353000		353000
26		WA			1134000	1134000
27	Sum of HW Sales	CA			1440000	1440000
28		FL		1020000		1020000
29		IL	850000			850000
30		MA		570000		570000
31		WA			1326000	1326000
32	Total Sum of SW Sales		584000	1263000	2670000	4517000
33	Total Sum of HW Sales		850000	1590000	2766000	5206000

In this example, the State and Region fields are to the right of the Data thus giving another view of the data.

Hands-On 13.8 – Rotate the column and row headings

In this exercise, you will rotate the row and column headings in the PivotTable. You could use the PivotTable Wizard to accomplish this, however, you will use another method. Keep in mind that these concepts can be difficult to understand. The best way to understand these concepts is to practice.

1. Use the following steps to turn the State column heading into a row heading.

❶ **Drag** the **State** heading below the Region heading and Excel will display a vertical row symbol as shown below.

❷ **Release** the mouse button and both the State and Region headings will be to the left of the Data heading as shown in the illustration on the following page.

20			State	
21	Region	Data	CA	FL
22	Central	Sum of SW Sales		
23		Sum of HW Sales		
24	Eastern	Sum of SW Sales		910000
25		Sum of HW Sales		1020000

Continued...

2. Use the following steps to turn the Region row heading into a column heading.

➊ *Drag the Region heading to the right of the Data heading and Excel will display a horizontal column symbol as shown here.*

➋ *Release the mouse button and the row and column headings will now be reversed as shown in the next illustration.*

20	State	Region	Data	
21	CA	Western	Sum of SW Sales	1536000
22			Sum of HW Sales	1440000

20			Region			
21	State	Data	Central	Eastern	Western	Grand Total
22	CA	Sum of SW Sales			1536000	1536000
23		Sum of HW Sales			1440000	1440000
24	FL	Sum of SW Sales		910000		910000
25		Sum of HW Sales		1020000		1020000
26	IL	Sum of SW Sales	584000			584000
27		Sum of HW Sales	850000			850000
28	MA	Sum of SW Sales		353000		353000
29		Sum of HW Sales		570000		570000
30	WA	Sum of SW Sales			1134000	1134000
31		Sum of HW Sales			1326000	1326000
32	Total Sum of SW Sales		584000	1263000	2670000	4517000
33	Total Sum of HW Sales		850000	1590000	2766000	5206000

This is the way your PivotTable should look after the row and column headings have been interchanged.

3. Feel free to experiment with the PivotTable by dragging the row and column headings to various locations. You can also click in the PivotTable and use the PivotTable Wizard 🔲 button. Then you can add, remove and reposition row and column headings as desired.

4. Save 🔲 the changes to your database when you have finished and continue with the end-of-lesson questions and exercises.

Leave the database open because it will be used in the end-of-lesson exercises.

Outlining

Many worksheets are structured hierarchically where groups of columns and/or rows form subtotals. The columns or rows that contribute to a subtotal are said to be subordinate to the subtotal. This hierarchical structure lets you take advantage of Excel's outlining tools. With outlining, you can easily display the level of detail you require. For example, you may want to view all columns and rows in a worksheet or only the subtotals and grand totals. You can easily expand and collapse an outlined worksheet to view your data in various ways. You expanded and collapsed an outline earlier in this lesson in the National Computing Solutions database.

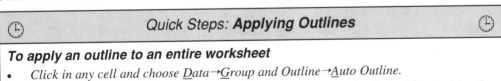

🕐	*Quick Steps:* **Applying Outlines**	🕐

To apply an outline to an entire worksheet

• *Click in any cell and choose Data→Group and Outline→Auto Outline.*
• *Use the row and/or column buttons on the outline to display the desired level of detail.*

To apply an outline to part of a worksheet

• *Select the desired range and choose Data→Group and Outline→Auto Outline.*
• *Use the row and/or column buttons on the outline to display the desired level of detail.*

Concepts Review

True / False

1. A database record is composed of many fields.   1. **T   F**

2. You should always give the name Database to a database.   2. **T   F**

3. The data form can be used to enter data into a database.   3. **T   F**

4. You can use the =, < and > operators in search criteria.   4. **T   F**

5. You should click in the field you wish to sort on prior to sorting a database.   5. **T   F**

6. Databases can only be sorted in ascending order.   6. **T   F**

7. AutoFilter creates both subtotals and totals for the control field you specify.   7. **T   F**

8. PivotTables automatically create subtotals and totals.   8. **T   F**

9. PivotTables let you view the same data in various ways.   9. **T   F**

10. You must use the PivotTable Wizard to rotate the row and column headings.   10. **T   F**

Multiple Choice

1. Which command is used to display the Data Form dialog box.
   a) Format→Form...
   b) Data→Form...
   c) Tools→Form...
   d) None of the above.   (   )

2. Which button would you use on the data form to search for a name such as Johnson, Will?
   a) Find Prev
   b) Find Next
   c) Criteria
   d) None of the above.   (   )

3. Which command is used to display subtotals?
   a) Format→Subtotals
   b) Tools→Subtotals
   c) Tools→Database Subtotals
   d) None of the above.   (   )

4. Which command is used to remove subtotals?
   a) Data→Subtotals
   b) Tools→Subtotals
   c) Format→Subtotals
   d) None of the above.   (   )

5. Which of the following tasks does a PivotTable do?
   a) Summarizes data
   b) Creates subtotals
   c) Creates totals
   d) All of the above.   (   )

Skills Builder 13.1

In this exercise, you will delete the PivotTable from the Hands-On Lesson 13 database. You will also display subtotals and totals in the database.

Delete the PivotTable

1. If necessary, open the Hands-On Lesson 13 database you created in this lesson.

2. **Select** the entire PivotTable by dragging the mouse over the row headings in rows 20 through the last row of the PivotTable.

3. Choose **Edit→Delete** from the menu bar.

    The PivotTable will be removed.

4. If necessary, widen the columns until all data is visible in the columns.

    The PivotTable may have caused the column widths to be reduced.

Create subtotals

5. **Click** cell **C5,** and then **click** the Sort Ascending [A/Z↓] button.

    Remember you must always sort on the field you want to base the subtotals on.

6. Choose **Data→Subtotals...** from the menu bar.

7. Set the **At Each Change in** field to **Position**.

8. Make sure both **SW Sales** and **HW Sales** are checked in the Add subtotal to list.

9. **Click OK** to complete the subtotals.

    Your subtotaled database should match the following example (although you may need to widen the columns slightly).

	A	B	C	D	E	F	G
1	National Computing Solutions						
2	1997 Sales Database						
3							
4	Name	Years Employed	Position	Region	State	SW Sales	HW Sales
5	Smith, Bob	3	Sales Rep	Western	CA	200,000	180,000
6	Williams, Michael	3	Sales Rep	Eastern	FL	120,000	340,000
7	Thomas, Will	2	Sales Rep	Central	IL	230,000	120,000
8	Wilson, Bernie	1	Sales Rep	Central	IL	120,000	170,000
9	Watson, Tom	8	Sales Rep	Eastern	MA	230,000	340,000
10			**Sales Rep Total**			900,000	1,150,000
11	Alivzo, Alex	7	Senior Sales Rep	Western	CA	450,000	340,000
12	Zain, Beth	7	Senior Sales Rep	Western	CA	340,000	800,000
13	Martinez, Carlos	4	Senior Sales Rep	Eastern	FL	450,000	450,000
14	Cain, Mary	5	Senior Sales Rep	Central	IL	234,000	560,000
15			**Senior Sales Rep Total**			1,474,000	2,150,000
16	Brown, Bill	3	Telemarketer	Western	CA	546,000	120,000
17	Hubbs, Daniel	4	Telemarketer	Eastern	FL	340,000	230,000
18	Smith, Michael	5	Telemarketer	Eastern	MA	123,000	230,000
19	Cray, Zip	6	Telemarketer	Western	WA	900,000	780,000
20	Richards, Paul	4	Telemarketer	Western	WA	234,000	546,000
21			**Telemarketer Total**			2,143,000	1,906,000
22			**Grand Total**			4,517,000	5,206,000

Leave the database open because you will continue to use it.

Skills Builder 13.2

In this exercise, you will remove subtotals from the database. Then you will use AutoFilter to filter the database in various ways. The Hands-On Lesson 13 database should still be open.

Remove the subtotals

1. **Click** anywhere in the database and choose **Data→Subtotals...** from the menu bar.

2. **Click** the **Remove All** button to remove the subtotals.

Use AutoFilter to filter the database

In the next few steps, you will use AutoFilter to display only the records where the Position is equal to Sales Rep and the Years Employed is greater than 2. AutoFilter lets you filter records based upon logical criteria such as Years Employed is greater than 2.

3. Choose **Data→Filter→AutoFilter...** from the menu bar.

4. **Click** the button ▼ to the right of the **Position** field and choose **Sales Rep** from the list.

   Only the records where the Position is equal to Sales Rep will be displayed.

5. **Click** the button ▼ to the right of the **Years Employed** field and choose **(Custom...)**.

   Excel will display the Custom AutoFilter dialog box. This dialog box lets you choose logical operators to use in filtering the records.

6. Use the following steps to set the Custom AutoFilter parameters.

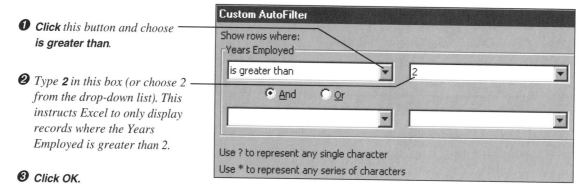

❶ **Click** *this button and choose* **is greater than**.

❷ *Type* **2** *in this box (or choose 2 from the drop-down list). This instructs Excel to only display records where the Years Employed is greater than 2.*

❸ **Click OK.**

   Excel should only display records where the Position = Sales Rep and the Years Employed is greater than 2. Once again, the second AutoFilter setting (Years Employed is greater than 2) created a subset of the first setting (Position = Sales Rep).

7. Choose **Data→Filter→AutoFilter** to remove the filtering.

8. Take five minutes to filter the database in various ways.

9. Remove filtering when you have finished experimenting.

   Leave the database open because you will continue to use it.

Skills Builder 13.3

In this exercise, you will create a PivotTable and subtotals in the database.

1. Choose **Data**→**PivotTable Report...**

2. **Click** the │ Next > │ button **twice** to bypass the first two steps in the wizard.

3. **Drag** the field buttons from the right side of the dialog box to the positions shown below.

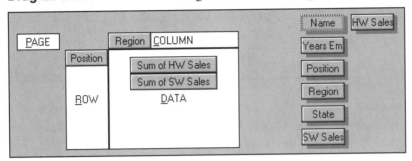

4. **Click** │ Next > │ to display the Step 4 of 4 dialog box.

5. Choose the ⊙ Existing worksheet │ option.

6. **Click** cell **A20** in the worksheet, and then **click** │ Finish │ .

   The PivotTable shown below should appear.

20			Region			
21	Position	Data	Central	Eastern	Western	Grand Total
22	Sales Rep	Sum of HW Sales	290000	680000	180000	1150000
23		Sum of SW Sales	350000	350000	200000	900000
24	Senior Sales Rep	Sum of HW Sales	560000	450000	1140000	2150000
25		Sum of SW Sales	234000	450000	790000	1474000
26	Telemarketer	Sum of HW Sales		460000	1446000	1906000
27		Sum of SW Sales		463000	1680000	2143000
28	Total Sum of HW Sales		850000	1590000	2766000	5206000
29	Total Sum of SW Sales		584000	1263000	2670000	4517000

Rotate the row and column headings

7. **Drag** the **Region** and **Position** headings until your PivotTable matches the following example.

20			Position			
21	Region	Data	Sales Rep	Senior Sales Rep	Telemarketer	Grand Total
22	Central	Sum of HW Sales	290000	560000		850000
23		Sum of SW Sales	350000	234000		584000
24	Eastern	Sum of HW Sales	680000	450000	460000	1590000
25		Sum of SW Sales	350000	450000	463000	1263000
26	Western	Sum of HW Sales	180000	1140000	1446000	2766000
27		Sum of SW Sales	200000	790000	1680000	2670000
28	Total Sum of HW Sales		1150000	2150000	1906000	5206000
29	Total Sum of SW Sales		900000	1474000	2143000	4517000

Modify the PivotTable

8. Modify the PivotTable until it matches the example on the following page.

   You will need to use the PivotTable Wizard.

Continued...

25			Position			
26	State	Data	Sales Rep	Senior Sales Rep	Telemarketer	Grand Total
27	CA	Sum of SW Sales	200000	790000	546000	1536000
28		Sum of HW Sales	180000	1140000	120000	1440000
29	FL	Sum of SW Sales	120000	450000	340000	910000
30		Sum of HW Sales	340000	450000	230000	1020000
31	IL	Sum of SW Sales	350000	234000		584000
32		Sum of HW Sales	290000	560000		850000
33	MA	Sum of SW Sales	230000		123000	353000
34		Sum of HW Sales	340000		230000	570000
35	WA	Sum of SW Sales			1134000	1134000
36		Sum of HW Sales			1326000	1326000
37	Total Sum of SW Sales		900000	1474000	2143000	4517000
38	Total Sum of HW Sales		1150000	2150000	1906000	5206000

Move the PivotTable to another worksheet

PivotTables are objects and they can be moved to other worksheets like charts and other objects. In the following steps, you will move the PivotTable to Sheet2.

9. **Click** cell **A20** (the first cell in the PivotTable) and the entire PivotTable will be selected.

10. **Click** the Cut ✂ button.

    The PivotTable will remain in this sheet until you paste it in the following steps.

11. **Click** the **Sheet2** tab, and then **click** the Paste 📋 button.

12. Now change the name of Sheet2 to **PivotTable**.

13. **Click** the **Sheet1** tab and notice the PivotTable is no longer there.

Create subtotals

14. Subtotal the database as shown below.

	A	B	C	D	E	F	G
1	National Computing Solutions						
2	1997 Sales Database						
3							
4	Name	Years Employed	Position	Region	State	SW Sales	HW Sales
5	Thomas, Will	2	Sales Rep	Central	IL	230,000	120,000
6	Wilson, Bernie	1	Sales Rep	Central	IL	120,000	170,000
7	Cain, Mary	5	Senior Sales Rep	Central	IL	234,000	560,000
8				Central Total		584,000	850,000
9	Williams, Michael	3	Sales Rep	Eastern	FL	120,000	340,000
10	Martinez, Carlos	4	Senior Sales Rep	Eastern	FL	450,000	450,000
11	Hubbs, Daniel	4	Telemarketer	Eastern	FL	340,000	230,000
12	Watson, Tom	8	Sales Rep	Eastern	MA	230,000	340,000
13	Smith, Michael	5	Telemarketer	Eastern	MA	123,000	230,000
14				Eastern Total		1,263,000	1,590,000
15	Smith, Bob	3	Sales Rep	Western	CA	200,000	180,000
16	Alivzo, Alex	7	Senior Sales Rep	Western	CA	450,000	340,000
17	Zain, Beth	7	Senior Sales Rep	Western	CA	340,000	800,000
18	Brown, Bill	3	Telemarketer	Western	CA	546,000	120,000
19	Cray, Zip	6	Telemarketer	Western	WA	900,000	780,000
20	Richards, Paul	4	Telemarketer	Western	WA	234,000	546,000
21				Western Total		2,670,000	2,766,000
22				Grand Total		4,517,000	5,206,000

15. Now change the name of Sheet1 to **Subtotaled Database**.

16. Feel free to experiment with your database, then **close** it and **save** the changes.

Assessment 13.1

1. Use the following guidelines to create the database shown below.

   – Enter the data in the same cells as shown below.

   – Format the titles and column headings as shown. You will need to use the Alt + Enter keystroke combination to create the multi-line entries in cells C4 and D4.

   – Format the numbers in columns C and D with the comma format shown.

   – Assign the range name **Database** to the range **A4:D17**.

2. **Click** the Save button and save the database as **Assessment 13.1**.

3. **Print** the database but leave the workbook open because you will continue to use it.

	A	B	C	D
1	**Westside Electric Supplies**			
2	*Employee Compensation Database*			
3				
4	**Name**	**Category**	**1996 Compensation**	**1996 Retirement Plan Contributions**
5	Jackson, Samuel	Salaried	45,000	4,700
6	Ellison, Linda	Salaried	32,000	2,500
7	Monroe, James	Hourly	34,000	4,250
8	Wilson, Larry	Salaried	89,000	21,890
9	Hughes, Ralph	Hourly	23,000	-
10	Peterson, Lisa	Hourly	31,000	2,300
11	Watson, Bill	Hourly	27,000	1,600
12	Templeton, James	Salaried	45,000	1,900
13	Barton, Lisa	Salaried	51,000	6,000
14	Erickson, Brian	Hourly	38,000	4,500
15	Thomas, Lynn	Salaried	34,000	2,700
16	Chin, Raymond	Salaried	56,000	3,450
17	Zurlow, Jack	Hourly	30,000	3,450

Assessment 13.2

1. Use the **File→Save As** command to save the Assessment 13.1 workbook as **Assessment 13.2**.
   This will create a copy of the workbook.

2. Subtotal the database as shown on the following page. Notice that the subtotals use the AVERAGE function instead of SUM as you have used thus far. The AVERAGE function is chosen in the Subtotals dialog box.

Continued...

	A	B	C	D
1	**Westside Electric Supplies**			
2	*Employee Compensation Database*			
3				
4	**Name**	**Category**	**1996 Compensation**	**1996 Retirement Plan Contributions**
5	Monroe, James	Hourly	34,000	4,250
6	Hughes, Ralph	Hourly	23,000	-
7	Peterson, Lisa	Hourly	31,000	2,300
8	Watson, Bill	Hourly	27,000	1,600
9	Erickson, Brian	Hourly	38,000	4,500
10	Zurlow, Jack	Hourly	30,000	3,450
11	**Hourly Average**		30,500	2,683
12	Jackson, Samuel	Salaried	45,000	4,700
13	Ellison, Linda	Salaried	32,000	2,500
14	Wilson, Larry	Salaried	89,000	21,890
15	Templeton, James	Salaried	45,000	1,900
16	Barton, Lisa	Salaried	51,000	6,000
17	Thomas, Lynn	Salaried	34,000	2,700
18	Chin, Raymond	Salaried	56,000	3,450
19	**Salaried Average**		50,286	6,163
20	**Grand Average**		41,154	4,557

3. **Print** the subtotaled database.

4. **Close** the database and **save** the changes.

Critical Thinking 13.1

Create an Excel database for Linda's Home and Garden Supply. Create rows in the database for 20 products. Each product should have a product ID, name, category, wholesale price and retail price. The category ID should indicate whether the product is for home or garden use. Calculate the retail price as a 200% markup over the wholesale price. Use Excel's subtotaling feature to compute subtotals for the wholesale price and retail price based upon the category field. The subtotals will instantly tell Linda the wholesale and retail values of her inventory for each category.

Critical Thinking 13.2

Create an Excel database that tracks returns for Parker Book Publishers, Inc. The database should have fields for the return authorization code, date, customer name, category, title, quantity returned and purchase price. Assume that Parker publishes four categories of books: Fitness; self-improvement; cooking and gardening. Also assume that one return may contain several different titles. This means there may be several records with the same return authorization code, date and customer name. Enter at least 20 records into the database using Excel's Data Form tool. Use a PivotTable to analyze the return data. Set up the PivotTable so that questions like the following can be answered.

– What is the total value of returns for each category?

– What is the total value of returns for each title within each category?

– What is the total value of returns for each customer?

Feel free to analyze the data in any other way you feel is appropriate.

14 New Tools and Advanced What-if Analysis

Objectives:

- Use data validation

- Consolidate worksheets

- Use natural language formulas

- Apply conditional formatting

- Use data tables

- Use Scenario Manager

The Project – Bob Johnson's Annual Bonus

In this lesson, you will help Bob Johnson, the Sales Manager of Seminar Solutions, develop a workbook designed to maximize his quarterly bonus. Seminar Solutions compensates Bob with a quarterly bonus that is based upon the sales and expenditures of the regions he manages. Bob is rewarded for maximizing sales and minimizing expenses. The workbook will receive data from subordinate workbooks using Excel's data consolidation feature. You will use Excel 97's new conditional formatting and data validation tools to control the data entry process. You will also use data tables and the Scenario Manager to perform what-if analysis. The what-if analysis will help Bob maximize his bonus. The illustration below shows the master worksheet and three subordinate worksheets that you will develop.

	A	B	C	D	E
1	Bonus Analysis				
2					
3					
4	Sales	Q1	Q2	Q3	Q4
5	Gross Sales	3,320,000	3,310,000	4,380,000	4,590,000
6	Returns	166,000	94,000	185,000	124,000
7	Net Sales	$3,154,000	$3,216,000	$4,195,000	$4,466,000
8					
9					
10	Expenses	Q1	Q2	Q3	Q4
11	Sample Costs	50,700	24,000	97,890	44,450
12	Trade Shows	107,490	6,700	122,000	96,000
13	Automobile	18,000	18,500	15,000	14,600
14	Cell Phones	10,800	12,900	11,140	11,100
15	Entertainment	17,900	20,100	11,700	10,200
16	Total Expenses	$ 204,890	$ 82,200	$ 257,730	$ 176,350
17					
18	Expenses vs Net Sales	6.50%	2.56%	6.14%	3.95%

Scenario Summary	Current Values:	Scenario 1	Scenario 2	Scenario 3	Scenario 4
Changing Cells:					
Net_Sales	2,000,000	1,000,000	1,000,000	2,000,000	2,000,000
Sample_Costs	17,000	10,000	10,000	17,000	20,000
Trade_Shows	12,500	10,000	20,000	12,500	20,000
Automobile	14,000	10,000	7,000	14,000	10,000
Cell_Phones	5,000	10,000	4,000	5,000	7,500
Entertainment	85,000	10,000	10,000	85,000	35,000
Result Cells:					
Expenses_vs_Net_Sales	6.68%	5.00%	5.10%	6.68%	4.63%

Notes: Current Values column represents values of changing cells at time Scenario Summary Report was created. Changing cells for each scenario are highlighted in gray.

Validating Data Entry

Excel 97's new data validation tool lets you restrict data entry in cells. You can restrict both the type and range of acceptable values. For example, you may want to restrict data entry to whole numbers between 0 and 100,000. You can also create both input messages and error alert messages. Input messages are displayed whenever the highlight is in a restricted cell. Error messages are displayed whenever data entry is attempted and the data is not of the correct type or within the accepted range.

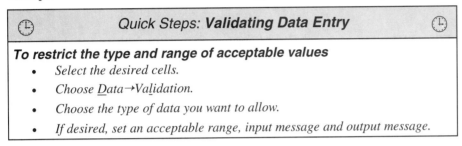

Quick Steps: Validating Data Entry

To restrict the type and range of acceptable values
- *Select the desired cells.*
- *Choose Data→Validation.*
- *Choose the type of data you want to allow.*
- *If desired, set an acceptable range, input message and output message.*

Hands-On 14.1 – Explore the workbook and assign range names

In this exercise, you will explore the structure of the master and supporting worksheets in the Seminar Solutions project. You will assign names to ranges and prepare the worksheets for data validation.

Explore the workbook
1. **Open** the workbook named **Hands-On Lesson 14**.

   Take a few moments to study the workbook. Notice there is a Master sheet and sheets for three regions. Notice that rows 5-6 and 11-15 in the Master sheet are empty. Later in this lesson, these cells will receive data from the Region1 – Region3 sheets through the data consolidation command.

2. **Click** the **Region1** sheet tab and notice this worksheet has the same structure as the Master sheet.

   The data consolidation technique is especially useful in workbooks with a uniform structure such as this. Also notice that the Region2 and Region3 sheets have the same structure.

Create range names
   In the next few steps, you will assign a range name to the ranges B5:E6 and B11:E15 in all four worksheets. These names will be useful as you develop the workbook.

3. **Click** the **Master** sheet tab.

4. Use the following steps to select the desired cells.

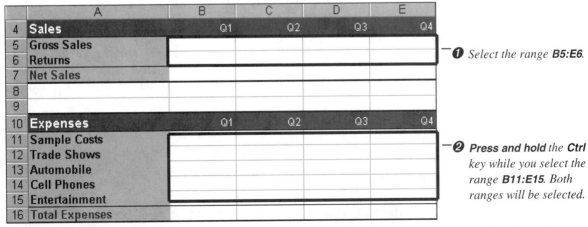

Continued...

5. **Click** in the Name box on the left end of the formula bar and type **Consolidation_Data** as shown below (make sure you use an underscore _ and not a space).

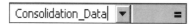

6. **Tap** (Enter) to complete the name (the name will **not** be displayed in the Name box).

7. **Click** the **Region1** tab.

8. Select the ranges **B5:E6** and **B11:E15** using the Ctrl key technique that you just used.

9. Assign the name **Region1_Data** to the range.

10. Assign the names **Region2_Data** and **Region3_Data** to the same ranges in the Region2 and Region3 sheets.

Hands-On 14.2 – Turn on data validation

In this exercise, you will restrict data entry in the Region1 – Region3 sheets.

1. **Click** the Name box drop-down button and choose Region1_Data as shown below.

    The range B5:E6 and B11:E15 should become selected in the Region1 sheet.

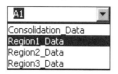

2. Choose **Data**→**Validation...** from the menu bar.

3. Use the following steps to set the data entry restrictions.

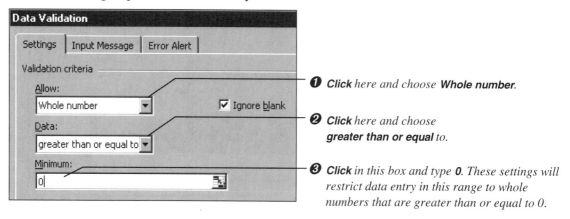

❶ *Click here and choose* **Whole number**.

❷ *Click here and choose* **greater than or equal** *to.*

❸ *Click in this box and type* **0**. *These settings will restrict data entry in this range to whole numbers that are greater than or equal to 0.*

4. **Click** the **Input Message** tab on the dialog box.

    Notice you can create an input message that appears whenever the highlight is in a restricted cell. You will not use this option in this exercise. You will use an error alert message instead.

5. **Click** the **Error Alert** tab.

6. Use the steps on the following page to set an error alert message.

Continued...

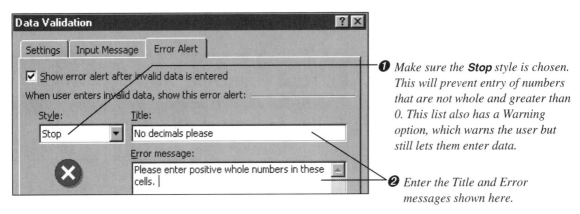

● *Make sure the* **Stop** *style is chosen. This will prevent entry of numbers that are not whole and greater than 0. This list also has a Warning option, which warns the user but still lets them enter data.*

❷ *Enter the Title and Error messages shown here.*

7. **Click OK** to complete the data validation steps.

Test the data validation

8. **Click** cell **B5** in the Region1 sheet.

9. Type the number **−1000** and **tap** ⌷Enter⌷.

   The error alert message you just created should appear. The data restrictions only allow you to enter positive whole numbers in this cell.

10. **Click** the **Retry** button.

11. Type the number **1000.50** and tap ⌷Enter⌷.

   Once again, this is not a whole number so it won't be accepted.

12. **Click** the **Retry** button and enter the original number **890000**.

13. Now apply the same data validation restrictions and error alert message to the ranges Region2_Data and Region3_Data.

   You can easily select the desired ranges by choosing the range name from the Name box.

14. Save 🖫 the changes and continue with the next topic.

Consolidating Worksheet Data

Excel lets you consolidate worksheet data in several ways. Consolidating combines values from supporting worksheets into a master sheet. For example, in the Hands-On Lesson 14 workbook, you will consolidate cells in the range B5:E6. The consolidation will add the values in cells B5:E6 of the Region1-Region3 sheets. The results will be displayed in cells B5:E6 of the Master sheet. The following illustration shows the consolidation of values in cell B6 of the Hands-On Lesson 14 workbook.

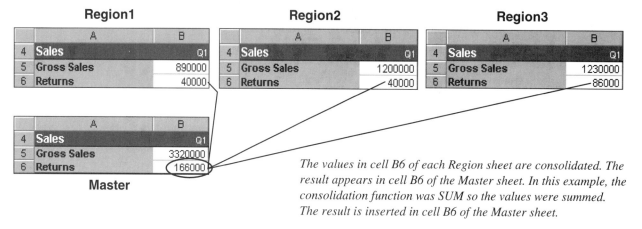

The values in cell B6 of each Region sheet are consolidated. The result appears in cell B6 of the Master sheet. In this example, the consolidation function was SUM so the values were summed. The result is inserted in cell B6 of the Master sheet.

You can use a variety of functions when consolidating

The SUM function is the most widely used consolidation function. In fact, it was used in the preceding illustration to obtain the sum of the region numbers. However, you can also use functions such as AVERAGE, MIN and MAX. The desired function is chosen in the Consolidate dialog box when the consolidation is set up.

There are 3 types of consolidation

You can consolidate data using three different methods. The following table describes the methods.

Consolidation type	Description
3-D referencing	You can use a function such as SUM to reference cells in multiple worksheets. This is known as 3-D referencing. For example, a SUM function in cell B6 of the Master sheet can be used to sum the values in cell B6 of each region sheet. This, in effect, consolidates the values into the Master sheet.
By position	Consolidating by position is useful if all worksheets have an identical layout. When consolidating by position, you specify the same range in all worksheets and Excel applies the consolidation function to each cell in the range.
By category	Consolidating by category is useful if the supporting worksheets have different layouts. Excel uses the row and column headings to determine how the data should be consolidated. The consolidation produces one row or column in the master sheet for each unique row or column encountered in the supporting sheets.

Hands-On 14.3 – Consolidate using 3-D references

In this exercise, you will use the SUM function with 3-D references to consolidate all cells in the range B5:E6 of the Master sheet.

1. **Click** the **Master** sheet tab, and then **click** cell **B5**.

2. **Click** AutoSum $\boxed{\Sigma}$.

   In the next few steps, you will build the SUM function by selecting the Region1 – Region 3 sheets and clicking cell B5. When you have finished, your SUM function will reference cell B5 in each of the region sheets. This is known as 3-D referencing.

3. **Click** the **Region1** tab.

   Notice the Region1 sheet name is displayed in the SUM function in the Formula bar.

4. **Press & Hold** the $\boxed{\text{Shift}}$ key on the keyboard while you **click** the **Region2** and **Region3** tabs.

5. Now **click** cell **B5** in the Region1 sheet and the expression =SUM('Region1:Region3'!B5) should appear in the Formula bar.

   Take a moment to study this expression and try to understand how it functions. You could also have built this expression by clicking the sheet tabs individually and then clicking cell B5 in each sheet.

6. Confirm $\boxed{\checkmark}$ the entry and the result should be 3320000.

Try it on another cell

7. **Click** cell **B6** in the Master sheet, and then **click** AutoSum $\boxed{\Sigma}$.

8. **Click** the **Region1** tab.

9. **Press & hold** $\boxed{\text{Shift}}$ while you **click** the **Region2** and **Region3** tabs.

10. **Click** cell **B6** in the Region1 sheet and confirm $\boxed{\checkmark}$ the entry.

    The result should be 166000.

Copy the formulas across the rows

11. Select cells **B5** and **B6** in the Master sheet.

12. Use the fill handle ✛ to copy the formulas across the row.

    Rows 1-7 of the Master sheet should now match the following example.

	A	B	C	D	E
1	Bonus Analysis				
2					
3					
4	Sales	Q1	Q2	Q3	Q4
5	Gross Sales	3320000	3310000	4380000	4590000
6	Returns	166000	94000	185000	124000
7	Net Sales				

Hands-On 14.4 – Consolidate by position

In this exercise, you will use the consolidation command to consolidate the range B11:E15 by position. This is possible, because all worksheets have the same layout.

1. **Select** the range **B11:E15** in the Master sheet.

   You begin this type of consolidation by selecting the consolidation range in the master sheet.

2. Choose **Data→Consolidate...** from the menu bar.

3. Use the following steps to explore the Consolidate dialog box.

   ❶ *Click this button and notice the various consolidation functions. Make sure Sum is chosen.*

   ❷ *Click in the Reference box. This box lets you specify the references you wish to consolidate in other worksheets. You will use this box in a moment.*

   ❸ *Notice these options (but don't choose them). The labels options are used when consolidating by category. The create links box creates links between data in the master and supporting sheets. This way, the master sheet is updated when data in the supporting sheets changes.*

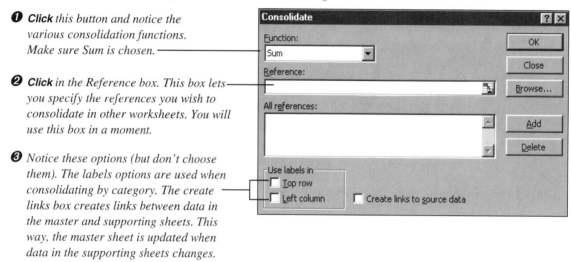

4. If necessary, move the Consolidate dialog box until you can see the range B11:E15 in the Master sheet and the sheet tabs at the bottom of the Excel window.

5. **Click** the **Region1** sheet tab.

   The expression Region1! will appear in the Reference box within the Consolidate box.

6. Use the mouse to select the range **B11:E15** in the Region1 sheet.

   The expression will now become Region1!$B$11:$E$15. This is the reference of the range B11:B15 in the Region1 sheet.

7. **Click** the [Add] button on the right side of the dialog box.

   This adds the reference to the All references list. You build a consolidation range by adding references to the All references list.

8. **Click** the **Region2** sheet tab.

   In the next step, you are instructed to select the range B11:E15. Don't be concerned if you see a flashing marquee in that range. Just select the data as instructed.

9. **Select** the range **B11:E15**.

10. **Click** the [Add] button to add that range to the All references list.

Continued...

11. Now **click** the **Region3** sheet tab, **select** the range **B11:E15** and **add** it to the list.

12. Click OK and Excel will consolidate the data.

Your Master sheet should have the consolidated numbers shown below.

	A	B	C	D	E
1	Bonus Analysis				
2					
3					
4	Sales	Q1	Q2	Q3	Q4
5	Gross Sales	3320000	3310000	4380000	4590000
6	Returns	166000	94000	185000	124000
7	Net Sales				
8					
9					
10	Expenses	Q1	Q2	Q3	Q4
11	Sample Costs	50700	24000	97890	44450
12	Trade Shows	107490	6700	122000	96000
13	Automobile	18000	18500	15000	14600
14	Cell Phones	10800	12900	11140	11100
15	Entertainment	17900	20100	11700	10200
16	Total Expenses				

Check out the results

13. Click any cell in the range B11:E15 in the Master sheet.

*Look at the Formula bar and notice a number is displayed. The consolidation command sums the values in the selected ranges and enters values in the master sheet. These numbers **will not** change if the data in the supporting worksheets changes (because they are not linked).*

14. Click any cell in the range B5:E6.

You created these 3-D SUM functions in an earlier exercise. These functions are linked to the supporting worksheets. The numbers in the master sheet will change if the supporting worksheet's numbers change.

15. Choose **Data→Consolidate...** from the menu bar.

Notice the references you created are still displayed on the All references list. These references will remain on the list even after you close and save the workbook. This is convenient, because you may want to add another worksheet at a later time. You could include the range B11:E5 from the new worksheet in the consolidation by adding it to the list.

Also notice the Browse button on the dialog box. This button lets you specify the location of workbooks on the computer system. This option is used when you are trying to consolidate data from other workbooks. You can consolidate from within a workbook (as in this exercise) or from other workbooks.

16. Close the Consolidate dialog box.

17. Save 🖫 the changes and continue with the next topic.

You will receive additional practice with consolidation in the end of lesson exercises.

Natural Language Formulas

Excel 97 lets you use row and column headings in formulas instead of cell references. This lets you create formulas using natural language expressions. For example, in the next exercise, you will create a formula in cell B7 of the Master sheet. The formula will calculate the Net Sales = Gross Sales − Returns. Until now, you would have been instructed to enter this formula as =B5-B6. With Excel 97, however, you can type the formula exactly as it is written =Gross Sales − Returns.

Hands-On 14.5 – Use natural language formulas

Compute the Net Sales

1.   **Click** the **Master** sheet tab, and then **click** cell **B7**.

2.   Type the formula **=Gross Sales - Returns** and confirm ✓ the entry.

     The result should be 3154000. At this point, you might be wondering why you have been instructed to use cell references in formulas throughout this course. This is because you may need to use an older version of Excel or perhaps a different spreadsheet program. The cell reference techniques you have learned can be used in all versions of Excel (and other programs). Natural language formulas are new in Excel 97 and they also have some limitations.

3.   Use the fill handle ✛ to copy the formula across the row.

4.   **Click** cell **C7** and notice the natural language formula has been copied to that cell.

Use AutoSum to compute the Total Expenses

5.   **Select** the range **B16:E16** and **click** AutoSum Σ.

     The Total Expenses in row 16 should be calculated. You could have used a natural language formula such as =SUM(Q1) and then copied it across the row. However, it is much easier to use AutoSum in this situation. Also, natural language formulas can be a little unpredictable when used with functions such as SUM.

Calculate the Expenses vs Net Sales

6.   **Click** cell **B18**, and then enter the formula **=Total Expenses / Net Sales**.

     The result should be .0649...

7.   Now use the fill handle ✛ to copy the formula across the row.

     At this point, rows 4-18 of your Master worksheet should match the example below.

	A	B	C	D	E
4	**Sales**	Q1	Q2	Q3	Q4
5	**Gross Sales**	3320000	3310000	4380000	4590000
6	**Returns**	166000	94000	185000	124000
7	**Net Sales**	3154000	3216000	4195000	4466000
8					
9					
10	**Expenses**	Q1	Q2	Q3	Q4
11	**Sample Costs**	50700	24000	97890	44450
12	**Trade Shows**	107490	6700	122000	96000
13	**Automobile**	18000	18500	15000	14600
14	**Cell Phones**	10800	12900	11140	11100
15	**Entertainment**	17900	20100	11700	10200
16	**Total Expenses**	204890	82200	257730	176350
17					
18	*Expenses vs Net Sales*	0.06496195	0.0255597	0.06143743	0.03948724

Hands-On 14.6 – Copy the formulas using 3-D selections

In this exercise, you will copy the formulas from the Master sheet to the Region1-Region3 sheets. You will copy and paste each formula just once using 3-D referencing.

Copy the formulas

1. **Click** the **Master** sheet tab and **select** the Net Sales totals in cells **B7:E7**.

2. **Click** the Copy button.

3. **Click** the **Region1** sheet tab.

4. **Select** the range **B7:E7**.

5. **Press & hold** ⌨Ctrl while you **click** the **Region2** and **Region3** tabs.

    This selects the same cells in all three worksheets.

6. **Click** the Paste button.

7. **Click** the **Region1**, **Region2** and **Region3** tabs and notice the formulas have been copied.

8. Now copy the Total Expenses and Expenses vs Net Sales formulas to Regions 1-3.

    Feel free to browse through the Regions 1-3 sheets and check out the results.

Format the cells

9. **Click** the **Name box** drop down button and choose **Consolidation_Data** as shown below.

    You created this name earlier in this lesson. The ranges B5:E6 and B11:E15 should be selected.

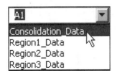

10. **Press & hold** ⌨Shift and **click** the **Region3** sheet tab.

    This will select all 4 sheets. Excel selects all sheets between the Master sheet and Region3.

11. Format the numbers as comma 🔲 with **0** decimals.

12. **Click** the various sheet tabs and notice the range is formatted in all sheets.

13. **Click** the **Master** sheet tab.

14. **Select** both the Net Sales and Total Expenses numbers in the ranges **B7:E7** and **B16:E16**.

15. **Press & hold** ⌨Shift and **click** the **Region3** tab.

16. Format the numbers as currency 🔲 with **0** decimals.

    Notice that all four sheet tabs are still active. Any range you select now will be selected in all four sheets. Formatting commands will affect all active sheets as long as they remain active.

17. **Select** the Expenses vs Net Sales numbers in the range **B18:E18**.

18. Format them as percent 🔲 with **2** decimals.

    Take a moment to browse through the worksheet, then continue with the next topic.

Conditional Formatting

Excel 97 lets you assign conditional formats to cells. Conditional formats are activated only when the conditions you specify are met. For example, in the next exercise, you will apply a conditional format to the Expenses vs Net Sales percentages in row 18 of the Master sheet. The conditional format will assign a red color to a cell if the percentage is greater than 6%. Conditional formats are often used as alarms. They let you draw attention to values that fall outside an acceptable range.

🕐	*Quick Steps:* **Conditional Formatting**	🕐

To apply conditional formats to cells
- *Select the desired cells.*
- *Choose Format→Conditional Formatting.*
- *Set the desired condition.*
- *If necessary, use the Add button to add additional conditions and click OK.*

Hands-On 14.7 – Apply conditional formatting

1. **Deselect** the sheet tabs by clicking one of the Region tabs.

2. **Select** the range **B18:E18** in the Master sheet.

3. Choose **Format→Conditional Formatting...** from the menu bar.

4. Use the following steps to apply the conditional format.

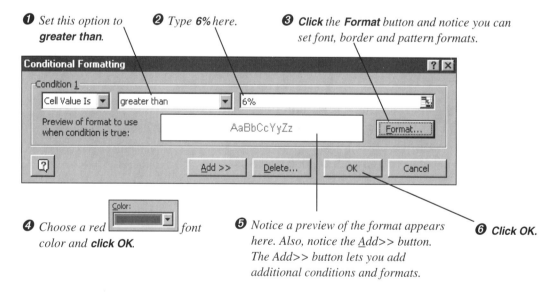

❶ *Set this option to* **greater than**.

❷ *Type* **6%** *here.*

❸ **Click** *the* **Format** *button and notice you can set font, border and pattern formats.*

❹ *Choose a red font color and* **click OK**.

❺ *Notice a preview of the format appears here. Also, notice the Add>> button. The Add>> button lets you add additional conditions and formats.*

❻ **Click OK.**

5. **Click anywhere** in the Master sheet to deselect the range.

   The conditional format should have been applied to cells B18 and D18.

6. Now **click** the **Region1** tab and **select** the range **B18:E18**.

7. **Press & hold** ⎰Shift⎱ and **click** the **Region3** tab.

8. Apply the same conditional format to these ranges.

   Once again, you can apply any format to 3-D selections. Now continue with the next topic.

Advanced What-If Analysis

Excel has a number of tools to let you perform advanced what-if analysis. In the following topics, you will use data tables and the Scenario Manager. You will help Bob Johnson, the Sales Manager of Seminar Solutions, develop a management strategy to maximize his quarterly bonus. Bob's bonus is dependent upon the Net Sales and Expenses vs Net Sales ratios of the regions he manages. Bob wants to analyze results from the previous year to help him make important management decisions in the current year. These decisions will help Bob maximize his bonus.

Data Tables

Data tables let you see the impact that changing variables have on a formula. For example, Bob's quarterly bonus is calculated as a function of two variables: Net Sales and the Expenses vs Net Sales ratio. You will use a two-variable data table to determine how these variables impact Bob's bonus. Excel supports both one-variable and two-variable data tables. You will work with a two-variable table in this section.

Setting up a two-variable data table

The following illustration discusses the layout and set up of a typical two-variable data table. Take a few moments to study this illustration carefully.

In this example, cells A2 and B1 are the input cells. Input cells are always empty in a data table. When you issue the data table command, Excel will substitute the Net Sales and Expenses vs Net Sales variables into the input cells.

Notice the formula in cell B2. This rather complex formula is used to calculate Bob's bonus. Also notice the input cells A2 and B1 are referenced in the formula.

B2		=	=A2*1%*(1-10*B1)			
	A	B	C	D	E	F	G
1			Expenses vs Net Sales				
2		0	1%	2%	4%	6%	8%
3	Net Sales	$ 1,000,000	9000	8000	6000	4000	2000
4		$ 2,000,000	18000	16000	12000	8000	4000
5		$ 3,000,000	27000	24000	18000	12000	6000
6		$ 4,000,000	36000	32000	24000	16000	8000
7		$ 5,000,000	45000	40000	30000	20000	10000

Expenses vs Net Sales are the row variables.

Net Sales are the column variables.

The data table command inserts these results into the table. The command substitutes one pair of variables into the input cells. The formula then calculates the result and inserts it in the table. This process continues until all the results are calculated.

A good way to understand data tables is to use a specific example. Look at the illustration above and notice the variable in cell C2 is 1% and the variable in cell B3 is $1,000,000. The result in cell C3 is 9000. When the data table command is issued, 1% is substituted into cell B1 and $1,000,000 is substituted into cell A2. The formula then calculates the result (9000) and inserts it in cell C3 (the intersection of the input variable cells). This process continues for all variable combinations in the table.

Hands-On 14.8 – Create a two-variable data table

In this exercise, you will set up the table discussed on the previous page.

Insert a new worksheet

1. **Click** the **Master** sheet tab and choose **Insert→Worksheet** from the menu bar.

2. Rename the sheet as **Bonus Analysis**.

Set up the table

3. Enter the following data into the new sheet and format the numbers as shown.

	A	B	C	D	E	F	G
1			Expenses vs Net Sales				
2			1%	2%	4%	6%	8%
3	Net Sales	$ 1,000,000					
4		$ 2,000,000					
5		$ 3,000,000					
6		$ 4,000,000					
7		$ 5,000,000					

4. **Click** cell **B2**.

   You will enter the formula in this cell. You always set up a two-variable data table in this manner. One set of variables is placed immediately to the right of the formula (the percentages in this example). The other set of variables is placed immediately below the formula (the dollars in this example). The Net Sales and Expenses vs Net Sales labels can be placed anywhere as long as they do not interfere with the table.

5. Enter the formula **=A2*1%*(1-10*B1)** in cell B2.

   *The result should be 0. This formula calculates Bob's quarterly bonus as 1% of Net Sales multiplied by a percentage. The percentage is calculated by the (1-10*B1) part of the formula. This component penalizes Bob as the Expenses vs Net Sales ratio increases. In other words, if Bob's regions spend too much compared to what they sell, then Bob gets penalized. Take a few moments to understand the way this formula works.*

Complete the data table

   The final steps in creating the data table are to select the table and use the Data→Table command.

6. **Select** the range **B2:G7** as shown below.

   When selecting the data prior to creating a data table, you must include the formula, variables and table cells in the selection.

	A	B	C	D	E	F	G
1			Expenses vs Net Sales				
2		0	1%	2%	4%	6%	8%
3	Net Sales	$ 1,000,000					
4		$ 2,000,000					
5		$ 3,000,000					
6		$ 4,000,000					
7		$ 5,000,000					

7. Choose **Data→Table...** from the menu bar.

Continued...

8. Use the following illustration to choose the input cells.

❶ *Type* **B1** *as the Row input and* **A2** *as the Column input.*

❷ **Click OK.**

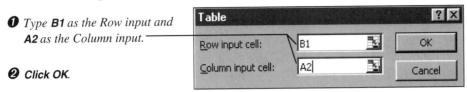

The data table will be completed as shown below. The Row input cell is the cell that you want the row variables (Expenses vs Net Sales) to be substituted into. Likewise, the Column input cell is where the column variables (Net Sales) will be substituted. If you look at the formula in cell B2, you will see that these substitutions make sense.

	A	B	C	D	E	F	G
1			Expenses vs Net Sales				
2		0	1%	2%	4%	6%	8%
3	Net Sales	$ 1,000,000	9000	8000	6000	4000	2000
4		$ 2,000,000	18000	16000	12000	8000	4000
5		$ 3,000,000	27000	24000	18000	12000	6000
6		$ 4,000,000	36000	32000	24000	16000	8000
7		$ 5,000,000	45000	40000	30000	20000	10000

Apply conditional formatting to the table

Bob has a "bottom line" when it comes to his quarterly bonus. He is unwilling to accept a bonus that is less than $20,000. For this reason, you will format the cells in the data table using a conditional format. Cells where the bonus is greater than or equal to $20,000 will be formatted with a blue color. This will let Bob instantly see the combinations of Net Sales and Expenses vs Net Sales that are acceptable.

9. **Select** the range **C3:G7**.

10. Choose **Format→Conditional Formatting...** from the menu bar.

11. Use the following steps to set the condition.

❶ *Set this option to* **greater than or equal to.**

❷ *Type* **20000** *here.*

❸ **Click** *the* **Format** *button, choose a* **blue font color** *and* **click OK** *in the Format Cells dialog box.*

❹ **Click OK** *in the Conditional Formatting box.*

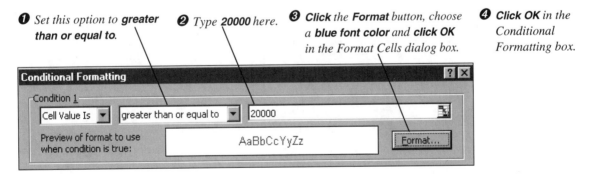

Only values greater than or equal to 20000 should appear in blue. As you can see, this data table and conditional formatting clearly show Bob which Net Sales and Expenses vs Net Sales ratio combinations are required to achieve a $20,000 (or greater) bonus.

12. Feel free to experiment with your data table.

Try changing the Net Sales variables in column B and the Expenses vs Net Sales variables in row 2. The data table will be recalculated each time you change a variable.

13. Save 💾 the changes when you have finished and continue with the next topic.

Scenario Manager

Data tables let you see the impact that changing variables have on a formula. Unfortunately, data tables are limited to just two variables. Excel provides the Scenario Manager for what-if models requiring more than two variables. In fact, the Scenario Manager can be used with up to 32 variables! This allows you to model virtually any what-if scenario.

What is a Scenario?

A scenario is a combination of values that are assigned to variables in a what-if model. The model calculates results based upon the values used in the scenario. Scenarios are given names to identify them and they are saved and organized using the Scenario Manager.

Managing Scenarios

The Scenario Manager lets you create and manage a large number of scenarios. This way, you can compare the various scenarios and the results they achieve. The Scenario Manager also lets you display and print out the results of multiple scenarios.

Hands-On 14.9 – Use the Scenario Manager

In this exercise, you will help Bob Johnson set up a model to further analyze expenses. Bob's data table has shown him that reducing expenses will increase his bonus. For this reason, Bob wants to take a closer look at each component of the expenses. You will set up a model that computes the Expenses vs Net Sales ratio using Net Sales and the expense components in rows 11 – 15 as variables. The Scenario Manager will be used to create multiple scenarios.

Set up the model
1. **Click** the **Bonus Analysis** sheet tab, and then **click** cell **B10**.

2. Enter the data shown below.

   You will need to widen column B as shown. Also, notice cell C18 is empty at this point.

	A	B	C
9			
10		Expenses vs Net Sales Model	
11			
12		Net Sales	1000000
13		Sample Costs	10000
14		Trade Shows	10000
15		Automobile	10000
16		Cell Phones	10000
17		Entertainment	10000
18		Expenses vs Net Sales	

3. **Click** cell **C18** and enter the formula **=SUM(C13:C17)/C12**.

   The result should be .05. Notice this formula sums the expenses and divides by the Net Sales.

4. Format the range **C12:C17** as **comma** with **0** decimals and cell **C18** as **percent** with **2** decimals.

   The completed model should match the example on the following page. This model will form the starting point from which you will create scenarios.

   Continued...

	A	B	C
9			
10		Expenses vs Net Sales Model	
11			
12		Net Sales	1,000,000
13		Sample Costs	10,000
14		Trade Shows	10,000
15		Automobile	10,000
16		Cell Phones	10,000
17		Entertainment	10,000
18		Expenses vs Net Sales	5.00%

Name the variable cells

In the next few steps, you will name the variable cells in the model using the Name Create technique. You learned this technique in an earlier lesson. Naming the variable cells is beneficial because the names will appear in the Scenario Manager dialog box.

5. **Select** the range **B12:C18** as shown below.

	A	B	C
9			
10		Expenses vs Net Sales Model	
11			
12		Net Sales	1,000,000
13		Sample Costs	10,000
14		Trade Shows	10,000
15		Automobile	10,000
16		Cell Phones	10,000
17		Entertainment	10,000
18		Expenses vs Net Sales	5.00%

6. Choose **Insert→Name→Create...** from the menu bar.

7. Make sure the Left column box is checked and **click OK**.

8. **Click** cell **C12** and notice the name Net_Sales appears in the Name box.

   All other variable cells have also been assigned names.

Create the first scenario

9. Select the range **C12:C17** as shown below (don't select cell C18).

   Only the variables will be adjusted in the Scenario Manager.

	A	B	C
9			
10		Expenses vs Net Sales Model	
11			
12		Net Sales	1,000,000
13		Sample Costs	10,000
14		Trade Shows	10,000
15		Automobile	10,000
16		Cell Phones	10,000
17		Entertainment	10,000
18		Expenses vs Net Sales	5.00%

10. Choose **Tools→Scenarios...** from the menu bar.

    The dialog box should indicate that no scenarios are currently defined.

Continued...

11. **Click** the **Add** button to add a new scenario.

12. Type the name **Scenario 1** in the Add Scenario box.

13. Notice the Changing cells box.

    This box determines which variable cells will be changed to create the scenario. This option should be set to C12:C17. This is because you selected those cells prior to starting the Scenario Manager. It is usually best to select the variable cells prior to starting the Scenario Manager (although you can always select them once the Add Scenario box is displayed).

14. **Click OK** and the Scenario Values box will appear.

15. Use the following steps to explore the Scenario Values box.

    ❶ *Notice the cell names are displayed to the left of the variable boxes. This is because you named the cells.*

    ❷ *Notice the variable boxes contain values. You create scenarios by entering values or formulas in these boxes.*

    ❸ **Scroll down** *until the Entertainment variable is visible. You can have up to 32 variables in a scenario.*

    ❹ **Click OK** *to close the dialog box.*

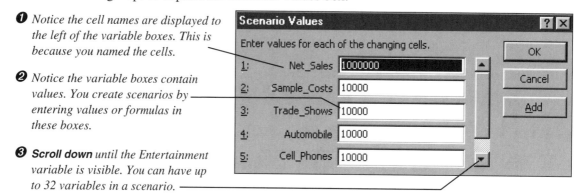

    The Scenario Manager dialog box will remain open. This scenario will serve as a starting point for other scenarios. The other scenarios you create will be compared to this one.

Add another scenario
16. **Click** the **Add** button.

17. Type the name **Scenario 2** and **click OK**.

18. Enter the following variables (there is no need to change the Entertainment variable).

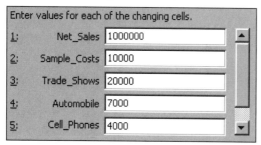

19. **Click OK** on the Scenario Values box.

    Scenario 1 and Scenario 2 will now appear in the Scenario Manager dialog box.

Show the results
20. Make sure Scenario 2 is chosen and **click** the **Show** button.

    Excel will substitute the scenario values into the model and the formula in cell C18 will calculate the result. The result should be 5.10%.

Continued...

21. Choose **Scenario 1** and **click** the **Show** button.

As you can see, the Scenario Manager lets you rapidly see the results of various scenarios.

22. Now add two new scenarios using the data in the following table.

Scenario name	Variable	Set to
Scenario 3	Net Sales	2000000
	Sample Costs	17000
	Trade Shows	35000
	Automobile	14000
	Cell Phones	5000
	Entertainment	85000
Scenario 4	Net Sales	2000000
	Sample Costs	20000
	Trade Shows	20000
	Automobile	10000
	Cell Phones	7500
	Entertainment	35000

23. Use the Show button to show the results of each scenario.

Edit a scenario

24. Choose **Scenario 3** and **click** the **Show** button.

The Expenses vs Net Sales should be 7.80%. The data table you created earlier shows that Bob's bonus will be around $4,000 for this scenario. Bob will not be happy with this! Fortunately, the Scenario Manager lets you adjust scenario values until a desired result is achieved.

25. Make sure Scenario 3 is chosen and **click** the **Edit** button.

26. Click OK on the Edit Scenario box.

27. Change the **Trade_Shows** number to **12500** and **click OK**.

28. Click the **Show** button again and the result should be 6.68%.

Bob can use these scenarios to determine which expense items to trim.

Display a summary of all scenarios

29. Click the **Summary** button.

Notice you can display a scenario summary and a scenario PivotTable. You will display a summary in the next few steps.

30. Choose the **Scenario summary** option and **click OK**.

Excel will insert the summary on a new worksheet.

31. Study the summary closely.

You can print a summary as you print any other worksheet. You can also delete a summary by deleting the summary worksheet.

32. Feel free to experiment with any of the topics you have learned in this lesson.

33. When you have finished experimenting, **close** the workbook and **save** the changes.

Continue with the end-of-lesson questions and exercises.

Concepts Review

True / False

1. Data validation cannot be used in cells that contain numbers.   1. **T F**

2. Data validation can provide error alert messages but it can't prevent a user from entering unacceptable data.   2. **T F**

3. Consolidation can only be used in worksheets that have an identical layout.   3. **T F**

4. Other functions besides SUM can be used when consolidating worksheets.   4. **T F**

5. All worksheets must have an identical layout when consolidating by position.   5. **T F**

6. Natural language formulas let you use labels instead of cell references in formulas.   6. **T F**

7. Conditional formats can apply colors to cells.   7. **T F**

8. You can use up to four variables in a data table.   8. **T F**

9. The variables cannot be changed once a data table is set up.   9. **T F**

10. You can have up to 32 variables when using Scenario Manager.   10. **T F**

Multiple Choice

1. Which command is used to turn on data validation?
   a) Tools→Validation
   b) Format→Validation
   c) Data→Validation
   d) None of the above.   (   )

2. Which command is used to set conditional formats?
   a) Format→Conditional Formatting
   b) Tools→Conditional Formatting
   c) Insert→Conditional Formatting
   d) None of the above.   (   )

3. Which of the following format categories can be applied with conditional formats?
   a) Fonts
   b) Borders
   c) Patterns
   d) All of the above.   (   )

4. What is the maximum number of allowable variables with Scenario Manager?
   a) 2
   b) 8
   c) 16
   d) 32   (   )

5. Which of the following statements is true?
   a) You can apply conditional formats using 3-D selecting.
   b) You cannot apply conditional formats using 3-D selecting.
   c) You can apply number formats using 3-D selecting.   (   )
   d) Both A and C.

Skills Builder 14.1

In this exercise, you will open a workbook that tracks compensation paid to independent contractors. Independent contractors are issued 1099 statements (similar to W2's) at the end of the year. The workbook has a Year-to-date sheet and sheets for each month. You will use the consolidate by category option to consolidate the months in the Year-to-date sheet.

1. **Open** the workbook named **Skills Builder 14.1**.

    Notice the Year-to-date sheet has column headings in row 3 but there is no data. The data will be inserted by the consolidation command.

2. **Click** the **January** sheet tab.

    Notice there are six 1099 recipients listed with the number of hours and compensation of each recipient. This recipient list is different for each month. This is because these temporary contractors come-and-go on a regular basis.

3. **Click** cell **C4**.

    Notice the compensation is calculated as the hours multiplied by $21.35. The consolidation command will consolidate the hours and compensation from the monthly sheets. You can consolidate cells with values or formulas (as in this example).

4. **Click** the **February** sheet tab.

    Notice there are seven recipients for February. Several of the recipients are different from those in the January sheet.

5. **Click** the **March** sheet tab and notice once again that the recipient list has changed.

    In the next few steps, you will use the consolidate by category command in the Year-to-date sheet. You cannot consolidate by position (as you did in the Hands-On Lesson 14 project) because the monthly sheets have different layouts (different recipients).

6. **Click** the **Year-to-date** sheet tab, and then **click** cell **A4**.

    Cell A4 will form the starting point for the consolidated data. When consolidating by category, it is best to click the starting point of the consolidated data prior to issuing the consolidate command.

7. Choose **Data→Consolidate...** from the menu bar.

    In the next few steps, you will specify the range references you wish to consolidate. You will do this by selecting the ranges in the various sheets and adding them to the All references list.

8. Make sure the insertion point is the Reference box and **click** the **January** sheet tab.

    You may need to move the dialog box out of the way.

9. Use the following steps to select the desired range.

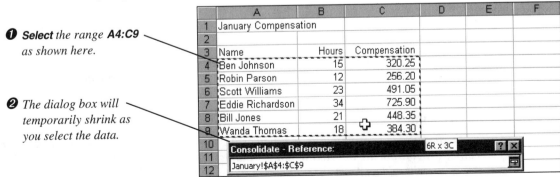

❶ *Select* the range **A4:C9** as shown here.

❷ *The dialog box will temporarily shrink as you select the data.*

Continued...

Notice that the row labels in column A were included in the selection. This is necessary because there are no row labels in the year-to-date sheet. The consolidate by category command will use these labels to determine which rows to consolidate from the monthly sheets.

Add additional ranges

10. Click the **Add** button.

11. Click the **February** sheet tab.

Notice that Excel inserts the reference February!$A$4:$C$9 into the Reference box and the marquee surrounds the reference in the worksheet. Excel assumes you want to reference the same cells as in the January sheet. This is an incorrect assumption. You will override Excel's proposal by selecting the correct cells in the next step.

12. Select the range **A4:C10** and **click** the **Add** button.

13. Click the **March** sheet tab and **select** the range **A4:C11**.

14. Click the **Add** button to complete the selection of references.

Consolidate the data

15. Click the **Left column** check box as shown below.

This instructs Excel to consolidate the data based upon the names in the left column of the selected ranges. Excel will create one consolidated row in the Year-to-date sheet for each name. For example, the name Ben Johnson appears in two sheets. Excel will create one Ben Johnson row in the Year-to-date sheet. This row will contain the consolidated numbers for Ben Johnson.

16. Click OK to complete the consolidation as shown below.

	A	B	C
1	1099 Recipient Compensation		
2			
3	Name	Hours	Compensation
4	Ben Johnson	27	576.45
5	Cheryl Lake	77	1,643.95
6	Robin Parson	67	1,430.45
7	Scott Williams	35	747.25
8	Eddie Richardson	46	982.10
9	Bill Jones	51	1,088.85
10	Wanda Thomas	65	1,387.75
11	Leslie Wilson	38	811.30
12	Ted Simpson	12	256.20
13	Ellen Ellis	10	213.50
14	Stewart Williams	8	170.80

Notice that each name appears just once in the consolidated list. Feel free to browse through the monthly sheets. You will notice that the consolidated numbers are the summation of the numbers for the individual months.

Add another worksheet

One of the benefits of consolidation, is it makes it easy to add data and worksheets at a later time. You can easily consolidate the data again by adding an additional consolidation range. In the next few steps, you will add an April sheet and reconsolidate the data.

Continued...

17. **Insert** a **new worksheet** and change the name to **April**.

18. **Drag** the **sheet tab** until it is positioned to the right of the March sheet.

19. **Click** the **March** sheet tab and use the Select All [ ] button to select the entire sheet.

20. Copy [ ] the sheet and **click** the **April** sheet tab.

21. Make sure the highlight is in cell **A1** and paste [ ] the sheet.

22. **Select** rows **6** and **7** and use the **Edit→Delete** command to remove them.

    Scott Williams and Eddie Richardson did not receive compensation in April.

23. Add the following new recipients to rows 10 and 11.

    You will need to copy the compensation formula from row 9 to rows 10 and 11.

| 10 | Pete Sanchez | 23 | 491.05 |
| 11 | Doness Yee | 21 | 448.35 |

Consolidate again

24. **Click** the **Year-to-date** sheet tab.

25. **Select** all the consolidated data in the range **A4:C14** and **delete** it by tapping the [Delete] key.

    It is best to delete the data before consolidating. This is because the new consolidation will overwrite the existing data. If the new consolidation has fewer rows than the original consolidation, then there will be leftover (and incorrect) rows at the bottom of the consolidated data.

26. **Click** cell **A4** and choose **Data→Consolidate** from the menu bar.

    Notice the consolidation ranges you chose before are still on the All references list. This is convenient because now you only need to add the April range.

27. Make sure the insertion point is in the References box and **click** the **April** sheet tab.

28. **Select** the range **A4:C11** and **click** the **Add** button.

29. **Click OK** to complete the consolidation.

    You should now have 13 unique rows of consolidated data.

30. Now **add** a **May sheet** (use whichever data you desire) and **consolidate** the data again.

31. Feel free to experiment further with this workbook.

32. **Close** the workbook and **save** the changes when you have finished.

Skills Builder 14.2

In this exercise, you will create a two-variable data table. The data table will calculate monthly payments on an automobile loan using various interest rates and terms.

1. Start a new workbook and enter the following data.

   Make sure the numbers in column B are formatted with percentages as shown.

	A	B	C	D	E	F	G
1	Automobile Loan Analysis						
2							
3			Months:				
4			36	42	48	54	60
5	Rate:	8.00%					
6		9.00%					
7		10.00%					
8		11.00%					
9		12.00%					
10		13.00%					
11		14.00%					
12		15.00%					

2. **Click** cell **B4**.

   In the next step, you will enter a formula that uses the PMT function. You used the PMT function in Lesson 11. The PMT function calculates payments using an interest rate, number of payments and opening balance as arguments.

3. Enter the function **=PMT(A4/12,B3,22000)** and confirm ☑ the entry.

   The result should be #DIV/0!. This message appears because cells A4 and B3 are empty. These are the input cells for the data table. The formula is interpreted as follows.

   - *The A4/12 reference is the interest rate argument. The A4 reference is divided by 12 because the PMT function requires a monthly rate and the rates in column B are annual rates. The formula references cell A4 because it is the input cell for the data table. The interest rates in column B will be substituted into cell A4 when the data table command is issued.*

   - *The B3 reference refers to input cell B3. The months in row 4 will be substituted into this cell when the data table command is issued.*

   - *The 22000 constant is the amount of the loan.*

4. Select the range **B4:G12** and choose **Data→Table...** from the menu bar.

5. Enter **B3** as the Row input cell and **A4** as the Column input cell.

6. **Click OK** and the table should be calculated.

   The numbers in the table will be negative. In Lesson 11, you learned that the PMT function returns a negative number. You will change this in the next few steps.

7. **Click** cell **B4**.

8. **Click** in the **formula bar** and insert a minus sign – between the equal sign and PMT function.

9. Confirm ☑ the change and the numbers should be positive.

10. Now **select** the range **C5:G12**.

Continued...

11. Format the numbers in the range **C5:G12** as **comma** with **0** decimals.

12. Apply a conditional format that changes the font color to blue when the value is less than or equal to 550.

We will assume you are trying to keep the monthly payment under $550.

13. Your completed worksheet should match the worksheet shown below.

	A	B	C	D	E	F	G
1	Automobile Loan Analysis						
2							
3			Months:				
4		#DIV/0!	36	42	48	54	60
5	Rate:	8.00%	689	602	537	486	446
6		9.00%	700	613	547	497	457
7		10.00%	710	623	558	508	467
8		11.00%	720	633	569	518	478
9		12.00%	731	644	579	529	489
10		13.00%	741	655	590	540	501
11		14.00%	752	666	601	551	512
12		15.00%	763	676	612	563	523

Change the loan amount

Now imagine that you want to see the same analysis but for a different loan amount. This is easily accomplished by changing the loan amount in the PMT function.

14. Click cell **B4**.

15. Click in the formula bar and change the 22000 number to **25000** in the PMT function.

16. Confirm ✔ the change and the data table will be recalculated.

The conditional formatting will also adjust to highlight only cells with a monthly payment of $550 or less.

17. Feel free to experiment by changing the loan amount, interest rates and months.

18. When you have finished, **close** the workbook and **save** it as **Skills Builder 14.2**.

Skills Builder 14.3

In this exercise, you will use the Scenario Manager to project the profit for a new children's toy manufacturer named KidCraft . Donna Williams, the founder of KidCraft, needs to set up the model as part of her business plan. She is trying to raise funds and a business plan and financial model are a crucial part of this process.

1. Start a new workbook and use the following guidelines to create the worksheet shown below.
   - *Enter the labels in column A and the values in the range B3:B8.*
   - *Use a SUM function in cell B9.*
   - *Use a natural language formula in cell B11 to calculate the Gross Profit as the Forecasted Revenue – Total Costs.*
   - *Use a natural language formula in cell B12 to calculate the Net Profit as the Gross Profit * 70%.*
   - *Format the values with the comma and currency formats shown.*

	A	B
1	KidCraft 1998 Projected Income	
2		
3	Forecasted Revenue	$ 345,000
4		
5	Employee Costs	62,000
6	Capital Expenditures	75,900
7	Manufacturing	58,650
8	Marketing & Sales	55,200
9	Total Costs	$ 251,750
10		
11	Gross Profit	$ 93,250
12	Net Profit	$ 65,275

Name the cells

2. Select the range **A3:B8**.

3. Choose **Insert→Name→Create...** from the menu bar.

4. Make sure the Left column box is checked and **click OK**.

Once again, this will assign names to the cells in column B. This will be helpful when using the Scenario Manager.

Create the first scenario

5. Click cell **B3**.

6. Press & Hold the ⌐Ctrl⌐ key while you **select** the range **B5:B8**.

This technique is necessary because cell B4 should not be included in the selection. You will create scenarios by changing the selected cells.

7. Choose **Tools→Scenarios...** from the menu bar.

8. Click the **Add** button.

9. Type the name **Scenario 1** and **click OK**.

10. Click OK on the Scenario Values box to choose the values displayed in the boxes.

Continued...

Add other scenarios

11. **Click** the **Add** button.

12. Type the name **Scenario 2** and **click OK**.

13. Change only the Forecasted Revenue number to **500000** and **click OK**.

14. Now add two new scenarios using the data in the following table.

Scenario name	Variable	Set to
Scenario 3	Forecasted Revenue	700000
	Employee Costs	80000
	Capital Expenditures	35000
	Manufacturing	98000
	Marketing & Sales	85000
Scenario 4	Forecasted Revenue	700000
	Employee Costs	80000
	Capital Expenditures	42000
	Manufacturing	85000
	Marketing & Sales	70000

15. Use the **Show** button on the Scenario Manager dialog box to show the results of each scenario.

Display a summary of all scenarios

16. **Click** the **Summary** button.

17. **Choose** the **Scenario summary** option and **click OK**.

Excel will insert the summary on a new worksheet. The summary is shown below. Notice the Scenario Manager assumed cell B12 as the Result Cell. This happens to be the correct assumption because it is the Net Profit in cell B12 that we are interested in seeing.

Scenario Summary	Current Values:	Scenario 1	Scenario 2	Scenario 3	Scenario 4
Changing Cells:					
Forecasted_Revenue	$ 700,000	$ 345,000	$ 500,000	$ 700,000	$ 700,000
Employee_Costs	80,000	62,000	62,000	80,000	80,000
Capital_Expenditures	42,000	75,900	75,900	35,000	42,000
Manufacturing	85,000	58,650	58,650	98,000	85,000
Marketing__Sales	70,000	55,200	55,200	85,000	70,000
Result Cells:					
$B$12	$ 296,100	$ 65,275	$ 173,775	$ 281,400	$ 296,100

Notes: Current Values column represents values of changing cells at time Scenario Summary Report was created. Changing cells for each scenario are highlighted in gray.

18. Feel free to create additional scenarios.

19. **Close** the workbook when you have finished and **save** it as **Skills Builder 14.3**.

Assessment 14.1

1. Use the following guidelines to create a new workbook with the sheets shown below and on the following page.

   - Make sure you enter the data in the correct cells. This is necessary because you will consolidate the data by position later in this assessment.

   - Make sure the column widths and cell formats are the same in all worksheets. You can accomplish this by setting up one sheet and copying it to the others.

   - Use the sheet names shown below.

   - The cells with hyphens should contain zeros 0. The hyphens appear because all values are formatted as comma with 2 decimal places.

	A	B	C	D	E	F
1	1997 Credit Card Transaction Summary					
2						
3	Card name	Purchases	Cash Advances	Interest	Payment	Credits
4	American Express					
5	National Bank Visa					
6	Western Visa					
7	Discover					
8	Norfolk Master Card					
9						

Year-to-date / January / February / March /

	A	B	C	D	E	F
1	January Transactions					
2						
3	Card name	Purchases	Cash Advances	Interest	Payment	Credits
4	American Express	125.00	200.00	25.78	100.00	-
5	National Bank Visa	500.00	-	35.00	250.00	50.00
6	Western Visa	-	-	-	-	-
7	Discover	450.00	125.00	125.65	200.00	35.98
8	Norfolk Master Card	25.00	-	-	60.00	-
9						

Year-to-date / January / February / March /

	A	B	C	D	E	F
1	February Transactions					
2						
3	Card name	Purchases	Cash Advances	Interest	Payment	Credits
4	American Express	679.56	-	30.23	350.00	85.89
5	National Bank Visa	345.00	900.00	38.90	200.00	-
6	Western Visa	400.00	-	-	-	-
7	Discover	345.00	-	130.35	500.00	-
8	Norfolk Master Card	-	-		25.00	-
9						

Year-to-date / January / February / March /

Continued...

	A	B	C	D	E	F
1	March Transactions					
2						
3	Card name	Purchases	Cash Advances	Interest	Payment	Credits
4	American Express	-	-	28.50	300.00	-
5	National Bank Visa	-	-	44.50	1,000.00	-
6	Western Visa	-	-	-	400.00	-
7	Discover	-	-	127.90	2,000.00	-
8	Norfolk Master Card	-	-	-	25.00	-
9						

Year-to-date / January / February \ **March** /

2. Use the consolidation by position command to consolidate the three monthly sheets into the Year-to-date sheet.

   The consolidated Year-to-date sheet should match the example below.

	A	B	C	D	E	F
1	1997 Credit Card Transaction Summary					
2						
3	Card name	Purchases	Cash Advances	Interest	Payment	Credits
4	American Express	804.56	200.00	84.51	750.00	85.89
5	National Bank Visa	845.00	900.00	118.40	1,450.00	50.00
6	Western Visa	400.00	-	-	400.00	-
7	Discover	795.00	125.00	383.90	2,700.00	35.98
8	Norfolk Master Card	25.00	-	-	110.00	-
9						

Year-to-date / January / February / March /

3. **Print** the workbook when you have finished.

4. **Close** the workbook and **save** it as **Assessment 14.1**.

Assessment 14.2

In this assessment, you will create the data table shown below. This table calculates monthly payments for a home mortgage using various interest rates and terms.

1. Use the following guidelines to create the data table.

   – Enter the interest rates in column B and the months in row 2 as shown.

   – Use the PMT function to create the formula in cell B2. You used the PMT function in Skills Builder 14.2. Assume the mortgage will be $200,000.

   – Do not enter the numbers shown in the range C3:F8. Excel will calculate these numbers when you issue the data table command.

   – Format the values in the range C3:F8 as comma with 0 decimals.

   – Apply a conditional format that changes the font color to blue when the value is less than or equal to 1,650.

2. **Print** the worksheet when you have finished.

3. **Close** the workbook and **save** it as **Assessment 14.2**.

	A	B	C	D	E	F
1			Months:			
2		#DIV/0!	180	240	300	360
3	Rate:	6.00%	1,688	1,433	1,289	1,199
4		6.50%	1,742	1,491	1,350	1,264
5		7.00%	1,798	1,551	1,414	1,331
6		7.50%	1,854	1,611	1,478	1,398
7		8.00%	1,911	1,673	1,544	1,468
8		8.50%	1,969	1,736	1,610	1,538

Critical Thinking 14.1

Create a data table that calculates the future value of an IRA (Individual Retirement Account). Assume that uniform monthly contributions will be made over a period of 25 years. Use interest rates as one of the variables in the data table. Use the amount of the monthly contribution as the other variable. Use interest rates that reflect the various investment vehicles that IRA funds can be placed in. For example, investing in utility funds represents low risk, however, the returns will also be relatively low (perhaps 3% - 6% per year). On the other hand, investing in high-growth technology companies is risky but the reward may be substantially higher (perhaps 10% – 15% per year). You will need to use the Future Value function as the formula in the data table. Your data table should show you the future value of the IRA for each combination of interest rate and monthly contribution. You can also adjust the period to see what the returns will be at 30 and 35 years.

Critical Thinking 14.2

Imagine that you are the director of fund raising for your church. You are asked to create and market a calendar that features artwork from children who attend the church. Create an Excel model that allows you to project the profitability of the project. Take at least five variables into consideration such as the development cost, printing cost, marketing cost, forecasted sales and selling price. Your model should contain a bottom-line profit number to help you decide which direction to proceed. Use the Scenario Manager to create four or five scenarios for your model. Display a summary of the scenarios so that you can compare and contrast them.

15 Connecting to Word and the World

Objectives:

- Learn about integration concepts

- Learn about object linking and embedding

- Link a worksheet to a Word document

- Create and use hyperlinks

- Use Excel's Internet tools

- Run Web queries

The Project – A Letter to a Financial Planner

In this lesson, you will help Shirley Washington compose a letter to Cindy Wilson, her financial planner. Cindy assists Shirley with long term planning, goals and objectives. However, Shirley has elected to manage her stock portfolio on her own using Microsoft Excel. Shirley sends Cindy a quarterly letter that details the holdings in her portfolio. You will help Shirley link the portfolio worksheet to the quarterly letter. This way, any changes made to the portfolio worksheet will automatically be reflected in the letter. The letter and linked worksheet that you will create are shown below.

Today's Date

Ms. Cindy Wilson
Wilson Financial Planning
500 Kellogg Avenue
Anaheim, CA 92807

Dear Cindy:

I have included an Excel worksheet containing my current stock portfolio. Please review my portfolio and compare it to the previous quarter.

Company	Symbol	Number of Shares	Purchase Price	Initial Value	Current Price	Current Value	Gain/Loss
IBM	IBM	500	30	15,000	94	47,000	32,000
Apple	AAPL	500	27	13,500	16	8,000	(5,500)
GM	GM	1000	39	39,000	57	57,000	18,000
Digital	DEC	300	72	21,600	38	11,400	(10,200)
Totals				$89,100		$123,400	$ 34,300
Average							$ 8,575

Please contact me if you have any questions. I look forward to hearing from you soon.

Best regards,

Shirley Washington

Integrating Office Applications

Microsoft Office 97 is composed of five main applications: Outlook; Word; Excel; PowerPoint and Access. The true power of Office 97 is in the integration of the programs. The old adage -The whole is greater than the sum of the parts- is especially relevant with Office 97. Office 97 has a variety of techniques and tools to let you share data between applications. Integration occurs between a **source** document and a **destination** document. For example, you may want an Excel worksheet to appear in a Word document. In this case, the Excel worksheet is the source document and the Word letter is the destination document. The following table lists the three most common integration methods.

Integration method	Description
Copy and paste	With copy and paste, the source document becomes part of the destination document. If you copy an Excel worksheet to a Word document, then the worksheet is converted to a Word table. You can edit the table in Word but it has no effect on the original Excel worksheet. Also, any formulas in the table will not be recalculated if the numbers in the table are changed.
Copy and embed	With copy and embed, the Excel worksheet becomes part of the Word document and it remains as a worksheet. You can edit the worksheet within Word using Excel's features. The worksheet formulas are recalculated if you change the numbers from within Word. However, the worksheet does not change in Word if you make changes to the original worksheet in Excel.
Copy and link	With copy and link, the Excel worksheet does not become part of the Word document. It appears to be part of the Word document, however, it is linked to the original Excel worksheet. Changes you make to the original worksheet in Excel are reflected into the Word document as well.

Hands-On 15.1 – Create a stock portfolio workbook

In this exercise, you will develop a stock portfolio worksheet for Shirley Washington. In a later exercise, you will link the worksheet to a Word document.

1. Start a new workbook and enter the data shown below.

    You will need to use the Alt + Enter keystroke combination to create the multi-line entries.

	A	B	C	D	E	F	G	H
1	Company	Symbol	Number of Shares	Purchase Price	Initial Value	Current Price	Current Value	Gain/Loss
2	IBM	IBM	500	30		94		
3	Apple	AAPL	500	27		16		
4	GM	GM	1000	39		57		
5	Digital	DEC	300	72		34		
6	Totals							
7	Average							

Continued...

Create the formulas

2. Create formulas in the worksheet as discussed below.

   – Calculate the Initial Value in the range E2:E5 as the Number of Shares * Purchase Price.

   – Calculate the Current Value in the range G2:G5 as the Number of Shares * Current Price.

   – Calculate the Gain/Loss in the range H2:H5 as the Current Value – Initial Value.

   – Calculate the totals in cells E6, G6 and H6 and the average in cell H7.

3. Format the values and narrow the columns as shown below. At this point, your worksheet should match the worksheet below.

	A	B	C	D	E	F	G	H
1	Company	Symbol	Number of Shares	Purchase Price	Initial Value	Current Price	Current Value	Gain/Loss
2	IBM	IBM	500	30	15,000	94	47,000	32,000
3	Apple	AAPL	500	27	13,500	16	8,000	(5,500)
4	GM	GM	1000	39	39,000	57	57,000	18,000
5	Digital	DEC	300	72	21,600	34	10,200	(11,400)
6	Totals				$89,100		$122,200	$ 33,100
7	Average							$ 8,275

Format the worksheet with AutoFormat

4. **Select** the range **A1:H7**.

5. Choose **Format→AutoFormat...** from the menu bar.

6. Choose the **Classic 3** style and **click OK**.

7. If necessary, widen the columns slightly until the worksheet is formatted as shown below.

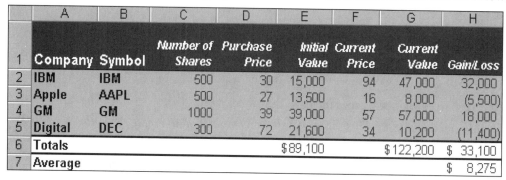

	A	B	C	D	E	F	G	H
1	Company	Symbol	Number of Shares	Purchase Price	Initial Value	Current Price	Current Value	Gain/Loss
2	IBM	IBM	500	30	15,000	94	47,000	32,000
3	Apple	AAPL	500	27	13,500	16	8,000	(5,500)
4	GM	GM	1000	39	39,000	57	57,000	18,000
5	Digital	DEC	300	72	21,600	34	10,200	(11,400)
6	Totals				$89,100		$122,200	$ 33,100
7	Average							$ 8,275

8. Save ⊟ the workbook as **Hands-On Lesson 15**.

Hands-On 15.2 – Create the Word document

In this exercise, you will create the Microsoft Word document shown below. The Excel worksheet will eventually be linked to this letter.

1. Start Microsoft Word and a blank new document will appear.

2. Set the font to **11** point.

3. Type the letter shown below.

    Don't be concerned if your text wraps at a different location than shown below.

Today's Date Enter
Enter
Enter
Enter
Ms. Cindy Wilson Enter
Wilson Financial Planning Enter
500 Kellogg Avenue Enter
Anaheim, CA 92807 Enter
Enter
Dear Cindy: Enter
Enter
I have included an Excel worksheet containing my current stock portfolio. Please review my portfolio and compare it to the previous quarter. Enter
Enter
Please contact me if you have any questions. I look forward to hearing from you. Enter
Enter
Best regards, Enter
Enter
Enter
Enter
Shirley Washington Enter

4. Save the document to your exercise diskette as **Cindy Wilson Letter**.

    Leave the document open because you will continue to use it.

Object Linking and Embedding

Object linking and embedding or OLE allows you to tie applications together. A description of both linking and embedding was given in the table at the beginning of this lesson. In the following exercise, you will link the Cindy Wilson letter to the stock portfolio worksheet.

Quick Steps: *Integrating Applications*

To copy and paste between applications
- *Select the desired data in the source application and click the Copy button.*
- *Switch to the destination application and click the Paste button.*

To copy and embed between applications
- *Select the desired data in the source application and click the Copy button.*
- *Switch to the destination application and choose Edit→Paste Special.*
- *Choose the Paste option, choose Microsoft Excel worksheet object and click OK.*

To copy and link between applications
- *Select the desired data in the source application and click the Copy button.*
- *Switch to the destination application and choose Edit→Paste Special.*
- *Choose the Paste link option, choose Microsoft Excel worksheet object and click OK.*

Hands-On 15.3 – Link the worksheet to the letter

In this exercise, you will link the stock portfolio worksheet to the letter.

1. **Switch to Excel** by clicking the Microsoft Excel button on the Windows 95 taskbar.

2. **Select** the range **A1:H7**.

3. **Click** the Copy  button.

4. **Switch to Word** by clicking the Microsoft Word button on the Windows 95 taskbar.

5. **Click** in the **blank line** between the two main paragraphs as shown below.

> I have included an Excel worksheet containing my current stock portfolio. Please review my portfolio and compare it to the previous quarter.
>
> *Click here* ——— |
>
> Please contact me if you have any questions. I look forward to hearing from you soon.

6. Choose **Edit→Paste Special...** from the menu bar.

7. Choose the ⊙ Paste link: option.

8. Choose **Microsoft Excel Worksheet Object** from the As list and **click OK**.

   The worksheet will be inserted. Notice the worksheet has sizing handles surrounding it. This is because you inserted it as a Microsoft Excel object and it is linked to the original worksheet. The only way you can edit the object is from within Excel. You can activate Excel by clicking the Excel button on the Taskbar or you can double-click the object in the Word document. Any changes you make to the object in Excel will be reflected in the Word document.

Continued...

Edit the worksheet in Excel

Notice the current price in cell F5 is 34. Imagine the share price has increased between the time you created this letter and the time you are ready to send it. You will make this adjustment by editing the worksheet in Excel.

9. **Double-click** the **worksheet** in the Word document and Excel will be activated.

    Notice the toolbars and all other screen elements belong to Excel.

10. **Tap** the (Esc) key on the keyboard to turn off the flashing marquee.

11. Change the value in cell F5 to **38**.

    The formulas in the worksheet will recalculate.

12. **Click** the **Microsoft Word button** on the Windows 95 taskbar.

    Notice the value in cell F5 has been updated to 38 and the formulas have been recalculated. This is because the Excel worksheet was inserted as a link. Any changes made in the worksheet will be reflected in the Word document.

13. Feel free to enhance the Word document in any way you feel is necessary.

    You may want to insert a hard return above the worksheet to push it down slightly.

Hyperlinks

Office 97 lets you insert hyperlinks in Excel worksheets and other office documents. A hyperlink sends you to another location whenever it is clicked. You can jump to a location within the same worksheet, to another worksheet, to a document in another program and even to the World Wide Web. Hyperlinks are a powerful way to tie your documents and applications together.

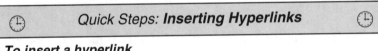

🕐 Quick Steps: **Inserting Hyperlinks** 🕐
To insert a hyperlink   • *Choose Insert→Hyperlink...*   • *Specify the filename of a file or the URL of a Web address in the Insert Hyperlink box and click OK.*

Hands-On 15.4 – Insert a hyperlink in the worksheet

In this exercise, you will insert a hyperlink in the stock portfolio worksheet. This link will open the Cindy Wilson Letter whenever it is clicked. This way, you can easily open the letter whenever you update the portfolio worksheet and wish to update the letter as well.

1. If necessary, switch to Microsoft Word.

2. Choose **File→Exit** and **save** the changes to the Cindy Wilson Letter.

3. **Switch to Excel** and **click** cell **A12**.

    You will insert the hyperlink in this cell.

4. Choose **Insert→Hyperlink...** from the menu bar.

Continued...

5. **Click** the **Browse** button and **navigate to your floppy diskette**.

6. **Locate** the **Cindy Wilson Letter** document and **double-click** it.

The pathname of the file will appear in the Link to file or URL box. If you were linking to a Web page, then you would have a Web URL such as http://www.labyrinth-pub.com (the Web site of Labyrinth Publications).

7. Notice the Named location in file box.

This box lets you specify a location within a file such as a cell or named range in a worksheet or a bookmark in a Word document. You will leave this box empty because the Cindy Wilson Letter is quite small. Going to a specific location in a small document has little practical use.

8. **Click OK** to complete the hyperlink.

Your hyperlink should appear in blue and be underlined.

Activate the link

9. Position the mouse pointer over cell A12 and it will have a pointing finger shape.

The pointer always has this shape when it is over a hyperlink.

10. Now **click** the hyperlink in cell **A12**.

Microsoft Word will start and the Cindy Wilson Letter will open.

11. Feel free to insert a hyperlink in the Cindy Wilson Letter that points to the Excel worksheet.

This way, you can easily move back and forth between these related documents.

12. **Close Microsoft Word** and **save** any changes you have made to the Cindy Wilson Letter.

Excel and the Web

Office 97 has a number of new features that let you connect to the world. Excel 97 is the first version of Excel that lets you access the wealth of information and data on the Internet. The following table discusses the new Internet related features in Office 97.

Feature	Description
Web toolbar	The Web toolbar lets you launch your Web browser and browse the Web from within Excel and other Office 97 applications. The Web toolbar is displayed with the **View→Toolbars** command.
HTML file creation	The **File Save as HTML** command launches an HTML wizard. This wizard guides you through the process of converting a worksheet to HTML format. Once this has been accomplished, you can post the worksheet on a corporate intranet or on the World Wide Web. An intranet is a large network within a company.
Web queries	Web queries let you download data from the Internet into an Excel worksheet.

More on Web Queries

Web queries let you download data from the Internet into an Excel worksheet. This powerful capability can be used to download stock prices, currency exchange rates and other types of data. Web queries are also a powerful way for employees to access data on corporate Intranets.

Excel 97 provides several Web queries

Excel 97 has several Web queries that are already set up for you. These queries are all designed to download stock market data and they are excellent for Web query demonstrations. Setting up Web queries is a rather involved task, so you will use one of the built-in Excel queries in the following exercise.

Hands-On 15.5 – Run a Web query

In this exercise, you will run a Web query that downloads up to 20 stock quotes at once. You will download the latest stock prices for the four stocks in Shirley Washington's portfolio. Keep in mind that this exercise will only work if you have a Web browser and an Internet connection.

1. If necessary, log on to your Internet service provider.

   This step shouldn't be necessary if you are in a computer lab with a permanent Internet connection.

2. If necessary, start Excel and open the Hands-On Lesson 15 workbook.

3. **Click** the **Sheet2** tab.

   You will download the stock quotation into this sheet.

4. Choose **Data**→**Get External Data**→**Run Web Query...** from the menu bar.

   The Queries folder should appear in the Look in box with four stock related Web queries listed. These queries are provided as part of Excel 97.

5. Choose **Multiple Stock Quotes by PC Quote, Inc** and **click** the **Get Data** button.

6. **Click OK** on the Returning External Data to Microsoft Excel dialog box.

   The Enter Parameter Value box appears. This is where you list the stock symbols.

7. Carefully type **IBM AAPL GM DEC** and **click OK**.

   You must type a space between each set of symbols. Depending on the speed of your Internet connection, the Web query may require a minute or more to run. The downloaded data will have a format similar to the following example. This data is updated constantly throughout the business day. You can always download "fresh" stock data using this technique.

	A	B	C	D	E	F	G	H	I	J
1	**Multiple Stock Quotes**									
2										
3										
4	Company Name & Symbol	Last Price	Net Change	Open	High	Low	Volume	Time	# of Outstanding Shares (Thou)	Market Cap
5	IBM INTERNATIONAL BUSINESS MACHINES (IBM)	89 1/4	1/4	88 3/4	90	88 5/8	2,667,000	6/97	1,035,092	$92,381,961
6	APPLE COMPUTER INC (AAPL)	15 1/2	- 5/16	15 7/8	15 7/8	15 3/8	1,196,500	6/97	124,669	$1,932,370
7	GENERAL MOTORS CORP (GM)	57 1/2	1/4	57 3/8	58	57 1/4	1,192,800	6/97	755,968	$43,468,160
8	DIGITAL EQUIPMENT CORP (DEC)	36 5/8	3/4	35 7/8	36 5/8	35 3/4	1,255,300	6/97	157,264	$
9										
10	All non-subscription data is delayed 20 minutes unless noted, and is believed accurate but is not warranted or guaranteed by PC Quote,Inc. All times are Eastern U.S.									
11	Data Provided by									
12	PC Quote, Inc.					Go to the PC Quote/Microsoft Excel Developer's Corner				

8. Feel free to enter the latest stock prices in your portfolio worksheet.

9. Try running the other built-in Web queries.

10. **Close** the workbook when you have finished and **save** the changes.

Concepts Review

True / False

1. Changes made to an Excel worksheet that is embedded in a Word document are reflected in the Word document. 1. **T F**

2. Changes made to an Excel worksheet that is linked to a Word document are reflected in the Word document. 2. **T F**

3. Hyperlinks can only be used to link documents that are created using the same application. 3. **T F**

4. Hyperlinks are underlined and usually appear in a blue color. 4. **T F**

5. Web queries can download data from the Internet. 5. **T F**

Multiple Choice

1. Which command is used to initiate object linking and embedding?
    a) Edit→Paste
    b) Insert→Paste
    c) Edit→Paste Special
    d) Insert→Paste Special   (   )

2. Which command is used to create hyperlinks?
    a) Insert→Hyperlink
    b) Edit→Hyperlink
    c) Tools→Hyperlink
    d) Edit→Paste Special→Hyperlink   (   )

3. Which command is used to display the Web toolbar?
    a) Insert→Web toolbar
    b) View→Toolbars
    c) View→Web Toolbar
    d) None of the above.   (   )

Off to Work™ With Excel 97
Quick reference guide

Moving the highlight
Home	Column A of active row
Ctrl + Home	Cell A1
PageDown	Down one screen
PageUp	Up one screen

Common function syntax
Current date	=TODAY( )
Average of range	=AVERAGE(range)
Minimum of range	=MIN(range)
Maximum of range	=MAX(range)
If	=IF(Test, True, False)
Sum of range	=SUM(range)
Vlookup	=VLOOKUP(argument, lookup table, column number
Linking formula	=Sheetname!reference
Payment	=PMT(rate, periods, loan amount)
Future Value	=FV(rate, periods, payment)

Selection techniques
Select a range	Drag mouse over cells
Select multiple ranges	Press Ctrl while dragging desired ranges
Select a column	Click column heading
Select a row	Click row heading
Select multiple rows/columns	Drag over the desired row/column headings
Select entire worksheet	Click Select All
Select multiple worksheets	Press Ctrl, click sheet tabs
Select using Shift key	Click first cell in range, press Shift, click last cell

COMMON COMMANDS
Absolute cell references	Use $ in front of references
AutoCorrect (Creating Entry)	**Tools→AutoCorrect**
AutoFilter	**Data→Filter→AutoFilter**
AutoFormat	**Format→AutoFormat**
AutoSum	Click Σ
Cancel cell entry	Click
Cell borders	Click
Cell comments	**Insert→Comment**
Chart Wizard	
Clip Art	**Insert→Picture...**
Conditional Formatting	**Format→Conditional**
Consolidation	**Data→Consolidate**
Copy text & number formats	Click or double-click 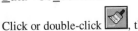, then drag over cells

Currency format (fixed)	Click $
Currency format (floating)	**Format→Cells,** choose Currency from Number tab, choose desired options
Confirm cell entry	Click
Data validation	**Data→Validation**
Data form (for database)	**Data→Form**
Decrease decimals	Click
Deleting Rows/Columns	**Edit→Delete**
Fill color	Click
Font color	Click
Freeze header rows/columns	**Window→Freeze Panes**
Headers & Footers	**File→Page Setup**
Hyperlinks	**Insert→Hyperlink**
Increase Decimals	Click
Insert rows/columns	**Insert→Rows/Columns**
Landscape orientation	**File→Page Setup**
Macro Play	**Tools→Macro→Macros**
Macro Record	**Tools→Macro → Record New Macro**
Margins	**File→Page Setup**
Merge and Center	Click
Multi-line text entries	Press **Alt + Enter**
Naming cells	Click in Name box, type name, tap Enter
Paste Function	Click fx
Pictures (Inserting)	**Insert→Picture**
PivotTables (creating)	**Data→PivotTable Report**
Protection options	**Tools→Protection**
Scenario Manager	**Tools→Scenarios**
Sorting	Click
Subtotals (in database)	**Data→Subtotals**
Templates (Using)	**File→New**
Templates (Editing)	Open template, change, save
Toolbars (Displaying/Hiding)	Right click any toolbar, choose desired toolbar from menu
Toolbars (Moving)	Point to the Move handle, drag to desired location
Undo	Click

Index